INSIGHT GUIDES

IRELAND

Discovery CHANNEL

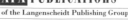
APA PUBLICATIONS   **L**
Part of the Langenscheidt Publishing Group

ABOUT THIS BOOK

INSIGHT GUIDE
Ireland

Editorial
Project Editor
Brian Bell
Principal Photographers
Geray Sweeney
Thomas Kelly

Distribution

UK & Ireland
GeoCenter International Ltd
The Viables Centre, Harrow Way
Basingstoke, Hants RG22 4BJ
Fax: (44) 1256 817988

United States
Langenscheidt Publishers, Inc.
36–36 33rd Street, 4th Floor
Long Island City, NY 11106
Fax: (1) 718 784-0640

Canada
Thomas Allen & Son Ltd
390 Steelcase Road East
Markham, Ontario L3R 1G2
Fax: (1) 905 475-6747

Australia
Universal Publishers
1 Waterloo Road
Macquarie Park, NSW 2113
Fax: (61) 2 9888-9074

New Zealand
Hema Maps New Zealand Ltd (HNZ)
Unit D, 24 Ra ORA Drive
East Tamaki, Auckland
Fax: (64) 9 273-6479

Worldwide
Apa Publications GmbH & Co.
Verlag KG (Singapore branch)
38 Joo Koon Road, Singapore 628990
Tel: (65) 865-1600. Fax: (65) 861-6438

Printing

Insight Print Services (Pte) Ltd
38 Joo Koon Road, Singapore 628990
Tel: (65) 865-1600. Fax: (65) 861-6438

©2005 **Apa Publications GmbH & Co.**
Verlag KG (Singapore branch)
All Rights Reserved
First Edition 1986
Sixth Edition (updated) 2005

CONTACTING THE EDITORS
We would appreciate it if readers
would alert us to errors or out-
dated information by writing to:
Insight Guides, P.O. Box 7910,
London SE1 1WE, England.
Fax: (44) 20 7403-0290.
insight@apaguide.co.uk

www.insightguides.com

This guidebook combines the
interests and enthusiasms of
two of the world's best known
information providers: Insight
Guides, whose titles have set the
standard for visual travel guides
since 1970, and Discovery Channel, the world's premier source of
nonfiction television programming.

The editors of Insight Guides provide both practical advice and general
understanding about a destination's
history, culture, institutions and
people. Discovery Channel
and its popular website,
www.discovery.com, help
millions of viewers explore
their world from the com-
fort of their own home
and also encourage them
to explore it first-hand.

How to use this book
For this new edition of
Insight Guide: Ireland, all

the maps have been redrawn, all the
Places chapters have been rewrit-
ten and the rest of the book has
been thoroughly updated. These
major changes were made in order
to reflect the speed at which Ireland
itself has been changing. In the
Republic, social reforms in areas
such as divorce have combined with
closer links with mainland Europe to
create a new confidence and dyna-
mism, and in Northern Ireland there
has been much renewal following decades of terrorist
bombings. *Insight Guide:
Ireland* reflects these
changes through its for-
mat of informative, en-
tertaining and well
written text paired with
vivid photojournalism.

The book is carefully
structured both to con-
vey an understanding of
the country and its cul-

Trinity College Dublin's Long Room Library.

ture and to guide readers through its many sights and attractions:

◆ To understand Ireland today, you need to know something of its past. The first section covers its history and culture in lively, authoritative essays written by specialists.

◆ The central Places section gives a full run-down of the attractions worth seeing. Places of interest are co-ordinated by number with the maps.

◆ The Travel Tips section is a point of reference for information on travel, hotels, restaurants, shops and festivals. Information may be located quickly by using the index printed on the back cover flap – and the flaps are designed to serve as bookmarks.

◆ Photographs are chosen not only to illustrate geography and buildings but also to convey the many moods of the country and the everyday activities of its people.

The contributors

This edition was produced by Insight Guides' editorial director, **Brian Bell**, an Irishman who began his publishing career as a journalist in Belfast. Most of the chapters on the Republic were revised by **Rachel Warren**, a West Cork-based writer with an encyclopedic knowledge of Ireland's attractions, and by Insight editor **Jason Mitchell**. **Tom Adair**, a prominent Northern Irish journalist, did the same job on the Northwest and Northeast chapters. The Dublin chapter was written by **Liam McAuley**, an editor on the *Irish Times*; he also wrote the piece on horses and is the author of the detailed *Insight Compact Guide: Dublin*. The Belfast chapter and the essay on food were written by Belfast journalist **Ian Hill**.

Other *Irish Times* contributors include **Eugene McEldowney** (Song and Dance), **Seamus Martin** (Pubs), and **Fintan O'Toole** (The Church). **Niall Stokes**, founder of the leading Dublin magazine *Hot Press*, wrote the chapter on Youth.

Much of the material for the chapters on Folklore, Sport and the Far West is based on the work of the late **Breandán O hEithir**, who wrote authoritatively for the first edition. Other writers whose work for earlier editions is partly retained include **Peter Kellner** and **Naomi May**. The Introduction and History chapters were written by **Brian Bell**.

Many photographers are represented in this book, notably **Geray Sweeney**, a Belfast photographer who has also shot Insight Compact Guides to *Dublin* and *The West of Ireland* and an Insight Pocket Guide to *Ireland's Southwest*, and the Limerick-born **Thomas Kelly**, who now lives outside Dublin.

Map Legend

– – ··	International Boundary
– – – –	County Boundary
⊖	Border Crossing
– • –	National Park/ Nature Reserve
– – – –	Ferry Route
✈	Airport
🚌	Bus Station
🅿	Parking
❶	Tourist Information
✉	Post Office
✝	Church/Ruins
	Mosque
✡	Synagogue
	Castle/Ruins
∴	Archaeological Site
∩	Cave
★	Place of Interest

The main places of interest in the Places section are coordinated by number with a full-colour map (e.g. ❶), and a symbol at the top of every right-hand page tells you where to find the map.

INSIGHT GUIDE
Ireland

CONTENTS

Maps

Ireland **136**

Dublin **138**

Dublin's Suburbs **161**

Around Dublin **166**

DART Rail System **337**

Southern Region **170**

Cork City **194**

Killarney **209**

The Midlands & West **230**

Northern Region **260**

Derry City **280**

Belfast **316**

Ireland **Front flap**

Dublin **Back flap**

Introduction

The Irish Character..................**15**

History

Chronology **22**

Ireland's Invaders **25**

The Making of a Nation............**33**

Living with Partition **45**

Ireland Today.........................**53**

Features

The Role of the Church **69**

The Youth Explosion **78**

Song and Dance **85**

The Irish Way with Words **93**

Fairies and Folklore **98**

Racing Certainties **105**

The Games People Play **110**

The Serious Business
of Drinking **119**

A Fresh Approach to Food **125**

Round tower at the Rock of Cashel, Co. Tipperary. About 70 round towers still exist in Ireland.

Insight on....

Ireland's Architecture..............62
Ireland in the Movies...............96
The Travelling People.............188
The Burren 228
The Men Who March 310

Places

Introduction 135
Dublin....................................141
Day Trips from Dublin 164
The Southeast.....................175
Cork City & Surroundings 193
The Southwest 201

The Shannon Region 219
The Midlands 235
The Far West 249
The Northwest 265
The Northeast 279
Belfast 315

Travel Tips

Getting Acquainted **330**
Planning the trip **331**
Practical Tips **333**
Getting Around **337**
Where to Stay **340**
Where to Eat **352**
Nightlife **361**
Cultural Attractions **363**
Festivals **366**
Shopping **369**
Sports **370**

Full Travel Tips index is on page 329

IRISH FINE ART

THE IRISH CHARACTER

Take generous portions of charm, wit, congeniality and loquacity. Then mix in melancholy, daydreaming and a tendency to violence. Stir gently

"How do you recognise an Irishman in a car wash?"
"He's the one sitting on the motorbike."

The Irish take a perverse delight in the universal jokes made against them. Indeed, they even print selections on linen tea-towels, which they sell at fancy prices in souvenir shops. That explains the perverse delight, of course: there's money to be made in conforming to a stereotyped image and, by appearing to be dim, the Irishman can benefit from the dimness of others.

Thus a guileful guide, deploying words like grapeshot, can charm the most sceptical travellers into paying good money to kiss the Blarney Stone in County Cork, at the same time reassuring them fulsomely that its promised ability to confer eloquence on all who kiss it is, in itself, just a bit of blarney.

Millions of visitors respond to this captivating charm by falling in love with Ireland at first sight. The national tourist slogan, *Céad Mile Fáilte*, fulfils its promise of "a hundred thousand welcomes" and the people's informal friendliness makes it exceptionally easy to take things easy. Rural values survive: after achieving independence from Britain in 1921, an event accompanied by bloody internal strife, the new Republic signalled its priorities in its currency, with coins displaying images not of rulers or tyrants but of pigs, hens, hares and salmon.

But only the coins of *the Republic*, of course, for there are two Irelands. One consists of the 26 counties of the Republic, which evoke images of black beer and green shamrock, of still sunsets over Galway Bay and statues of the Virgin Mary that, according to thousands of eyewitnesses, miraculously move. Then there

are the six counties of British-administered Northern Ireland, a harder place where a celebrated slogan daubed on the side of a derelict house asked: "Is there life *before* death?"

Endless paradoxes ambush the unwary. It doesn't take long for the enquiring visitor to begin pondering such puzzles as why a Dublin

Roman Catholic will in all probability hate the British but respect the English, while a Belfast Protestant will badmouth the English yet swear eternal loyalty to the British. Non-residents should enter this debate only if they relish taking sides in marital conflicts.

Such stereotypes, naturally, soon turn into absurd over-simplifications. An English journalist, for instance, despatched to Northern Ireland to seek out why its Protestant and Roman Catholic communities were at each other's throats, reported: "They are incomparably more pleasant to the outsider than any other people in the British Isles. Even the terrorists have excellent manners." It was the German writer

PRECEDING PAGES: wall mural in Killarney Town; art store in Inishshannon, County Cork; farm children, Connemara; an evening out at Bad Bob's bar, Dublin. **LEFT:** the Republic's flag at a football game at Croke Park, Dublin. **RIGHT:** the Long Room of the Old Library, Trinity College, Dublin.

Heinrich Böll who identified the two turns of speech most characteristic of the Irish as "It could be worse" and "I shouldn't worry." In a world where worries proliferate daily, Ireland has more to offer than pigs, priests, potatoes and patriots: it has insane optimism.

Naturally the Irish have written down this philosophy on linen tea-towels, which they will sell to passers-through at a decent profit. It reads: "There are only two things to worry about: either you are well or you are sick. If you are well, then there is nothing to worry about. But if you are sick, there are two things to worry about: either you will get well or you will die.

image of the stage Irishman, a clownish character with a liking for alcohol and argument, preferably indulged in simultaneously. But the Irish readily collaborated.

Unarguably, there is a strong theatricality about their character. There's a recklessness, a tendency towards exaggeration. There's a love of "codology", the Irish equivalent of "leg-pulling." But there's an introversion, too, the proneness to melancholy captured by George Bernard Shaw in *John Bull's Other Island*, a play set in the land of his birth: "Your wits can't thicken in that soft moist air, on those white springy roads, in those misty rushes and brown

If you get well, then there is nothing to worry about. If you die, there are only two things to worry about: either you will go to heaven or to hell. If you go to heaven, there is nothing to worry about. But if you go to hell, you'll be so damn busy shaking hands with friends, you won't have time to worry. Why worry!"

A strong theatricality

Not that the Irish won't give you cause enough for perplexity. Their character is as elusive as the fairy gold to be found at the end of Irish rainbows and the conversation as elliptical as an incomplete jigsaw puzzle. Hollywood, as so often, is partly to blame; it perpetuated the

bogs, on those hillsides of granite rocks and magenta heather. You've no such colours in the sky, no such lure in the distance, no such sadness in the evenings. Oh the dreaming! the dreaming! the torturing, heartscalding, never satisfying dreaming, dreaming, dreaming."

You can sometimes sense this aspect of the Irish character in a pub when, after the talk – once called "a game with no rules" – has achieved an erratic brilliance, the convivial mood abruptly changes to one of wistfulness and self-absorption, and you know it's time to go. This contradictory character led the 19th-century philosopher Søren Kierkegaard to muse that, if he hadn't been a Dane, he could well have been an Irishman: "For the Irish have not the heart to baptize their children completely, they want to preserve just a little paganism, and whereas a child is normally completely immersed, they keep his right arm out of the water so that in after-life he can grasp a sword and hold a girl in his arm."

The Irish themselves look less whimsically at their native land. The poet Louis MacNeice, for example, described it as a nation "built upon violence and morose vendettas". Today, because of

THE EXPATRIATE IRISH

Almost 3 million Irish citizens live outside Ireland, including 2 million in Britain, 500,000 in the US, 213,000 in Australia and 74,000 in Canada.

Micheál MacLiammóir, "no European island lies in so lamentable and hostile a solitude as Ireland, who has no neighbour on her right hand but her conqueror, and nothing at all on her left hand but the desolate ocean, not one dry step until you get to America."

This "wretched little clod, broken off a bigger clod, broken off the west end of Europe," as Shaw called it, has had a turbulent history, whose unfinished state is reflected in the island's partition. The current "Troubles" blighting Northern Ireland

the guerrilla warfare that has been waged in the northeast of the island since 1969, this dark side of the Irish character is much more in evidence than it was half a century ago, when John Wayne and Maureen O'Hara rollicked their way through the virulently green landscapes of *The Quiet Man*. As one commentator observed: "The quiet Irishman is about as harmless as a powder magazine built over a match factory."

Perhaps the island's location is to blame. "With the exception it may be of Malta and of Iceland," wrote the actor and theatre director

LEFT: the wearing of the green.
ABOVE: traditional rural cottage and locals.

were at first seen by the world as a curious religious conflict, an inexplicable throwback to the Reformation. In reality, religious affiliation has been mostly a symbol. The conflict has had little to do with God but everything to do with nationalism. The doctrine of the Transubstantiation may be debated from the pulpits of fundamentalist preachers, but what everyone else is arguing about is the conflicting secular loyalties of 1 million Protestants, who want to stay British, and half-a-million Roman Catholics, who feel a bond with the Republic. It's partly a question of insecure national identity, partly a realisation that, in an area with too few jobs to go round, each tribe has to fight for its fair share.

What these divisions indicate is that there is more than one "Irish" character. The Northern Protestant is generally regarded as being more earnest, more unimaginative than the Northern Catholic, who is in turn seen as less outgoing, less impulsive than the Southern Catholic. The Irish refine these distinctions even further, giving the sense of place an importance seldom found elsewhere in the world.

But is too small a place for many. In *Mother Ireland*, the novelist Edna O'Brien described the constricting parochialism and the awful predictability that led her to flee to London: "Hour after hour I can think of Ireland, I can imagine without going too far wrong what is happening in any one of the little towns by day or by night... I can almost tell you what any one of my friends might be doing, so steadfast is the rhythm of life there."

A strong theatricality

It's a rhythm, though, that's well liked by most visitors. It is an echo of an 18th-century pace of life that has not completely faded away, a psychological climate in which a racehorse attracts more admiring glances than a Rolls-Royce. It reflects the values of the railway guard answering a traveller who complained that the train was already half an hour late: "You must have a very narrow heart that you wouldn't go down to the town and stand your friends a few drinks instead of bothering me to get away."

It's this attitude to life, never far beneath the surface, that makes Ireland such a rewarding place to visit. As the American-born novelist J. P. Donleavy, an exemplar of the less folksy style of Irish writing, expressed it winsomely in *The Ginger Man*: "When I die I want to decompose in a barrel of porter [*dark beer*] and have it served in all the pubs of Dublin. I wonder would they know it was me?" ❑

THE IRISH DIASPORA

As many as 70 million people throughout the world can claim Irish descent, and the Irish are generous in granting citizenship. It can extend to the grandchildren and great-grandchildren of people born in Ireland, the argument being that they were prevented from being Irish only because their forebears had to emigrate for economic reasons.

RIGHT: traditional music is a big draw in many pubs.

IRLANDIÆ REGNUM.

Decisive Dates

ca 7000BC Archaeological evidence of Mesolithic hunter-fisher people (flints, etc) along the coast dates from this period.

From ca 3000BC The Neolithic period sees megalithic tombs appear. Signs of prolonged settlement, agriculture and cultural sophistication (portal tombs) grow more frequent.

From ca 500BC The migration of Celts from Britain marks the start of Ireland's Iron Age.

ca AD300 Stone-carved inscriptions appear in the 'Ogham alphabet', a rune-like script.

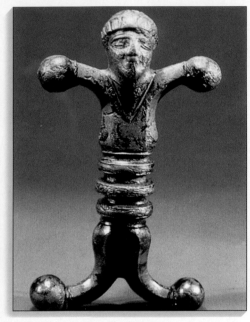

431 The Pope sends Palladius as a bishop to Ireland. This implies that Christian communities existed before St Patrick arrived.

ca 432 St Patrick (later to become Ireland's patron saint) comes back to Ireland as a missionary. At 16, he had been abducted from Britain to Ireland, but later fled to France.

From ca 800 Viking attacks begin. After a series of raids (many monasteries are plundered) the Norsemen found settlements which grow into harbour towns (e.g. Dublin).

976–1014 Brian Ború, crowned King of Munster in 976, proclaims himself High King of Ireland in 1002 and defeats the Vikings near Clontarf in 1014. After his murder that same year, the kingdom falls apart again.

From 1169 Anglo-Normans – sent to Ireland by the English king Henry II after a request from Dermot MacMurrough, who is losing the fight for the Irish throne – conquer large areas of the island and settle there. Feudalism is introduced and castles built.

1366 The Statutes of Kilkenny represent an attempt by the English crown to stop its barons from assimilating, marrying Irishwomen or speaking the Irish language.

From 1541 England's Henry VIII declares himself King of Ireland and begins asserting British supremacy over the Irish clan princes.

1607 The most powerful Irish clan princes flee to Spain (the "Flight of the Earls"), marking the end of Gaelic supremacy.

1608 James I starts systematic settlement of Protestant Scots and English ("the Plantation of Ulster").

1641–53 A rebellion by Irish Catholics against the English settlement policy is initially successful. In 1649, after his victory in the English Civil War, Oliver Cromwell conquers Ireland in a merciless campaign.

1690 England's Catholic King James II loses his throne to William of Orange at the Battle of the Boyne in 1690, and the period of "Protestant Ascendancy" begins.

1691 The Irish-Protestant parliament in Dublin passes the "Penal Laws" which exclude Catholics from public office, deprive them of their property and hence of their right to vote, and make it difficult to practise their religion.

1791 Influenced by the revolutions in France and America, the United Irishmen movement is formed in Belfast. Its leading light, Wolfe Tone, is a Protestant coachbuilder's son.

1800 The Act of Union makes Ireland part of the United Kingdom. The parliament in Dublin is dissolved and Ireland is represented by 100 MPs in the House of Commons.

1829 A Catholic politician, Daniel O'Connell ("the Liberator"), forces the London parliament to pass a law emancipating Catholics.

From 1840 Nationalist movements gain strength (Irish Republican Brotherhood founded in 1858, Irish National Land League founded in 1879). There is a renewed interest in Gaelic culture (Gaelic League formed in 1893).

1845–51 The Great Potato Famine deprives more than one-third of the Irish population of their main source of nutrition (the unusually warm winters mean that the fungus blighting the crops cannot be destroyed). An estimated 1 million people die between 1846 and 1851 of malnutrition, typhus and other diseases; 1 million others emigrate.

From 1880 The Land League and the Irish Home Rule Party led by Charles Stuart Parnell employ parliamentary means in their struggle for Irish autonomy and land reform. In 1886, the first of several draft resolutions for Irish independence is rejected.

1905–08 The group known as Sinn Féin ("We Ourselves") is formed "to make England take one hand from Ireland's throat and the other out of Ireland's pocket".

1912 Almost three-quarters of all Ulster Protestants sign a solemn pledge to stop all attempts at autonomy "by all necessary means". The Ulster Volunteer Force is formed in 1913 to enforce the pledge.

1916 On 24 April around 1,800 volunteers, led by Pádraig Pearse and James Connolly, occupy public buildings in Dublin and declare the formation of an Irish Republic. This "Easter Rising" is put down six days later. Britain's harsh response backfires and support strengthens for the nationalist cause.

1918–23 In elections to the UK Parliament, Sinn Féin wins 73 of 105 Irish seats. Their MPs announce the formation of an Irish parliament in Dublin, with Éamon de Valera as president; the British government sends in troops. During the Anglo-Irish War of 1919–21 the Irish Republican Army gradually gains the upper hand against the British. In 1922 the Irish Parliament narrowly accepts the Anglo-Irish treaty for the foundation of an Irish Free State excluding the six counties of Northern Ireland with Protestant majorities. Civil war ensues between forces in favour of a Pan-Irish Republic and the pro-treaty Free State government, which wins.

1937 The Free State (now known as Éire) adopts its own constitution.

1939 Éire declares its neutrality during World War II. Germany tries to damage Britain's interests by supporting the IRA.

1949 Éire leaves the British Commonwealth to become the Republic of Ireland.

1969–70 A demonstration by the Northern Irish

Civil Rights Movement is attacked by loyalists in 1969. The IRA, which has been fighting for a united Ireland since the 1930s, splits into two factions in 1970. The Provisional IRA intensifies its "armed struggle" in Northern Ireland.

1972 The situation becomes volatile when 13 demonstrators are shot dead by British soldiers on "Bloody Sunday". The parliament in Belfast is dissolved and Northern Ireland is henceforth ruled directly from London.

1973 The Republic joins the European Economic Community along with Great Britain.

1990 Mary Robinson becomes the first woman president of the Republic of Ireland.

1994 IRA declares ceasefire in Northern Ireland (ends in 1996 with bomb in London).

1997 In the Republic, divorce becomes legal, a Fianna Fáil-led coalition wins the general election and Mary McAleese, a Northerner, becomes president. The IRA declares another ceasefire.

1998 A Northern Ireland peace treaty is signed by all parties, including Sinn Féin. David Trimble and John Hume receive Nobel prize.

1999 An all-party Assembly with limited powers set up in Northern Ireland.

2002 The Republic adopts the euro. In the North, trust breaks down between Unionists and Nationalists and direct rule from London is reimposed.

2004 A £26 million bank robbery in Belfast is blamed on IRA and helps keep the Assembly on ice. ❑

PRECEDING PAGES: Ireland in 1606 as portrayed by an Amsterdam atlas, the Mercator-Hondius.
LEFT: an ancient dagger hilt. **RIGHT:** monument in Dublin's O'Connell Street to Charles Stewart Parnell.

IRELAND'S INVADERS

*First the Celts came, then the Vikings and Normans. The English decided
to stake a strategic claim, and that's when the trouble really began*

Ireland, it is said, has no ancient annals: all its history is contemporary because yesterday's myths mould today's thought in an astonishingly direct way. In the words of the 19th-century historian Thomas Babington Macaulay, dealing with Ireland is like stepping "on the thin crust of ashes beneath which the lava is still flowing."

It's an easy proposition to prove. Volunteer, at an Irish dinner party or in a bar, a statement about any aspect of the country's turbulent past, and a catalogue of heroism and hatreds, claims and counter-claims, murderers and martyrs, decisive dates and disputed deeds will pour out with vehemence and wit, populated with a cast of characters ranging from Brian Ború to Oliver Cromwell, from William of Orange to O'Connell the Liberator, from Henry VIII to Margaret Thatcher. Nowhere else does the ordinary citizen delight in interpreting today's political deeds through such detailed and comprehensive reference to centuries old events.

The next-door neighbour

The reason for this lack of historical perspective lies in the extraordinary love-hate relationship that Ireland has had with its more powerful neighbouring island to the east. Ireland's history, in a nutshell, is its resistance to England. In this geographically forced marriage, the dominant partner sometimes deliberately abused the weaker, more often unthinkingly ignored her; yet the Irish, while hating the English for their arrogance and neglect, also admired them for their character and achievements and, until a surprisingly late stage, had no great wish for the marriage to be totally dissolved.

It is a tragic national drama, full of tantalising might-have-beens, and the English have long been resigned to the fact that they are cast as the villain. "Go into the length and breadth of the world," England's reforming prime minister William Ewart Gladstone told his parliament a century ago, "ransack the literature of all countries, find if you can a single voice, a single book... in which the conduct of England towards Ireland is anywhere treated except with profound and bitter condemnation."

Those seeking to understand rather than condemn must begin by travelling back several cen-

turies before the birth of Christ. It was then that Ireland's first conquerors, the Celts (or Gaels), quick-tempered masters of horsemanship, came west from the mainland of Europe, mainly from France and Spain, to this wild, wet island at the continent's outermost fringes. They brought with them a loose tribal structure, the blueprint for building a civilization, and had little trouble in overcoming the natives, an obscure, primitive people called the Firbolg ("Big Men").

But old traditions of magic and wizardry survived so strongly that to this day you can find reverence for holy wells and for clumps of trees inhabited by "the fairies". Evidence of much earlier inhabitants survived, too, in the form of

---

LEFT: The Arrest of Christ from the *Book of Kells*.
RIGHT: Tara brooch from the 8th century.

thousands of megalithic burial chambers. The Newgrange passage-grave in the Boyne valley, near Dublin, for example, is thought to be 5,000 years old. From the Bronze Age, when Ireland was one of the world's largest metal producers, beautifully crafted leaf-shaped swords and gold ornaments are preserved.

Europe's next conquerors did not get as far as Ireland. The Roman legions, hard pressed to hold southern Britain against incursions by Picts and Scots,

HEAVY REIGNS

Because kingship was elective, not hereditary, power struggles were inevitable, especially since there were as many as 150 kings in a population of 500,000. They reigned, it was said, but didn't always rule.

Christianity had been brought to the island by an English-born rustic missionary, St Patrick, who had been kidnapped as a youth and taken to Ireland to tend sheep. Later, he travelled widely in France and Italy, returning to Ireland in 432 to spread the word of Christ through the trackless forests. He found, in this land of which he was to become the patron saint, a largely peaceable people, though there was intermittent feuding between various provincial kings.

were disinclined to take on more trouble by adding the Gaels to their empire. Their inaction had far-reaching consequences: if Julius Caesar had successfully ventured west, it is unlikely that Ireland's character today would be so distinct from Britain's. What's more, the roads might have been better.

The Golden Age

The divergences between the two cultures widened still further when the fall of the Roman Empire plunged Europe into the Dark Ages. Ireland, in contrast, entered its Golden Age, becoming a lone beacon of learning and civilization – "the Land of Saints and Scholars".

In the absence of a Roman substructure of towns and cities, monasteries became centres of population. The kings kept their treasures there, which made the monasteries a target for plundering bands of Vikings, who sailed to Ireland in their high-prowed ships from northern Scandinavia. Tall round towers, many still standing, were built by the monasteries to serve as lookouts and refuges as well as belfries. Also surviving are some of the monks' exquisitely illuminated manuscripts, such as the *Book of Kells*, which the Vikings, being unable to read, ignored. Ireland's strong tradition of storytelling dates from this period. It can be seen on the many sand-stone high crosses, designed to teach

Bible stories by means of elaborate carvings.

The Norse tyranny was destroyed at the Battle of Clontarf in 1014 by the most celebrated of the High Kings, Brian Ború, who saw himself as Ireland's Charlemagne. But he himself died in the battle as he was praying for victory.

Less destructive but no less ambitious visitors were the Norman adventurers such as Strongbow, who came looking for land. His real name was Richard, second Earl of Pembroke, and he was answering a call for help from Dermot MacMurrough, a local chieftain, who had outraged rivals by stealing another prince's wife – an offence which, not for the first time, was to change the course of history.

England gets involved

The Norman lords' pedigrees were longer than their purses. Having gained a toehold, they began enriching themselves by building a power base, complete with fortified stone castles. This alarmed England's king, Henry II. He promptly paid a visit to Ireland, inaugurating an involvement between the two countries that was to last, with immeasurable bloodshed, for 800 years.

Over the next three centuries, the Normans, intermarrying with the natives, expanded their influence. Many of the country's elaborate castles, such as Blarney in Co. Cork and Bunratty in County Clare, date from this time. In 1429, Henry VI subsidised each new castle to the tune of £10, then a sizeable sum.

But, as the barons thrived, the English Crown's authority gradually shrank to an area around Dublin known as "the Pale". It was Henry VIII, determined finally to break the local nobles' power, who proclaimed himself "King of this land of Ireland as united, annexed and knit for ever to the Imperial Crown of the Realm of England". Henry tried to make himself the source of all land ownership by demanding that the lords surrender their lands to him, then have them "regranted by the grace of the king". When many refused, Henry seized their lands, resettling them with loyal "planters" from England and Scotland.

His daughter, Elizabeth I, fought four wars in Ireland. As well as trying to impose the Refor-

mation on the country, she wanted to protect England's right flank against an invasion from her principal opponent, Spain.

Later, James I defeated a particularly powerful baron, Hugh O'Neill, Earl of Tyrone, at the Battle of Kinsale and planted new settlers on O'Neill's lands in six of the nine counties of the ancient province of Ulster. The new settlers were Protestants, firm believers in the Calvinist work ethic, and the racial mix that they created is still causing strife in Ulster today.

An early sign of the troubles ahead came in 1641, when Ulster Roman Catholics, hoping to recover their confiscated lands, rebelled at Por-

tadown. The facts of the rebellion were rapidly overwhelmed by the legend as lurid tales spread of a drunken Catholic pogrom against the God-fearing settlers, with 12,000 Protestants knifed, shot and drowned, pregnant women raped, and infants roasted on spits. Whatever the death toll really was, the Protestants were never to forget the threat represented by 1641.

The Gaelic Irish had further cause to worry when, after Charles I was beheaded, the new Puritan Parliament in England began suppressing the Roman Catholic religion. Fanned by the flames of this resentment, a new Catholic revolt began to spread. This "Great Rebellion" was ruthlessly suppressed by the English Protector,

---

LEFT: England's Richard II made two expeditions to Ireland, in 1394–95 and in 1399. **RIGHT:** Walter Devereux, 1st Earl of Essex, was despatched in the 1570s by Elizabeth I to colonise Ulster.

Oliver Cromwell, whose 20,000 Ironside troops devastated the countryside. By 1652, about a third of the Catholic Irish had been killed. Much of their land was handed over to Protestants.

When the monarchy was restored, Charles II disappointed Catholics by throwing his support behind the Protestants, on whom he depended for power. His successor, James II, himself a Roman Catholic, raised hopes by introducing an Act of Parliament that would have ousted the Protestant settlers; but, before it could be put into practice, James was defeated in 1690 at the Battle of the Boyne, near Dublin, by William of Orange. William had been called in by the Eng-

was broken up between all his sons instead of passing to the eldest – unless one son turned Protestant, in which case he got the lot. By the middle of the 18th century, only 7 per cent of land was in Catholic hands.

The land problem

Any threat from the trading class was removed when swingeing restrictions were imposed on commerce between Ireland and England. The country was left with only the land to rely on and the peasants put in the position of slaves. No hope of redemption was offered: if a tenant worked hard to improve his holding, the land-

lish establishment to end James's "Popish ways" and his success in doing so is still commemorated annually on 12 July with mammoth parades by Protestant Orangemen throughout Northern Ireland.

From that day in 1690, Roman Catholics became a persecuted majority in Ireland. Their share of land ownership tumbled to just 15 percent. New anti-Catholic legislation, the "penal laws", barred them from all public life and much social activity. They weren't allowed to buy land or rent it profitably. When a Catholic landowner died, his property

THE POVERTY TRAP

The king's representative, the Viceroy, reported in 1770 that Irish peasants were "amongst the most wretched people on earth".

lord would raise his rent.

But the people blamed their plight not on the king but on the landlords. Even the Catholic gentry did not resent the king's control; indeed, when the American colonies declared their independence in 1776, the Catholics reaffirmed their allegiance to George III. Also, many of the middle-class "Ascendancy" were prospering. Arthur Guinness, for instance, introduced his famous stout in 1759.

But trouble was inevitable and, gradually, violent groups of men began to ride out at night avenging themselves on their oppressors –

maiming landlords' cattle, burning barns, firing shots through windows. These secret societies, with names such as the Whiteboys and the Ribbonmen, deflected much of the masses' energy from more political aims. Jonathan Swift, the Irish-born dean of St Patrick's Protestant Cathedral in Dublin and the author of such incisive satires as *Gulliver's Travels*, had a more political sensibility: he endorsed the call to his fellow countrymen to burn everything English except their coal, and he advocated a separate parliament for Ireland.

THE FRENCH LESSON

The echoes of the French Revolution of 1789 were heard loudly in Ireland.. Fashionable Dubliners addressed one another as "Citizen". Demands grew for Catholic emancipation.

fourths of the population) were still denied any political role and the extensive patronage at the disposal of the English parliament allowed it easily to manipulate policy in Dublin.

The government in London thought it had done rather well to pass two Catholic Relief Acts giving Roman Catholics limited voting rights and allowing them once more to own or lease land. As so often in Ireland, however, a well-meaning policy gave birth to anarchy. Catholics began buying land in Ulster, forcing up

Pressure for political change was applied by Protestant patriots such as Henry Grattan. The threat of physical force was added in the shape of the Irish Volunteers, 80,000 strong by 1782. London caved in and agreed to a separate parliament in Dublin. At last Ireland was an independent nation – although only legislatively, since allegiance was still owed to the British Crown. Also, a fatal flaw in the new arrangement was that the Catholic majority (three-

LEFT: William of Orange, victor at the Battle of the Boyne in 1690. **ABOVE:** Powerscourt, in Co. Wicklow, was one of the grandest English-built mansions.

prices and alarming the Protestants, who formed a vigilante outfit, the Peep o' Day Boys, to burn out Catholics in dawn raids. The Catholics set up their own vigilante force, the Defenders. The lines of a long conflict were drawn.

A secret society is born

Yet Ulster was the cradle in 1791 for a brave attempt by Protestants and Catholics to fight together for reform. Wolfe Tone, the son of a respectable Protestant coach builder, set up the first Society of United Irishmen club in Belfast and a second soon opened in Dublin. It began well, largely as an enlightened debating society, but was suppressed within three years when

William Pitt, the British prime minister, feared an alliance between Ireland and France, with whom Britain was then at war. Tone, condemning England as "the never-failing source of all our political evils", fled to America.

Government anxiety increased when the United Irishmen, largely a middle-class Protestant group, began forging links with the Defenders, who were mostly working-class Catholics. And soon an even more threatening alliance was being forged: the United Irishmen persuaded Tone, who had been thinking of settling down near Philadelphia as a farmer, to sail to France and rally support against Britain. Tone assured

Catholic Irish peasants, began arresting the organisation's outlawed leaders, identifying them as a result of information partly provided by informers, partly extracted through brutal beatings. Soon Ulster was in the grip of terror and the stage was set for a significant new group to enter the Irish drama. These were the Orangemen, whose role in Ulster remains central today.

The movement began in 1795 after a bitter clash between Protestant Peep o' Day Boys and Catholic Defenders at the Battle of the Diamond, near Armagh, in which 30 men died. The Protestants, fearing worse was to come, reorganised as the Orange Society, named after their

the French that their arrival in Ireland would trigger a national uprising, supported by the Irish militia, and on 16 December 1796 a French battle fleet of 43 ships set sail.

It was the weather that came to England's rescue. Severe storms dispersed the fleet, and the few troops who landed at Bantry Bay, on the southwest coast, were greeted rather unenthusiastically by the Irish peasants, who believed that the French really had been sent by the northern Protestants to suppress them further.

In the end, it was the United Irishmen who were suppressed. Pitt, fearing a second French expedition, imposed harsh martial law in Ulster. The army, four-fifths of whom were themselves

hero, William of Orange, and preyed as lawless bandits on Catholics. In defeating the United Irishmen, the government was glad of their vicious support.

The Great Rebellion

Disaffection with English rule climaxed in May 1798 in a major rebellion. But by then so many of the United Irishmen's leaders had been arrested that most of the risings throughout the country were too ill-organised to succeed. Also, the native yeomanry, revealing a disturbing aspect of the Irish character, reacted by torturing and shooting indiscriminately, often butchering the rebels after they had surrendered.

Within six weeks, it was all over. Perhaps 50,000 had died, giving birth in the process to countless ballads commemorating a small nation's struggle for freedom.

The notion of an Irish patriotism independent of England's fortunes was taking root with a vengeance.

Napoleon Bonaparte, pressed by Wolfe Tone not to abandon French support for Ireland, belatedly agreed to another expedition, which set sail that August. But again the French had been misinformed. When one party

MASSIVE CORRUPTION

Irish leaders who wavered about union with England found themselves offered peerages, offices of state and huge financial bribes.

Pitt's exasperated response was to propose a full union between Britain and Ireland. The 300-seat Irish parliament in Dublin would be abolished and 100 seats for Irish representatives would be created within the Imperial Parliament in London. Englishman, Irishman, Welshman and Scot would be treated equally. Opinion in Ireland was split, less on any patriotic principles than on cool appraisals of individual self-interest and economic prospects. But London's mind was made up and, after a period of

landed at Killala, County Mayo, having been led to expect enthusiastic, disciplined battalions, they found instead supporters whom they could at best regard as rapacious simpletons. Tone landed with another party at Donegal, was captured and died in prison after an attempted suicide. His martyrdom was assured, but the French declaration of an Irish republic was as insubstantial as so many other Irish dreams before and since.

political wheeler-dealing on an ambitious scale, a majority of five voting *against* the union was turned into a majority of 46 voting *for* it. Ireland's parliament had, in effect, abolished itself.

On 1 January 1801, with all the pomp and circumstance that attend such occasions, Britain and Ireland entered, in Pitt's phrase, their "voluntary association" within the Empire with "equal laws, reciprocal affection, and inseparable interests". As with most marriages, the intentions were good. Perhaps the two partners might even live happily ever after.

It was not to be. No one present on that day early in a promising new century could have imagined the terrible suffering that lay ahead. ❏

LEFT: Protestant prisoners are executed at Wexford in 1798 in what was regarded as a "murder without sin" (MWS). **ABOVE:** Thomas Robinson's *Battle of Ballinahinch* portrays a clash the same year in County Down.

THE MAKING OF A NATION

The union with Britain brought little happiness to either partner. And the divorce would involve more than a century of bitter bloodshed

None of Ireland's basic problems had been solved by the union. The peasants who worked the land still had no rights to it and no alternative employment had been created. They did not applaud or even notice the new arrangement, and agrarian disturbances continued, as the Anglo-Irish historian William Lecky put it, "like the passing storms that sweep so rapidly over the inconstant Irish sky".

This was the situation that Robert Emmet found when he returned from France in 1802 after the Peace of Amiens had ended hostilities between Britain and France. Emmet, a Protestant doctor's son, had been much influenced by the United Irishmen and concocted a plan to seize Dublin Castle, the seat of Britain's administrative power in Ireland, in July 1803.

The rebellion, like so many others, misfired. For one thing, Emmet had kept it such a well-guarded secret that too few supporters knew it was happening; for another, the last-minute organisation produced a comic opera of incompetence, with fuses for grenades being mislaid and only one scaling ladder being completed. Thirty people died in fitful rioting. Emmet, soon captured, was sentenced to be hanged, drawn and quartered. It could have ended there, but for the condemned man's inspiring speech from the dock. "Let no man write my epitaph," said Emmet. "When my country takes her place among the nations of the earth, then and not till then let my epitaph be written."

The rise of Daniel O'Connell

A more democratic approach was taken by Daniel O'Connell, a Catholic lawyer from a well-off Kerry family. Like many of his contemporaries, he had been educated in France and the ideals of the French Revolution had entered his thinking. He wanted no revolution in Ireland, though, not even a separation from the British Crown. What he campaigned for,

---

LEFT: emigrants bound for a new life in America.
RIGHT: absentee landlords continued to evict the poor who didn't keep up with their rents.

with powerful oratory, was the right of Catholics to become Members of Parliament. Soon landlords were alarmed by the success of O'Connell's Catholic Association, particularly when its leader, standing for parliament in 1828 as a "Man of the People", had an overwhelming victory. Sir Robert Peel, Britain's prime

minister, was forced to introduce a Catholic Emancipation Bill, which was passed.

Once in the House of Commons, O'Connell, by now "the uncrowned king of Ireland", began to rally support for his next cause: a repeal of the union. When his appeals struck few chords in parliament, he took his arguments to his fellow country-men, holding monster rallies throughout Ireland. At one meeting attended by 300,000 at Tuam, a Union Jack flew from the cathedral spire to underline O'Connell's insistence that Ireland did not wish to relinquish its loyalty to King or Empire but merely sought the right to run its own internal affairs. Also, he told the crowds, there must be no violence.

Ireland's greatest disaster

At that point, fate intervened in the form of the Great Famine that began in 1845. In reality, it wasn't a true famine at all; rather a failure of the potato crop. At its height, wheat and barley were being freely shipped to England, together with tens of thousands of cattle, sheep and pigs. But such produce was beyond the pockets of the peasants, whose every penny went towards paying rent to the series of middlemen – often as many as seven – who stood between them and their land's ultimate owner. All they could afford was the humble potato. When it was blighted, they starved.

The crop failed again and mothers were reported to be eating flesh from their dead babies. The *Mayo Constitution* reported: "The streets of every town in the country are overrun by stalking skeletons." And, all the while, food exports to England remained buoyant.

England's refusal to provide relief is regarded today as a horrifying failure of imagination, one of the worst in its colonial history. Even compassionate and otherwise enlightened men lacked the vision to question the wisdom of the prevailing economic orthodoxy, the rigid belief that it would make matters even worse to interfere with natural economic forces. The same

Twenty years before the famine, the novelist Sir Walter Scott had written of the Irish peasantry: "Their poverty has not been exaggerated: it is on the extreme verge of human misery." And, as their numbers grew – the population doubled to 8 million between 1800 and 1840 – so their misery deepened. Evictions began as the first potato crop's failure left tenants unable to pay their rents. An English MP described one large-scale eviction as "the chasing away of 700 human beings like crows out of a cornfield".

THE GREAT HUNGER

A Mayo curate wrote in 1846 of the people's plight: "They are to be found in thousands, young and old, male and female, crawling in the streets and on the highways, screaming for a morsel of food."

principle was applied to the industrial working classes in England's factories, but their lot was less desperate than that of the Irish peasants.

A million people died in the Great Hunger and well over a million set off in squalid emigrant ships for a new life in America, where they would pass down to future generations a deep anti-British resentment. Around a third of the land in Ireland changed hands as estates went bankrupt, but the new landlords, who were mostly Irish (of both religions, now that

Catholics were allowed to buy land), were even harsher than their predecessors in increasing rents. O'Connell's talk of non-violent nationalism seemed quite irrelevant and a group of his middle-class supporters broke away to form the Young Ireland movement, which was prepared to use the threat of violence. O'Connell himself died in 1847, aged 71, his dreams shattered.

In 1848, a year which saw nationalist uprisings in several countries of Europe, an attempted rising in Kilkenny was easily put down; it was a bungled fiasco, with little support from a weakened populace and none at all from the influential priesthood. A few wild

WHAT KARL MARX THOUGHT

In a letter to Friedrich Engels in 1856, Karl Marx analysed Ireland's down-trodden populace in terms of a class struggle: "By consistent oppression they have been artificially converted into an utterly demoralised nation and now fulfil the notorious function of supplying England, America, Australia, etc with prostitutes, casual labourers, pimps, thieves, swindlers, beggars and other rabble."

plans, like one to kidnap Queen Victoria during her visit to Dublin in 1849, didn't materialise. The Irish genius seemed to be for theatricality, not for effective action. As one disconsolate patriot put it: "God knows, if eloquence could free or save a people, we ought to be the freest and safest people on the face of the globe."

Revolution in the air

Tenant rights were talked about regularly by Irish MPs in the House of Commons, but good

LEFT: the formidable Daniel O'Connell, "the Liberator"; an Irish kitchen in the 1840s was far from primitive.
ABOVE: cows shared space with a cottage industry.

harvests after 1851 seemed to lessen the urgency. In 1856, James Stephens, a Kilkenny railway engineer, came home from France and took what he called his "3,000-mile walk" through south and west Ireland talking of an independent republic. But, failing to interest either the gentry or the tenant farmers, he concluded that perhaps only the labourers could be stirred to revolution. On St Patrick's Day, 17 March 1858, Stephens founded a society which later came to be known as the Irish Republican Brotherhood, dedicated to the idea of an independent democratic republic and branding its opponents as "ruthless tyrants" and "an alien aristocracy". An American branch was set up, called the Fenians after ancient Gaelic warriors. The American Civil War, Stephens noted, had given his supporters there valuable experience of battle. After a skirmish in Canada, Fenian participants were referred to as "The Irish Republican Army." It was the IRA's first appearance on the world stage.

Stephens was deposed as leader after his failure to organise an army of liberation from the United States, but by 1867 armed and well-drilled bands had been set up throughout Ireland to revolt. During one of the risings, some trains were derailed, marking the arrival in the country of a strategy that would shape Ireland's strug-

other Irishmen from Clerkenwell prison in London killed 12 Londoners and maimed 30.

The fight for Home Rule

But it was not terrorism that was to further Ireland's cause most at this time. The two principal engines of change were driven by William Ewart Gladstone, who came to power as Britain's prime minister in 1868, and Charles Stewart Parnell, an English-educated Protestant landowner from County Wicklow.

Gladstone's approach was far removed from the indifference of his predecessors. "My mission," he said, "is to pacify Ireland." He began

gles until the present day: guerrilla warfare. A ship, *Erin's Hope*, sailed from New York carrying much needed modern rifles and ammunition, but it reached Ireland too late and nobody could be found to receive the consignment.

The same year, too, England learned for the first time what it meant to have Ireland's grievances brought to its own door-step. A prison van carrying two captured revolutionary leaders was ambushed near Manchester, a police sergeant being shot dead in the raid. When three of the rescuers were caught and sentenced to death, an emotional appeal from the dock about the nobility of their cause transformed them into martyrs. Soon afterwards, an explosion meant to spring

in 1869 by removing one chronic grievance. Since the Reformation, the Protestant church had been the established church in Ireland, although it represented only a sixth of the population. Gladstone abolished this privileged position. Next, he introduced a land Bill designed to make it less easy for landlords to evict tenants. Sensing new hope, nationalists began to demand once more that Ireland should have its own parliament to administer Irish affairs, leaving international matters to the Imperial parliament in London. This aspiration became known as Home Rule.

Parnell, son of an Irish father and an American mother, had an arrogant personality and a political pragmatism that enabled him to take on even Gladstone without the slightest sense of inferiority. On reaching the House of Commons, in 1875, he scorned its cozy, club-like conventions and perfected filibustering techniques for blocking parliamentary business: proposing endless amendments, and making speeches lasting several hours. In one case, he forced an infuriated House into a continuous 41-hour session.

He had reason for concern

BOYCOTT'S LEGACY

An effective technique was to ostracise anyone who took over an evicted man's land; it was applied so successfully to a Captain Boycott in County Mayo that his surname entered the English language.

emigrated to Lancashire in England, where Davitt lost an arm in a factory accident when he was 11. By the time he returned to Ireland, he had embraced Fenianism, completed a term of penal servitude, and was convinced that the only hope for tenants was to have rents reduced by law to a realistic level and then to devise a scheme enabling them gradually to own their own land.

Once again, across Ireland, massive demonstrations were held. Funds from America

about Ireland. After several relatively good harvests, 1877's summer was wet and a flood of cheap grain carried from America by the new fast steamships was lowering prices to a point where tenants could no longer afford their rents. A new wave of evictions was threatened. With Michael Davitt, Parnell set up the National Land League of Ireland.

Davitt's parents, evicted from their Mayo landholding in 1852 when he was five, had

LEFT: two great opponents in the London parliament, William Ewart Gladstone (left) and Charles Stewart Parnell. ABOVE: an 1874 St Patrick's Day parade in New York features a bust of Daniel O'Connell.

flowed in to help the victims of oppression and threats of violence, frequently carried out, gave teeth to the Land League. In parliament, Parnell officially deplored the violence, and one Irish MP condemned the practice of shooting landlords because the gunmen often missed and hit the wrong person. At home the agitators gained some invaluable allies: the Catholic priesthood, which had previously stood aside from nationalist movements. Soon no-go areas were established within which justice was in the hands of the Land League.

Gladstone's 1881 Land Act was regarded as revolutionary. It granted fixity of tenure to tenants who paid their rent; laid down that a tenant should be paid when he vacated a holding for improvements he had made; and decreed that fair rents should be defined not by the landlord but by a Land Court. Progress seemed possible. But then Lord Frederick Cavendish, the new Chief Secretary for Ireland and Gladstone's nephew by marriage, was knifed to death in Dublin. Reform slid down the agenda.

Parnell's next move was to found the Irish National League to campaign uncompromisingly for Home Rule. A general election in 1885 gave him control of 85 of the 103 Irish seats in the House of Commons and ensured that he held the balance of power between Gladstone's Lib-

erals and Lord Salisbury's Conservatives. Suddenly, Home Rule became the main issue in English politics.

The Conservatives found it hard to regard Home Rule as anything other than the thin end of the wedge of full independence. After all, they argued, Home Rule would still leave the Imperial parliament controlling international affairs, war and peace, even customs and excise. How could any Irishman be satisfied with that? And yet the writings of the time show that most educated Irishmen, including nationalists, were happy to remain within the British Empire. All that self-respect required was that they should control their domestic affairs. Had Home Rule

been granted in 1886, therefore, Ireland might well still be part of the United Kingdom, having "a distinct but not separate identity" rather like Wales and Scotland. It is one of the big "ifs" of Irish history.

Ulster goes on the alert

But one significant group would have hotly opposed such an outcome. A million Protestants still lived in Ireland, almost half of them in the northeast area of Ulster, and Home Rule would have severely limited the power of this influential minority. These Ulstermen saw themselves as different, as indeed they were. Their Presbyterian tradition had always been more radical than the loose Protestantism of their southern co-religionists and had given them a formidable self-reliance. Although security of tenure had always been greater in the northeast, the Protestant descendants of the 17th-century Scots settlers felt far from settled; they had retained an ineradicable tribal fear of being dispossessed of their lands by the Catholics.

What's more, they had a lot to lose. England's Industrial Revolution, which had been stopped from spreading to most of Ireland by trade restrictions, had taken root in Ulster. The linen industry, permitted to flourish because there was no equivalent industry for it to compete with in England, had brought prosperity to Belfast. Then, in the 1850s, shipbuilding became a major employer. In those few years, Belfast was permanently differentiated from Dublin. Some saw the city as a New Jerusalem created largely by jerry-builders; others regarded it as an outpost of industrial Britian. Northern Protestants saw their prosperity being threatened by anyone who wanted to weaken the link with England.

This uncertainty was a tonic to the Orange Order, whose belligerent cry of "No Popery, No Surrender" succinctly defined, and still defines, its attitude. Leaders such as the Earl of Enniskillen gave the movement a veneer of respectability, but signs of the Orangemen's violent origins weren't hard to find. Lord Randolph Churchill ringingly reassured the northern Protestants on behalf of the Conservatives that,

---

BELFAST'S STUPENDOUS GROWTH

Belfast's population jumped from 20,000 to 100,000 between 1800 and 1850, making it Ireland's first – and only – industrial city.

ULSTER'S PLEDGE

More than 440,000 Ulster people in 1912 signed declarations, many in their own blood, that they would not recognise the authority of a Home Rule parliament.

if Home Rule were imposed, "Ulster would fight, and Ulster would be right." But the first Home Rule Bill was voted down in 1886.

England's values, so precious to the Orangemen, were being rejected in the south. A literary revival was growing, creating a new appreciation of Celtic culture and myths and a new respect for the Irish language, hitherto regarded as a fast-dying vulgar tongue. W.B. Yeats, the son of a Protestant Irish artist, published collections of folk tales such as *The Celtic Twilight,* conferring a new dignity on the often ridiculed Irish peasantry. A Gaelic League was set up, declaring itself the archer that would slay the plundering crow of the English mind, its arrow being the Irish language. It was time, said the League, for the Irishman to stop being a "West Briton".

In the political arena, however, there were setbacks. Parnell lost political support when the scandal of his long-time affair with Kitty O'Shea, who had borne him three children, erupted in 1889. Parnell died two years later, after being soaked with rain at a political rally in Galway. Gladstone himself retired from the scene in 1893, aged 84, having failed to get his second Home Rule Bill, which had been approved narrowly by the House of Commons, through the Upper Chamber, the House of Lords. It was time for the baton of the Irish cause to pass to a new generation.

The 20th century

As a new century dawned, a Conservative government in England held out no hope of Home Rule. Queen Victoria's visit to Dublin in 1900 and Edward VII's in 1903 were well received, but new forces of nationalism were being assembled by Arthur Griffith, a Dublin printer and journalist, and John McBride, a Mayo-born republican who had fought against the British in South Africa's Boer War. Griffith and

McBride demanded "an Irish Republic One and Indivisible".

Two general elections in Britain in 1910 left the Liberals and Conservatives almost equally split in parliament. Once again the Irish Party, now led by the moderate John Redmond, used its balance of power to press for a new Home Rule Bill. Such a Bill was introduced in 1912 by prime minister Herbert Asquith and looked likely to become law in the foreseeable future.

The Protestants in Ulster began arming themselves. They found as leader a Dublin MP and brilliant lawyer, Sir Edward Carson, who had been Solicitor General in a Conservative gov-

ernment and who had earlier acted as prosecuting counsel against Oscar Wilde in the writer's celebrated homosexuality trial. What, asked Carson, was the point of Home Rule now that most Irishmen owned their farms, all major grievances had been removed, and even a Catholic university had been set up?

In 1913 recruiting started for a 100,000-strong Ulster Volunteer Force and large consignments of rifles were imported. "This place is an armed camp," said Carson. The southerners responded by setting up a counter-force, the Irish National Volunteers, whose badge carried the Letters "FF", for Fianna Fáil, a legendary band of warriors. The problem, then as now,

---

LEFT: Orangemen opposing Home Rule march to Belfast's City Hall in 1886. **RIGHT:** Sir Edward Carson, a Dubliner, rallies Protestant Ulster against Home Rule.

could be simply stated. The Protestant majority in the northeast wished to remain full British subjects and were prepared to fight Britain to retain that status. The Catholic minority in the area, like the Catholic majority in the rest of the island, sought a more Irish identity. The two attitudes seemed irreconcilable.

Sir Winston Churchill, then a Liberal Minister, was first to voice publicly one possible solution. Six of the ancient province of Ulster's nine counties – those most heavily settled by Protestants in the early 1600s – might be excluded from any Home Rule agreement. Redmond, under pressure to get results, conceded that

these six counties could *temporarily* be excluded for six years, after which time he hoped the Unionists would see the wisdom of rejoining their fellow Irishmen. From the nationalists' point of view, it was a fatal concession.

The Great War intervenes

Larger problems than Ireland loomed for Britain in 1914 with the outbreak of World War I. A deal was rapidly done under which a Home Rule Act was passed, together with an order suspending its operation for the duration of the war or until such time as an amendment could be added to take account of Ulster's concerns. Ireland was thus bought off, to the extent that a greater pro-

portion of Irishmen volunteered for the British army than any other part of the United Kingdom's population. Irishmen won 17 Victoria Crosses in the first 13 months of the war. Surely, Redmond reasoned, such courage would eradicate even Ulster Unionist worries.

The reality was different. Carson, now a member of Britain's War Cabinet, saw the Ulster regiments' heavy losses in the war, particularly during the Battle of the Somme in 1916, as a subscription towards permanent membership of the UK. In Ireland, many still remembered the old adage that England's misfortune is Ireland's opportunity, and nationalists led by Arthur Griffith began grouping under the broad banner of Sinn Féin (pronounced *shin fayne* and meaning, self-reliantly, "We Ourselves").

James Connolly, a tough-minded labour organiser born into a poor Irish family in Scotland in 1868 and a soldier in the British army at the age of 14, had embraced socialist thinking, setting up an Irish Citizens' Army to defend striking workers against brutal police suppression. Pádraic Pearse, a shy and austere school-master, had developed a mystical belief that bloodshed was needed to cleanse Ireland, in the same way as Jesus Christ, by shedding his blood, had redeemed mankind. Philosophy and physical force came together on the sunny spring holiday morning of Monday, 24 April 1916.

The Easter Rising

As Pearse, commander of the patriots determined to liberate Ireland, set out to march down Dublin's Sackville Street, his sister pleaded with him to "Come home, Pat, and leave all this foolishness." Most Irish people would probably have echoed her sentiments if they'd had an inkling of the ambitions of the small band of unrepresentative middle-class intellectuals behind the Easter Rising. But Pearse proceeded and, with 150 others, armed with a variety of venerable rifles and agricultural implements, took over the city's General Post Office and solemnly read out, to the apathy of bystanders, the proclamation of the new Irish Republic.

Another 800 or so civilian soldiers took over a brewery, a biscuit factory, a lunatic asylum and other key points. Eamon de Valera, a young mathematics teacher born in America of an Irish mother and a Spanish father, liberated a bakery against the wishes of its workers, who had felt that even in a republic people had to eat.

As usual in Irish politics, dissension among the rebel components was rife, some regarding the revolt as "rampant neurotic romanticism". The Rising, planned for the Easter Sunday, had to be postponed for a day, and the chaos meant that only in Dublin was it possible to organise anything, and even there only 800 of a hoped-for 3,000 soldiers showed up.

Soon Dublin ground to a halt. Alarm and rumours spread. The poor looted stores and children ran-

REACTION TO THE RISING

The Rising was unexpected. A quarter of a million Irishmen were fighting in France at the time, and Dublin housewives, regarding the rebellion as treachery and madness, made tea for the troops sent in to quell it.

Sinn Féiners," one leading Irish MP wrote to his party leader, Redmond. "But a reaction might very easily be created." He then added the prophetic words: "Do not fail to urge the government not to execute any of the prisoners."

But Redmond's urgings went unheeded and on 3 May the first three leaders, including Pearse, were shot at dawn. The next day, four more were shot. On 5 May, one more. On 8 May, four more. On 12 May, two more – including Connolly, who,

sacked sweet shops. A British gunboat on the River Liffey began to shell the rebel strongholds. The inevitable end, when it came, was swift. The British set fire to the area around the GPO, burning out the rebels. By the time Pearse surrendered on the Saturday, 64 rebels, 134 police and soldiers and at least 220 civilians had died. The centre of Dublin lay in ruins. Martial law was imposed and 4,000 jailed. "So far the feeling of the population in Dublin is against the

LEFT: James Connolly, labour organiser and one of the rebel leaders in 1916. **ABOVE:** Dublin's O'Connell Street in ruins after being shelled by British gunboats during the Easter Rising; the pillared Post Office survived.

because a bullet during the fighting had fractured his ankle, sat in a chair before the firing squad. Nobody knew how long the executions would go on. It was, someone said later, "like watching a stream of blood coming from beneath a closed door". Slowly, in Ireland, derision for the upstarts turned to sympathy, then support. As Yeats wrote in a famous poem, the rebels had been "changed, changed utterly. A terrible beauty is born."

That Christmas, as a goodwill gesture, David Lloyd George, the "Welsh wizard" who was now Britain's charismatic prime minister, released 560 Irish internees from prison in England. Among them were Arthur Griffith, Sinn

Féin's founder, and a 27-year-old west Cork man, Michael Collins, formerly a clerk in London with the British civil service. Another batch of prisoners given an amnesty at Easter 1917 included Eamon de Valera, the sole surviving Easter Rising commandant. The cast was in place for the climactic act of Ireland's drama.

The hunger strikes begin

The new men wrote a script which was to be revived with uncanny fidelity in the 1970s and 1980s. They opposed Redmond's party at by-elections with Sinn Féin candidates, who began winning. Jailed supporters, on having their

Church's hierarchy condemned conscription – which turned out to be unnecessary anyway, as the war was soon to end – and the Irish Party walked out of the House of Commons. Sinn Féin had found a rallying cry, which it put to effective use, winning sweeping victories in the post-war general election of December 1918.

The new MPs boycotted the House of Commons forming their own parliament, Dáil Eireann, in Dublin's Mansion House. As president of their new "republic", they elected de Valera; the fact that he was languishing in jail at the time was probably worth an extra vote or two.

Standing behind Sinn Féin were the Volun-

demand to be recognised as political prisoners turned down by the authorities, staged hunger strikes. When one striker died after being force-fed, Collins organised a show funeral, massively attended. Arms were stockpiled. Lawlessness reminiscent of the 18th century started spreading in rural areas. By the time Redmond died (of natural causes) in March 1918, his hopes of bringing about Ireland's independence peaceably had turned to dust.

The next month, panicked by a setback in the war in France, Britain finally extended conscription to Ireland, throwing in as a sop new Home Rule legislation based on partitioning the island. It was a foolish move. The Catholic

teers, known in the countryside as the Irish Republican Army, who increasingly saw violence as an effective weapon. They began killing anyone in uniform who stood in their way, then progressed to selective assassinations. Like so many Irish conflicts, this one rapidly took on some of the characteristics of a civil war. The corpses found labelled "Spy – Killed by IRA" were usually those of Irishmen.

After an attempt was made in broad daylight on the life of Viceroy, the king's representative in Ireland, England, perplexed as ever, suppressed Sinn Féin. "The English government in Ireland," jeered Arthur Griffith, "has now proclaimed the Irish nation, as it formerly proclaimed the Catholic Church, an illegal assembly." Undeterred, Sinn Féin did well in the municipal elections held in January 1920.

When some of the boycotted police force – about one in 10 – resigned, they were replaced by recruits from England, many of them demobilised soldiers hardened to killing on the battlefields of France. Forming motorised anti-terrorist squads, they hit back quickly at any sign of trouble. But there were areas into which even they dared not go. In these, policing was taken over by the trench-

> ## A NEW COUNTRY
> The 1921 Treaty styled the 26 counties the Irish Free State, a literal translation of the Gaelic word *Saorstat*.

Sunday", Michael Collins had 12 British officers shot dead, mostly in their beds. That afternoon, at a Gaelic football match in Dublin's Croke Park, police shot dead 11 civilians. In the countryside, fearful families took to sleeping in hedgerows to escape the revenge killings. Guerrilla warfare spread, out of control.

In May 1921 Britain tried out a new idea, holding elections for two Irish parliaments, one in the North, one in the South. Sinn Féin swept the board in the South and the Unionists dominated the North.

coated Volunteers, who arrested and sentenced petty criminals such as house breakers and cattle stealers and enforced licensing laws. The government, with 10,000 police and 50,000 troops, was humiliated.

Run-up to a Republic

Before long, the police began fighting back, carrying out undisciplined reprisals after every IRA atrocity. On 21 November 1920, "Bloody

LEFT: Ireland's independence did not end the bloodshed on the streets of the capital. **ABOVE:** children in Dublin wave American flags to celebrate the ending of the Anglo-Irish war in 1921.

Partition appeared inevitable. That October, a conference was called in London at which Britain and Ireland, faced with the prospect of declaring war on each other, sat down to thrash out a settlement.

The compromises were agonising. But on 5 December 1921, at 2.20 in the morning, a deal was done, a document signed. The consequences would be enormous, for this was the first fissure, signalling the eventual break-up of the British Empire. To those present, the significance was somewhat narrower. Eight centuries of attempts by England's monarchs and ministers to rule their neighbouring island had, with surprising abruptness, come to an end. ❑

LIVING WITH PARTITION

Instead of coming together, the Catholic South and the Protestant-dominated North ignored each other for 50 years. Then civil strife erupted in the North

To David Lloyd George's dexterous political mind, the fact that the Anglo-Irish Treaty gave everyone *something* they wanted but nobody *everything* they wanted meant that it must stand some chance of success. This was the old mistake: the belief that the Irish were really Englishmen with brogues. In reality, the two peoples' expectations were quite different and, after eight centuries during which Irishman had fought Irishman over conflicting national allegiances, the first fruit of independence was true civil war.

The treaty gave the nationalists more than many had expected: an Irish Free State with a dominion status within the British Empire similar to Canada's. This was far greater freedom than Home Rule had ever promised.

The border question

But one dark cloud cast a shadow over the deal. Six counties of Ulster – Antrim, Down, Tyrone, Fermanagh, Armagh and Derry – were retained within the United Kingdom, the British having recognised that even the deluge of a world war had not softened the resolution of the northern Protestants. Sir Winston Churchill expressed the dilemma graphically: "As the deluge subsides and the waters fall short, we see the dreary steeples of Fermanagh and Tyrone emerging once again. The integrity of their quarrel is one of the few institutions that has been unaltered in the cataclysm which has swept the world."

To sell the long-resisted division of Ireland to nationalists, the government added a proviso: a Boundary Commission would decide which Roman Catholic-dominated areas of Northern Ireland would later be incorporated within the 26 counties of the Free State. This promise permitted patriots such as Michael Collins to swallow the bitter pill of partition: after the Catholic areas of Tyrone, Fermanagh and south Armagh

---

LEFT: a farewell to empire as Queen Victoria's statue is removed from outside Ireland's parliament building.
RIGHT: the new nation looked to the Gaelic language to help mould a new identity.

had been removed, they reckoned, what would remain would not leave the new north-eastern state a viable entity.

But Collins's hopes, faint though they were, were not universally held. Ferocious arguments split the infant Free State, laying bare long suppressed personal animosities. On the one side

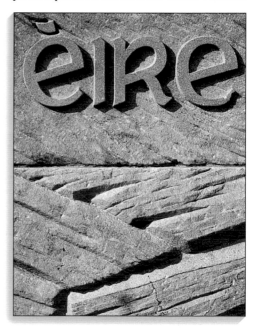

stood the pro-Treaty provisional government led by Arthur Griffith; on the other, the anti-Treaty forces massing behind Eamon de Valera. After a bitter 12-day parliamentary debate, the Treaty was carried by 64 votes to 57.

It was too narrow a margin to ensure peace, especially since the Irish Republican Army, mirroring the split in the country, was marching in opposite directions; about half with Collins, transforming itself into the regular army of the Free State, and the other half refusing to recognise the new government, relying instead on force to win them a free and united Ireland.

By 1922 Dublin's O'Connell Street was in flames again, with 60 dying in eight days of savage fighting. Northern Protestants, looking on, vowed to have nothing to do with any redrawing of borders, declaring: "What we have, we hold." Fighting broke out in Northern Ireland, too, with the death toll rising to 264 within six months.

The new Ireland's first prime minister did not live to see the end of the struggle: in August 1922, heavily overworked, Griffith collapsed and died. Collins had a more violent end, being shot dead in an ambush on the Macroom to Bandon road in his

STATE EXECUTIONS

The Free State government, in its first six months, executed 77 Republicans – far more than had been shot by the British in the preceding Anglo-Irish War.

effective surrender. But it was to dominate every aspect of political life in the Free State for the next half-century. The country's two main political parties today, Fine Gael (meaning *Tribe of Ireland*) and Fianna Fáil (*Warriors of Ireland*) are direct descendants of the pro- and anti-Treaty forces.

In 1927, de Valera entered parliament (the Dáil) at the head of Fianna Fáil. He came to power in the 1932 election, ushering in a new era of pious respectability and vowing to reinstate the ancient Gaelic lan-

native County Cork. He had been expecting just such an outcome: after putting his name to the Anglo-Irish Treaty, he had written to a friend: "Will anyone be satisfied with the bargain? Will anyone? I tell you this – early this morning I signed my death warrant."

De Valera's vision

The Boundary Commission recommended only minor adjustments, and even these were never implemented. De Valera's view of the border as "an old fortress of crumbled masonry, held together with the plaster of fiction" had proved false. Permanent partition had arrived.

The civil war ended in 1923 with de Valera's

guage and culture. "No longer," declared de Valera, "shall our children, like our cattle, be brought up for export." His vision was later spelt out in a famous St Patrick's Day address, in which he described his ideal Ireland as "a land whose countryside would be bright with cozy homesteads, whose fields and villages would be joyous with the sounds of industry, with the rompings of sturdy children, the contests of athletic youths and the laughter of comely maidens, whose firesides would be forums for the wisdom of serene old age." It was a noble enough aim. It just didn't particularly belong to the 20th century.

In the following three decades, de Valera built

Fianna Fáil into a formidable populist political movement, drawing support from small farmers, the urban working class and the newly moneyed. Fine Gael's heartland was among larger farmers and the professional classes. The Labour Party, which pre-dated partition, found it hard to build support: the trade unions, while nominally pro-Labour, often did deals with Fianna Fáil, and the Church's anti-communist propaganda encouraged a fear of the Left.

Endless emigration

"Dev", as he became affectionately known, pursued a policy of economic nationalism, raising

social scale from the farmhands, the once affluent Anglo-Irish – sometimes called the Protestant "Ascendancy" – fell into decline and their "Big Houses" at the end of long, tree-lined avenues began to look dilapidated.

Many southerners began to question the wisdom of following their leader's "Small is Beautiful" signposts. "It was indeed hard," said one observer, "to muster up enthusiasm for the cargeen moss industry, in the possible utilisation of the various parts of the herring's anatomy, down to the tail and the fin, in portable, prefabricated factories themselves made of herringbone cement along the west coast."

tariff barriers against England, which retaliated. A tax was even imposed on English newspapers. Yet not everyone was thrilled when, for example, Dev announced that Ireland was self-sufficient in shoelaces. Emigration, mainly to England and America, claimed yet another generation of younger sons unable to inherit the family farm and younger daughters unable to find husbands. In the early 1920s, an astonishing 43 per cent of Irish-born men and women were living abroad. At the opposite end of the

LEFT: Eamon de Valera's vision for a new Ireland had a strong rural emphasis. **ABOVE:** a turf gatherer in the remote west of Ireland

But what was the alternative? Certainly not to imitate the United Kingdom, Dev insisted, and, to emphasise the point, he produced a constitution in 1937 which abolished the oath of allegiance to England's king and claimed sovereignty over all 32 counties of Ireland. But it also underlined the pervasive influence of the Roman Catholic Church, thus alienating northern Protestants for good. The poet W. B. Yeats, a member of the Irish Senate, had warned him of the dangers. "If you show that this country, Southern Ireland, is going to be governed by Catholic ideas and by Catholic ideas alone, you will never get the North," said Yeats. "You will put a wedge into the midst of this nation."

The new constitution created a curious equilibrium. The bishops in the South and the Orangemen in the North each exercised a sectarian and politically conservative pressure on their respective parliaments.

Although the Unionists would have been happy to remain an integral part of Britain, Lloyd George, emphasising Ulster's "otherness", had given them their own parliament, Stormont – built on the outskirts of Belfast in the style of Buckingham Palace, only grander. And they had lost no time in making their makeshift state impregnable. London, relieved to be rid of the perennial Irish problem, did mended Catholic pipes. An all-Protestant part-time special constabulary (the "B" Specials) maintained close links with the Orange Order and helped the police keep dissension under control. The IRA, making little headway in Ulster, began a campaign in English cities in 1938, setting off suitcase bombs.

World War II

While Irish history was repeating itself, European history concocted another world war. The Unionists felt their self-interest had been justified when, as soon as Britain declared war on Germany in 1939, de Valera announced that

nothing to stop them. Nor, fatally, did the Roman Catholics' elected representatives, who boycotted Stormont. The assembly, the Unionists boasted, was "a Protestant parliament for a Protestant people." The historic hatreds between the two communities were left unhealed.

If anything, they were deepened. Taking advantage of the nationalists' boycott, the Unionists made sure that the plum jobs and the best housing went to their own supporters. Two distinct communities developed: Protestant dentists pulled Protestant teeth, Catholic plumbers

WARTIME VOLUNTEERS

Although the Free State stayed neutral in the war, 50,000 southern Irishmen joined the British forces.

Southern Ireland would remain neutral. Behind the scenes, Sir Winston Churchill, Britain's new wartime leader, offered de Valera a united Ireland at some point in the future if Ireland were to enter the war and allow the British navy to use its ports. De Valera said no.

Churchill's fears had not been unfounded. The Germans had been planning an invasion of Ireland, "Operation Green", as a springboard to an assault on Britain. In a handbook designed to brief their battalions, they noted that "the Irishman supports a community founded upon equality for all, but associates with this an extraordinary personal need for independence which easily leads to indiscipline and pugnacity."

Northern Ireland became a target. A ferocious night raid on Belfast in April 1941 killed more than 700 people. The Unionists claimed that the neutral South's lack of a blackout helped German bombers pinpoint their targets in the darkened North. Another grudge was chalked up on the blackboard of Irish history.

Over the years even the name of the Free State had been fiercely argued about. Both the English and the Irish seemed to find "Eire" (Gaelic for "Ireland") acceptable. But in 1948

also by the restrictions placed on entertainment. In 1954 a record 1,034 books were banned, and cinemagoers, if they wished to follow the plots of many films, had to cross the border to see the unscissored versions. London's more lurid Sunday newspapers published tamer Irish editions.

Northern Protestants looked askance at what they saw as the southern state's unacceptable intrusion into personal freedoms – its outlawing of divorce, for example, and its ban on the importation of contraceptives. Northern Ireland, Britain had pledged when the Republic left the Commonwealth, could remain part of the United Kingdom as long as a majority of its

a coalition government fixed the name of the country as the Republic of Ireland. Britain declared that, as a result, Ireland was no longer part of the Commonwealth. At last, Ireland – or at least 26 counties of it – was truly free.

Politically free, at least. Economically and culturally, Ireland remained chained. Emigration reached epidemic proportions, triggered not only by the loneliness, dullness and generally unattractive nature of life in rural Ireland but

LEFT: Stormont, symbol of power in British-ruled Northern Ireland. ABOVE: Nelson's pillar in Dublin's O'Connell Street was illegally blown up in 1966 to mark the 50th anniversary of the Easter Rising.

people wished. Since Protestants outnumbered Catholics by two to one in the Six Counties, that might mean forever. Some Protestants were so fervently "loyalist" that they would not even think of setting foot in the alien republic.

The green consumers

As Britain rebuilt its economic strength in the 1950s, Northern Ireland began to feel the benefit of its welfare state and industrial incentives, while the Republic remained essentially a humdrum peasant economy. In 1958, under the premiership of Sean Lemass, Ireland decided to rejoin the 20th century. He set out vigorously to create new jobs by opening up the economy to foreign investment, attracting light engineering, pharmaceutical and electronics companies. The dream of Eamon de Valera – who was now president, a largely symbolic office – faded fast. Interest in Gaelic language and culture waned and the voice of management consultants was heard in the land. The Irish, embracing consumerism with relish, seemed destined to become indistinguishable from the English.

Even the IRA failed to command much support in its continuing fight for a united Ireland. A campaign of border raids between 1956 and 1962 netted a few arms hauls but gradually petered out. By 1965, it seemed the most nat-

ural thing in the world for Lemass to have a good-neighbourly meeting with Northern Ireland's premier, Captain Terence O'Neill. But it seemed shockingly unnatural to hardline Unionists. Uncompromising voices, including those of several Cabinet colleagues and a popular fundamentalist preacher, the Reverend Ian Paisley, reminded him that Lemass's Republic still claimed jurisdiction over the Six Counties.

O'Neill, with his upper-class background, was ill-equipped to cope with the Pandora's Box that was opened just three years later. It began routinely enough, when a Unionist-controlled council in Caledon, County Tyrone, where many Catholic families were badly in need of

housing, allocated one of its dwellings to a young, single Protestant girl. Local nationalists, following the example of blacks in the United States, first staged a sit-in, then a civil rights march. A second march was planned for October 1968, inside the walled city of Londonderry. This is a symbolic place for Unionists, who still commemorate the breaking of the city's siege in 1689 when Protestant supporters of William of Orange defeated Catholic supporters of James II, thus cementing Protestant supremacy (Nationalists, equally tutored in the city's history, reject its "English" name in favour of the original Derry).

O'Neill's government, viewing the march not as a civil rights protest but as a nationalist conspiracy, banned it. Two thousand people marched anyway, and were met by the massed forces of the Royal Ulster Constabulary, complete with two mobile water cannon. Television viewers around the world were treated to the ensuing battle, as the RUC took their truncheons to the demonstrators with what looked suspiciously like enthusiasm. "It was as though they had been waiting to do it for 50 years," said a young civil rights leader, Bernadette Devlin.

Further marches ended in violence and O'Neill, having seen his dreams for a civilised relationship between the two Irelands consumed by the fires of sectarian hatred, was forced out of office by militant Unionists.

British troops march in

Almost inevitably, the Protestants' annual march through Londonderry in August 1969 sparked off violence. Petrol bombs were hurled, along with broken-up paving stones. The police replied with CS gas. Fighting spread to the Catholic Falls Road and the Protestant Shankill Road. The RUC, hopelessly out of its depth, appealed for reinforcements and, on 16 August, a reluctant British government sent troops on to the streets of Derry and Belfast "in support of the civil power". What was the choice? Northern Ireland was, after all, part of the UK.

It was an emergency measure, a temporary arrangement. Nobody imagined, in their wildest nightmares, that the troops would still be there three decades later. ❑

LEFT: Bernadette Devlin, the fiery civil rights leader who became an MP. **RIGHT:** the Rev. Ian Paisley, rallying Protestants in the late 1960s.

IRELAND TODAY

Leaving the North to fight its ancient battles, the South looked to Europe,
transforming in the process its economic and social values

At first the British soldiers arriving in what was technically British territory were welcomed as saviours. Catholic housewives, many of whom had been preparing to take refuge in the Republic, plied them with endless cups of tea. Girls smiled sweetly at them. Perhaps, it seemed for a moment, all would be well. But it was already too late for such hopes, for this latest chapter of Ireland's Troubles had caused a fearful resurrection: that of the IRA.

As a fighting force, the Irish Republican Army had virtually ceased to exist in 1962. By the late 1960s the declared aim of the small group of Marxists who constituted the rump of the IRA was to overthrow the conservative establishments in both parts of Ireland, then set up an ill-defined workers' republic. Lacking modern weaponry, they were acutely conscious of their failure to protect Catholic communities against Protestant mobs, a failure brought painfully home by graffiti which interpreted IRA as "I Ran Away".

The IRA is reborn

After a stormy meeting in the Republic, the movement split into two groups: the Official IRA, which had Marxist leanings and was interested in infiltrating conventional politics, and the Provisional wing, which combined a more simplistic nationalism with a faith in the efficacy of violence.

Recruitment to the Provisionals ("Provos") soared when the British army embarked on late-night arms searches in Catholic areas. Guns and explosives were found, but the sympathy of moderate Catholics was lost. To keep the two communities apart, the troops erected a ramshackle barrier of building blocks and corrugated iron, "the Peace Line". No one thought that the line would become a semi-permanent concrete and steel fortification, a Berlin Wall within the United Kingdom.

LEFT: Ulster's wall art conveys a sinister sectarian message. RIGHT: a Belfast loyalist publicly states her opposition to closer links with the Republic.

Trust and understanding between nationalists and Unionists have always been difficult because the two cultural traditions have so few points of contact. Protestant children still attend Protestant schools supported entirely by the state, while Catholic children go to schools largely financed by the state but managed by

their church. Catholic children are taught Gaelic games, Protestants play cricket. Catholics learn Irish, Protestants don't. Integrating the schools, a policy which might in the long term lessen the inheritance of hate, has proved an impossible nettle to grasp. The Roman Catholic Church in particular argues strongly that Catholic children must have the spiritual nourishment of a Catholic education. And, in any case, so few communities remain in which Protestants and Catholics live side by side that integrated schools would mean bussing thousands of children from one area to another.

In the anarchy of the early 1970s, relationships within Ulster were corroded further as shopkeepers in both Catholic and Protestant areas were visited regularly by vigilantes from their own communities demanding what amounted to protection money. Most paid up; those who didn't frequently found their premises burned to the ground soon afterwards. Gangsterism, divorced from any political objective, was added to the witches' brew of violence.

The IRA's armed offensive gathered pace, spreading terror by means of snipers' bullets, booby-trapped vehicles and bombs placed in crowded bars.

DIVISIONS RUN DEEP

Even underground, Ulster's communities are divided. Republicans work in the sewage tunnels in Catholic areas and Loyalists in the tunnels in Protestant areas.

of it, 13 civilians lay dead, shot by paratroopers. The date, Bloody Sunday, became yet another Irish anniversary to be commemorated violently. The following month, as a reprisal, a bomb exploded at Aldershot Barracks in England, killing seven people. As in the 1850s and the 1930s, the Troubles had spread inexorably across the Irish Sea.

Ireland joins Europe

In the Republic of Ireland, where many IRA men on the run took refuge, leading politicians

In the Catholic ghettos, the initial songs of praise for the British army had turned into a ghoulish refrain: "If you kill a British soldier, clap your hands." Protestant vigilante and terrorist groups such as the Ulster Defence Association and the Ulster Volunteer Force began to match violence with violence. Britain introduced internment of suspected terrorists without trial – a drastic remedy, but one which had worked before. It didn't work this time. The army, having arrived as mediator, was now in many areas the enemy.

The situation worsened dramatically when, on 30 January 1972, shooting broke out at an anti-internment rally in Londonderry. At the end

condemned the continuing violence in the North but were careful to ensure that the South would not easily be drawn into it. For, as bombs and bullets ripped Northern Ireland's economy to shreds, the Republic was enjoying unprecedented affluence. The inward investment policy had brought real, not fool's, gold to the end of the Irish rainbow. Large Mercedes and Toyotas sped German and Japanese executives through rural lanes, adding further unpredictability to Ireland's devil-may-care driving conditions.

After the country's entry into the European Economic Community at the beginning of 1973, financial subsidies descended, as seemingly inexhaustible as Ireland's rain. Former farm labourers, much to their delight, found themselves earning good money assembling electronics components, and one euphoric trade minister dared to describe Ireland as "the sunbelt of Europe".

Culturally, too, the climate was brightening. Writers and artists, once forced to emigrate in scarch of intellectual freedom, were exempted from paying income tax on their royalties. Some well-known names, such as thriller writer Frederick Forsyth, moved to Ireland to take advantage of the concession. One or two more provocative authors found it peculiar that, while one arm of the government was allowing them

London takes control

In the North, the sky was darkening further. Two months after Bloody Sunday, Britain abolished the 50-year-old Stormont parliament, imposing direct rule from London, and began attempts to persuade Protestant and Catholic leaders to set up a power-sharing executive. To the English, power-sharing seemed a perfectly sensible compromise. But to both tribes in Ulster, it was anathema: the Protestant extremists saw it as the first step towards a united Ireland, and the IRA saw it as a permanent hindrance to such unity. It collapsed and direct rule was reimposed

As atrocities multiplied, the death toll passed

to live free of income tax, another was banning their books.

Feminism reached Dublin, flourishing richly in a climate long hostile to female initiative. In one celebrated protest against the ban on importing contraceptives into the Republic, groups of women staged well-publicised shopping trips by train to Belfast. On returning to Dublin, they made a point of declaring their unlawful purchases to Customs officers and, on being asked to hand them over, informed the embarrassed young men that they were wearing them.

LEFT: In the North, the security forces were very visible.
ABOVE: In the South, poverty remained very visible too.

2,500 and an entire generation reached adulthood without ever having known peace. British governments suggested political formula after political formula, but none was accepted. Even well-tried nationalist tactics were failing to work any more: a hunger strike in an Ulster prison was ignored by Britain's prime minister, Margaret Thatcher, and 10 men starved to death.

British politicians sent across the Irish Sea recalled the plea of one 19th-century predecessor who wrote to the then prime minister, Benjamin Disraeli: "Ireland is an infernal country to manage, statemanship wholly out of place. The only way to govern is the old plan (which I will not attempt) of taking up violently one faction or the other, putting them like fighting cocks, and then backing one. I wish you would send me to India. Ireland is the grave of every reputation."

The truth was that most people in Northern Ireland had adapted to the level of violence. As the estimated 300 to 400 republican gunmen concentrated their fire on police and military targets, it was possible for the average citizen to live a relatively uneventful life. Indeed, it was reported that statistically the combined risk of being killed in the Troubles and on the roads was, at 22 per 100,000 population, much less than the combined risk of being murdered or of being killed on the roads in France (30) or the United States (32).

Hard times

Economic recession, and the reluctance of industrialists to site factories in Northern Ireland, made unemployment seem as great an evil as terrorism. And in this respect the South was faring little better. As the effects of the 1970s oil crisis became felt, industrial unemployment rose and inflation neared 25 per cent. Both governments were chasing the same investors. The North had the bad luck to win the tussle over who should build John de Lorean's gull-wing

CHARLES HAUGHEY: CHARISMA AND CONTROVERSY

Charles J. Haughey's personality would dominate and divide politics in the Republic throughout the 1980s. Well before becoming Taoiseach, he had caused controversy. In 1970, when Minister for Finance, he had been accused – and acquitted – of conspiring illegally to import arms for use in Northern Ireland.

He was also charismatic, as this pen portrait by the historian J.J. Lee makes clear: "An accountant by profession, with a capacity to master a brief quickly, he had abundant flair and imagination, immense public self-control, an ability to cut through red tape with an incisiveness that infuriat-

ed those wedded to the corruption of bureaucratic mediocrity, and an energy capable of sustaining his insatiable appetite for power. He was plainly Taoiseach material. Yet, widely admired for his talents, he was also widely distrusted for his use of those talents. He radiated an aura associated in the public mind with a Renaissance potentate – with his immense wealth (discreetly acquired after his entry to politics), his retinue of loyal retainers, his Florentine penchant for faction fighting, his patronage of the arts, his distinctive personality, at once crafty and conspiratorial, resilient and resourceful, imaginative but insecure."

sports car: the Belfast factory closed after the UK had poured £17 million into it.

The parlous state of the Republic's economy was not helped when Fianna Fáil, out of power since 1973, successfully wooed the electorate in the 1977 general election with an irresponsibly profligate manifesto. State spending, much of it on creating non-productive public service jobs, soared out of control and the state's foreign debt became mountainous.

The Haughey era

At one stage in 1981–82, there were three elections within 18 months. The country's complex system of proportional representation meant that Fianna Fáil minority administrations, now led by the charismatic Charles Haughey, *(see panel, facing page)* alternated with Fine Gael-Labour coalitions led by Garret FitzGerald, whose genial manner concealed a sharp political brain.

The last of these coalitions, from late 1982 to 1987, had one major achievement: it succeeded in negotiating, with the British Prime Minister Margaret Thatcher, the Anglo-Irish Agreement. This gave the Irish Government a consultative role in the administration of Northern Ireland, while committing British and Irish law and security forces to work together against terrorism and reaffirming that the Six Counties would remain part of the United Kingdom as long as a majority of their people favoured that option.

It was a Haughey administration that eventually introduced fiscal measures brutal enough to halt the Republic's economic deterioration. Public services were cut and unemployment soared, but the ground was laid for better times in the 1990s. That decade was ushered in by the election as Ireland's president of the left-wing Mary Robinson, a leading lawyer and feminist who stood for liberal and pluralist values. In her seven-year term, she was to transform the presidency from being a dumping ground for retired politicans to a force for social change.

Suspicions grew about Charles Haughey's financial probity and in 1992 he was forced from office, to be replaced by Albert Reynolds, a homelier, less charismatic figure. Five years later Haughey was charged for having received while in office more than £1m of undeclared funds from supermarket tycoon Ben Dunne.

LEFT: Charles Haughey, a cunning political magician.
RIGHT: Ireland's first female president, Mary Robinson.

The abortion debate

The 1992 election, which resulted in a coalition led by Reynolds, also involved voters adjudicating by referendum on a bizarre debate about abortion. The controversy had erupted when it emerged that the attorney-general (the Government's chief legal advisor) had sought an injunction to prevent a 14-year-old rape victim going to England to have an abortion.

To many people, the proposal seemed both hypocritical and irrelevant since an estimated 4,000 Irish women travelled to Britain each year for abortions. But after a vitriolic public debate, the Constitution was amended to support the

attorney-general's view and defend the right to life of the unborn.

The issue would not die down, and three proposals were put to the electorate. The first guaranteed freedom of travel (thereby ensuring that women could continue to go abroad for abortions). The second promised freedom of information "relating to services lawfully available in another state." The third, and most contentious, outlawed termination of pregnancy unless it was necessary "to save the life, as distinct from the health, of the mother." It also specifically excluded the risk of suicide acknowledged by the Supreme Court.

After an acrimonious debate, this last proposal was defeated; the others, on freedom of travel and information, were passed. Abortion therefore remained legal, but in narrow and ill-defined circumstances.

Divorce at last

The most striking feature of the abortion debate was that it was carried on by powerful cliques – politicians, lawyers, clerics, doctors – consisting overwhelmingly of men. But the ground was shifting significantly and a 1995 referendum on divorce gave the pro-divorce faction the slimmest of majorities: less than 1 percent. Such a result would have been inconceivable a

citizenship. But, as traffic jams in Belfast were caused for the first time in 25 years not by security checks but by coachloads of Christmas shoppers from provincial towns and from Dublin, there was an intense popular desire to avoid any return to violence.

Political see-saw

As hope spread in the North, confusion reigned in the South as Albert Reynolds's Fianna Fáil-led coalition collapsed. After weeks of political horse-trading, a new coalition emerged led by Fine Gael's leader, John Bruton, portrayed as a colourless politician and more sympathetic

decade earlier. Despite the closeness of the vote, enough politicians of all parties were emboldened to ensure that divorce finally became legal in the Republic two years later.

A truce is declared

Suddenly, in 1994, it seemed an end might be in sight to the troubles in the North: the IRA declared a ceasefire and, after initial scepticism, the Loyalist terrorists did the same. As tentative talks began between the British and the Irish, it was unclear what had really changed: Republicans still wanted an end to British rule in any part of the island and Ulster Unionists still refused to contemplate abandoning their British

HYMNS ANCIENT AND MODERN

The traditional rigid division between God and Mammon became more and more blurred as the millennium approached. Newpaper columnist Gene Kerrigan summed up the new attitude rather well: "The best-selling album in Ireland right now is a compilation of old church hymns called Faith of Our Fathers. A decade or so ago, I would have revolted against that album – seeing it as a symbol of repression. Now I enjoy it – because it's nostalgic, and it reminds me of hymns I sang as a kid. Buying a record of hymns nowadays doesn't mean that you're married to the values they represent."

THE ENDLESS CONFLICT

The writer Dervla Murphy cleverly summed up British and Irish impatience towards the Northern Ireland drama: "They want the play to end – and who can blame them? It has gone on too long, the plot has become too confusing, it is very expensive to produce and the critics are not impressed."

than most to Ulster Unionist fears. But he was lucky, too: the economy began to flourish as never before, as did artistic creativity, and the combination gave the Irish a jaunty confidence.

The European Union was largely responsible

well-educated workforce and generous grants and tax incentives lured more than 300 electronics companies to the Republic. Computer giants such as Dell and Gateway began assembling computers there, and Microsoft established its European operations centre in Dublin. Thanks to the wonders of satellite transmission, women in remote villages plagued for decades by unemployment began to be offered jobs keying in data for American hospitals and life insurance companies – they were so much cheaper than typists in the United States.

The buoyant job market eroded one of the Republic's most distinctive characteristics: the

for the economy's upturn. Economically, jobs were created and roads built as billions of pounds poured into the country from the European social fund. Cheques from Brussels made up almost half the income of Irish farmers. Psychologically, any lingering inferiority complex towards Britain was eroded as the new wealth reduced the country's economic dependence on trade with its larger neighbour.

Ireland began promoting itself as the Silicon Valley of Europe. Its combination of a youthful,

LEFT: women in Dublin protest against anti-abortion laws. **ABOVE:** youthful vandals became a major social problem on Dublin housing estates in the 1980s.

fatalism with which young people emigrated – at a rate of some 30,000 a year in the 1980s – mainly to Britain and the United States. Suddenly many of those who had gone in the 1980s came home, flaunting the experience they'd gained abroad and grabbing many of the new jobs. This unaccustomed immigration had one negative effect: it meant that overall unemployment stayed high, at around 12 or 13 percent.

As the transformation of the economy became known abroad, Ireland became a magnet for refugees. Having exported people for centuries, Ireland was unprepared to import them, yet refugees from destinations as diverse as Romania and Zaire, learning of Ireland's comparatively liberal immigration laws, arrived in Dublin. Applications for asylum, which had been only 30 to 40 a year at the beginning of the decade, soared to several thousand a year. Politicians feared a backlash if the immigrants proved to be economic migrants rather than political refugees. Perhaps, they mused, Mary Robinson would be able to lend a hand: in 1997 she gave up the Irish presidency to become the United Nations High Commissioner for Human Rights.

A love affair with Europe

Happily, Europe loved Ireland just as much as Ireland loved Europe – if nothing else because

its support acted as a useful counterweight to Britain's often antagonistic attitude. Being small and remote lent enchantment, too: Ireland could never have got away with offering corporate tax incentives that made a mockery of EU harmonisation if it had been a serious economic competitor to France or Germany.

The effects weren't wholly beneficial. For example, because agricultural subsidies favoured sheep farming, the republic's sheep population more than trebled to over 5 million and some lush parts of the west looked like being turned into rocky hillsides by overgrazing.

Tourism benefited, though, as Ireland suddenly became a chic tourist destination. Part of this popularity could be traced to the success of bands such as U2 and the international success of Riverdance, the show that sexualised traditional Irish dancing. The Irish talent for making merry was also highlighted by the creation of more than 1,000 Irish theme pubs overseas, from Durty Nellie's in Amsterdam to O'Kims in Seoul. For the first time, a £30 million advertising campaign promoted both the Republic and Northern Ireland as a joint destination.

Social changes

On the political front, a change of government in Britain in 1997 encouraged the IRA to declare a second ceasefire, and peace talks – this time involving Sinn Féin – were resumed. The optimistic climate, however, did not do John Bruton's centre-left coalition much good in the Republic's general election that year and a centre-right coalition of Fianna Fáil and the Progressive Democrats came to power. The coalition's leader, 45-year-old Bertie Ahern, was notable for being the first Irish Taoiseach to be separated from his wife and living openly with another woman. This underlined how quickly Ireland had developed into a more liberal, pluralist society – one that might even, some day, win the approval of Ulster Unionists.

The Alice in Wonderland nature of Irish politics was also highlighted in 1997 by the election of Mary McAleese, a Belfast academic with strong nationalist sympathies, to the presidency. Being a citizen of Northern Ireland, Mrs McAleese could not cast a vote in the Republic's presidential contest, yet she could legally stand as a candidate – and win.

But the Emerald Isle hadn't quite become the Garden of Eden. Dublin in particular was bedevilled by criminal racketeering, much of it centred on the lucrative drug trade. The scale of the problem became apparent to the outside world only in 1996 when the gangs gunned down Veronica Guerin, the country's leading

---

THE GAELIC REVIVAL

Although as many as 500,000 people can speak Gaelic with some degree of fluency, it is the everyday language of fewer than 20,000 people. But efforts to promote it continue and in 1996 a subsidised Irish-language TV station, Teilifís na Gaeilge, began broadcasting from a base in Connemara.

investigative journalist. In addition, there were disturbing reports of racial violence as gangs in Dublin declined to extend Ireland's traditional "hundred thousand welcomes" to immigrants.

The Irish had few qualms about embracing the euro in 2002, however (although Northern Ireland, as part of the UK, retained the pound). But the rules surrounding the common European currency restricted their domestic economic options, and a world downturn in trade finally tranquilised the Celtic tiger. In particular, American companies severely cut back their Irish operations.

In Northern Ireland, a peace agreement has been signed in the early hours of Good Friday

now Minister of Education – in charge of the teaching of both Protestant and Catholic children – seemed to symbolise the remarkable progress that had been made,

But the foundations of trust remained shaky, not helped by a continuing low level of violence in both communities and a refusal by terrorists to destroy their weapons. Direct rule from London was reimposed, and in 2003 the stalemate hardened significantly when elections favoured the two parties at either end of the political spectrum: Ian Paisley's Democratic Unionist Party and Gerry Adams's Sinn Féin.

A record-breaking £26 million bank robbery

1998 by all the main political parties, including Sinn Féin, and the Republic changed its constitution to renounce its territorial claim to the North. However, the Unionists refused to participate in any governing body until the IRA began handing over its weapons and it was not until late 1999 that an all-party assembly, with Unionists and Republicans facing each other for the first time, was set up to provide demonstrably fair government. The fact that Martin McGuinness, a former IRA leader in Derry, was

LEFT: primary colours in Dublin's Temple Bar.
ABOVE: prime minister Bertie Ahern casts his vote in favour of expanding European Union membership..

in Belfast at the end of 2004 was blamed on the IRA, and shortly afterwards IRA members admitted to the brutal murder of a Catholic in a Belfast pub brawl, alienating many of their remaining sympathisers in both Ireland and the United States. This high-profile criminality torpedoed hopes of Sinn Féin taking part in any revived assembly in the immediate future, and so direct rule from London continued.

Hope and despair, those familiar partners in Irish affairs, kept the future uncertain. Realists knew that Macauley's words remained as true as ever: beneath the thin crust of today's events, the hot lava of history, 800 years of it, refuses to stop flowing. ❑

IRELAND'S ARCHITECTURE

Ireland has history like dogs have fleas, and its buildings reflect not only a catalogue of conquest but also its roots as a purely agrarian economy

"Never accept a commission in Ireland," a 19th-century English architect warned his colleagues. His fear was that only the most rugged buildings could withstand the rain and the wind sweeping in from the Atlantic. In the 20th century, two even greater threats emerged: bitter warfare which would see many of the great Anglo-Irish manors burnt to the ground, and the rapacity of property developers which would devastate Dublin's Georgian heritage.

Ireland's buildings reflect a history of conquest. From the 12th century, Anglo-Norman fortresses were designed to intimidate. But Ireland proved hard to subjugate and fortified tower houses, obsolete in the rest of Europe, continued to be built in Ireland until the end of the 17th century. In the 18th century, the British imported Palladian and Georgian styles of domestic architecture.

Neo-classical influences spread to humble farm houses, which embraced symmetry by adopting a central doorway. But the crude thatched cottage didn't die: it evolved into the crude modern bungalows which disfigure the countryside today.

△ **ROMANTIC CASTLE**
Lemaneagh Castle is a striking ruin of an extended tower house, dating from 1480 and attached to a 17th-century four-storey mansion. It can be found in the Burren area of Co. Clare, on route R476 from Kilfenora through Killinaboy.

△ **THE ROMANTIC IMAGE**
The English tradition of fine carpentry did not extend to Ireland, and the limestone or clay thatched cottage was not built to last. Traditional long-houses combined a dwelling with a shelter for animals. Cottages were built where there was shelter from the wind and a spring could provide water. An open hearth fuelled by turf provided both cooking and heating facilities.

▷ **GEORGIAN ELEGANCE**
Dublin became a showpiece city in the 18th century, with areas such as Fitzwilliam Square (right) conveying an elegant simplicity that implied social status. It was clearly a European capital. By contrast, Belfast was an industrial city, whose rapid growth in the 19th century produced some grand civic edifices but mainly utilitarian Victorian buildings.

◁ **PALATIAL SPLENDOUR**
Bantry House in Co. Cork is about as far as you can get from the cliché image of an Irish cottage, and hints at the lifestyle enjoyed by the Anglo-Irish aristocracy. When the 2nd Earl of Bantry inherited this Georgian house in 1845, he began turning it into a repository for the art and antiques he collected on his world travels. An amateur architect, he had a theatrical sense of design. Parallels with the Capitol Building in Washington DC reinforce the claims of Charles Frederick Anderson, who emigrated to the US, that he had a hand in both. Its collection of carpets, tapestries and furniture is open to the public, and it offers one of the best views over Bantry Bay.

▽ **POLITICAL RETREAT**
Avondale House, a classic Georgian building in Co. Wicklow, was the birthplace of the leading politician Charles Stewart Parnell (1846–91). Now a museum, it is surrounded by a forest park.

THE FIGHT FOR OLD DUBLIN

Dublin in the 18th century was one of the ornaments of Europe, its Georgian buildings expressing a distinctive graciousness. In 1757, it established the Wide Streets Commission, Europe's first town planning authority.

Much of that heritage was destroyed in the unregulated explosion in property speculation during the 1960s. Whole streets were razed and replaced by often unsympathetic office blocks. Classic Georgian terraces vanished. Protests peaked in the late 1970s after an important Viking site at Wood Quay was obliterated in order to build offices for city officials.

The recent record has been better. CIE, the state transport authority, began buying up property in the Temple Bar area south fo the Liffey with the intention of building a huge bus depot. They temporarily rented out some of the small shops to artists, designers and restaurateurs and the district took on a bohemian atmosphere. Eventually public pressure killed off the bus depot scheme and the narrow cobbled streets of Temple Bar have now become the city's liveliest artistic and gastronomic quarter. The tide may have turned.

◁ **COUNTRY LIVING**
Kilruddery House in Bray, Co. Wicklow, is an example of a grand country house within easy reach of Dublin. Built in the 17th century, it was later remodelled along neo-Elizabethan lines. A conservatory was added in 1852, its walls being masonry instead of glass because it was meant to house not only plants but also the statues collected by its owner, Lord Meath.

THE ROLE OF THE CHURCH

Once, when a priest pronounced on any subject, no-one dared question his authority. Then, suddenly, the Church's power began slipping away

In English, the days of the week take their names from a curiously promiscuous collection of gods – Roman, Viking, and Pagan – from Saturn to Woden and the Moon. In Irish, three days are named after, not Gods, but penitential religious practices. The Irish for Wednesday translates as "first fast", for Friday as "the fast", and for Thursday as "the day between the two fasts". Wednesday and Friday were, in the great Irish monasteries, days of fasting and mortification. Thus, in Ireland, the everyday has been literally defined, not by wandering gods, but by religious practice. For much of Irish history, the sacred and the secular have been virtually indistinguishable.

Church and State

Catholicism in Ireland has long been a nationality as much as a religion. The words "Irish Catholic" do not denote merely a person of a specific faith born in a specific country. They have also come to stand for some third thing born out of the fusion of the other two – a country, a culture, a politics. Catholicism in Ireland has been a matter of public identity more than of private faith, and the struggle to disentangle the two is what defines the Irish Church now.

In Ireland, as in some other atypical European countries such as Poland and Croatia where political nationality was often tenuous or submerged, the Church became a kind of surrogate state, the only organised expression of nationality. Modern Ireland, in its attempt to become a European republican democracy, has had to struggle with the fact that the Church was there *before* the state, that it can claim, and often has claimed, prior rights over the territory. The state is young and fragile, with less than 80 years behind it. The Church is old and seasoned – so old that its language and culture, its imagery and its power, have seeped into the society.

PRECEDING PAGES: pilgrimage to Croagh Patrick mountain; church procession on the Aran Island of Inishmore.
LEFT: a cross on Inishmore. **RIGHT:** a detail from the pulpit in St Werburgh's Church, Dublin.

It is not just a matter of a strongly religious culture, though it remains true that Ireland is exceptionally religious by the standards of the western world. More people attend church once a week (86 per cent of the overwhelmingly Catholic population) than in any other Judeo-Christian society in the world. Asked how important God is in their lives, the Irish come out far ahead of any nation in Europe.

When it comes to belief in the existence of the soul, in life after death, in heaven, in prayer, the Irish score so much higher in surveys than the rest of the developed world as to seem not part of that world at all. Yet even this is not what is at issue, for such things remain, however deeply-held, still matters of private belief.

It is the public nature of Catholicism in Ireland that has really marked it off. The founding act of the modern Irish State – the 1916 Rising – was a religious as much as a political act, and was conceived by its leader, Pádraic Pearse, as such. Its symbolic occurrence at Easter and its conscious imagery of blood sacrifice and redemption shaped a specifically Catholic political consciousness that belied the secular republican aims of many of the revolutionaries.

Irish nationalism, the primary driving force of Irish politics for most of the 20th century, became, in both its constitutional and its violent manifestations, intimately entwined with Catholicism. Eamon de Valera, the nationalist politician who dominated the State's politics for 40 years, saw fit to get John Charles McQuaid, the Catholic Archbishop of Dublin, to help him to write the Constitution. In the early 1980s, IRA prisoners in Northern Ireland staged a

hunger strike whose imagery and effect were inextricable from Irish Catholicism's traditions of penitence and martyrdom.

In less directly political ways, too, the Church had an enormous public presence. The sociologist Tom Inglis has pointed out that in Ireland it was the Catholic Church which, in the 19th century, taught the peasant Irish not merely what to believe but how to behave. It was the Church which took an agricultural people used to landscape and the rhythms of the farming day, and taught them how to inhabit public spaces and respect modern, industrialised time-keeping.

And if the Church "civilised" the Wild Irish, it also provided the trappings of a state where

there was no state. The Church successfully outmanoeuvred the British government's attempts to construct a secular education system, and built its own mass education system under the control of religious brothers and nuns. It founded its own universities and hospitals.

Having built all of these institutions as alternatives to British rule, the Church retained them in an independent Ireland, and remains a massive temporal power, controlling most of the health and education systems and having a large influence in all other social services. Most primary schools are in Church ownership, as are 90 per cent of secondary schools. Teacher training is Church-controlled, as are most of the training hospitals in which nurses and doctors are formed.

Loss of authority

Yet this great monolith is not all that it seems. The Irish Catholic Church is also a troubled institution, suffering a serious loss of authority. Its strengths throughout the centuries have also become weaknesses in the Ireland of the 1990s. It is afflicted with a paradox: it cannot hope to retain power without giving up power.

The first strength that is now becoming a weakness lies in the very nature of Irish Catholicism itself. It achieved and retained its power through the centuries not by being simply the rock of Peter, but by being something much more like a geological section in which layer after layer of rock is submerged beneath the surface. It grew and consolidated itself not by obliterating what was there before, but by adding another layer to its surface.

Early Irish Christianity, for instance, flourished not by wiping out the earlier Celtic beliefs, but by adapting them. To this day, the annual

FROM THE CRADLE TO THE GRAVE

Irish people were, and are, likely to be born in a Catholic hospital, educated at Catholic schools, married in a Catholic church, have children named by a priest, be counselled by Catholic marriage advisors if the marriage runs into trouble, be dried out in Catholic clinics for the treatment of alcoholism if they develop a drink problem, be operated on in Catholic hospitals, and be buried by Catholic rites. In a sense, the Roman Catholic Church in Ireland anticipated European social welfare systems.

pilgrimage on the last Sunday in July up Croagh Patrick mountain in County Mayo re-enacts the worship of the mountain gods in a Catholic context. Early Irish Christian spirituality is marked by both the intimacy of a tribal society and by a use of natural imagery bordering on pantheism. John Scotus Eriugena (the name meaning John the Irishman, born in Eire), the greatest philosopher and theologian of the early Middle Ages, was indeed accused of pantheism, his great book *De Divisione*

MOVING EXPERIENCES

From time to time, there are outbreaks of superstitious enthusiasm, such as the craze for "moving" statues of the Blessed Virgin which swept much of the country in 1985 and 1986.

At a popular level, and often to the discomfort of the Catholic hierarchy, early pagan Catholicism remains very much alive. In many rural areas, acts of devotion at, for instance, holy wells, vestigial shrines of forgotten water spirits, survive in a Christianised form. In some places, such as Knock, in County Mayo, visited by Pope John Paul II in 1979, this religion of magic has been fully institutionalised by the Church. But in others, it remains on the fringe of Catholicism, barely

Naturae burned in 1210 and banned in 1685.

This tendency to localism and independence, to build on what is in Ireland rather than on a simple universalism, helped Irish Catholicism to survive under centuries of British rule. But it also forged a kind of Catholicism that is highly dependent on the nature of Irish society. So long as the society remained relatively stable, this rootedness was a huge strength. But, in a shifting society, the Church's very close relationship to the place and the people means that the Church feels the pressure of change intimately.

FAR LEFT: a pilgrim on misty Croagh Patrick mountain.
ABOVE: St Teresa's Church, off Dublin's Grafton Street.

accommodated by a church all too aware of its capacity to take on a life of its own.

The modern Irish Church, however, was built in the 19th century by the imposition on this native layer of religion of a particularly harsh and autocratic combination of sexual puritanism and centralised bureaucracy. Both owed their success to the trauma of famine, the catastrophe of the mid-19th century which halved the population in a few decades. Because the Famine had been caused at least in part by over-population, the new combination of French Jansenism and English Puritanism which the Church adopted made a kind of bitter economic sense and eventually led to a situation in the 1950s where Ireland had the lowest marriage rate in the world.

At the same time, the institutionalisation of the Church as an obedient, highly organised, highly efficient bureaucracy also had economic roots in the Church's position after the Famine as one of the few sources of wealth, development and social services that the Catholic Irish had. On the one hand, the jobs of priest and nun provided an acceptable economic status for surplus children. On the other, the massive church and school building programmes undertaken in the latter half of the 19th century were Ireland's form of infrastructural development.

A religion that had been local, intimate and more spiritual than devotional became a massively effective power structure. Between 1850 and 1900, Mass attendance rose from an estimated 30 to 40 per cent to the 90 per cent level which it retained up to the 1980s. However, as the Redemptorist priest Father John J. O'Riordain has put it: "The whole progress of the 19th century in Ireland, with its renewal of church structures, training of clergy, building of churches, expansion of religious life, and devotional revolution, might well be seen as one triumphal march. But the truth, to my mind, is less flattering. Success there was beyond doubt. But the progress was not so much earned as gained

in a somewhat dishonest manner. At best it was a display of wealth by somebody who had received a legacy."

That legacy, though, lasted well into the 1980s. The groundwork laid down in the 19th century was the basis for the Church's triumph in independent Ireland.

Holding on to power

Yet this very success also carried the seeds of failure. Because its triumph was so complete, the Irish Catholic Church did not have to develop the kind of complex lay culture which the Catholic Church built in other European Catholic countries such as France, Spain and Italy.

Because the media was mostly very respectful towards the Church, there was no need for specifically Catholic newspapers or broadcasting stations. Because the trade unions were only marginally "infested" by Marxism or secular radicalism, there was no need for specifically Catholic trade unions. Because all of the functioning political parties were fundamentally Catholic, there was no need for a specifically Catholic political party. Thus, Ireland, the most unequivocally Catholic society in Europe, has none of these things to this day.

Essentially, the Catholic Church exercised its power at the top and at the bottom, but not in the middle of the social process. At the top, there were secret meetings with Government Ministers and political leaders at which the Church could exercise great influence. At the bottom, there was the long-term power of controlling education and shaping minds. But in the middle, there was no genuinely Catholic intelligentsia and no Catholic civil society.

In the 1980s, the top and bottom layers of influence ran into deep trouble. At the top, the Church's political influence has become

THE CHURCH'S NEW INFLUENCE

After Ireland achieved independence, the Catholic Church became the effective arbiter of social legislation, having a ban on divorce inserted into the Constitution, encouraging the introduction of draconian censorship of books and films, delaying the legalising of artificial contraception until 1979, retaining largely unquestioned control over schools and hospitals funded by the taxpayer, resisting the slow development of a welfare state.

steadily more marginal. The Church scored two great political victories: by using its influence in favour of a constitutional amendment to ban abortion, and against a constitutional amendment to permit divorce. In both cases, it was on the winning side, and succeeded in holding the line against the march of secular liberalism.

Both victories were Pyrrhic, however, achieved at the cost of a break in the politico-moral consensus that ultimately undermined the Church's authority as being "above politics". By 1990, it was possible for the leader of one of Ireland's major political parties, aligned to the Christian Democrats in Europe, to refer to an

the Supreme Court, faced with the case of a 14-year old girl who had been raped and was pregnant and suicidal, decided that, under the "pro-life" clause itself, she had the right to an abortion in Ireland.

In the subsequent referendum to roll back this judgement, the Church, for the first time in living memory, was clearly divided and marginalised, with the bishops collectively telling the faithful that they could vote either way, but with individual bishops, including the powerful Archbishop of Dublin, Desmond Connell, taking a much harder line. The magisterial authority of the Church had been fatally undermined.

unnamed bishop in public as a "bastard".

In 1997 Ireland finally had to introduce divorce laws – almost inevitable after a 1995 referendum gave the advocates of legalising divorce a wafer-thin majority. In the case of abortion, the 1983 "pro-life" amendment to the Constitution recognising the right to life of the unborn foetus not only made abortion a matter of public controversy and thus increased public support for it in certain circumstances; it also led to the legalisation of abortion itself. In 1992,

LEFT: religious statues can be seen even in central Dublin. **ABOVE:** a Madonna at Ballinspittle, Co. Cork, created a sensation when it was said to move in 1985.

Too few priests

For different reasons, the bottom layer of influence has also become much more tenuous. Keeping control of schools, hospitals and other public services is a highly effective way of maintaining power, but it is also highly labour-intensive. It requires the kind of mass recruitment of clergy and nuns which made it possible up to the early 1970s for most Irish families to boast a member in holy orders. Such recruitment fell away almost completely during the 1970s, and has not recovered since.

The shock troops of Church control in education, the Christian Brothers, are moribund, with barely enough recruits to look after aged members in retirement, never mind teach in hundreds of schools. Likewise with most orders of nuns and priests. In the 1990s, the Church has retreated further into management of schools and hospitals, leaving the groundwork to lay personnel who are increasingly hard to control.

At the same time, there is increasing radicalism among those who do join or stay in religious orders. The extraordinary missionary tradition which sent thousands of Irish priests and nuns to a "spiritual empire" in Africa, Asia, and Latin America has, in a sense, reversed itself, with returned missionaries importing ideas which threaten, rather than reinforce, the

remember that "male geriatric dictatorship may well have been what finally toppled Communism in Eastern Europe."

Recognising that its power was threatened at the top and at the bottom in these ways, the Irish Church began to slowly accommodate itself to what was in the middle: the new Irish civil society which emerged from urbanisation and industrialisation in the 1960s. By the early 1970s, the Church was trying to jettison paternalism and present the image of bishops who could sing on TV chat shows.

It had, however, underestimated the omnivorous power of the new media. By 1992, the

Church's place within Irish power structures. Much of the most radical campaigning on poverty and exclusion in Ireland has come from the Conference of Major Religious Superiors, representing the large orders of priests and nuns.

A woman's place

Perhaps even more profoundly threatening to the institutional power of the Church is the quiet spread of feminism within its ranks. Nuns, for so long the obedient servants of the magisterium, have begun to threaten its authority, causing the eminent Catholic sociologist Father Liam Ryan to remark that the Church treats women like second-class citizens but must

bishop who was best at singing on chat shows, Bishop Eamonn Casey of Galway, appointed as the friendly face who could win through media charm the authority which the Church had previously maintained by haughty power, himself became a victim of the ultimate resistance to authority of the modern media. The *Irish Times* uncovered the fact that Bishop Casey had used diosecan funds for payments to the mother of his secret son in America. A sex scandal in the highest ranks of of the Irish Catholic Church, the last unthinkable event, had happened, and the Church discovered it could not be both magisterial and populist, that if you tried to show a friendly face, you could not control what might be revealed. An avalanche of reports on priestly misdemeanours followed: one died in a sex club for gays, another was tried for child abuse…

This final loss of authority has placed the Irish Church on an inexorable path of institutional change. It also explains why the Church cannot retain power without giving up power. At the level of institutional, bureaucratic and political power that it attained for itself in the 19th century, the Irish Church is mortally wounded. Its institutions are challenged from

HE WAS WRONG

In the early 1960s the Archbishop of Dublin, John Charles McQuaid, told his Irish flock: "Allow me to reassure you; no change will worry the tranquillity of your Christian lives."

decline. The Church on which it imposed itself – the intimate, pantheistic and spiritual Church which had shown itself to be virtually invulnerable to persecution and poverty even if Mass attendance was relatively low – shows no sign of rapid decline.

What Father Liam Ryan describes as the four deadly sins of Irish Catholicism – "an obesssion with sexual morality, clerical authoritarianism, anti-intellectualism or, at best, non-intellectualism, and the creation of a ghetto mentality" – will,

within, and its political power, though still exercised, is on the wane. The demands of a young, educated population and the needs of a pluralist society to disentangle itself from the tribalism that has made violence endemic in Northern Ireland both mean that the Church's grip on power will continue to weaken.

What the future holds

But it is important to remember that it is really only this 19th-century Church that is in sharp

LEFT: pilgrims in Knock, Co. Mayo, "the Lourdes of Ireland". **ABOVE:** pro-abortion protests called into question the traditional moral authority of priests.

ironically, become less important as the faithful vote with their feet and choose simply to ignore Church teaching on sexuality, to disregard clerical authority, to develop their own intellects, and step out of their ghettoes.

In a sense, the more easily Irish Catholics are able to reject the Church for its sins, the more easily will the religious culture which, like it or not, they have inherited, sit with them. Indeed, the Irish Church at the dawn of the 21st century looks remarkably similar to what it looked like at the dawn of the 19th: a focus for a relaxed but nevertheless deep spirituality in which the broad culture is what matters, not the minutiae of devotional and behavioural rules. ❑

THE YOUTH EXPLOSION

With half the population under 25, old values are coming under attack

"This is no country for old men." This dramatic assertion by the poet William Butler Yeats, framed in the opening lines of *Sailing to Byzantium* in 1926, would have seemed like a sad anachronism to the vast majority of young people reared in post-war Ireland. This was no country for *young* men and women in the 1950s, and the mail boat to England claimed some of the brightest talents of a generation.

Not that emigration was confined to the educated classes; it cut right to the core in a society which had been conned by the provincialism of the Republic's founder, Eamon de Valera, out of its colour, its vibrancy, its life force – and out of much of its potential. Socially, Ireland was a drab grey landscape, morose in its conservatism, backward-looking and defensive.

The tunnel of grey

All the while, the country's lack of resources (and so of employment) ensured a constant seepage. Those who went, however, were to return, bringing with them intimations of other cultures, other influences, other possibilities.

By the 1960s the Irish reached the end of the long tunnel of grey. The driving force was money: it was an era of economic expansion and many in Ireland wanted a slice of the international cake. Foreign capital was flowing in as investment. Export markets were opened. Aerials sprouted on roofs as RTE television programmes began. They sprouted especially high so that they could pick up TV programmes from Northern Ireland and Britain. It was a period of extraordinary excitement, and new influences were afoot.

Emigration dwindled with the economic expansion, and the population began to expand. The Irish were producing children faster than anyone else in Europe and, as infant mortality

PRECEDING PAGES: first Communion, Killorglin, County Kerry.. **RIGHT:** the average size of families has fallen, but there's still a need to create jobs for the young.

fell, the children grew up to find jobs in the Republic and to procreate as well. The changes wrought were profound. Although legislatively backward, Ireland by the 1980s had become in most respects a modern, vibrant young society. International culture had made an impact, sometimes sitting uneasily alongside traditional values, sometimes embracing them.

In search of the grail

The effects were most tangible in the area of music, where there had been a rich folk tradition. Pop audiences' interest in folk music during the 1960s had brought new enthusiasts to

traditional music sessions throughout the country. But while the wave peaked and faded elsewhere, interest continued in Ireland. The transcendent magic of the music attracted many thousands of American, British and, above all, European young people to come in search of the grail. To many, Ireland seems the last refuge of the irrational – and in many ways it is. Modern institutionalism hasn't penetrated too deeply into the countryside or psyche, and even Dublin retains a sense of community rare in cosmopolitan capitals. The characteristic Irish qualities of spontaneity and gregariousness have begun to reassert themselves. Visitors provoke inquisitiveness rather than paranoia.

With such a significant proportion of the population younger than 25 – the figure is just below 50 per cent – the rate of change is accelerating. These children of the 1960s generation entered their teens with totally different expectations. International pop culture vies with school, church and parents as the dominant influence in their lives. The new range of "youth" magazines and TV and radio programmes has made young people more sophisticated, more cosmopolitan, more informed – and more demanding. It hasn't yet made them more radical politically, though that change may come soon.

Young people are no longer prepared to sit around and wait for things to be done. The success of pop groups such as U2 and the fund-raising for famine relief of Bob Geldof are mirrored in the energy being invested in music, film, video and radio by thousands of youngsters. This energy was vividly captured in Alan Parker's 1991 film *The Commitments*, the tale of the rise and fall of a Dublin band that gained credibility not only through its realistically scatalogical dialogue but also because it managed to avoid tacking on a Hollywood-style happy ending. Riverdance, which debuted by filling an interval in the Eurovision Song Contest, became an international phenomenon. It's clear that, if the Irish have special gifts and aptitudes, it's in the area of communications and music.

Ireland's real appeal

These qualities act as a magnet each year for thousands of curious young visitors. The grandeur of the west coast appeals to those who have searched in vain throughout civilised Europe for a taste of gritty authenticity. West Cork, Dingle in Kerry, the Burren in Clare, Connemara in Galway and Gweedore in Donegal – each has its special charm; but the secret of real satisfaction lies in stopping long enough in one spot to get the feel of the authentic culture.

Despite the fresh air blown into the country in the past 30 years, Ireland is still too much a place for old men, with many lingering attitudes that Yeats would readily recognise. But the beauty of the new Ireland is that it has increasingly become a place for young people too. ❑

LEFT: a scene from *The Commitments*, Alan Parker's 1991 hit movie set in Dublin. **RIGHT:** more opportunity for leisure in districts such as Dublin's Temple Bar.

SONG AND DANCE

Irish musicians from the Dubliners and the Chieftains to U2 and Van Morrison
have had global success. And Riverdance has reinvigorated Irish dancing

An English traveller, writing from Ireland in the 17th century, had this to say of rural diversions on a Sunday afternoon: "In every field a fiddle, and the lasses footing it till they are all of a foam." No doubt the writer exaggerated, for if a fiddle was to be provided for every field in the country, it would have kept several factories operating around the clock. But his comment echoes the experience of thousands of visitors to Ireland in the intervening years and bears out the general view that the Irish are a remarkably musical people. Time after time, in letters and reminiscences, we find references to music, dance and song.

You'll still find in every town and hamlet, particularly at weekends, a traditional music session taking place in some pub or other. And it won't be laid on for tourists: it will reflect an authentic tradition going back hundreds of years, mixing haunting airs, lively jigs and soul stirring ballads, and revealing the influences of classical, Italian and even Spanish music.

Reinventing tradition

While other countries have seen their traditional music wither under the assault of mass-produced pop music, Ireland has witnessed a minor miracle: thousands of youngsters have been picking up the old tunes and songs and carrying them forward into the 21st century. With the international success of such groups as the Chieftains, Clannad, and the Furey Brothers, Irish music has taken on a new lease of life at home and abroad, and the Riverdance troupe catapulted Irish dancing into the 1990s in spectacular fashion. In the pop charts, the remarkable success of Irish groups such as U2, Boyzone, the Corrs and B*witched sent record producers scurrying to Dublin to sign up the next pop phenomenon.

But what exactly *is* Irish traditional music? Since the Irish are a disputatious people, there is no single answer. True *aficionados* would prob-

ably frown on songs such as "Galway Bay" and "Danny Boy", songs regarded internationally as typically Irish. Although "Danny Boy" undoubtedly has deep roots, the folk music purist would consider such songs too modern. To the purist, material can be properly classified as traditional only if it is several hundred years old and fits a

closely defined style of playing or singing.

Yet, in fairness, it is common at traditional music sessions to hear quite modern melodies, such as emigrant songs or patriotic songs of the past 100 years, or even songs composed in recent times such as the haunting anti-war song "The Band Played Waltzing Matilda".

The national instrument

Indisputably, the instrument most associated with Ireland is the harp. As the national emblem, it even appears on the coinage. References to the harp can be found in documents dating back to the 11th century, when it was used to accompany the poetry of the Irish bards at the courts

---

PRECEDING PAGES: traditional music in Hughes Bar, Dublin and, **LEFT,** in the street. **RIGHT:** traditional Irish dancing at the Galway Oyster Festival.

of the Gaelic kings and princes. However, as the ancient Gaelic civilization began to break down under English pressure in the 17th century, harpists had to find a new role. Many, taking to the roads, travelled the country, entertaining the aristocracy in the "Big Houses" of the time.

Other instruments used by the ancient Irish include the bagpipes, which were similar to the modern Scottish equivalent. In time, though, these gave way to a uniquely Irish instrument, the uillean or union pipes. These are played by using a bellows rather than blowing to inflate the bag. They are outstanding among the pipes of the world for their sweetness of tone, and are one of the principal instruments used by today's leading traditional musicians. Others include the fiddle, concertina, flute, tin whistle, guitar and bodhran (a round goatskin tambourine or drum played with a small stick).

Pipers call the tune

Closely allied to the playing of traditional music was Irish dance, which came into its own in the late 18th century. Travellers of the period have remarked that dancing was so widespread among the poor that dancing masters would tour the countryside from cabin to cabin, accompanied by a piper or fiddler, and would be paid by the peasants to teach their children to dance.

Each master had a defined territory and would settle into a district for up to six weeks, ensuring that there would be a festival of music and dancing for the duration. Stories are told of rivalry between various dancing masters for control of certain districts, and at fairs and sporting events they would often hold solo exhibitions of their prowess to decide who was best. A visitor to a town in County Kilkenny recounts seeing a large crowd gathered around two dancers who were taking it in turns to perform on the soaped head of an upturned barrel. They were, he was informed, dancing masters contesting which of them should "own" the parish.

The main occasions for dancing appear to have been Sundays, fair days, at sporting events – and, of course, at weddings, where the musician would be paid for his performance. For many of them, indeed, it was their only means of livelihood. The dances themselves involved communal and group dancing between the sexes to a variety of tunes and tempos which are

LEFT: blowing with brio at Enniscorthy, Co. Wexford.

known today as jigs, reels and hornpipes.There was also great interest in individual prowess, such as dancing within a confined patch of ground. When it was raining, the events were held in barns. In fine weather, they would take place in level fields, or often at a crossroads.

Many of the tunes and songs heard on these occasions had been handed down from one musician to another. A lot would have been lost to modern ears, though, if it hadn't been for the dedicated work of several great music collectors who began to travel the country in the early 19th century annotating and writing down the tunes.

Spurred on by nationalism

Another boost to tradition came at the end of that century from the growth of nationalism and a revival of interest in the Irish language and culture generally. After the founding of the Republic, the teaching of folk music and traditional dancing in schools was emphasised. The new state's broadcasting station, Radio Eireann, devoted much air-time to the native culture. More recently, interest has been stimulated by respected composers such as the late Sean O'Riada and his group Ceoltoírí Chualann, the forerunner of the Chieftains. The Clancy Brothers were a great popularising influence.

But perhaps the greatest credit should go to the Comhaltas Ceoltoírí Eireann, the body which looks after traditional music and song. It has hundreds of branches, in every county of Ireland and abroad, and organises regular festivals which culminate every summer in a three-day event called the All-Ireland Fleadh Ceoil. Usually held in a town in the west of the country, it can attract more than 100,000 people and answers the wildest prayers of local publicans.

Major centres such as Dublin, Belfast and Cork hold their own festivals. In addition, there are specialist festivals such as the one devoted to uillean piping. This event, held in Milltown Malbay in County Clare each July, is named after a famous Clare piper, Willie Clancy.

In the tourist season, many hotels lay on after-dinner dancers and traditional musicians. Medieval castles do the same sort of thing in grander style: near Shannon airport in the west of the country, for example, you can find Knappogue Castle, Quin, County Clare; Dunguaire Castle, Kinvara, County Galway; and Bunratty Castle, Bunratty, County Clare. But for authenticity you can't beat the musicians who sing and play primarily for their own pleasure rather than for the tourist coach parties – and you'll mostly find them in plain, unadorned pubs.

Reliable venues

Dublin alone has dozens of regular events, most held in the backrooms of pubs. In the city centre, pubs such as O'Donoghue's in Merrion Row have long been a magnet for lovers of traditional music. It was from O'Donoghue's that the world-famous Dubliners were launched in the early 1960s, and most nights of the week a lively session gets under way in the same back room. Other reliable venues include the Brazen Head, one of the city's oldest pubs, located in Lower Bridge Street; Slattery's of Capel Street; An Beal Bocht in Charlemont Street; and the Wexford Inn, Wexford Street.

To the north of the city, in the picturesque fishing village of Howth, the Abbey Tavern's reputation for traditional music and song (and good food and drink) is still justified despite increased commercialisation in recent years. On the south side of the city, the headquarters of the Comhaltas in Monkstown hosts regular events. ❏

LEFT: exuberant performers dominate a Dublin pub, but traditional music **(RIGHT)** remains very popular.

THE IRISH WAY WITH WORDS

Whether in the theatre or the street, in parliament or the pub, the Irish are renowned for having the gift of the gab. Where did they get it from?

The Irish are noted for their ability to perform remarkable conjuring tricks with the English language, written and spoken. This gift ranges from the calculated blarney of the professional tourist guide or the frothy whimsicalities of a Dublin pub through masters of conversation like Oscar Wilde and Sir John Mahaffy to some of the greatest names in world literature, from Jonathan Swift to George Bernard Shaw, Edmund Burke to Samuel Beckett.

And yet James Joyce, the ultimate virtuoso of the English language, noted wryly in *A Portrait of the Artist as a Young Man* the cultural alienation that underlies its use by an Irishman. In this novel, Joyce's *alter ego*, Stephen Dedalus, uses a word unfamiliar to the Dean of Studies at his university. The Dean, Father Darlington, an Englishman, suspects wrongly that the word is Irish in origin, which prompts Stephen to reflect: "The language in which we are speaking is his before it is mine. How different are the words *home*, *Christ*, *ale*, *master* on his lips and on mine! I cannot speak or write these words without unrest of spirit. His language, so familiar and so foreign, will always be for me an acquired speech. I have not made or accepted its words. My voice holds them at bay. My soul frets in the shadow of his language."

A minority language

Indeed, few visitors realise how recent is the general use of English in Ireland. Few know that Irish, not English, is still the official first language of the state and that, in matters of law, the Irish-language version of the constitution holds superior authority.

In 1835 there were an estimated 4 million Irish speakers, most of whom belonged to a deprived rural class devastated by the Great Famine of the 1840s and subsequent mass emigration. By 1891 the number of Irish speakers

had tumbled to 680,245. Today, the everyday use of Irish is almost exclusively confined to the officially designated Gaeltacht areas along the western seaboard, whose combined population is around 75,000. Yet over a million people claim some knowledge of the language, thanks to compulsory instruction at school.

The ancient Irish language survived repeated waves of invasion by Vikings, Normans and English planters. In 1366, so many of the Anglo-Irish settlers had "gone native" that the Statutes of Kilkenny forbade the use of Irish in a vain attempt to stop Celtic customs and language spreading among the colonisers.

The decisive abandonment of Irish in the 19th century was brought about not just by the impact of the famine but by the introduction of the National School System in 1831. This system decreed that English would be the proper language of instruction, and children who spoke the native tongue were beaten or gagged. Surprisingly, the system was condoned by national

PRECEDING PAGES: a performance in Dublin's Abbey Theatre of Sean O'Casey's play *Shadow of a Gunman*. **LEFT:** Oscar Wilde and, **RIGHT**, George Bernard Shaw, two Irish-born playwrights who found fame in Britain.

leaders such as Daniel O'Connell, who, although a native Irish speaker himself, declared that he was "sufficiently utilitarian not to regret its gradual abandonment."

Far different was the attitude of the 20th-century leader Eamon de Valera, who somewhat surprisingly said that "Ireland with its language and without freedom is preferable to Ireland with its freedom and without its language." The virtual extinction of Irish as a living language was certainly a tragedy because its structure was so closely linked to a distinctive mode of thinking. *Gan teanga, gan tír* was the slogan of the revivalists – "No language, no country" – and a certain element of the Irish identity withered as English took over.

Why Irish is unique

Irish had a venerable tradition, being the earliest variant of the Celtic languages and the earliest language north of the Alps in which extensive writings survive. It had a special alphabet of distinctive, beautiful characters. This script was, in a strange quirk of history, carried over into print by order of England's Queen Elizabeth I, who commanded a fount to be cut in 1571 for an Irish version of the Protestant catechism.

Unfortunately this elegant script was officially superseded by Roman script in the 1960s in an attempt to make the language more "modern" and accessible, and the use of Irish script is now rare. Outstanding examples can be seen in the *Book of Kells* or the *Book of Armagh*, kept in Dublin's Trinity College library, or in the *Book of the Dun Cow* in the Royal Irish Academy.

The 19th-century shift from Irish to English was so sudden and so resented that the mark of the earlier language was imprinted on its successor. Initially, Irish was regarded as "talk", the language of communication and imagination, whereas English was a necessary and utilitarian, but not fully understood, vehicle. During the 19th century it became commonplace for many people to think in Irish, then translate their thoughts into English. This process led to the development of the so-called Hiberno-English dialect, and sometimes produced effects of great beauty and elegance, even in the simplest phrases. Thus the bald statement in English "that is true" becomes either "'Tis true for you" (Hiberno-English) from *Is fíor é sin* (Irish) or

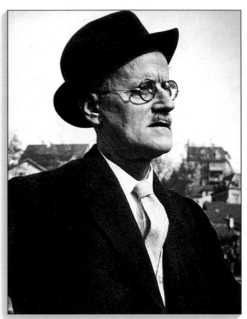

PLAYING WITH WORDS – AND WINNING

A classic illustration of the Irish love of language is the story of a battle of words between the patriot Daniel O'Connell and an old Dublin fishwife, reported to have the most virulent flow of invective in Ireland.

A colleague bet O'Connell that even he could not best this woman in dispute. He accepted the challenge and, on the appointed day, a quarrel was deliberately engineered. The old harridan attacked O'Connell with all the considerable verbal venom at her disposal. He bided his time and, when she was finally exhausted, let fly at her, eschewing vulgar obscenity, employing instead only the terms of Euclidian geometry. When he reached a climax of mathematical abuse, describing her as a shameless parallelogram, an inveterate isosceles triangle and an unregenerate hypotenuse, she collapsed in tears, protesting her virtue. O'Connell was the victor.

It is no accident that it was an Irish playwright, Richard Brinsley Sheridan, who created the immortal Mrs Malaprop in his comedy *The Rivals* (1775). She resents "an aspersion to my parts of speech" and avers that "if I reprehend anything in the world it is the use of my oracular tongue and a nice derangement of epitaphs."

"There's not a word of a lie in it" from *Níl aon focal bréige ann.*

What's more, received standard English is a language that is imperial and rational, its preoccupations administrative and its social tone most characteristically represented by the genius of Jane Austen. No Irish hand could have written the celebrated opening line of *Pride and Prejudice*: "It is a truth universally acknowledged that a single man in possession of good fortune must be in want of a wife." For all its wit and elegance, it is too precise, too conscious, and, above all, too lacking in the essentially subversive irreverence. Anglo-Saxon precision is

alien to the Irish mind, which would be more at home with Humpty-Dumpty's dictum: "When I use a word it means just what I choose it to mean – neither more nor less."

In the 20th century, a new generation of writers rediscovered the collision of sensibility between the Irish mind and the English language, and set out to explore its literary potential. William Butler Yeats and Lady Gregory, instrumental in founding Dublin's Abbey Theatre, decided that the Irish peasant was essen-

LEFT: James Joyce, who arm-wrestled English into startling new forms. **ABOVE:** Sean O'Casey, who dramatised 20th-century Ireland's political anguish.

tially a noble creature, and they determined to correct the balance of earlier representations by giving him a speech that was real and melodic rather than phonetic and contrived.

John Millington Synge (pronounced *sing*) had the added benefit of being fluent in Irish, and carried the experiment even further, although his lilting stage speech was sometimes dismissed as "Synge-song". In the preface to his controversial play *The Playboy of the Western World*, he wrote:"Anyone who has lived in real initimacy with the Irish peasantry will know that the wildest sayings and ideas in this play are tame indeed when compared with the fancies one may hear in any little hillside cabin in Geesala or Carraroe or Dingle Bay."

A web of lyricism

Synge manufactured a convincing theatrical language from a small number of Irish-derived constructions: ending a phrase with *surely* as in "It's destroyed he'll be surely"; using *do be* in the sense of a continuous present, as in "In the big world the old people do be leaving things after them for their sons and children"; and inserting the adverbial *and*, as in "There were two men and they rowing." Synge used these simple devices as a frame over which he stretched the web of a remarkable new lyricism.

When one considers the contribution of Irish writers to literature in this century, even an incomplete list astonishes: Yeats with his poetry of the Celtic Twilight and beyond; Sean O'Casey with his miraculous ear for the cadences of the Dublin slums; Frank O'Connor's powerfully humorous but unsentimental stories of childhood in Cork; the plays of Samuel Beckett and George Bernard Shaw; Somerville and Ross's world of the Irish RM (resident magistrate), in which tweedy English officialdom gets its come-uppance from the brilliant improvisations on language of the Irish peasantry; the poetry of Patrick Kavanagh, Brendan Kennelly and Seamus Heaney.

The fine tradition of short-story writing is carried on by practitioners such as Neil Jordan (better known as a film director), John McGahern, Brian Friel, Benedict Kiely and William Trevor.

Although very different in their genius, most of them share one thing in common: an almost physical delight in words that springs from a sharpened sensitivity to a language that is never entirely their own. ❑

IRELAND IN THE MOVIES

Bejasus, it's them leprachauns again! The cinema has played a big part in reinforcing the stereotyped image of the Irish. Do they care? No, it spells profit

Ireland's first dedicated cinema, the Volta in Dublin's Mary Street, was opened in 1909 by none other than James Joyce – an indication that the Irish have always valued the word more than the visual. But the country had no film studio until 1958, when Ardmore Studios opened in Bray, Co. Wicklow. Significantly, its first effort was an international production, *Shake Hands with the Devil*, starring James Cagney.

It was thus left to Hollywood to portray Ireland to the world, and it did so by peddling whimsicality to the huge audience of urban Irish-Americans who had a sentimental attachment to the pastoral ideal most potently portrayed in John Ford's *The Quiet Man*. The Irish, who were in reality facing economic hardship and chronic emigration, didn't object to such a benign portrayal: indeed, they proceeded to build a thriving tourist industry on it.

Attempts at realism were suspect: Alan Parker's faithful 1999 version of *Angela's Ashes*, Frank McCourt's account of growing up in Limerick, was felt locally to have overstated the level of poverty.

COMING TO GRIPS WITH CRIME

Three decades of terrorism have produced a muted response from international film makers – Neil Jordan's *The Crying Game* was a rare success. Dublin's gangland featured in John Boorman's *The General* and Thaddeus O'Sullivan's *Ordinary Decent Criminal*, but some felt that these films – like many Mafia dramas – had too much sympathy for violent lawbreakers.

◁ **POTS OF GOLD**
A pre-007 Sean Connery (complete, as always, with Scottish accent) sang and danced with Janet Munro and gangs of leprachauns (above) in *Darby O'Gill and the Little People* (1959). No cliché was left unturned, but the pot of gold at the rainbow's end went to Walt Disney.

▽ **FIGHT FOR FREEDOM**
Michael Collins (1996) was dubbed Ireland's first national epic film, yet it was financed by Warner Bros. Although director Neil Jordan sacrificed historical detail for dramatic impact, Liam Neeson in the title part conveyed the mixture of romanticism and ruthlessness that characterised Ireland's fight for freedom.

◁ **REVIVING THE DEAD**
Veteran Hollywood director John Huston, who came of Irish stock and had a home in Ireland, captured the country's Chekovian melancholy in his last film, James Joyce's *The Dead* (1987), starring his daughter Anjelica Huston.

▽ **WAYNE'S WORLD**
The movie that did most to cement the image of the Irish as fighting boyos with a pre-feminist outlook was John Ford's 1952 production *The Quiet Man*, in which John Wayne slugged it out with Victor McLaglan and Maureen O'Hara in a virulently green landscape. The Irish loved it.

HERBERT J. YATES *presents*
JOHN FORD and MERIAN C. COOPER'S
Argosy Production

"THE QUIET MAN"

starring

John Maureen Barry
Wayne **O'Hara** Fitzgera[l]

with Ward BOND, Victor McLAGLEN, Mildred NATWICK, Francis FORD
Colour by **TECHNICOLOR**
Directed by **John FORD**

A HOME-GROWN FILM INDUSTRY

In 1990 Richard Harris (above) played a farmer in *The Field*, a grim story of life on the land in the 1920s. It was part of a spate of local films which had begun with the launch of the Irish Film Board in 1981 and included such varied offerings as Neil Jordan's moody IRA thriller *Angel* (1982) and *Eat the Peach* (1986), the quirky tale of one man's bid to build a motorcycle wall of death.

Irish governments had long realised that film-making created employment and attracted foreign investment. But actively encouraging the industry had been difficult as long as the Catholic church exercised a tight grip on moral values: in the first 40 years of the Republic's independence, an average of 75 films a year were banned and another 200 censored.

With the Irish box office representing less than 0.5 per cent of the global market there was limited scope for purely Irish films. So the government tempted in foreign producers with tasty tax breaks. This persuaded Mel Gibson, for instance, that, although his 1995 *Braveheart* portrayed a legendary Scottish hero, the stirring battle scenes would look no less patriotic if they were filmed in Ireland.

△ **SINGING THE BLUES**
Although directed by an Englishman (Alan Parker) and financed from America, *The Commitments* (1991), from the novel by Roddy Doyle, captured the mood of modern young Dubliners, expletives and all. This was no feel-good tale of a pop group on the make – it chronicled their disaffection with life in Dublin and referred to Ireland as a Third World country.

▽ **WHIMSICAL HUMOUR**
The 1990s saw some gentler films taking a fanciful and melancholy view of Irish life. Albert Finney made a convincing Irishman in *The Playboys* (1992) and, below, *A Man of No Importance* (1994). *Hear My Song* (1991),with Ned Beatty as tenor Josef Locke, was a return to whimsicality.

◁ **MODERN MAYHEM**
Movies dealing with IRA violence tended towards melodrama, but Neil Jordan's *Angel* and, left, his 1992 hit *The Crying Game* analysed the often conflicting emotions in Ireland's killing fields. Here the IRA man (Stephen Rea) prepares to kill a captured British soldier. The movie was filmed partly on location in Bettystown and Laytown, Co. Meath.

FAIRIES AND FOLKLORE

From leprechauns to giants, there are Irish tales to suit all tastes

During the summer of 1985 thousands of people began to go on pilgrimages to Marian shrines, in various parts of the country, because people claimed to have seen them move. After a time the phenomenon became a national and international news story; much to the indignation of the country's advanced liberals who saw these pilgrimages as a further manifestation of national obscurantism. The Catholic Church authorities, in the areas where pilgrims collected, counselled caution. They advised people to seek physical and rational explanations for what was happening rather than supernatural ones. But still the thousands travelled until the strange happenings ceased just as suddenly as they had commenced.

By then a book had been produced, in which, tucked away among the eyewitness accounts from the contemporary pilgrims and descriptions of apparitions from the past, there was a contribution by a lecturer in the Department of Folklore in University College, Dublin. This erudite essay showed that the phenomenon of moving statues originated in the early Middle Ages, was well-known in Ireland, and was the subject of many tales and legends.

Heroic tales

This is just one manifestation of Irish folklore, as well as being an example of the past returning to embarrass the present. Other forms of folklore were used to good effect by writers such as W. B. Yeats and J. M. Synge. Then there were the heroic tales concerning Fionn MacCool, leader of Fianna Eireann, and his band of warriors. They defended Ireland against invaders, hunted and indulged in feats of strength between May and November. Then, for six months, they retired to the winter quarters where they feasted, told tales, listened to the harp and played chess. The ancient Irish had

RIGHT: Irish illustrator Jim Fitzpatrick's drawing of an early Norse invader from *The Silver Arm*.

only two seasons, summer and winter, and in rural Ireland May Day and Hallowe'en still mark the beginning and end of the agricultural year. Potatoes that have not been dug before Hallowe'en will remain in the ground, and children will not pick blackberries after that date.

Other writers drew inspiration from tales of spirits, benign and malign, and the little people, sometimes called leprechauns, who guarded hidden treasure and had a thousand tricks to distract the greedy mortals who sought it. They also indulged in games of hurling, sometimes borrowing a champion from the world of mortals to assist them. If they won, he was suitably

tales, concerning personages such as "The King of Ireland's Son" and his adventures in Spain and Africa, could take more than two hours in the telling. About six really top-class storytellers still survive and their art has now been preserved on film for posterity.

One of the principal reasons why so much of Ireland's past lives on today is to be found in the method St Patrick used to propagate the Christian message when he arrived in 432. He found a people immersed in pagan beliefs and rituals. His debates with the Druids (the pagan priests) enliven much of early Irish literature. He even debated with Oisín, son of Fionn MacCool, who

rewarded. It was believed in Sligo that the great traditional fiddle player Michael Coleman, who recorded all his music in New York, had learned his flawless bowing technique from a band of little folk whom he had befriended.

The oral tradition

The storytellers who preserved most of these tales, before the scholars came to write and record them, were custodians of a very ancient oral tradition. They were called *seanachaidhe* from the Irish *seanachas* meaning lore. Some could relate more than 300 tales, learned by rote from their elders, and could recite them without changing a word or an emphasis. Some of these

had unwisely returned from the land of Eternal Youth only to become an old man as soon as he touched the soil of Ireland.

St Patrick helped preserve Ireland's social structure and many of its customs even as he changed fundamental beliefs. He clearly did not believe in the politics of confrontation – which is as good a proof as any, some say, that he was not an Irishman. When he ascended Croagh Patrick, Ireland's holy mountain in Co. Mayo, the peak was sacred to the pagan god Crom. When he descended, after battling for 40 days and nights with a legion of evil spirits, including the Devil's mother, he declared the summit sacred to the Christian God. The people were to continue paying homage, but in a new form. So it came about that every year tens of thousands of pilgrims, from all parts of the country and beyond, converge on Croagh Patrick on the last Sunday in July (still called Black Crom's Sunday in the Irish language). They climb at dawn, many of them barefoot, to the oratory on the summit.

But what is sometimes regarded as mere superstition is often based on something very different. For example, the white thorn bush frequently found growing on wheat and barley

PAGAN TRADITIONS

Many holy wells, where people come to pray and pay penance, were also deemed to be holy in pre-Christian times.

in which one finds that received wisdom and superstition have become inextricably mixed.

How is it that only a member of the Doogan clan can guarantee that earth from Tory Island, off the Donegal coast, will banish all rodents from your home by handing it to you? Why is the seventh son of a seventh son capable of curing certain ills and ailments, depending on which family he comes from? If he is a Shanaghan, for instance, he has the cure for whooping cough. Why is it that direct acceptance of

fields is untouched by the farmer supposedly because "it is a fairy tree and bad luck will quickly follow the person who disturbs it." But the truth is that "fairy forts" are old burial places and the picturesque tale merely serves to strengthen reverence for the dead.

Folk medicine

Another form of folklore, which is now getting a new lease of life because of the increased interest in herbs and alternative medicine, is the area of folk cures and folk medicine. It is an area

LEFT: a fairy ring, said to possess magic powers.
ABOVE: a holy well, keeping alive old superstitions.

financial reward will remove the capacity to cure, while indirect payment, or payment in kind, will not?

Of course, folklore never ceases to evolve in an island the size of Ireland in which traditions linger on and emerge in new guises when least expected. Television may have hastened the death of the gatherings around the storyteller at the fireside, but it has not yet fully demolished the delight Irish people take in listening to a tall tale well told. Contemporary moving statues have created enough stories to ensure that another generation will have another folk-memory passed on to them orally. That is how it all begins; and that is how it all began. ❑

RACING CERTAINTIES

Whether they're breeding them, racing them, exporting them or betting
on them, the Irish have an extraordinary affinity with horses

In County Cork in the year 1752, a Mr Edmund Blake and a Mr O'Callaghan raced each other on horseback across the countryside from Buttevant Church to the spire of St Leger Church 4½ miles away, jumping hedges, walls and ditches on the way. As a result, a new word, "steeplechasing", entered the English language, and a new sport was created.

Steeplechasing was soon all the rage. Races were run, like the original, across open country from one point to another with the precise course to be taken left largely to the discretion (or indiscretion) of the riders. A 19th-century Englishman returning from a holiday in Ireland wrote that steeplechasing was "a sort of racing for which the Paddies are particularly famous, and in which, unless the rider has pluck and his prad (*horse*) goodness, they cannot expect to get well home." Fortunately, Ireland had no shortage of plucky riders and good horses. *The History and Delineation of the Horse* recorded in 1809 that "the Irish are the highest and the steadiest leapers in the world." They still are.

Great breeding

The pre-eminence of Irish-bred steeplechasers and hurdlers on the racecourses of Britain today is undisputed; and it is remarkable, given the legions of horses exported annually to trainers in England, that the greatest steeplechasers of modern era have also been trained in Ireland. Perhaps the greatest of all was Arkle, who won the Cheltenham Gold Cup, British steeplechasing's equivalent of the Derby, three years in succession in the 1960s, in the process humiliating the cream of the English racehorses to the undisguised glee of all Ireland.

All horse-racing is sport, but some forms are more sporting than others. The Irish prefer the reckless and often threadbare thrills of steeplechasing to its rich relation, racing "on the flat". Whereas top-class flat-racing throughout the

world is dominated by the commercial requirements of the multi-million dollar bloodstock industry, this aspect is absent from racing "over the sticks" for nearly all jumpers are geldings.

The winner of a great flat race like the Irish Derby may become worth tens of millions of dollars because he may breed future winners of

great races. The winner of a great jump race earns his owner only the prize-money – modest by comparison – the proceeds of a winning bet, perhaps, and the glory. But what glory. Had Arkle been entered in a referendum for the Irish presidency, the world might well have had its first equine statesman since Caligula.

The origins of horse-racing "on the flat" are lost in pre-history. We know that the Red Branch Knights of pre-Christian Ireland raced each other on horses and that horse-racing was an essential part of public assemblies or fairs in the early centuries AD. According to John Welcome's history, *Irish Horseracing*, "these fairs were held for the purpose of transacting all sorts

PRECEDING PAGES: a race at Leopardstown.
LEFT: a bloodstock sale in Co. Kildare.
RIGHT: studying form at the Dublin Horse Show.

of business—marriages were celebrated, deaths recorded, laws debated and defined, methods of defence agreed; but always they were followed by sports and games, and of these sports and games the most popular was horseracing." The greatest fair was held at the Curragh – a wide, grassy plain in what is now County Kildare, across which a horse can gallop to exhaustion.

Racing went on, especially at the Curragh, through Norman and Elizabethan times, and

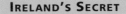

IRELAND'S SECRET

Horses are said to thrive in Ireland because of the moist climate, which produces some of the world's lushest pastures, and the limestone subsoil, which makes the grass rich in bone-building calcium.

Its headquarters, naturally enough, are at the Curragh, still the heartland of Irish racing. Its 6,000 windswept acres (2,400 hectares) are the home of many training stables. On most days, the gaunt grandstands of the Curragh racecourse overlook the plain silently, like a stranded liner; but on big race days, they overflow with a restless throng of owners, trainers, spectators, bookmakers and various hucksters.

A race meeting is a heady mixture: the lean, hard-muscled

through the succeeding centuries, despite an attempt by Oliver Cromwell's Puritans to stamp it out as a work of the devil. But it wasn't until the middle of the 18th century that the results of races at the Curragh were recorded. In 1790, Irish racing was organised under the aegis of a governing body, the Turf Club. Today it continues to be responsible for the integrity of horse racing at Ireland's 27 tracks, licensing and registering all participants, and overseeing the annual race calendar. The Irish Horse Racing Authority, a semi-state body, was set up in 1994 to oversee the financing or racing and the provision of Totaliser betting on the 25 courses in the Republic.

horses, the small, scrawny jockeys in their vivid silks, the eager gamblers thrusting handfuls of banknotes at the bookmakers, who shout and signal to each other constantly, chalking up odds on their blackboards and rubbing them out again with an air of obsessive duty. Wealthy women in their finery, bowler-hatted remnants of the Anglo-Irish gentry, down-at-heel city-dwellers, red-faced farmers... all human life is there.

The thrill of the race

Just before the start of each race, there is a last flurry in the dance around the book-makers. Then a tense stillness as the race commentator's voice echoes over the stands. Batteries of binoculars are trained silently on the runners. But as the horses round the final bend, a murmuring in the crowd rises like a gathering storm until the commentator's voice is drowned in a cacophony of supplication, triumph and despair. Hats are thrown in the air in delight, losers' betting tickets fall to the ground like confetti.

The Curragh is the setting for all the Irish classic races: the 2,000 and 1,000 Guineas, the Derby, the Oaks and the St Leger. The most valuable of these, in terms of prize-money, is the Derby, sponsored since 1986 by the US brewer Budweiser. The total prize fund is now IR£750,000, and can be expected to keep rising.

Although it is contested by fewer runners than its English counterpart, the race is arguably a truer test of a horse's ability, as the Curragh has none of the topographical eccentricities of the Epsom Downs. Winners include some of the world's greatest racehorses: Nijinsky, Shergar, El Gran Señor, Zagreb and Desert King.

The Derby is always a thrilling spectacle. Like all classic races today, it is also a superb shop-window for the international bloodstock industry, in which Irish breeders play a vital and

LEFT: signing a cheque at the Ballinasloe Horse Fair. **ABOVE:** to some, fashion is as important as fillies at the Dublin Horse Show.

growing role. Ireland developed into Europe's leading nursery for thoroughbred racehorses: in 1985, for the first time, more foals were born in Ireland than in Britain.

In spring, the migration of birds from their winter quarters to sunnier climates is paralleled by a migration of hundreds of mares (mainly from the US, Britain and France) to be mated with the many former leading males of the turf who have retired to stallion duties in Ireland.

The recent prosperity of the Irish bloodstock industry owes much to a 1969 government concession under which fees received for the services of thoroughbred stallions are fully exempt from tax. Its effect was shown dramatically in the turnover of Ireland's leading bloodstock auctioneers, Goffs of Kildare, which rose from around IR£2 million in 1974 to more than £40 million a decade later, settling at an average of about £35 million. Nice work if you can get it.

An affinity with horses

Then there's the natural ability of many Irish people to understand and handle horses, whether as breeders, stud managers, stud and stable hands, jockeys or trainers. This justly celebrated Irish way with horses was apotheosised in the dapper and diffident personage of Vincent O'Brien, who, until he retired in 1993, had a training record that stretched credulity and defeated even Irish superlatives. His son-in-law, John Magna, carries on the family tradition at Coolmore Stud where he continues to dominate the stallion world, thanks partly to his extraordinary premier stallion, Sadler's Wells.

Summertime visitors to such top-class tracks as the Curragh and Leopardstown are likely to see runners entered by leading trainers such as Aidan O'Brien (no relation to the legendary Vincent) and John Oxx. Most likely two-year-olds are introduced to the duties and rigours of racing life before being sent across the Irish Sea in search of a big-race win to set them on their planned careers as classic victors and, later, top-priced stallions. But their odds are likely to be prohibitively short – and, as racegoers quickly learn, favourites don't always win.

Other leading Irish trainers include Dermot Weld and Jim Bolger. The most successful jockeys of recent years have been Michael Kinane – whose services are in demand worldwide – John Murtagh and Christy Roche.

Apart from the aforementioned tracks, there

is racing "on the flat" and "over the sticks" at 25 other racecourses throughout Ireland. They include Fairyhouse, venue for the Irish Grand National, held on Easter Monday; Punchestown, which holds an historic three-day festival meeting in late April; Killarney and Galway, both of which hold meetings in holiday-time high summer with a festive, not to say Bacchanalian, tinge.

A race across the beach

Perhaps the unlikeliest venue is Laytown, a small holiday resort on the east coast, about 30 miles (50 km) north of Dublin. Racing is held there on only one day a year, in July or August, on a date determined as much by the tidal movements of the Irish Sea as by the Turf Club – for when the tide is in at Laytown, the racecourse lies under a metre or more of water. The Laytown Strand Races is Europe's only official race meeting to be held on a beach.

There is no grandstand at Laytown – and, strictly speaking, no racecourse at all, just a long, gently-sloping beach. A group of marquees serve as the racecourse offices, tea-room and bar. The racetrack is marked out with flags on the sands at low tide.

The atmosphere is extraordinary. In the field above the beach, horses parade in the paddock, owners and trainers confer, punters debate the form, bookmakers shout the odds, drinkers drink – all much like an ordinary race meeting.

But down on the beach hucksters sell candy floss and fish-and-chips and fizzy drinks and toys and raffle-tickets and souvenirs; small-time bookmakers splash barefooted through small pools left by the receding tide; children run about yelling and eating ice-cream; strangest of all, huntsmen on horseback in their red-coated regalia ride back and forth, policing the crowds clear of the racetrack. At times, the races themselves seem a bit like a sideshow.

Laytown is a world away from the Curragh on Derby Day, from big prize-money and bafflingly high bloodstock prices. It has none of the glamour of the top meetings – and little of the tension. But, although the Laytown Races are unfashionable by the standards of today, they are maybe not so far in spirit from the races that thrilled fair-goers in ancient Ireland. ❏

LEFT: the extraordinary Laytown Races, Europe's only official race meeting to be held on a beach.

THE GAMES PEOPLE PLAY

Hurling and Gaelic football make soccer

seem tame by comparison. And then

there are oddities like road bowls

All the major international sports are played to some extent in Ireland and only a few are affected by the political division of the island: the main exceptions being soccer, athletics and hockey. But the most popular sports in the island are the native ones of hurling and Gaelic football. These are truly amateur games, organised on the smallest social unit of population, the parish, and controlled by a body called the Gaelic Athletic Association.

The GAA was founded in 1884, in Thurles in County Tipperary, by Michael Cusack, a fiery nationalist from the Burren in County Clare, who was immortalised by James Joyce as "The Citizen" in *Ulysses*. Its purpose was as much political as sporting: to revive the native games, under native control, as a means of strengthening national self-respect at a time when national morale was at a low ebb. The association also organised athletic contests in opposition to the Ascendancy-controlled organisation which banned "artisans" from its competitions and, because of a mixture of exclusivity and Sabbatarianism, held its contests on Saturdays. At the time, all but the professional classes worked a six-day week and Sunday was the only day left for organised games.

How to understand hurling

Hurling has been played in Ireland since prehistoric times and the oldest sagas tell of hurling matches that went on for days. It is the fastest of all field team games and its rules are relatively simple, although those who see it played for the first time have some difficulty following the flight of the ball.

Played between teams of 15 a side, it gets its name from the stick, a hurley, used by the players. Made from ash, the hurley is about 3½ ft (1 metre) long with a crooked blade which is about

RIGHT: hurling, one of the world's toughest, fastest and most exciting ball games.

3 inches (8 cm) across at its broadest. The ball consists of yarn, tightly wound round a ball of cork and covered with hard leather, stitched along the outside in a ridge to facilitate handling. The goal-posts stand 21 ft (6.4 metres) apart and are 21 ft high, with a crossbar 8 ft (2.5 metres) from the ground. A goal (three points) is scored when the ball is sent between the posts under the bar. A single point is scored when the ball goes between the posts and over the bar.

The ball can be propelled along the ground or hit in the air. It can only be

> ### FOOTBALLING ICONS
>
> In Kerry, photographs of famous Gaelic football teams and players hang on the walls in the company of the Sacred Heart of Jesus, the Pope and Jack Kennedy.

a ball similar to that used in soccer, Gaelic football is to a great extent an invented game. The rules are therefore imperfect and subject to constant revision. Players can handle the ball, lift it off the ground with the foot, run with it while passing it between hand and foot, kick it, or fist it, or play it with the feet on the ground as in soccer. Its main flaw is that there is no clear method of dispossessing a player in possession. But it is a spectacular game, and attracts the biggest crowds of any sporting event in Ireland.

taken into the hand if caught in flight, or if lifted from the ground with the stick. Skilled players can take the ball onto the hurley, from the ground, while running at full speed and carry it, balanced or bouncing, on the broad end before passing or scoring. The main traditional hurling areas remain south of a line from Dublin to Galway, with a small pocket in the Glens of Antrim. Cork and Kilkenny are the top hurling counties.

Football, Gaelic-style

Gaelic football is also played by teams of 15 a side and the layout of the pitch and methods of scoring are the same as for hurling. Played with

Australian Rules, although played with an oval ball on an oval pitch, has features similar to those of Gaelic football. Irish emigrants were no doubt responsible for the long kicking and the great leaps in the air to catch the ball. In an attempt to gain an international dimension for a game played only in Ireland (with the exception of Irish emigrants in the USA and Britain) the GAA has organised tours to and from Australia, with games played under compromise rules. The fact that the Australian players are all professionals have so far given the contests more bite than was anticipated. Professional players do not like being beaten by amateurs.

Hurling and Gaelic football are organised in a

variety of competitions, graded according to age up to senior level, for county and then provincial championship. The high point of the GAA year is in September with the All-Ireland hurling and football Finals in Dublin's Croke Park, which now incorporates a museum devoted to uniquely Irish sports.

Bowling along

Road bowling is a strange game, played only in South Armagh, Cork and parts of Waterford and Limerick. The game is very simple: two players throw or bowl an iron ball along an ordinary public road, and the winner is the one who covers a

Hares and horses

Greyhound racing (on tracks) and coursing in enclosed fields with live hares are very popular sports in Ireland. The breeding and export of grey-hounds is a minor industry and prize-money is now increased by sponsorship. The fact that races are over in a matter of seconds is no deterrent to the small army of punters who attend. Bookmakers attend all kinds of dog- and horse-races, in competition with the more impersonal tote. In their offices, these "turf accountants" take bets on almost anything, from the World Cup to the papal election.

Coursing is a winter sport which has come

set distance with fewer throws. The bowl, or "bullet," can be 28, 21 or 16 ounces (between 800 and 450 grammes). One of the skills of the game is the negotiation of a bend in the road, either by lofting the bowl over the corner or by curving the throw. If the bowl leaves the road, the player is penalised.

It is a great betting sport and large sums change hands when two noted players meet. Not only are bets laid on the result of the contest; side-bets are also laid on individual shots. Road bowling is illegal as sections of public roads are barred to traffic during the contest. But prosecutions are rare.

under fire from animal-rights campaigners because of cruelty to hares. Two dogs are slipped simultaneously to chase a hare. Points are scored by deflecting the hare from its course, or by killing it before it gets to the escape exit at the end of the field. Protests have resulted in greyhounds being muzzled by law.

Casual perusal of the sports pages of any Irish daily newspaper will show that an extraordinary range of sports, both national and international, is covered. And, while spectators far outnumber participants, a surprising number excel in a variety of sports at the highest level.

To mention just a few: Sean Kelly dominated the world of professional cycling throughout the

LEFT: greyhound racing attracts Ireland's gambling fraternity. **ABOVE:** Dublin's Hermitage Golf Club.

1980s, and in 1987 Stephen Roche won the sport's ultimate prize, the gruelling Tour de France. In professional boxing, world titles were held by Barry McGuigan and Dave McAuley. Alex Higgins and Denis Taylor both claimed the world championship at snooker. To that list can be added two players with the most international appearances: Mike Gibson, in rugby football, and Pat Jennings, as a soccer goalkeeper. In 1998 Sonia O'Sullivan crowned an already illustrious career in athletics by winning both the 5,000-metre and 10,000-metre European championship titles, while Michele Smith de Bruín brought back three gold medals and one silver from the 1996 Olympics.

In international rugby Ireland fields a team drawn from Northern Ireland and the Republic. It's the one international sport (except for professional boxing) that unites all political elements on the island, at least temporarily.

Soccer, the great working-class game, is split by the internal political border. The island fields two international sides: Ireland, as the Northern Ireland team is officially designated, and the Republic of Ireland. Despite limited resources, both have impressed: Northern Ireland qualified for the final stages of the World Cup in both 1982 and 1986, while the Republic caught the eye in the finals of the 1988 European Championships and in the 1990 and 1994 World Cup.

Where golfers link up

Golf is another national passion. Because of the availability of courses, it is played by everyone interested enough to buy a set of clubs. The country is dotted with courses: inland courses like the Curragh (the oldest), Mullingar, Tralee (designed by Arnold Palmer) and the picturesque one at Killarney. There is also a chain of seaside links round the coast from Rosses Point in Sligo, to Lahinch in Clare, to Ballybunion and Waterville in Kerry, Portmarnock and Royal Dublin in the capital, Beltray in Louth and Royal County Down in Newcastle.

So let the non-golfer be warned: Ireland has a higher percentage of golf bores than any other European country. Most of them, though, are also interested in hurling, Gaelic football, soccer, racing, snooker and boxing. Let the non-sportsman be warned. ❑

LEFT: Gaelic football, a spectacular game; the rules, such as they are, are frequently revised.

THE SERIOUS BUSINESS OF DRINKING

The so-called Irish pub has conquered the world. But the only authentic Irish pubs are in Ireland, and their most intoxicating product is talk.

A common stereotype of the Irishman abroad is that of a maudlin drinker seated at a bar in London or New York or Chicago, gazing dolefully into his glass and mouthing inanities to himself about the green fields and the clear mountain streams of his native land. An ill-chosen word from a stranger will quickly rouse his anger and, in the twinkling of an eye, a rip-roaring riot is in progress.

This image of the Irish exile, conveyed principally by movies of a certain vintage, has a strong element of truth in it and so too has the stereotype of the Irish when they are at home. The same movies portray the home-based Irish as jovial, garrulous, welcoming in the extreme and brilliant at the art of conversation. A more realistic view is that the Irish are sad abroad and happy at home because of the drink.

The mystique of Guinness

What makes the Irishman surly in foreign climes is, usually, the lack of quality in, or the total absence of, Guinness. This brew, a strongish black beer with a creamy white head, is, even more than Irish whiskey, the country's national beverage. Brewed in Dublin since 1759, it is a temperamental drink, needing great care in pouring from the tap to the glass. Constant temperature in the cellars, the distance from cask to tap and the frequency of the flow are all considered important factors in the art known as "the pulling of a good pint".

If the pint isn't good, it is sent straight back. Experts embark on long discussions on the pint's quality in different bars throughout the country. Dubliners, who travel frequently inside Ireland, make lists of the provincial pubs which have the best pints. The visitor's best criterion is this: if the place is crowded with locals, then the pint is probably good. And you'll know a good pint when you get one. It won't taste like what passes for Guinness in Britain where the

beer is sloshed into the glass by insensitive barmen, or like the Guinness in America, where the long sea journey from Dublin does nothing for the quality. It will taste, in a good pub in Ireland, as smooth as velvet.

There are other Irish beers, too. Harp, brewed in Dundalk, sells well internationally, particu-

larly in Britain. Smithwick's Ale, lighter than Guinness and darker than Harp, is also popular.

As far as spirits are concerned, the Irish rank highly as connoisseurs. One French Cognac house was surprised to discover that some of the highest sales per head for its premium brandies were in a less than affluent Dublin suburb. But it's Irish whiskey (note the extra "e") which reigns supreme on its home territory. Triple-distilled for purity and lightness, Irish whiskey was overtaken by Scotch on the world market during World War II. One main reason was selfishness on the part of the Irish.

It was an Irishman, Aeneas Coffey, who invented the patent still in the 1830s. This per-

PRECEDING PAGES: Dublin's Brazen Head, a traditional pub. **LEFT:** perfectly poured Guinness. **RIGHT:** enjoying a pint at the home of Guinness, Dublin.

mitted the mass production of blended whiskies. Scottish distillers, in the main, switched to the new method. The Irish and the smaller Scottish malt-whisky producers stuck with the old tried and tested "pot still" method, which involved a single whiskey acquiring its mellowness through long ageing. In the 1940s, the Scots diverted their production to export and rationed the sale of their whiskies at home. The Irish did the opposite, keeping their whiskies to themselves. The result was disastrous. GIs from all over America acquired their taste for Scotch in Europe's theatre of war and brought the taste home. Irish whiskey, whose popularity in the royal courts of Europe had inspired Russia's Peter the Great to describe it as "the best of all the wines", went into a decline from which it has only recently begun to recover.

Maturing the malts

The comparative affluence and sophisticated tastes of recent years have stimulated the demand for Ireland's more traditional whiskies as well as Scotland's rarer malts. There are 15 or so different whiskies on sale in Ireland. John Power's Gold Label is by far the most popular. Next come Jameson, Bushmills, Coleraine (which sells in Northern Ireland), Paddy,

HOW THE IRISH PUB CONQUERED THE WORLD

If America can persuade the world to eat McDonald's hamburgers, can Ireland persuade it to drink Guinness? It seems to be doing just that, judging from the explosive international spread of "traditional" Irish pubs. There are more than 1,000 of them now, from Durty Nellie's in Amsterdam to Finnegan's in Abu Dhabi, from Shifty O'Sheas in Leicester, England, to O'Kims in Seoul, Korea. Most have rumbustious music, and some carry the theme to absurd lengths by incorporating in the decor such Irish Catholic icons as a pulpit and confessional. But they all seem to have one thing in common: they sell lots of beer.

How did it all start? Some trace the trend to the 1994 World Cup when Irish football fans descended on bars around the world, creating the convivial atmosphere of a pub back home. The popularity of Irish culture since then has helped things along.

Never slow to spot an opportunity, brewers such as Guinness set up companies to export the Irish pub concept. They'll help entrepreneurs anywhere in the world to design their hostelry – you can pick a standard model such as Country Cottage, the Victorian Dublin or the Brewery – and also to locate authentic fittings and recruit staff. But of course they're nothing like the genuine article in Ireland.

Hewitt's and Dunphy's. Murphy's sells mainly in the United States, and Tullamore Dew, a particularly light brand, does well in Europe.

Two popular premium brands are Black Bush (from Bushmills in County Antrim, the world's oldest distillery) and Crested Ten, matured for 10 years in the Jameson stable. At the top of the range are liqueur whiskies, among the most exceptional drinks on earth. Bushmills Malt is a single 10-year-old; Jameson 1780 is aged for 12 years; and Redbreast, also 12 years old, is

HOW TO DRINK MALTS

The best Irish malts should be sipped neat like fine Cognacs or Armagnac, although the foreigner is permitted to add just a dash of pure Irish water.

prepared, this secretly distilled drink can seriously damage your health.

But it's not only the drink itself that's important: it's where you drink it. Ireland's rural bars are usually functional in design; nothing to look at from the outside, but warm, cosy and well filled inside.

Picture a bar in a small village on the Atlantic coast. It is 2am, long after the official closing time. There is a rap on the door, sharp enough to suggest authority. A local police sergeant enters, in full uniform, torchlight

matured in wood by the house of Gilbey, renowned for its wines, ports and sherries. To put ice in these last three whiskies is an act of sacrilege to an Irishman.

While all the major international brands of gin, vodka and other spirits are readily available, the Irish are inclined to stick to the home products. Thus Cork Dry Gin far outsells the more famous British gins. One often-mentioned drink, poteen, isn't on sale anywhere legally. Some of it can be quite good; but, if carelessly

in hand. Yet no-one present interrupts the conversation – except for a few visiting English and Americans. Half an hour later, the scene has changed entirely. Not a murmur of conversation is to be heard. The sergeant, his cap placed on the bar in front of him, is clasping a pint of Guinness and, with eyes closed, is singing the old lament "The Blackbird of Sweet Avondale".

This sort of scene can be found easily enough anywhere on the west coast, where the summer tourist season is short and the after-hours trade compensates for the meagre takings in the desolate winter months. In the main cities, however, this laxity does not exist. Drinking-up time is now extended to midnight, Monday to Saturday

LEFT: singing and supping at Megaw's pub in Brookeborough, Co. Fermanagh. **ABOVE:** dogs are welcome, especially at this bar in Crookhaven, Co. Cork.

in summer, while it's back to 11.30pm in winter. Sunday closing all year round is 11pm. The law is strictly enforced. Well, fairly strictly.

City pubs are different, too. In Dublin some bars are richly caparisoned in brass and mahogany, with antique mirrors proclaiming the merits of whiskies long since defunct. Some such pubs look much as they did in 1850.

Classic pubs

To experience the value placed on the traditional, visit Doheny and Nesbitt's in Dublin's Baggot Street. This is an old-fashioned pub, long and narrow with a "snug" at each end. A

snug is a small area partitioned off from the rest of the bar in which up to 10 people can drink in almost complete privacy. It even has its own private service hatch, and is a hangover from the days when women who fancied a tipple didn't want to be seen consuming it. The atmosphere is one of talk and more talk, for if there is one thing that is as important as the drink in a Dublin pub it is the conversation. The general appearance is dowdy enough, with hard bar stools and not the slightest attempt at plushness. Yet this bar is the haunt of government ministers, senior public servants, prominent journalists and a group of economists known informally as "the Doheny and Nesbitt School".

Nesbitt's, as it's known for short, fulfills the function that private clubs play in most capital cities, with the distinct advantage that any member of the decent Irish drinking public is free to walk in from the street and join the company.

Other Dublin pubs with good character and conversation include Mulligan's of Poolbeg Street, Neary's of Chatham Street and Ryan's of Parkgate Street. Mulligan's, which welcomed its first customer in 1782, is also divided into sections.The entrance to the left of the building leads into the older part of the pub. Here one finds students, the occasional retired docker and photographers from the *Irish Press,* whose head office is nearby. The door to the right of the building leads to the first of two bars in the slightly more modern section. The first is occupied by newspaper and TV people. Go through to the far bar and you are in left-wing territory.

Neary's is a beautifully furnished old-style pub which attracts permanently posing actors from the Gaiety Theatre. Ryan's, situated in an area a little distance from the centre of Dublin's action, is a real gem: its clients are those who appreciate good conversation, good atmosphere and the traditions of Dublin pub life.

Salmon and singing

Along the Atlantic coast is a tremendous selection of fine pubs, but none better than those in north and west Clare, not far from Galway. In the spa town of Lisdoonvarna, Curtin's "Roadside" tavern smokes its own salmon and has fresh shellfish in season. At night, there are traditional fiddlers, pipers and flute players.

There are about 12,000 pubs on the island, and in them visitors can see something of the real Ireland, both its strengths and its weaknesses. Drinkers will usually respect a stranger's privacy, talking only when a willingness to talk is shown. Those who join in, however, won't forget the experience: the talk's even better than the scenery.

But do the Irish really appreciate what they've got? The curious thing is that, while the rest of the world is discovering the joys of the Irish pub, the latest growth phenomenon in Dublin is the continental café, modelled along the lines of Amsterdam's "brown cafés", where the young and trendy go to converse. ❑

LEFT: a convivial chat in Kenmare, Co. Kerry.
RIGHT: unambiguous message on a Donegal pub door.

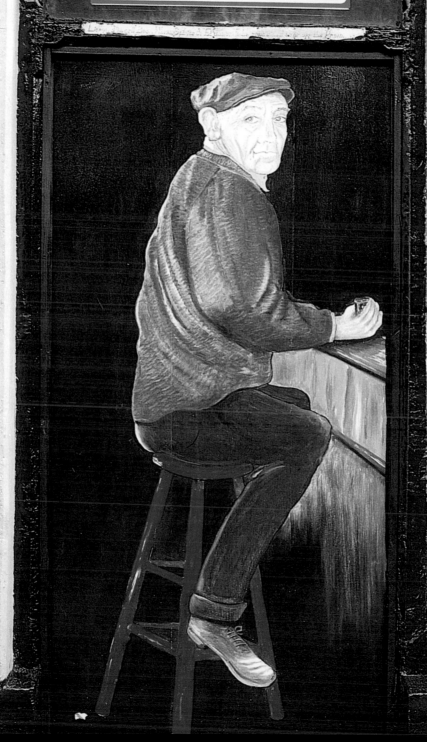

A FRESH APPROACH TO FOOD

*Despite an abundance of fresh ingredients, the Irish have never
shown much interest in haute cuisine. Until now...*

When Irish food is good it is, like the little girl in the nursery rhyme with the curl in the middle of her forehead, very very good. But when it is bad it is horrid.

The distinction begins with the day's first meal. The short-order cry goes out to the cook: "Two breakfasts – one a gentleman's, the other a lady's." Blazing hot plates arrive on the linen tablecloth. Everything on them is fried, not grilled, for this is calorie-cholestrol country. On top of the piles of potato-bread and soda-bread farls, beside the rashers and sausages and black pudding culled from organically managed stock, the tomatoes fresh from the greenhouses, are free-range eggs. The gentleman gets two eggs, his lady one.

If the accommodation is a country house hotel rather than a bed-and-breakfast bungalow, the silver teapot may bear the family crest, and the fried breads – plus the wheaten toast in the rack and the gooseberry jam – come from the house's own walled garden, where the red-faced master of the house, clad in Beford cords and Tattersal checked shirt, forks the soil his ancestors preferred to leave to the gardeners.

The harsh reality

But such heaven is not always available. For, curiously, these simple country skills – bread and jam making, patting butter, letting hens range free – are the exception, not the norm, and they are more likely to have been preserved by what used to be called "the gentry". At too many breakfasts, the juice offered is pasteurised, tasting more of its container than of any orange. Pale flaccid bacon, flecked with a whitish ooze, lies in grease. The eggs' yokes are pale, the store-bought sausages anatomical in colour, shape and aroma. The coffee is stewed, harsh, often instant, poorly disguised by its serving jug.

It's all a long way from the promising "A Taste of..." descriptions in the tourist brochures.

LEFT: the fish should be fresh – Ireland's surrounded by them. **RIGHT:** the country's other culinary glory is its wonderful range of home-baked bread.

Those same brochures promise even greater delights by showing alluring platters of seafood: a salmon, probably, fine as any on an heraldic shield, amongst a throng of lobster, crab, oysters and speckled brown trout.

And so it should be on an island surrounded by relatively unpolluted water. Ireland's coastal

bays are dotted with brightly coloured floats marking pots set to catch European, squat and Norway lobster, and common and spider crab. Vacationing anglers and offshore nets bring wild Atlantic salmon to the table. Raft-hung ropes glisten with plump mussels. Dredgers haul up queen and fan-shell scallops, Venus clams and the one the French call *palourde*. Spanish holidaymakers dig for razorshells on breath-taking strands or scuba-dive for the elusive, scrumptious goose-barnacle (known to locals as the devil's fingernails).

Away from the sea, dun cows browse the wild-flower water meadows, piglets and lambs gain flavour on purple, heathery mountain slopes. Carrots, onions and potatoes prosper in the drumlin's gravelled loam.

But the truth is different. Unlike France's Brittany or Spain's Galicia – both also Catholic, Celtic and projecting into the western Atlantic – Ireland has no hereditary passion for food, seafood in particular. The Anglo-Norman colonists who changed the landscape for ever brought with them tastes more Anglo than Norman-French: woodcock, venison, pheasant, snipe. The Scots Planters who came as their servants and tradesmen did little to redeem the situation: they brought to the table an attitude of Calvinist rigour, not rapture.

The result? In all too many hotels, chicken, overcooked steak with chips, or "meat and two veg" – both overcooked as well – are the best a traveller may expect. The "fresh" salmon is all too often dull farmed fish, as are the muddy rainbow trout. The increasingly ubiquitous burger bars, pizza parlours and Chinese take-aways are rarely models of their kind, leaving the traditional "fish supper" – heavily battered fish 'n' chips – the best bet.

Another serving of tourist iconography, proferred on so many postcards, are the traditional Irish foods: boxty (raw and cooked potato mashed with butter, buttermilk, flour, then baked), champ (potato boiled and mashed with butter, milk, scallion, salt), colcannon (champ and cabbage), Dublin coddle (bacon, ham-bone, onion, potato, sausage), Irish stew (mutton, carrot, leek and potato). They're excellent if you can get them – but authentic versions are available in only a handful of places, such as Gallagher's Boxty House in Dublin's *rive gauche*, Temple Bar, or in Belfast's famed Crown Liquor Saloon.

So where does all the fine produce go? Much of it, bought almost before it is caught or killed, is off that night, express, to the markets of Rungis in Paris and Madrid's Maravillas, which between them display more Irish-caught seafood than you'll find on any given day in the whole of Ireland.

The modern approach

Fortunately, there are some saviours at hand. For, just as the great English food writer Elizabeth David rescued her country from roast beef, so the Allen dynasty, from Cork east, have liberated a new generation of Ireland's chefs. Myrtle Allen's Ballymaloe Country House and Restaurant led the revolution, drafting small bands of suppliers together, letting the fine local produce – lamb filets and kidneys in a walnut-oil salad tiede, free-range chicken baked with cucumber, grilled scallions and buttered turnips – speak for themselves. Books, a TV series and a cookery school have helped spread the gospel.

These shops are usually well-stocked with Ireland's other new culinary delight: a great range of farmhouse cheeses. Soft or hard, from cows', goats' or sheep's milk, their arrival on the shelves marks a watershed in the country's new attitude towards its own food products. Fresh herbs, venison and boar sausage, mountain honey and organically grown vegetables compete for shoppers' attention.

There's money to be made, of course, in the new food consciousness. Shannon Basket of Fine Foods in Limerick can export you a preview, or mail you a memory. In September, Galway's riverbank Clarinbridge festival and the Galway International Oyster Festival are splen-

---

FOOD FOR THOUGHT

The novelist William Makepeace Thackeray wrote about Ireland: "We can feel the beauty of a magnificent landscape, perhaps: but we can describe a leg of mutton and turnips better."

did events, as is mid-October's harbourside Kinsale Gourmet Festival.

Now many of the country house hotels – most of which are listed by the Irish Country House Association or by its competitor, Hidden Ireland – are unfurling the fine produce banner. Among the current leaders is Gerry and Marie Galvin's Drimcong House Restaurant in Moycullen, Co. Galway.

Innovative cooking – at a price

Dublin, in particular, has a good spread of first-class restaurants. Some, such as Patrick Guilbaud's eponymous establishment, fly the classic

Belfast, once a foodies' wasteland, has begun providing the lead in a revolution which may even supplant that of its southern competitors. In their restaurant Roscoff, for example, Jeannie Rankin, the Canadian honorary consul, and her Belfast-born husband Paul are aiming to change the face of dining out in Ireland. Surrounded by minimalist decor, fine linen and glass, the Rankins' cuisine embraces marinated olives, oven-hot breads, lobster and herb risotto, char-grilled lamb and couscous. Disciples in Northern Ireland include Shanks, Deane's, Beech Hill Country House, Macnean's and Ardtara Country House.

French flag. Others, including Les Frères Jacques, promote the French provincial style. Johnny Cooke melds Italian and Pacific Rim with panache in Cooke's Café. The Temple Bar *arrondissement* is jammed with multinational tastes and there's an almost Italian quarter, a little south, off Wicklow Street. Visitors, however, can be shocked by the high prices, partly the result of the high rates of value-added tax and duty on wine.

LEFT: tasting time at the Clarenbridge Oyster Festival.
ABOVE: the traditional utensils behind Irish Stew; today's chefs have learned that visitors prefer their meat not to be overcooked.

At a less elevated level, the baking of bread and cakes anywhere in Ireland is almost always reliable. Brown soda bread made from stoneground wheaten flour is crusty, yet soft inside, and is the perfect accompaniment to seafish. Potato cakes, most popular in the north, are served with bacon and eggs for breakfast. A Barm Brack is a currant loaf traditionally eaten at Hallowe'en (31 October).

Pubs, the social heart of Irish communities, serve food of varying standards. You'll find scary re-heated and re-chilled "lasagnes", but you'll also find excellent home-made sandwiches and the finest of oysters and steaks. And the Guinness is likely to be very reliable. ❑

PLACES

*A detailed guide to the entire island, with principal sites
clearly cross-referenced by number to the maps*

W hat other city but Dublin, capital of the Republic of Ireland, could boast a General Post Office as a national shrine? Where else but Belfast, capital of Northern Ireland, could have endured a quarter of a century of sporadic terrorist activity and remain so bustling, so commercially alive, so welcoming? How can a country with a tiny population and a reputation for anarchy convince some of the world's biggest computer manufacturers to set up shop there? Why does the South say that the border between the two states has 252 crossing points, while the North insists it has 287?

"Sure," the Irishman will tell you, "it's only apathy that's saving the country from chaos but don't you worry your head at all about it now, the situation may be desperate, but sure it's not serious." Forget the statistics, therefore. Bring a raincoat, an umbrella and sturdy walking boots, but leave your preconceptions at home.

What you'll discover is a beguiling Irish stew of hidden loughs and ancient towns, prehistoric burial chambers and strange stone crosses, round towers and ruined castles, holy wells and high-spirited waterfalls. Racehorses are the local heroes and the villain is anyone too hurried to bid the time of day to a neighbour in a civilised manner. Kerry beckons with opulent valleys, nurturing arbutus, wild fuchsia and scented orchids; Killarney, with jaunting cars and leprachaun lore designed to charm the punts from tourists' pockets; the remote Irish-speaking Gaeltacht in the far west, with its mile after mile of magnificent emptiness; Dublin, increasingly anglicised, americanised and hamburgerised, yet still the least lonely of cities; rivers like the Galway and the Shannon where you could knock a dozen salmon senseless with a single brick; Fermanagh's resplendent lakeland, where boats are still gloriously few and far between; and County Clare's bleak but fascinating Burren.

It is a small country but, like vintage wine, should be savoured slowly. A signpost may present you with three ways of getting to a destination or it may show none. Ask a passer-by and, if he decides you look a bit tired after a hard day's sightseeing and comparing pints of Guinness, he'll probably assure you that it's "just a wee way ahead" because he doesn't wish to distress you by telling you it's really 40 miles by a narrow, twisting road.

The tensions of the modern world have not bypassed Ireland, but a remarkable capacity for enjoyment has survived. The island, in the end, is less a place on a map than a state of mind, induced by exposure to its restful yet excitable people, who routinely view life as a chaotic comedy. The inevitable, they promise, never happens in Ireland and the unexpected constantly occurs. Be prepared. ❏

PRECEDING PAGES: walkers in the Mourne Mountains, County Down; the ancient dolmen at Poulnabrone, County Clare; a traditional Connemara farmer – an increasingly rare sight these days.
LEFT: sheep farming at Glenmalure, Co. Wicklow.

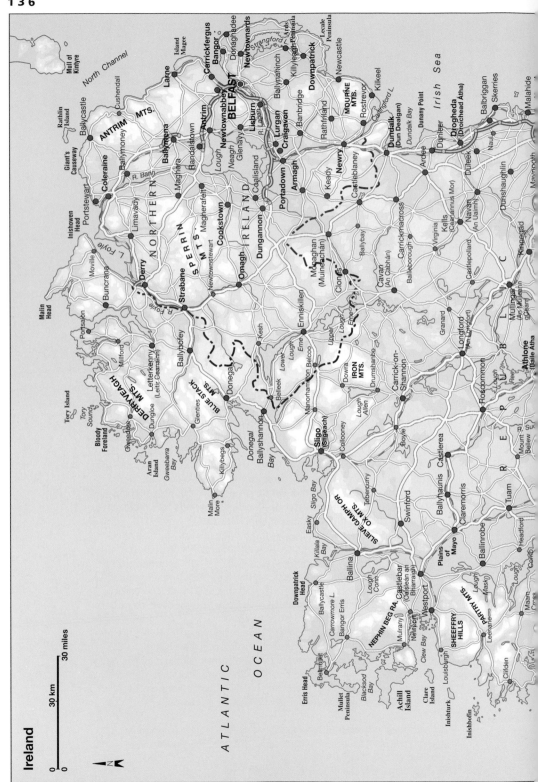

Ireland

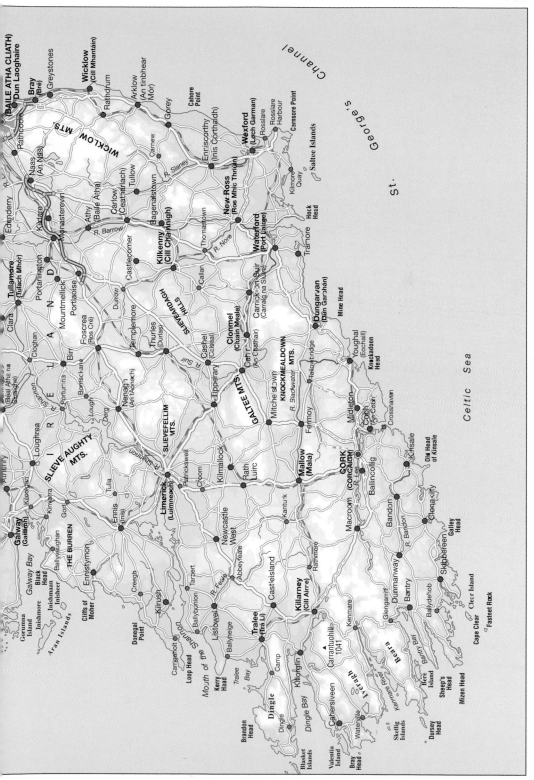

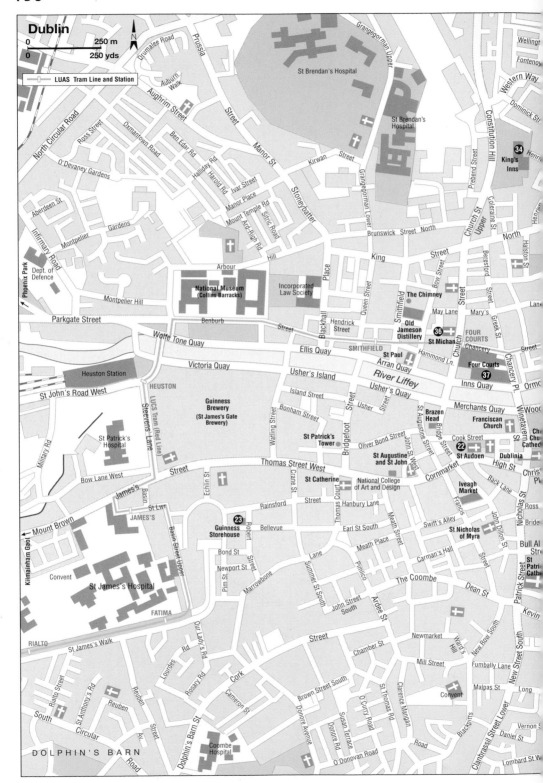

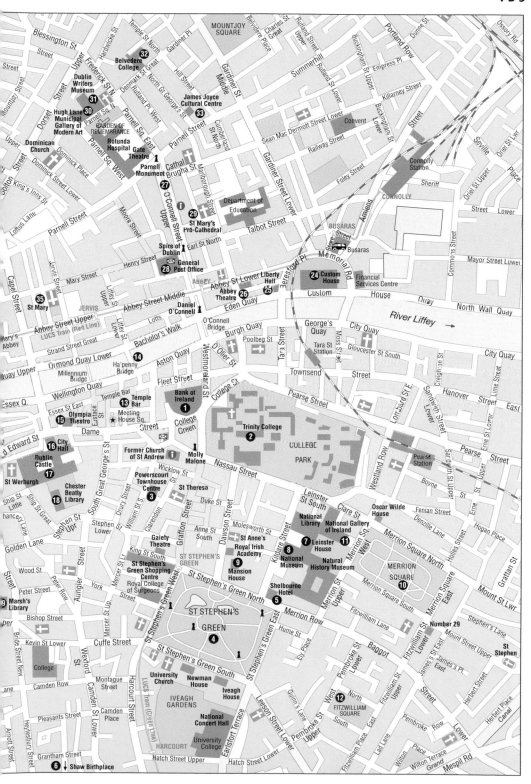

DUBLIN

It's a small capital and not an especially pretty one – but the vivacity of its citizens and the hospitality they show to visitors have made it one of Europe's most popular destinations

Map, page 138

Dublin means many things to many people. For some, it is a city of writers, the city of Jonathan Swift, Oliver Goldsmith, James Joyce, William Butler Yeats, Sean O'Casey, Brendan Behan, and even Bram Stoker, creator of Dracula. For others, it is a shrine of Irish nationalism. For some, it is the gateway to the fabled Irish landscape. For others, it is a city of talkers, its pubs overflowing with Guinness and jokes. Some come to wander in its Georgian streets, squares and gardens. Keith Ridgway listed some of its facets in his 2003 novel *The Parts*: "Working Dublin, queer Dublin, junkie Dublin, media Dublin, party Dublin, executive Dublin, homeless Dublin, suburban Dublin, gangland Dublin…"

The first thing that strikes nearly all visitors – weather permitting – is its superb natural setting, on a wide plain bisected by the **River Liffey**, overlooked by hills and headlands and facing a broad sweeping bay. By contrast, the city itself has an untidy, abstracted elegance, as if its mind is on something more important than looking attractive. The once-fashionable clothes are now a little threadbare, thanks to poor urban planning, but it can still sparkle when it tries.

A divided city

Dublin is divided by the River Liffey that flows through its centre and also by the social differences which the river delineates. In the early 18th century, the rich moved north across the river from the old medieval city with its teeming slums to the fine new terraces and squares that were then springing up, such as **Henrietta Street** and **Mountjoy Square**. But within decades they doubled back again to establish fashionable residences on the south side in **Merrion Square** and **Fitzwilliam Square**, continuing in Victorian times through the suburbs of **Ballsbridge** and out along the coast to **Dun Laoghaire** and **Dalkey**.

There are still middle-class enclaves on the northside, but by and large southsiders are better-off, better-dressed and (to their own ears) better spoken. They are also determined and skilful in the preservation of their privilege. Like any snobbery, of course, the north–south chauvinism works both ways, and just as many southsiders "wouldn't be seen dead on the northside", northsiders are inclined to judge that the southside is a wasteland of snobbery and pretension and that "them'uns are welcome to it."

Paradoxes of history

Dublin began by the banks of the Liffey, where Celtic settlements and churches existed at least from early Christian times, near a causeway crossing from which the city's Gaelic name, *Baile Atha Cliath*, "The Town of the Hurdle Ford", is derived. But towns as such did not figure in the old Celtic way of things, and it is gen-

LEFT: windy perch on the GPO in O'Connell Street. **BELOW:** one of the city's flashy malls – this one's at St Stephen's Green.

The Four Courts, the work of Thomas Cooley and James Gandon, was completed in 1796. The original Four Courts were those of Chancery, Common Pleas, Exchequer and King's Bench.

BELOW:
Dublin Castle.

erally accepted that Dublin was founded in the 9th century not by the Irish, but by the Vikings, who were plundering and colonising all the coasts of Northern Europe. They built a garrison port on the south bank of the river where its tributary, the Poddle, joined it to form the black pool (*dubh-linn*) that gave the city its name. The Poddle, once a fair-sized river, is now an underground stream.

Dublin was soon a lucrative base for both raiding and trading and the Danes hung on to it – despite persistent attacks by local chieftains and a great defeat at the Battle of Clontarf in 1014 – gradually intermarrying with the Irish and adopting Christianity. The Anglo-Normans arrived in the 12th century. But, until Elizabethan times, direct English rule was restricted to a ribbon of land on the east coast known as "the Pale", running roughly from Dundalk to the north to a little way south of Dublin.

The colonisation by landlords from Britain in the 17th and 18th centuries, however, established a stability of Anglo-Irish rule under which the city started to flourish for the haves, if not the have-nots. The 18th century was Dublin's "golden age", when many great buildings were erected and the city's social life was as fashionable as any in Europe. Legislative independence was granted under the English Crown in 1782, but the Irish parliament in College Green was short-lived. After the rebellion of the United Irishmen in 1798, inspired by the ideals of the French and American revolutions, Britain brought Ireland under direct control again and began a long period of decline in Dublin life.

The city was at the heart of the political and cultural ferment that led to the Rising of 1916, the subsequent War of Independence and the establishment of the Free State in 1921. The next 40 years were a time of economic struggle in a puritan atmosphere that was often culturally and socially stifling. All that

changed in the 1990s, as Dublin led the way in Ireland's economic renaissance and became one of Europe's most thriving artistic capitals.

Map,
page 138

City centre elegance

A good place to begin a walking tour is O'Connell Bridge. Turn your back on the inviting breadth and bustle of **O'Connell Street** and instead walk down **Westmoreland Street** into **College Green**, which contains two of Dublin's most impressive and historic buildings: the **Bank of Ireland** ❶ and Trinity College. You might think that the bank, with its curving, columnar, windowless facade, exudes loftier ideals than those of commerce, and you would be right. It was begun in 1729 to house the Irish Parliament, whose builders could not have foreseen how brief would be its age of glory.

The statue of Henry Grattan, the parliament's greatest orator, stands in the middle of College Green, frozen in mid-gesture, apparently delivering one of his ringing speeches. "Nations," he once said, "are governed not by interest only, but by passion also, and the passion of Ireland is freedom." The eastern front of the bank was added in 1785 by James Gandon. The building is open during banking hours; and conducted tours are held on Tuesday at 10.30am, 11.30am and 1.45pm.

Trinity College ❷, whose sober facade is topped by a surprisingly bright blue clock, was founded in 1592 by Elizabeth I on the site of a confiscated monastery, but the frontage was built between 1755 and 1759. The porch inside the main gate leads to a spacious, cobbled quadrangle, on the right of which is the Theatre, or Examination Hall (1779–91), which contains a gilt oak chandelier from the old parliament and an organ said to have been taken from a Spanish ship at Vigo in 1702. On the left is the Chapel (1792) and beyond it the Dining

ABOVE: the Bank of Ireland. **BELOW:** capturing attention in O'Connell Street: a lady preacher and pioneer labour leader James Larkin (1876–1947).

Hall (1743). The 100-ft (30-metre) campanile which dominates the quadrangle was designed by Sir Charles Lanyon and erected in 1853 on a spot supposed to mark the centre of the medieval monastery church.

To the right of the second quadrangle is the **Old Library** (1712–32), containing in a glass case the *Book of Kells*. This magnificently ornate 9th-century manuscript copy of the gospels in Latin is the centrepiece of an exhibition "Turning Darkness into Light" (Mon–Sat 9.30am–5pm year round, Sun Oct–Apr 12–4.30pm May–Sept 9.30am–4.30pm; entrance fee) and should not be missed. It is the greatest artefact of the flowering of Irish culture between the 7th and 9th centuries, the era when Ireland was famed as "the land of saints and scholars" and Irish monks re-Christianised Europe after the Dark Ages. Also in the library are the *Book of Durrow* (7th-century), the *Book of Dimma* (8th-century) and the *Book of Armagh* (*circa* 807). Upstairs is the breathtaking **Long Room**, nearly 210 ft (64 metres) in length and containing 200,000 of the college's oldest books. It holds temporary exhibitions which highlight the library's fine collection.

Embracing a more modern form of communication, the college also houses in the nearby Arts Block the inevitable **Dublin Experience**, a 45-minute multimedia show that catalogues the city's history (daily shows begin on the hour, 10am–4pm, May–Sept).

Leaving Trinity by the main gate and turning left, you face the mouth of **Grafton Street**, the southside's principal shopping thoroughfare, now pedestrianised, teeming with people and home to a pavement café culture which is beginning to rival the city's legendary pubs for custom – proof positive that Ireland has received more from joining the EU than just new roads and farm subsidies. A statue at the junction with Suffolk Street depicts Molly Malone who, in the famous song *In Dublin's*

ABOVE: Bewley's as it used to be.
BELOW: statue of Edmund Burke outside Trinity College.

Fair City, "wheeled her wheelbarrow through streets broad and narrow." With typical Dublin wit, the statue was dubbed "the tart with the cart". Worth a visit for its gregarious atmosphere is **Bewley's Oriental Café**, one of a chain of large, old-fashioned coffee-shops/restaurants that has become a justly beloved Dublin institution. Upstairs the Bewley's café-theatre presents daily a 50-minute lunchtime play (the ticket price includes soup and sandwiches). **Johnston's Court**, a narrow alley off Grafton Street to the right, leads to the rear entrance of the **Powerscourt Centre ❸**, a three-storey collection of stylish shops and cafés under the roof of the former Powerscourt Townhouse, built in 1771–74 for Viscount Powerscourt.

St Stephen's Green

On returning to Grafton Street, a right turn and a short walk takes you to the corner of **St Stephen's Green ❹**, a delightful small park bordered by some fine houses, though there has also been some ruinous modern development – particularly on the westside, where the only surviving historic building is the neo-classical **Royal College of Surgeons** (1806). The green, formerly an open common, was enclosed in 1663, but it was not surrounded by buildings until the late 18th century, when it became very fashionable. The gardens, laid out as a public park in 1880, are a relaxing refuge from the traffic and contain several interesting sculptures.

On the Green's south side are two elegant Georgian houses: **Newman House**, numbers 85 and 86 (tel: 475 7255; June–Aug Tues–Fri, guided tours begin at 11am and 12, 2 and 4pm and last 45 minutes; entrance fee), once the seat of the Catholic University of Ireland at which James Joyce, Flann O'Brien and Gerard Manley Hopkins worked or studied; and **Iveagh House**, numbers 80 and 81, which was built for the Bishop of Cork, once housed the Guinness family, and is now part of

Map, page 138

Newman House's interior shows how European tastes influenced Irish craftsmen.

BELOW: the statue of Molly Malone in Grafton Street.

the Department of Foreign Affairs. The main attraction of Newman House is its fine interior plasterwork. In 1856 John Henry Newman, the English theologian who was rector at the forerunner of University College Dublin, directed the building next door of **University Church**, designed in a colourful neo-Byzantine style.

On the north side of the Green is the **Shelbourne Hotel** ❺, built in its present splendid form in 1865. Dublin's hotels have an important role in the social life of the middle classes as places to meet and be seen. In **Earlsfort Terrace**, which branches from the southeastern corner of the green, is the **National Concert Hall** *(see Travel Tips page 364)*. The building, beautifully renovated, has first-rate acoustics.

Fans of George Bernard Shaw (1856–1950) can divert about a mile southwest to the **Shaw Birthplace** ❻ (tel: 475 0854 May–Oct, Mon–Sat 10am–5pm, Sun 11am–5pm, closed 1–2 lunch) at 33 Synge Street. Since Shaw moved to England at the age of 20, there's little here to indicate his writing activities, but the house nicely evokes the domestic world of Victorian Dublin.

The House of Representatives (Dáil) has 166 members (Teachtaí Dála, usually abbreviated to TD), and is directly elected every five years.

Official Dublin

Back on the north side of St Stephen's Green, **Kildare Street** leads past the left-hand side of the Shelbourne Hotel and a block of modern state buildings to **Leinster House** ❼, built as a townhouse for the Duke of Leinster in 1746 and now home of the Dáil Eireann (Irish parliament). It is flanked by two, nearly symmetrical, edifices with columnar entrance rotundas. These are the **National Library** and **National Museum** ❽, both built in 1890. Apart from more than 500,000 books, the library has an extensive collection of old newspapers and periodicals and a recently opened gallery housing temporary exhibitions of its collection (tel: 603 0200; www.nli.ie; exhibition area open Mon–Wed 10am–8pm, Thur–Fri 10am–4.45pm, Sat 10am–

BELOW: the National Library.

12.30pm). The large, musty reading-room is also well worth a look. The National Museum (tel: 677 7828, www.museum.ie, Tues–Sat 10am–5pm, Sun 2–5pm) has exhibits ranging from prehistory through the early Christian period and the Vikings to the Independence struggle. Exhibits include such treasures as the Ardagh Chalice and the Tara Brooch, plus fine prehistoric gold artefacts.

Map, page 138

Directly opposite Leinster House is **Molesworth Street**, and a few yards along it is **Buswell's Hotel**, a popular haunt among politicians and political journalists. At its far end the street meets **Dawson Street**, which contains several stylish shops. **Cafe Trí D** at No. 3 is part of a new educational centre which offers short intensive Irish language courses. Staff are bilingual and you can order a cup of tea *as Gaeilge* (in Irish) if you wish. Turning left at the corner you find **St Anne's Church** (1720), a venue for concerts as well as religious services. A few metres up the street is the **Mansion House ❾**, the residence since 1715 of the Lord Mayors of Dublin. A Queen Anne-style house, dating from 1705, it was decorated with stucco and cast iron in Victorian times.

At the other end of Dawson Street (towards Trinity College), you can turn right along **Nassau Street** which quickly becomes **Clare Street**, past the Kilkenny Design shop *(see Travel Tips page 370)* and Greene's fine old bookshop, into **Merrion Square ❿**, one of Dublin's finest. Laid out in 1762, it has had many distinguished inhabitants, Sir William and Lady "Speranza" Wilde, surgeon and poetess, and parents of Oscar, lived at number 1 (tel: 662 0281, now partially restored and open for guided tours on Mon, Wed and Thurs at 10.15 and 11.15am, entrance fee); Daniel O'Connell lived at number 58; W. B. Yeats, who was born in the seaside suburb of Sandymount but grew up mainly in London, lived at number 52 and later at number 83; Sheridan Le Fanu, author of the seminal vampire story *Carmilla*, lived at number 70. The Duke of Wellington, victor over Napoleon at the Battle of Waterloo, was born at number 24 Merrion Street Upper, which runs off the southwest corner of the square towards Merrion Row and St Stephen's Green. The lush gardens in the square are open to the public.

BELOW: the nursery of Number 29 Fitzwilliam Street.

Turn right from the end of Clare Street, along the western side of the square, to visit the **National Gallery of Ireland ⓫** (tel: 661 5133, www.nationalgallery.ie, Mon–Sat 9.30am–5.30pm, Thur to 8.30pm, Sun 12–5pm, guided tours Sat at 3pm, Sun at 2.15pm, 3pm and 4pm, free, fee for exhibitions). The statue on the lawn is of William Dargan, who organised the 1853 Dublin Exhibition on this site and used the profits to found the collection. To the left of the entrance is a statue of George Bernard Shaw, who said he owed his education to the gallery and left it a third of his estate. Apart from a range of Irish work, the gallery has some Dutch masters and fine examples of the 17th-century French, Italian and Spanish schools. The "Amorino" is the work of the Italian sculptor Canova. The **Yeats Museum** is a tribute to the artistic achievements of the Yeats family, especially Jack B. Yeats. The millennium wing houses temporary exhibitions and a very good café.

Leaving the gallery and turning right up **Merrion Street Upper** past the lawns of Leinster House, there is a fine view to your left along the southside of Merrion Square towards the distant cupola of St Stephen's Church (1825). Passing the **Natural History Museum**

on your right (an eclectic collection of dead animals), you reach the imposing gates of Government Buildings, which house the office of the Taoiseach (prime minister) and the Cabinet room. Tours are available on Saturdays; tickets from the National Gallery.

A left turn at the next intersection along Baggot Street, then a right up **Pembroke Street** leads to **Fitzwilliam Square ⓬**, the city's smallest, latest (1825) and best-preserved Georgian square. Jack B. Yeats lived at number 18, on the corner of Fitzwilliam Street, the longest Georgian street in Dublin. In an infamous piece of state vandalism, 26 houses on its eastern side were demolished in 1965 to make way for a new Electricity Supply Board HQ. Perhaps out of shame, the ESB helped restore **Number 29**, (open Tues–Sat 10am–5pm, Sun 1–5pm; entrance fee) in Fitzwilliam Street Lower, as an elegant middle-class house of the late 1700s.

Wander back now to Trinity College, a good starting point to begin exploring the oldest part of the city.

Some of the converted Temple Bar buildings have retained their elaborate friezes.

BELOW: conviviality at Temple Bar.

Temple Bar

With your back to the facade of Trinity and the Bank of Ireland on your right, walk along **Dame Street**, passing on your right the imposing, layered structure of the modern **Central Bank**. The network of small streets between the Central Bank and the river quays, known as **Temple Bar ⓭**, has undergone a remarkable renaissance in the past few years to become Dublin's "Left Bank", its cobbled streets full of studios, galleries, second-hand book, clothing and music stores, pubs, clubs, cultural centres, restaurants and craft shops. This is very much the "buzz" area of Dublin, especially for young people. It even has its own marketing department (www.templebar.ie).

There's no "best route" through Temple Bar; it's essentially a place for browsing. The area's renewal has been planned around two new public squares: **Temple Bar Square**, a meeting point for shoppers, and **Meeting House Square**, a cultural centre and performance space. Just off Temple Bar Square, Merchant's Arch – a favourite spot for buskers – leads to the river quay and the **Ha'penny Bridge** ⑭ (1816) – so-called because of the toll once charged for crossing it. This cast-iron pedestrian walkway across the Liffey has become one of the best-known symbols of the city. It is a valuable link between Temple Bar and the bustling shopping streets of the Henry Street area across the river. Further west a companion footbridge spans the Liffey between the Ormond Quay and Wellington Quay.

The route from Temple Bar Square to Meeting House Square goes through the newly built Curved Street, which houses the the the **Temple Bar Music Centre**, which is both a training centre/workshop and a venue for concerts (www.tbmc.ie). You emerge in Eustace Street, which contains the **Ark**, a cultural centre for children (www.ark.ie). Just up the street from the Ark, a covered passageway leads into Meeting House Square, an outdoor performance venue, used in summer for concerts, theatre and film shows.

To one side of it are two of the area's main cultural attractions: the **Irish Film Institute** – an art house cinema with a bookshop, café/restaurant, bar and film archive (www.ifc.ie) – and the **Gallery of Photography**, which shows both Irish and international work and has an interesting range of postcards and books (www.irish-photography.com). Just off the other side of the square is the **Temple Bar Information Centre** (tel: 677 2255, www.temple-bar.ie, useful for details of current events). Continuing along Essex Street East, you pass the rear of the Clarence Hotel *(see Travel Tips page 341)*, which fronts onto the river quay. The hotel's current owners include members of the U2 rock band, and its stylish Octagon Bar is a fashionable meeting place.

At the riverside end of Parliament Street is Sunlight Chambers, a building with a beautiful Victorian frieze displaying the world according to the priorities of Lever Bros, soap manufacturers: men's toil makes clothes dirty, women's toil (and Sunlight Soap) makes them clean again!

Ancient Dublin

Beyond Parliament Street, Essex Street ends at its junction with **Fishamble Street**, the medieval "fish shambles", or market, whose existence can be traced back to 1467 and which winds upwards from the quay alongside the Civic Offices. This otherwise unprepossessing street is celebrated as the venue of the first performance of Handel's *Messiah*, conducted by the composer in 1742 in the Charitable Music Society's Hall, long since demolished. Because the hall was cramped and the attendance large, ladies were asked not to wear hooped petticoats and gentlemen not to wear their swords. *Messiah* was an instant success in Dublin, though London audiences remained cool towards it for several years. A new hotel, named after the composer, stands beside the original site, and the *Messiah*'s birth is celebrated at this spot by a statue of the composer (in the nude) and at noon every 13 April by members of Our Lady's Choral Society (fully clothed), who sing a selection of choruses.

Map, page 138

The only constants are the sea, the play of light and the same green curve of hills the Vikings saw when they arrived."
—Peter Somerville-Large

BELOW: understatement is not a characteristic of Temple Bar.

Back on Dame Street, opposite City Hall, you see on your right the ornate Victorian doorway of the **Olympia Theatre** ⓯. Despite its modest frontage, it is Dublin's largest theatre; its programme mixes plays, musicals and concerts.

Dublin Castle

Dublin's medieval city once occupied the area between City Hall and Bridge Street, bordered by the riverbank to the north and defensive walls which stretched as far as Bride Street in the south. **City Hall** ⓰ (tel: 672 2204; Mon–Sat 10am–5.15pm, Sun 2–5pm, entrance fee) was designed in 1769 as the Royal Exchange by the London architect Thomas Cooley (who won a £100 prize for the plan) and served as a prison for rebels in 1798, as a military depot, and as a corn exchange, before being taken over by the Corporation of Dublin in 1852. The entrance rotunda has a splendid illuminated dome. On the mosaic floor is the city's coat of arms, with the rubric in Latin, "Happy the city where citizens obey" – not perhaps the most apposite motto for Dubliners. A multimedia exhibition in the basement traces 1,000 years of Dublin's history.

Dublin Castle ⓱ (Mon–Fri 10am–5pm, Sat–Sun 2–5pm, fee applies to guided tours), just behind City Hall, was built between 1208 and 1220 on the site of an earlier Danish fortress and was the symbol of English rule in Ireland for almost eight centuries. The building as it now stands is mainly 18th-century; the largest

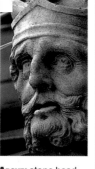

ABOVE: stone head in the chapel of Dublin Castle.
BELOW: the interior of Dublin Castle.

visible remain of the Norman structure is the **Record Tower**, in the lower Castle Yard, which contains the present-day State Paper Office. The **Bermingham Tower**, tallest in the castle, was originally early 15th-century, but was rebuilt after an explosion in 1775. Many celebrated rebels were imprisoned here, including Red Hugh O'Donnell and Henry and Art O'Neill, who escaped on Christmas Eve, 1591.

The most impressive parts of the castle are the **State Apartments** (viewed by guided tour only) – St Patrick's Hall, 25 metres long and 12 metres wide, with a high panelled and decorated ceiling, is probably the grandest room in Ireland. It was used by the British for various state functions and since 1938 has been the scene of the inauguration of Irish presidents. The Gothic-style Church of the Most Holy Trinity was built as the Chapel Royal between 1807 and 1814 to a design by Francis Johnston; it was taken over by the Catholic Church in 1943. The exterior is decorated with more than 90 carved heads of English monarchs and other historical figures. To the castle's rear the Clocktower building has been extended to accommodate the **Chester Beatty Library** ⓲ (tel: 407 0750, www.chl.ie, Tues–Fri 10am–5pm all year, May–Sept only Mon 10am–5pm, Sat 11am–5pm, Sun 1–5pm, free). Named European Museum of the Year in 2002, it has a fine collection of Chinese, Japanese, Persian, Indian and Middle Eastern manuscripts, paintings and ornaments. Audio-visual programmes provide background.

Leaving the castle, head a short way down Dame Street towards Trinity College and turn right up busy **South Great George's Street**; on the left side is a Victorian shopping arcade containing many interesting and colourful shops and stalls. Continuing into **Aungier Street**, you see on your right the **Church of the Carmelite Fathers**, the only church in Dublin to be re-established on its pre-Reformation site – the order had a church here in the 13th century. Thomas Moore, the 19th-century poet and songwriter, was born at number 12 Aungier Street. John Field, Ireland's greatest composer and pianist, was born nearby in **Golden Lane** in 1782. He created the nocturne and originated the style of romantic pianism which culminated in Chopin's work.

Swift's self-penned epitaph in Latin reads: "He is laid where bitter indignation can no longer lacerate his heart."

Continue now into **Wexford Street**, turn right, and cross **New Bride Street** into **Kevin Street Upper**, where you find **Marsh's Library** ⓳, the oldest public library in Ireland and named after its founder, Archbishop Narcissus Marsh (1638–1713). Among its 25,000 interesting items is Jonathan Swift's copy of Clarendon's *History of the Great Rebellion*, with Swift's pencilled notes.

BELOW: Boyle family monument in St Patrick's Cathedral.

The next junction marks the beginning of the **Liberties**, an area so named because it lay outside the jurisdiction of medieval Dublin. One of the city's oldest and most characterful working-class areas, it was also filled with some of the worst 19th-century slum tenements. The **Coombe** road, which runs westward into the Liberties, was once the "coomb" (river valley) of the Poddle.

Make a note to sample the character of the Liberties another time and turn right along Patrick Street to **St Patrick's Cathedral** ⓴ (Mon–Fri 9am–6pm; Sat Nov–Feb 9am–5pm Mar–Oct 9am–6pm; Sun Nov–Feb 10am–3pm Mar–Oct 9am–6pm; entrance fee). Dedicated in 1192, it has been restored many times and, like Dublin's other cathedral, Christ Church, has belonged to the Church of Ireland since the Reformation. Swift, Dean from 1713 to 1745, is buried in it, near his beloved "Stella", Esther Johnson. "Living Stones", a permanent exhibition, explores the history of the cathedral.

Continue now along Patrick Street and then Nicholas Street to **Christ Church Cathedral** ㉑ (Mon–Fri 9.45am–5pm, Sat–Sun 10am–5pm, entrance fee). It was founded by Sitric, the Danish King of Dublin, about

Map, page 138

1040, and greatly expanded from 1172 onwards under the aegis of Strongbow and St Laurence O'Toole. The central tower was built about 1600 after storm and fire damage to the original steeples. Lambert Simnel, 10-year-old pretender to the English throne, was crowned here by his supporters in 1487. Christ Church became Protestant in 1551, though the Mass was restored for a short period under James II. The structure was greatly rebuilt in Gothic revival style in the 1870s. Two of the cathedral's many tombs are said to be those of Strongbow and his son, whom, according to legend, he killed for cowardice in battle.

Linked to the cathedral by a covered bridge is **Dublinia** (Apr–Sept, daily 10am–5pm; Oct–Mar, Mon–Sat 11am–4pm, Sun and public holidays 10am–4.30pm, entrance fee), an exhibition, run by the non-profit Medieval Trust, which recreates the medieval city's growth from 1170 to 1540. Exhibits include a scale model of the old city, artefacts from the Wood Quay excavations including the skeleton of a 12th-century woman, and a multi-screen historical presentation. From the top of the 200-ft (60-metre) St Michael's Tower, you can enjoy a panoramic view over the city. Admission to Dublinia includes entry to the cathedral via the bridge, but you can also enter Christ Church directly. Across the river to your left is the stately dome of the **Four Courts** *(see page 159)*; save it for a later tour.

High Street, which runs off the westside of **Christchurch Place**, was the backbone of medieval Dublin. Part of the old city wall and the only surviving city gate have been uncovered near the partially ruined **St Audoen's Church ㉒**, (June–Sept daily 9.30am–5.30pm, fee includes guided tour). It was named by the Normans after St Ouen of Rouen. Its aisle contains a font dating from 1194; the tower is 12th-century and three of its bells were cast in the early 15th century, making them the country's oldest. On the other side of High Street, in **Back Lane**, is **Tailors' Hall**,

ABOVE: Arthur Guinness. **BELOW:** the brewery tower; the Custom House.

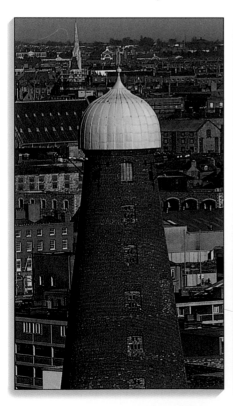

the only surviving guild hall in Dublin, and now the offices of **An Taisce**, which works to preserve the country's natural and architectural heritage.

One part of the national heritage which seems well able to look after itself is enshrined half-a-mile (1km) to the west along Thomas Street: **Guinness's Brewery**, the biggest in Europe, churning out 2½ million pints of its celebrated black stout every day. The brewery doesn't admit visitors, but the **Guinness Storehouse ㉓** (tel: 408 4800, daily, entrance fee) lets you explore – through sight, touch, taste and smell – the making and history of the world's most famous stout. The building also houses gallery and exhibition areas, events venues, an archives room and the highest bar in Dublin, with a panoramic view of the city. The admission ticket entitles you to a complimentary pint in the rooftop bar – probably the best-tasting Guinness to be had anywhere, since it hasn't had to travel.

If you don't feel like walking quite so far for a drink, you may enjoy a visit to the **Brazen Head** *(see Travel Tips page 355)*, nearer at hand in Bridge Street. There is said to have been a tavern on this site since Viking times, though the present premises date from only 1688. It was once a meeting place for the United Irishmen. As well as being old, it's odd. On your way back to O'Connell Street Bridge, you could cross over the narrow, arching footpath of the "**Ha'penny Bridge**", from which there are fine river views, especially at sunset. Alternatively, you can use its brand-new neighbour, the Millennium Bridge.

Discover how Ireland's famous brew and its barrels are made.

North of the Liffey

O'Connell Bridge is again your starting-point to explore Dublin's northern half, but before acquainting yourself with the main features of O'Connell Street, stay a little longer on the southside, walking east along **Burgh Quay** and under the railway bridge for a view across the river to the **Custom House ㉔**, one of the masterpieces of James Gandon, the greatest architect of 18th-century Dublin. Although English, Gandon looked to the Continent for architectural models and it is easier to imagine the Custom House transposed to the banks of the Seine than to the Thames. Finished in 1791, the building was extensively damaged in a fire started by Republicans to mark the Sinn Féin election victory in 1921 and has been largely rebuilt. The central copper dome, 120 ft (38 metres) high, is topped by a statue of commerce by Edward Smyth. The keystones over the arched doorways flanking the Doric portico represent the Atlantic Ocean and 13 principal rivers of Ireland.

BELOW: the Ha'penny Bridge.

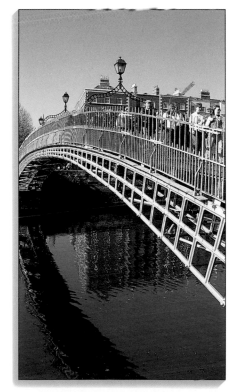

Gandon went on to design Carlisle Bridge (widened and rebuilt in 1880 and renamed **O'Connell Bridge**), the Four Courts, the eastern portico of Parliament House (Bank of Ireland) and the King's Inns.

The gleaming new building just downstream of the Custom House is the **Financial Services Centre**, erected in the late 1980s. The tall, 1960s edifice a little way upstream of the Custom House is **Liberty Hall ㉕**, headquarters of the country's largest trade union, the Services, Industrial, Professional and Technical Union. Its more modest predecessor was a nerve-centre of the labour struggle. It stands at one end of a crescent laid out by Gandon and named **Beresford Place** after his patron in the building of the Custom House, John Beresford,

Chief Commissioner for the Irish Revenue. At the far end of the place is the **Busaras** (central bus station), a daring work by Dublin standards when built in 1953. More recently it has been described, rather unfairly, as a "hideous edifice".

Walk towards O'Connell Bridge along the north bank and turn into **Marlborough Street**, where you find the **Abbey Theatre ㉖**, Ireland's national playhouse (www.abbeytheatre.ie). The present building was erected in 1966 to replace a predecessor destroyed by fire. The Abbey, founded in 1904 by W. B. Yeats, Lady Gregory and their collaborators, played a vital role in the cultural renaissance of the time and quickly earned a world reputation through the great works of Synge and O'Casey and for its players' naturalistic acting style. Performances were often turbulent: the most celebrated uproar was that caused at a performance of Synge's *The Playboy of the Western World* by the use of the word "shift" (petticoat). Downstairs in the Abbey is its sister theatre, the **Peacock**, used for experimental work.

O'Connell Street

O'Connell Street **㉗** itself is not what it was, though the latter-day rash of fast-food joints, amusement arcades, ugly modern buildings, billboards and signs cannot quite obscure its inherent grandeur. It was planned (as Sackville Street) in the mid-1700s by the first Viscount Mountjoy, Luke Gardiner, who widened the existing narrow roadway, Drogheda Street, and planted trees on a central mall. In 1794, the construction of Carlisle Bridge turned it from a fashionable residential promenade into the city's main north-south artery. A tall column surmounted by a statue of Horatio Nelson, like that in London's Trafalgar Square, was erected in 1815 to mark the famous sea victory over Napoleon; republicans blew it up, neatly, by an explosion one night in 1966 to mark the 50th anniversary of the Easter Rising.

TIP

Book well ahead for Abbey performances. Tel: Dublin 878 7222.

BELOW: conviviality powers Dublin pubs,

The **statues** still lining the centre of the street are (from the bridge end): Daniel O'Connell (1775–1847), a great leader of constitutional nationalism; William Smith O'Brien (1803–64), leader of the Young Ireland Party; Sir John Gay (1816–75), proprietor of the *Freeman's Journal* and organiser of the city's water supply; James Larkin (1876–1947), a great trade union leader; Father Theobald Mathew (1790–1856), the "Apostle of Temperance"; and Charles Stewart Parnell (1846–91), inspiration of the Home Rule movement and a tragic victim of intolerance whose career was ruined by the outcry over his union with Kitty O'Shea, who happened to be married to another Irish politician.

City planners, eager to mark the city's millennium in 1988 (the date was somewhat arbitrary, chosen more to boost tourism than to mark any significant historical event), supplied Dubliners with an easy target for wit by installing a large aquatic sculpture in O'Connell Street's central promenade. The female figure – a representation of Anna Livia, the river goddess of the Liffey who featured in James Joyce's *Finnegans Wake* – was instantly christened "the floozy in the Jacuzzi". The floozy has now been displaced in favour of the **Spire of Dublin**, an aspirational 390-ft (120-metre) stainless steel pillar which was immediately dubbed "the stiffy by the Liffey".

Centrepiece of the street is the imposing Ionic portico of the **General Post Office ㉘** (1815), headquarters of the 1916 Rising and the place where the rebels proclaimed the republic in ringing terms, to the initial bemusement of Dubliners – a reaction, in Yeats's words, "changed utterly" by the subsequent execution, one by one, of 15 captured leaders. The GPO's pillars are still pock-marked by bullets; although the building survived the fighting, much of the street was wrecked by British artillery and it suffered further in 1922 during the Civil War.

Map, page 138

Daniel O'Connell, presiding over the street named after him.

LEFT: James Joyce statue in Earl Street, off O'Connell Street. **BELOW:** the General Post Office.

Inside the GPO (open Mon–Sat 8am–8pm, Sun 10.30am–6pm) is a fine bronze statue of the ancient Irish hero Cuchulainn, with the Proclamation of the Republic on its base.

But those struggles are not the principal cause of O'Connell Street's fall from grace: it was rebuilt well enough in the 1920s but, as the journalist Frank McDonald wrote in *The Destruction of Dublin*, "the dignified and noble facades... got scant attention from the developers who descended on the street during the late 1960s and early 1970s." In McDonald's angry words: "This magnificent thoroughfare could have become Dublin's answer to the Champs Elysées, lined with fashionable shops and terrace cafés where people could sit and watch the world go by. Instead, the capital's main street was transformed into a honky-tonk freeway, cluttered with fast-food joints, slot-machine casinos, ugly modern office blocks, vacant buildings and even the odd derelict site."

Moore Street market

Off O'Connell Street, just past the GPO, **Henry Street** is the northside's main shopping street. Its tributary to the north, **Moore Street**, is filled with fruit and vegetable stalls staffed by colourful and vociferous women. It also has a remarkable battery of butchers' shops and has recently added ethnic food outlets to cater for Dublin's ever-expanding immigrant population. It is well worth visiting for a dose of down-to-earth Dublin. On the opposite side of O'Connell Street, walk down Earl Street and turn left into Marlborough Street to visit **St Mary's Pro-Cathedral** ㉙ (1816–25), the city's main Catholic Church. John Henry Newman first publicly professed Catholicism here in 1851. The area was once a notorious red-light district, known as "Monto" (James Joyce's "Nighttown").

At the north end of O'Connell Street are the late 18th-century **Rotunda Rooms**, occupied in recent years by a cinema. The **Rotunda Hospital** to the left (Europe's first maternity hospital) was financed by concerts in the Rooms. Built in con-

BELOW: Moore Street market.

junction with the hospital, the **Gate Theatre** at the bottom of Parnell Square East was founded in 1928 by Micheál MacLiammóir and Hilton Edwards; the teenage Orson Welles made his first professional appearance here (www.gate-theatre.ie).

A few yards past the Gate, the **Garden of Remembrance** (1966) commemorates Ireland's martyrs. The sculpture by Oisin Kelly, beyond the central lake, is based on the myth of the Children of Lir, who were changed to swans.

On the northside of Parnell Square is the **Hugh Lane Municipal Gallery of Modern Art** ③⓪ (Tues–Thur 9.30am–6pm, Fri–Sat 9.30am–5pm, Sun 11am–5pm, free). Its nucleus is formed by the mainly Impressionist collection of Sir Hugh Lane, who died when the liner *Lusitania* was torpedoed in 1915. As a result of a wrangle over his will, the collection was split, each half being alternated every five years between Dublin and London's Tate Gallery. In 1998 the gallery employed a team of archaeologists to painstakingly dismantle the London studio of Dublin-born artist Francis Bacon and faithfully reconstruct it here.

At 18–19 Parnell Square North, the **Dublin Writers Museum** ③① (Mon–Sat 10am–5pm, until 6pm Jun–Aug, Sun 11am–5pm, entrance fee) displays photographs, paintings, busts, letters, manuscripts, first editions and other memorabilia relating to celebrated deceased writers such as Swift, Shaw, Yeats, O'Casey, Joyce, Beckett and Behan. The first-floor **Gallery of Writers** is splendidly decorated.

The **National Wax Museum** (tel: 872 6340, Mon–Sat 10am–5.30pm, Sun noon–5.30pm), around the corner in Granby Row, caters for eclectic tastes.

Return to Parnell Square East, turn left and then right into Great Denmark Street. On the left is **Belvedere College** ③② a fine 18th-century mansion which has been the Jesuit Belvedere College since 1841. James Joyce, who was a pupil here, described its atmosphere in *Portrait of the Artist as a Young Man.*

Map, page 138

ABOVE: Yeats painting in Dublin Writers Museum. **BELOW:** an exhibit at the Municipal Gallery of Modern Art.

The main James Joyce commemorations centre on Bloomsday, held on 16 June.

BELOW: convent in Henrietta Street.

Turn into **North Great George's Street,** where many grand Georgian houses have been saved from decades of decrepitude. At number 35 is the **James Joyce Centre ㉝** (year round Tues–Sat 9.30am–5pm, tours must be pre-booked; tel: 878 8547). This addition to the literary tourist trail is located in a beautifully restored late 18th-century townhouse which features in *Ulysses* as the venue for dancing classes. The centre's most interesting exhibit is a set of biographies of real Dublin people fictionalised in Joyce's masterpiece. There are photographs and storyboards about Joyce's family and the many homes they inhabited. And, in a suitably Joycean collision of fact and fiction, you can view the front door of No. 7 Eccles Street, home of Leopold Bloom and his wife Molly, the central characters of *Ulysses* (the house itself was demolished). The centre's interior has splendid stucco ceilings.

Returning past the Municipal Gallery to Parnell Square West, turn right, then left into Bolton Street, then right again at **Henrietta Street**, the oldest and once, it is said, the finest of the city's Georgian streets, the home of archbishops, peers and Members of Parliament. It is now mostly decrepit. At its far end are the **King's Inns ㉞**, the Dublin inns of court, where, in the English tradition, newly qualified barristers must eat a prescribed number of meals. The building was designed by Gandon at the turn of the 19th century (tours by appointment only, tel: 874 4840).

Continue down Bolton Street bearing left into **Capel Street**. To the left in Mary Street is **St Mary's Church ㉟**, built from 1697 by Thomas Burgh, architect of Trinity College library. Here, in 1747, John Wesley preached his first sermon in Ireland. Theobald Wolfe Tone (1763–98), founder of the United Irishmen and father of Irish republicanism, was born nearby in a street now named after him.

To the other side of Capel Street, Mary Street leads via Mary's Lane to Church Street, where you find **St Michan's Church ㊱**, (Mon–Sat, fee for tour of vaults)

founded in 1095 as a Viking parish church. The present structure dates from the late 1600s, but it was much restored in 1821 and again after the Civil War. Handel is said to have played on its organ. In the vaults are 17th-century mummified bodies, preserved because the limestone walls absorb moisture from the air.

Leaving the church, turn down May lane and left into Bow street which will bring you to the **Old Jameson Distillery** (daily 9am–5.30pm, tours are continuous), a museum sited in the old warehouse of the 1791 whiskey factory.

A small lane will then take you to **Smithfield village**. Its distinctive architecture incorporates a 175-ft (53-metre) chimney built in 1895 and now an observation platform giving interesting views of the city.

Return to the quays and turn left to end this section of the tour as you began it: with a look at a Gandon masterpiece. The **Four Courts** ㊲ (visitors allowed to witness most court proceedings, Mon–Fri 10am–1pm and 2–4pm) was built between 1786 and 1802. The dominant lantern-dome is fronted by a six-columned Corinthian portico surmounted by the statues of Moses, Justice and Mercy, and flanked by two wings enclosing courtyards. In 1922, after the building was barricaded by anti-Treaty republicans, troops of Michael Collins's new government shelled it from across the river. In the ensuing fire, the Record Office was burnt, destroying many priceless documents. Restoration was completed in 1932.

West Dublin

Board the westbound Red Line of LUAS at the rear of the Four Courts. After three quick stops, you'll be at Heuston Station. From here it is only a five-minute walk west along St John's Road before turning north onto Military Road and the entrance to **Kilmainham Royal Hospital**, founded by Charles II (1680–84)

**Map,
page 138**

Unlike many English architects, James Gandon liked Dublin and chose to live in Ireland. He finally retired there and died in 1823.

BELOW: St Michan's Church vaults; the Four Courts.

A Kilmainham Jail plaque lists the executions in 1916.

TIP

Guided tours run every Saturday to Aras an Uachtaráin from the visitor centre at the north end of Phoenix Park.

BELOW: interior of Kilmainham Jail.

"for the reception and entertainment of antient (*sic*) maimed, and infirm officers and soldiers." It now houses the **Irish Museum of Modern Art** (Tues–Sat 10am–5.30pm; Sun noon–5.30pm, free, fee for special exhibitions, www.modernart.ie), which combines Irish and international 20th-century art with educational and community programmes and performing arts. The permanent collection is patchy, but the temporary exhibitions can be interesting.

Exit the museum the way you came in, a right turn onto Military Road and a right again onto Bow Bridge brings you to the South Circular Road and **Kilmainham Gaol** ❸ (Apr–Sept daily 9.30am–6pm, Oct–Mar daily 9.30am–5.30pm, entrance fee), which has been intimately connected with Ireland's struggle for independence from its construction in the 1790s until it ceased to be a prison in the 1920s. Visitors are invited to browse in the museum, which explores 19th-century notions of crime, punishment and reform through a series of well-captioned displays. The upstairs section is devoted to the nationalist figures, some famous, some obscure, who were imprisoned here, many awaiting execution.

A guide then leads visitors into the vaulted east wing of the jail, with its tiers of cells and overhead catwalks, and upstairs to the prison chapel, where an excellent audio-visual summary of the nationalist struggle is shown. Visitors are then brought to the "1916 corridor", containing the cells that housed the captured leaders of the Rising, and finally led to the stone-breakers' yard where 14 of them were shot between 3 and 12 May of that year.

If you prefer a walk in the park to time in jail, turn left on Bow Lane from Military Road and left again on **Steeven's Lane**. Head past Heuston Station and cross the river to visit **Phoenix Park** ❹, whose southern boundary extends west on the Liffey's north bank for about 3 miles (5 km). At 1,760 acres (712 hectares), it is over five times as large as London's Hyde Park. Its name is a corruption of the Gaelic *fionn uisce* ("clear water").

Among its features, all signposted, are: the **Wellington Monument**, an obelisk 60 metres high, erected after Waterloo; the **Zoological Gardens**, the third oldest public zoo in the world (1830), well known for the breeding of lions (it supplied the MGM announcer); the President's residence, **Aras an Uachtaráin**, formerly the Viceregal Lodge (1751–54); the US Ambassador's residence; and the "15 acres", an open space actually of 200 acres containing paths and playing fields, the duelling ground of 18th-century Dublin gentlemen.

On the way back to the city, on the north side of the quays, is the former **Collins Barracks**, now the **National Museum extension** for decorative arts with displays of Irish silver, glassware, musical instruments and Japanese art (www.museum.ie).

Southside suburbs

Most places mentioned in this section are served by various buses departing from **Eden Quay**, beside O'Connell Bridge, and by the excellent DART suburban trains.

Travelling out through Merrion Square North, along Northumberland Road past the squat, circular block of the **American Embassy** (1964), you reach the prestigious suburb of **Ballsbridge** ❹, named after the bridge over the River Dodder. The large greystone buildings to the right on Merrion Road, just past the bridge, are the headquarters of the **Royal Dublin Society** ("the RDS", www.rds.ie), the sponsor of improvements in agriculture and stock breeding and the venue for the **Dublin Horse Show** (in August). The RDS's Simmonscourt Extension is used for exhibitions and concerts.

The main road south soon skirts the coast, affording fine views of the bay, and passes through **Blackrock ㊶**, where Eamon de Valera studied and later taught at the boys' college. A couple of miles further on is the town and port of **Dun Laoghaire ㊷** (pronounced *Dunleery*), departure point for ferries to Britain. The harbour, with its long, granite piers, was built between 1817 and 1859.

The next promontory, within easy walking distance, is that of **Sandycove**, with its **Martello tower** where Joyce lived for a short time in 1904. He used it as the setting for the opening scene of *Ulysses* and it is now a **Joyce Museum ㊸** (open Apr–Oct Mon–Sat 10am–5pm, Sun 2–6pm, closed between 1–2pm). The nearby **Forty Foot** bathing place has been for generations a spartan haven of nude bathing for men, though feminists have made incursions.

A bit further on is **Dalkey ㊹**, a meandering old village of great charm and some *cachet*. **Dalkey Castle** (tel: 285 8366), a medieval tower house, has been restored and houses a heritage centre. Its battlements give excellent views of the surrounding land and seascape. From nearby **Coliemore Harbour** there are boat trips in summer to **Dalkey Island**, a stone's throw offshore; it contains another Martello tower and the ruins of a Benedictine church. The island is a bird sanctuary. From Vico Road, which continues along the coast, you can enter **Killiney Hill Park**; motorists should drive instead up Dalkey Avenue, to the public car-park.

At the summit of the park is a Victorian obelisk commanding splendid views of the broad sweep of **Killiney Bay** (often likened to the Bay of Naples), **Bray**

Map, page 161

The Round Room at the Joyce Museum. Tel: Dublin 280 9265.

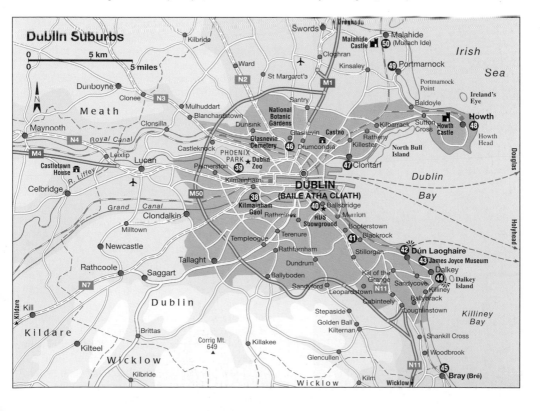

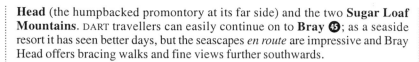

Map,
page 161

Head (the humpbacked promontory at its far side) and the two **Sugar Loaf Mountains**. DART travellers can easily continue on to **Bray** ⑮; as a seaside resort it has seen better days, but the seascapes *en route* are impressive and Bray Head offers bracing walks and fine views further southwards.

Northern suburbs

The attractions of the northside are more diffuse. But it's worth visiting the suburb of **Glasnevin** ⑯ (buses 13 and 19 from O' Connell Street) to see the beautifully arranged **Botanic Gardens** (summer Mon–Sat 9am–6pm, Sun 10am–6pm, winter Mon–Sat 10am–4.30pm Sun 10am–4.30pm, free, fee for guided tours) in the former demesne of Joseph Addison, the English essayist and founder of *The Spectator* magazine who lived in Dublin as secretary to the Earl of Sutherland.

ABOVE: Cyril Fry
Model Railway
Museum. **BELOW:**
quayside meeting.
RIGHT: relaxing
at Malahide.

The coastal route northeast by the Custom House leads past **Fairview Park** to the middle-class enclave of **Clontarf** ⑰, site of the battle in 1014 in which Brian Ború defeated the Danes. **Malahide Road** branches off to the left and to the left again is the recently restored **Casino**, once part of the seaside estate of Lord Charlemont, whose town house is now the Municipal Gallery. It is a small Palladian building, a gem of its kind, with several unusual features: the roof urns are actually chimneys and the columns are hollow, serving as drains.

Beyond **Clontarf** the coast road passes the **North Bull Island**, a huge sandbank growing from the North Wall of Dublin Port and containing two golf courses: **St Anne's** (www.stanneslinksgolf.com) and the famous **Royal Dublin** (www.the royaldublingolfclub.com). It is also an important sanctuary for winter migrant birds.

Carrying on via the isthmus at the suburb of **Sutton** you reach **Howth Head** (also accessible by DART and bus), whose rugged brow overlooks the northern entrance to Dublin Bay. You can go directly to the village of **Howth** ⑱ or start instead at The Summit and walk to the village around the nose of the promontory by a splendidly scenic cliff path, which descends steeply to the fishing harbour. The novelist H.G. Wells called the view from the head "one of the most beautiful in the world." The offshore island of **Ireland's Eye** was the site of a 6th-century monastery and is now a bird sanctuary. Howth is the most fashionable place to live on the northside, and it is easy to see why. The gardens at nearby **Howth Castle** are beautiful, especially if you like rhododendrons.

Five miles (8 km) north of Howth lies the resort of **Portmarnock** ⑲, which has fine beaches and a championship golf course (www.portmarnockgolfclub.ie). West of here is **St Doulagh's Church**, claimed to be the oldest still in use in Ireland; its high-pitched stone roof is 12th-century. **Doulagh Lodge**, nearby, was the home of the landscape painter, Nathaniel Hone (1831–1917).

At **Malahide** ⑳, a pleasant resort and dormitory town 7 miles (11 km) north of Howth, is **Malahide Castle** (daily, entrance fee), inhabited by the Talbot family from 1185 until 1976, except for a short period when Oliver Cromwell was around. The castle, now publicly owned, houses many portraits from the collection of the National Gallery. In its gardens is the **Fry Model Railway Museum**; (Apr–Sept Mon–Sat 10am–5pm, Sun 2–6pm, closed Oct–Mar and for lunch between 1–2pm) the models of trains and stations are meticulous. ❑

DAY TRIPS FROM DUBLIN

*To the south lie the Wicklow Mountains, to the north the
remarkable prehistorical burial chambers of Newgrange,
and to the west some of the world's best racehorse country*

It is easy for Dublin dwellers to take for granted the wild beauty of the **Wicklow
Mountains**, just a few miles to the south. As one writer has pointed out, it is, for
a Londoner, as if the Lake District began at Golders Green. The "hills" are great
outcrops of granite thrown up by ancient earth movements. In the Ice Age, glaci-
ers smoothed and rounded their peaks and carved deep, dark, steep-sided glens
whose wide floors glitter with rivers and lakes. The region is sparsely inhabited –
just a few villages, scattered farms and cottages, and the occasional great house.

The chief attractions of Wicklow are well served by coach tours from Dublin.
If you are driving, take the N81 southwest, through the bleak new suburb of **Tal-
laght**, to **Blessington**, a 17th-century village consisting mainly of one long, broad
street. Just past the village, the large artificial lake of **Poulaphouca**, which supplies Dublin with water, lies to the left. A popular scenic road encircles the lake.

Two miles (3 km) on is **Russborough ❶** (tel: 045 865 239 Apr and Oct Sun
and public holidays 10am–5pm, May–Sept daily 10am–5pm; visits by guided
tour only; ongoing renovation may effect opening times and exhibits), a Palladian house built in the 1740s by Richard Castle for the Earl of Miltown. Its 700-
ft (210-metre) frontage is the longest in Ireland; inside is the Alfred Beit art
collection, with works by Vermeer, Goya, Reubens and Velasquez.

BELOW: the 11th-
century round
tower, Glendalough.

Four miles (6 km) south at Hollywood, a left turn leads into the wild heart of the mountains through the Wicklow Gap to **Glendalough ②**, a secluded, seductive valley, steep-sided and well-wooded, where in 545 St Kevin founded a great monastic settlement between two lakes. The sight of the ruins – a cathedral and several churches, dominated by a 110-ft (33-metre) round tower – evokes that deep longing for peace and solitude central to the monk's idea of sanctity. Guided tours available from the Glendalough visitors centre (tel: 0404 45325; daily all year from 9.30am, closing at 5pm Oct–Mar and at 6pm Apr–Sept)

Driving south through **Rathdrum** you reach **Avondale**, the beautiful Georgian home of the politician Charles Stewart Parnell (1846–91); it is now a museum surrounded by public parklands. A couple of miles further south is the celebrated **Vale of Avoca**, where the Avonmore and Avonbeg rivers join, supposedly described in Thomas Moore's song, *The Meeting of the Waters*. At **Avoca** village (better known to some as TV's Ballykissangel and home to the Avoca weavers), you can turn northwards again and drive, via the unremarkable county town of **Wicklow ③**, to the village of **Ashford**, near which there are two spots of great beauty: to the south, the **Mount Usher Gardens**, a lush display of trees, subtropical plants and shrubs; to the northwest, the **Devil's Glen**, a deep chasm with spectacular walks above the rushing Vartry river.

Return to Dublin via **Roundwood** and **Enniskerry**, where you can divert to visit the magnificent landscaped gardens at **Powerscourt ④** (daily 9.30am–5.30pm), an 18th-century mansion badly damaged by fire in 1974 and re-opened in 1997 to incorporate a restaurant, visitor centre and stylish shops. Nearby **Powerscourt Waterfall** is the highest in these islands (90 metres). You now drive directly back to Dublin or divert again through the magnificent valley of **Glencree**.

 Map, page 166

ABOVE: catering for visitors to the Glendalough ruins. **BELOW:** Powerscourt House and Garden.

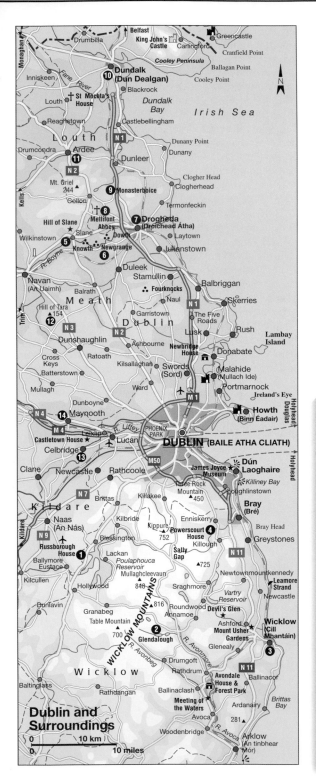

Dublin and
Surroundings

Excursions north

A half-hour's driving on the N2 road across the rolling fields of Meath takes you to the beautiful old village of **Slane** ❺, built on a steep hill above a bridge on the **River Boyne**. The grounds of the nearby castle have been used to stage concerts by the likes of Bob Dylan and the Rolling Stones. The **Hill of Slane**, where St Patrick proclaimed Christianity in Ireland by lighting a paschal fire in 433, is on the northern outskirts of the village. The ruins of a 16th-century church stand on the site of the church he founded. The view over the plain is striking.

A few miles east along the north bank of the Boyne is one of Europe's most remarkable prehistoric sites: the burial chambers of **Newgrange** ❻, **Knowth** and **Dowth** (entry to chambers via the Brú na Bóinne visitor centre, daily Mar, Apr and Oct 9.30am–5.30pm, May and Sept 9am–6.30pm, June–Aug 9am–7pm, Nov–Feb 9.30am–5pm, entrance fee). Although the Dowth burial mound is

inaccessible, conducted tours of the other two chambers provide fascinating insight into the 5,000-year-old Boyne Valley culture. At Newgrange, a 20-metre passage leads into the central burial chamber. A small aperture over the entrance is aligned so that the sun's rays penetrate to illuminate the chamber only at the winter solstice – a powerful symbol of rebirth and renewal. The chamber is older than the Pyramids of Egypt. The road on to Drogheda passes the site of the Battle of the Boyne (1690).

Drogheda ❼, a large town and port dating from Viking and Norman times, was a frontier outpost of the Pale. Oliver Cromwell is still accursed here: during his campaign of suppression in 1649 he captured the town and slaughtered 2,000 people – "a righteous judgement of God upon those barbarous wretches".

The main features of the town are: the **Millmount**, a prehistoric mound surmounted by an 18th-century barracks, now including a museum; **St Lawrence's Gate**, one of the best-preserved town gates in Ireland; the ruins of several medieval churches; the 18th-century **Tholsel**, or town hall, now a bank; and the 19th-century high Gothic **St Peter's Church**, erected in memory of Oliver Plunkett, a Meath man who became Catholic Archbishop of Armagh. He was martyred in London in 1681, and canonised in 1975. His head is preserved in a shrine at the church.

You have now crossed into **Louth**, Ireland's smallest county. Six miles (10 km) northwest of Drogheda, by the River Mattock, stand the ruins of **Mellifont Abbey** ❽ (1142; May–Sept daily 10am–6pm), Ireland's first Cistercian foundation. Remains include those of a square tower, a large church, and a lavabo, an octagonal building where the monks used to wash. At **Monasterboice** ❾, a few miles northeast, are the remnants of a 5th-century monastic settlement founded by St Buithe: a round tower, two churches, three sculptured crosses, two early grave-slabs and a sundial.

The head of the martyred Oliver Plunkett is preserved in St Peter's Church.

LEFT: the Neolithic passage grave at Newgrange.
BELOW: Drogheda.

Map, page 166

TIP

West of Navan along the R163 and R154 lie the Loughcrew Neolithic passage tombs. Not as famous as Newgrange, they are likely to be less crowded. One of the largest, Cairn T, has some impressive examples of prehistoric art and Sliabh Na Caillige, the highest peak, gives splendid views (open daily all year, tours mid-June to mid-Sept).

You can now join the main N1 route north to **Dundalk** ⑩, a busy border town and a good centre for exploring the picturesque **Cooley Peninsula**. This area features prominently in the great epic legends of ancient Ireland. At **Carlingford** village, a fine Norman castle commands the entrance to the sea inlet, Carlingford Lough. A corkscrew road through the nearby forest park climbs to a viewing point near the summit of **Carlingford Mountain**, providing splendid views of the Mournes to the north. **Greenore** and **Omeath** are small resorts.

The N52 road southwest from Dundalk leads to **Ardee** ⑪, or Irish *Baile Atha Fhirdiadh*, "The Town of Ferdia's Ford". It is here that Cuchulainn slew his friend Ferdia, the champion of Queen Maeve, in the great epic story of the Cattle Raid of Cooley. Continuing through Meath's county town of **Navan** on the N2, you then take the N3 to **Kells**, where St Colmcille founded a monastery in the 6th century (this is where Trinity College's famous *Book of Kells* was created, *see page 144*). The extant remains are more recent: a round tower and a high-roofed 10th-century building known as **St Colmcille's house** are the most interesting.

Trim, a pleasant town 16 miles (26 km) to the southeast, has the largest Anglo-Norman fortress in Ireland: its complex and well-preserved remains cover 2 acres and the surrounding moat was filled from the River Boyne. The ragged outline of the so-called **Yellow Steeple** (1358), part of a collapsed abbey, stands on a ridge opposite the castle. There's an interpretative centre in Mill Street (tel: 046 9437227).

Return now to Navan and take the main Dublin road, which passes near the **Hill of Tara** ⑫, the cultural and religious headquarters of ancient Ireland. A great assembly or *feis* was held there every three years to pass laws and settle disputes. By the 6th century, when Niall of the Nine Hostages founded the house of O'Neill that was to rule Ulster until the Plantations, Tara had become pre-eminent among

BELOW: Hill of Tara.

Ireland's five kingdoms, but its influence declined soon after as Christianity took root. It has remained a powerful symbol of Irish unity, expressed in the Thomas Moore (1779–1825) song, *The harp that Once through Tara's Halls*, and Daniel O'Connell chose it in 1843 as the venue for one of his "monster meetings" to demand repeal of the Corn Laws. A million people attended, according to *The Times*. On top of the hill is a modern statue of St Patrick and a pillar-stone said to have been used in the coronation of the ancient kings.

Map, page 166

Excursions west

Kildare, the county to the west of Dublin, is the "horsiest" part of Ireland, but there are many charms even for those whose blood does not rise at the sound of hoof-beats. **Naas**, the county town, is a handy centre for touring the county.

You can drive there quickly over one of the Republic's few modern highways, or via **Celbridge** ⓭, an attractive village which was the home of Esther Vanhomrigh, the "Vanessa" who competed with "Stella" (Esther Johnson) for the affections of Jonathan Swift. He often came here to visit her and you can see the seat by the river where they sat and talked. Nearby is the magnificent Palladian mansion of **Castletown House** (1722) (tel: 01 628 8252; Easter–Sept daily 10am–5pm; Oct Mon–Fri 10am–5pm, Sun and public holidays 1–5pm; Nov Sun 1–5pm, closed Nov–Easter).

For more about Kildare's horse culture, see the feature on pages 105–9.

Drive west from Naas through Newbridge to reach the great expanses of the **Curragh**. Apart from the racecourse and many training stables, it has contained a military camp, established in 1646. This was the scene of the "Curragh Mutiny" of 1914, when British officers threatened to refuse orders to fire on Edward Carson's Ulster Volunteers, who had armed to oppose Home Rule.

Near the road south to Kilcullen is a depression, **Donnelly's Hollow**, where a small obelisk commemorates an 1815 prize fight in which Dan Donnelly, the giant Irish champ, beat England's George Cooper.

BELOW: market in Trim, Co. Meath.

Kildare town, 6 miles (10 km) from Newbridge, was the site of a monastery founded by St Brigid (*circa* 450–520), the most revered Irish saint after Patrick. Her attributes have been reinforced by others borrowed from the great goddess of the same name, who was venerated also in Britain and Europe. The **Cathedral of St Brigid**, begun in 1229, has been rebuilt many times, most substantially in 1875. A mile from the town, at **Tully House**, is the **National Stud** (*see also page 182*).

At **Athy**, 16 miles (26 km) south of Kildare, a 15th-century tower, Whitescastle (now a private house) overlooks a fine old bridge over the **River Barrow**, once an important commercial waterway to Dublin. But the town's main attraction is the striking, fan-shaped **Dominican Church** (1963–65). The painter George Campbell designed the stained glass and the stations of the cross. The town hall in the centre square houses the Heritage Centre (tel: 059 8633075; May–Sept Mon–Sat 10am–5.30pm, Oct–Apr Mon–Fri 10am–5pm).

Returning to Dublin from Naas, it is worth diverting via **Maynooth** ⓮, where Ireland's Catholic diocesan clergy are trained at **St Patrick's College**. It was founded in 1795 and became a college of the National University in 1908. An ecclesiastical museum can be seen by prior arrangement. ❑

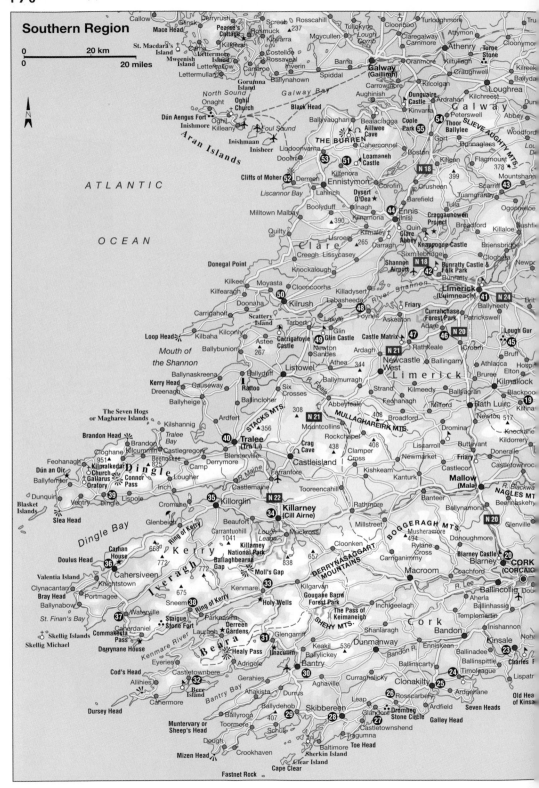

Southern Region

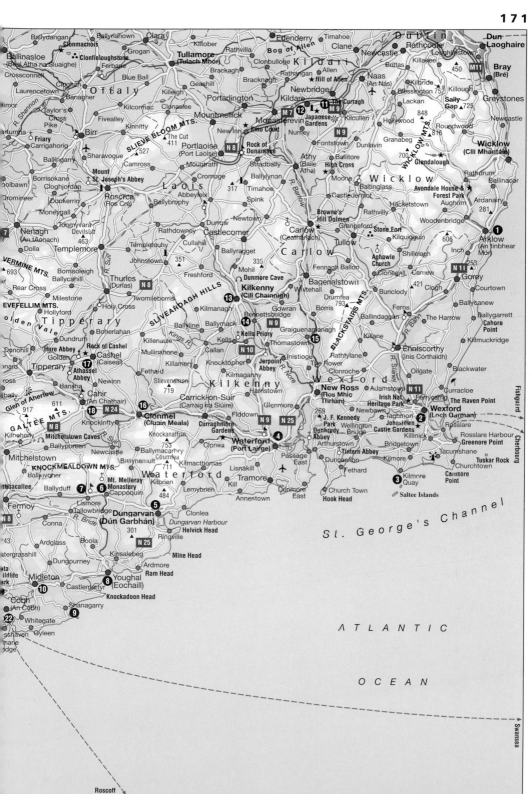

THE SOUTHEAST

*Between Dublin and Cork, you can find opera in Wexford,
crystal glass in Waterford, horse-racing at the Curragh,
and ancient historical sites at Kilkenny and Cashel*

Map,
page 170

The southeast is the least typical region of Ireland. Its climate is mild and sunny, and it has the lowest average rainfall in the whole island. In contrast to the wild and rugged west, the coast of south county Wicklow, county Wexford and county Waterford is mainly flat and sandy, with small, hilly dunes. Inland counties Carlow, Tipperary and Kilkenny consist of undramatic, restful country – rich farmland and low hills intersected by winding rivers.

Because of its proximity to mainland Europe, the history of the southeast is marked by invasions. Inland, the Rock of Cashel was an important ceremonial centre from the 7th century, while other monasteries thrived at Lismore, Ardmore and Kilkenny. The Vikings, who regularly raided Ireland's coastal monasteries, began to settle here in the 9th century, founding the towns of Waterford and Wexford. Two hundred years later the same cities were among the first to be conquered by the Normans. Most of the region's churches were ruined during Oliver Cromwell's Irish campaign in 1650.

It is now 200 years since the 1798 Rebellion, whose decisive battle took place at Vinegar Hill near Enniscorthy, when 20,000 rebels armed only with pikes were cut down by British cannon fire. However, this unsuccessful bid for a united Ireland, inspired by the French Revolution of 1789, remains vividly alive in folk memory, and is commemorated by numerous monuments in the region.

PRECEDING PAGES:
Lismore Castle,
Co. Waterford.
LEFT: the view from
Mount Leinster,
Co. Kilkenny.
BELOW: the national
colour, hard to avoid.

Option 1: Dublin to Cork via the coast

The first tour travels from Dublin to Cork, through Wexford, Waterford, Dungarvan and Youghal. This route takes 4½ hours – about an hour longer than the main N7/N8 route, but it is far more scenic, with frequent sea views, and far less congested. Take a full day for the drive, or plan one or two overnight stops.

Leave Dublin on the N11 Bray road, and follow this through Rathnew to **Arklow ❶**. This is a small but lively fishing port and seaside resort on the estuary of the River Avoca known for boat building and for its pottery that makes everyday tableware.

Gorey, the first town in county Wexford, has a more genteel ambience than Arklow. It is not actually on the sea, but nevertheless is chiefly a holiday resort. The seaside cottages will be found by turning left in Gorey on to the R742, a pleasant alternative route to Wexford.

The R742 passes **Curracloe Strand** 7 miles (11 km) northeast of Wexford Harbour. The totally unspoilt strand is backed by dunes, and stretches for 6 miles (9 km). It "stood in" for the Normandy beaches when Speilberg filmed *Saving Private Ryan*. In winter it is home to numerous Canada geese. Information on the birds of the region can be found at the **Wexford Wildfowl Reserve** (tel: 053-23129, admission free.) which is

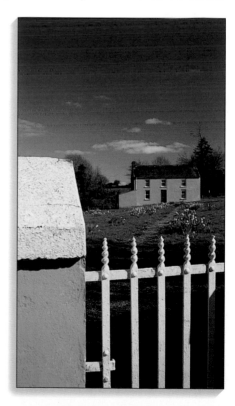

signposted off the R741 just outside Wexford. The harbour is partly silted up, and its mud flats attract a variety of ducks, geese and swans.

Wexford: opera and heritage

Wexford ❷ is a small, easy-to-explore town consisting of a series of quays parallel to the water, with a compact network of smaller streets parallel to the quays. Head for the **Westgate Tower** which is a short walk inland from the main bridge. This red sandstone building is the only remaining of five fortified gateways in the Norman town walls. It now houses the **Westgate Heritage Centre** (tel: 053-46506, admission fee), which has a 30-minute audio-visual display on the town's history.

Wexford, which has an interesting selection of small, old-fashioned shops and pubs, is at its best in October during the three-week run of the **Festival Ireland Wexford Opera** (tel: 053-22144). Three full-length operas are performed at the **Theatre Royal** with an international cast of up-and-coming stars. The tradition is to choose little-known works, with consistently interesting results. A series of fringe events guarantee musical entertainment from 11am to midnight.

The **Irish National Heritage Park** (tel: 053-20733, admission fee) at Ferrycarrig, 3 miles (5 km) northwest of Wexford on the N11 Enniscorthy road, is an open air theme park on the banks of the River Slaney. A couple of hours among its life-size replicas of typical dwelling places will make you an expert on Irish history and architecture, from Stone Age man, around 6000BC, up to the 12th-century Norman settlements.

Follow the N25 for 3 miles (5 km) in the Rosslare direction to visit **Johnstown Castle Gardens**. The castle is a grandiose grey stone Gothic building dating from the mid-19th century. Only the entrance hall is open to the public but the

Wexford was founded by the Norsemen, who used the inlet as a good base from which to plunder the area. Later they turned to trading.

BELOW: the Irish National Heritage Park, Wexford.

attractively landscaped gardens can be visited. The **Irish Agricultural Museum** (tel: 053-42888, admission fee) is in the stables. It has extensive displays of artefacts from Ireland's rural past, and a collection of Irish country furniture.

Map, page 170

The scenic way to Waterford

The N25 travels to Waterford via New Ross, but we suggest this scenic alternative route to Waterford. Take the N25 in the Rosslare direction and turn off at Piercetown for **Kilmore Quay** ❸. This quaint little fishing village of thatched, whitewashed cottages and friendly pubs is built between the dunes and a stone harbour wall, and looks out to the uninhabited **Saltee Islands**, one of Ireland's most important bird sanctuaries. In late spring to early summer, 3 million birds from 47 species stop here, and can be observed from local boats.

Heading west, the R736/R733 will take you to the **Hook Head Peninsula** and its lighthouse which forms the eastern side of Waterford harbour. Beyond Arthurstown is **Ballyhack**, a picture-book pretty waterside village on the estuary of the River Barrow, dominated by **Ballyhack Castle**, a 16th-century tower house. Continue north on the R733 for 3 miles (5 km) to **Dunbrody Abbey** (tel: 051-388 603, admission fee), an impressive ruined Cistercian Abbey dating from 1175. A further 5 miles (8 km) north is the **John F. Kennedy Memorial Forest Park and Arboretum** (tel: 051-388 171, admission fee). Planted in 1968, the 4,500 species of trees and shrubs are now reaching maturity. The farmhouse near Dunganstown from which US President John F. Kennedy's grandfather emigrated to Boston is now the **Kennedy Homestead** (daily May and Sept 11.30am–4.30pm, June–Aug 10am–6pm, or by appointment, tel: 051-388 246). From here the shortest route to Waterford is back to Ballyhack for a five-minute car ferry to the Waterford side.

BELOW: Kilmore Quay, Co. Wexford.

ABOVE: Reginald's Tower, a Norman tower built on a Viking site and named after Waterford's first Viking ruler.

BELOW: Waterford's crystal glass plant, open to visitors.

Waterford ❹, a city of 49,000 inhabitants, has a proud past as an important European port but nowadays its wide, stone quays look grim. Its heyday as a port was in the 18th century, when the famous glass-manufacturing industry was established. The Tourist Office is on Merchants Quay. **Waterford Treasures** (tel: 051-304 500, admission fee), in the same building, is an exhibition and audio-visual presentation covering the town's rich history from its first Viking conqueror Regnall (after whom Reginald's Tower is named) up to the 19th-century American Civil War hero Thomas Francis Meagher. From across the street, you can see the distinctive landmark **Reginald's Tower** (tel: 051-304 220, admission fee), a massive, 12th-century cylindrical tower built by the Normans on a former Viking site. It is said that when the Norman Strongbow married the daughter of Dermot McMurrough, thus peacefully uniting the Norman invaders and the native Irish, the wedding took place here.

Georgian Waterford is only a short walk from Reginald's Tower, up **The Mall**. The **City Hall** (open office hours, admission free) is a neo-classical building dating from 1788, which contains some good examples of early Waterford crystal, including a huge chandelier. Just beyond it is **Bishop Foy Palace,** originally an imposing town house, which is also used by the Corporation as offices. Behind the palace is **Christ Church Cathedral** which replaced an older church in 1773.

Waterford Crystal Factory (tel: 051-373 311, admission fee) offers tours of its glass-cutting and glass-blowing workshops which most first-time visitors seem compelled to take. Tours last 40 minutes and include an audio-visual display and a chance to buy crystal. The factory is a mile from the town centre on the N25 Cork road. Groups of more than 10 people should book in advance.

The main N25 takes a fast inland route to Dungarvan. If you have time, take

the coastal route leaving Waterford on the R684 for **Dunmore East**. This pretty cliff-side fishing village and holiday resort of thatched cottages is on the open sea at the head of Waterford Harbour.

Tramore is a total contrast, with a long flat sandy beach, a fun fair, caravan parks and other facilities aimed at the budget holiday market. The coast road continues through a series of villages with good beaches – **Annestown**, **Bunmahon** and **Clonea**. Elsewhere in the sandstone cliffs secluded coves can be reached by foot. **Dungarvan ❺**, situated on Dungarvan Harbour and backed by wooded hills, is the county town of Waterford. It has some lively waterside pubs, and is increasingly popular as a centre for activity holidays.

If you're headed for Cork, skip to Ardmore below. Those heading for Killarney, or with time for a scenic detour into the **Blackwater Valley**, should pick up the N72 Cappoquin road outside Dungarvan.

Vee Gap: the scenic route to Lismore Castle

Cappoquin ❻ is a quiet village nicely situated on a wooded hillside on the River Blackwater, a beautiful salmon and trout river. About 3 miles (5 km) north of the village is **Mount Melleray** (tel: 058-54404), a Cistercian abbey dating from the mid-19th century that welcomes visitors in search of solitude. The Vee Gap route is signposted form here, going north on the R669 into the Knockmealdown Mountains. The Vee Gap is at the summit, from which you can see the Galtee Mountains in the northwest, and in good visibility the Rock of Cashel due north, rising out of the Tipperary Plain. Turn back here, and take the R668 to Lismore.

Lismore ❼, a pretty wooded village of 900 inhabitants approached over a stone bridge, was an important monastic centre from the 7th to the 12th centuries, which

Map, page 170

The Cistercians, a Roman Catholic monastic order founded in 1098 in France, were introduced to Ireland by St Malachy in 1142.

BELOW:
Dungarvan Harbour.

is why it has two cathedrals. **St Carthage's** (1633) has some interesting effigies. Nowadays the village is dominated by the grey stone turrets of **Lismore Castle** (tel: 058-54424, admission fee; gardens open Easter–mid-Oct). Built on a rock overhanging the river in the mid-18th century, it is a dramatic and imposing building. The castle is used as a summer residence by the Duke of Devonshire, and is not open to the public. The gardens, which are, include an 800-year-old yew walk.

If you are heading for Killarney, follow the Blackwater valley on the N72 from Lismore to Fermoy to Mallow, and on to Killarney, about a two-hour drive.

Beyond Dungarvan the main tour joins the N25, which climbs the **Drum Hills** giving good views back across Dungarvan harbour. **Ardmore** involves a 5-mile (8-km) detour, but is worth the effort. St Declan established a monastery here in the 5th century. Today the remains of a medieval cathedral and round tower stand on the site of the original foundation, a cliff top with stunning views over Ardmore Bay. The 12th-century cathedral with its sturdy, rounded arches is a prime example of the Hiberno-Romanesque style, while the slender round tower with its conical roof is an elegant contrast. There are also interesting stone and carvings. The tiny village is at the bottom of the cliff, and is a pleasant place with good sandy beaches.

Youghal ❽ (pronounced *yawl*), famous for its long sandy beaches and historic town centre, found fame in the 1950s when John Huston filmed the New Bedford scenes of *Moby Dick* here. The Youghal Tourist Office (Market Square, tel: 024-92447) houses a heritage centre. The **Clock Tower** is a distinctive landmark built in 1776 as a jail, that straddles the road in the town centre. The steps beside it lead to a street with excellent harbour views, and to the 13th-century **St. Mary's Collegiate Church**. Sir Walter Raleigh lived next door, where he smoked the first tobacco and planted the first the potato plant in Ireland – a claim disputed by several other places.

Quaker connections

Turn left off the N25 in Castlemartyr for **Shanagarry ❾**, a tidy village built of grey stone with many Quaker connections. To the east of the village is the famous hotel, **Ballymaloe House**. The **Ballymaloe Cookery School Gardens** (tel: 021-464 6785) in the village centre have a geometric potager, a formal fruit garden, a Celtic maze and a shell house. **The Emporium** is a large factory outlet for Stephen Pearce's pottery which also stocks hand-made crafts from around the world. **Shanagarry House** where William Penn, the founder of Pennsylvania, grew up, is opposite the Emporium.

Ballycotton, 3 miles (5 km) beyond Shanagarry is a fishing village built on a cliff top overlooking a small island and lighthouse. There are good cliff walks, and numerous nesting seabirds can be seen in early summer. The brightly-coloured fishing fleet supplies much of Cork city's fish.

Midleton ❿, a pleasant market town, is the home of Ireland's largest distillery. A new distilling complex was built in 1966, and the **Old Midleton Distillery** (tel: 021-461 3594, admission fee) now houses an audio-visual display and an optional guided tour which explains the distilling process of Irish whiskey. Afterwards you can sample a drop of the famous product in a traditional Irish pub. Admirers of industrial architecture will enjoy

the carefully restored 11-acre (4.5-hectare) 18th-century site. Most of the buildings are of cut stone, and the original waterwheel still functions. The N25 continues for 15 miles (24 km) into Cork City.

Map, page 170

Option 2: Kildare to Cashel via Kilkenny

This is an alternative, inland route from Dublin to Cork, visiting some of the southeast's most interesting historical sites. Kildare, with its Japanese Gardens and National Stud, has a 16th-century Cathedral and a 12th-century Round Tower associated with St Brigid. The historic medieval town of black marble, Kilkenny, lies 23 miles (37 km) south of Kildare, and has a magnificently restored castle.

You can linger in the Kilkenny area exploring the pretty riverside villages of the Nore and the Barrow, or continue to Clonmel, a compact market town on the River Suir, and head into the Nire Valley for a taste of unspoilt hill and bogland. Both options lead to Tipperary, and the spectacular ecclesiastical ruins on the Rock of Cashel. At Cahir, there is a massive castle to visit, and quiet woodland walks in the relatively unfrequented Glen of Aherlow.

Leave Dublin on the main N7 Limerick motorway, taking the Kildare exit. The road cuts through **The Curragh ⓫**, a broad plain of 6,000 acres (2,400 hectares). The **Curragh Racecourse** is the heart of the Irish racing world, and the Irish Derby is held here every June. If you are lucky, you might see a string of race horses galloping by. Otherwise, the plain is used for exercises by the Irish Army who have a large camp here.

St Brigid founded a religious settlement in **Kildare ⓬** in the 5th century. The present **Cathedral** dates partly from the late 17th century and partly from the 19th century. The 108-ft (33-metre) **Round Tower** beside the cathedral belongs

The Curragh means The Racecourse in Gaelic (An Currach). It was once known as St Brigid's Pasture Land.

BELOW: a race at The Curragh.

to a 12th-century monastery. You can climb to the top for excellent views of the surrounding country.

Nowadays Kildare is a prosperous town, closely associated with the horse racing business, with dozens of small studs in the area. Admission to the most prestigious of them all, the **National Stud**, where top-class breeding stallions are stabled, and the **Irish Horse Museum** (tel: 045-521 617, admission fee, closed Nov–Feb; www.irish-national-stud.ie) also allows you to visit the rather strange **Japanese Gardens** that were laid out here in the early 20th century by the Japanese landscape artist Eida. The gardens trace a symbolic journey through life, and are considered by experts to be among the finest in Europe.

Also in the National Stud grounds is the newly opened **St Fiachra's Garden**, designed by Professor Martin Hallinan, gold medal winner for his Irish Garden in Expo 90, held in Japan. St Fiachra, a 6th-century Irish monk, is the patron saint of gardeners.

To see the most interesting part of **Monasterevin**, turn right at the traffic lights in the centre of town. Immediately ahead, the **Grand Canal** crosses the River Barrow on a 19th-century aqueduct in an interesting feat of industrial engineering. There are a couple of very pleasant, old-fashioned little pubs with waterside gardens hidden away on this side road.

Return to the traffic lights and turn left, back towards Dublin, keeping an eye out for a right-hand turn, the R417 Athy road. If you look hard enough, you'll find the remnants of a fine Georgian town in **Athy** (pronounced a-*thigh*), which was once an important fording place on the River Barrow. There's also a striking, fan-shaped Dominican church (1963–65). Athy Heritage Centre (tel: 059-863 3075; May–Sept Mon–Sat 10am–5.30pm, Oct–Apr Mon–Fri 10am–5pm) in the town hall has an

For more about the National Stud, see the feature on horses on pages 105–8.

BELOW: the Japanese Gardens at Kildare.

audio-visual presentation covering a wide range of historical data, including the exploits of Ernest Shackleton, the Antarctic explorer who was born locally.

Map, page 170

Medieval Kilkenny

Kilkenny ⓭ was founded as a monastic settlement by St Canice in the 6th century. In 1641 a Catholic parliament, the Confederation of Kilkenny, attempted to organise resistance to the persecution of Catholics. Cromwell's destructive 1650 campaign put a brutal end to such aspirations. While **Kilkenny** likes to promote itself as "Ireland's medieval capital", its rich heritage is not immediately obvious. Start at the Tourist Information Office in **Shee Alms House**, Rose Inn Street (tel: 056-775 1500; www.southeastireland.com) where you can equip yourself with free maps. This charming stone house with mullioned windows was built in the mid-17th century as a hospital for the poor. Frequent walking tours leave from here daily between March and October.

The sites of medieval Kilkenny start with St Canice's Cathedral at one extreme and end with the Castle at the other. Between them is a **Tholsel** (town hall) dating from 1761, the ruins of a 13th-century friary, the **Black Abbey**, and **Rothe House**, a 16th-century merchant's townhouse.

Kilkenny Castle (tel: 056-772 1450, admission fee; guided tours only) has recently been sumptuously restored. The grey stone, turreted landmark towers over the River Barrow which serves as its moat. It dates from 1820, but there has been a Butler family castle here for over 500 years. The furnishings are mainly 19th-century. The stableyard of the castle is occupied by the **Kilkenny Design Centre** which has a big display of local and national crafts and several workshops.

St Canice's Cathedral dates from the 13th century and is built in the Early

ABOVE: Kilkenny's Design Centre.
BELOW: Kilkenny Castle; shop fronts in Kilkenny town.

English style. The Gothic interior is remarkable for its wealth of medieval monuments and life-size effigies, many of them carved from a locally quarried black marble. The 6th-century **Round Tower** in the Cathedral grounds is the only remnant of St Canice's monastery. On a clear day it is possible to see seven counties from its top – or so they say.

Riverside villages and craft trail

ABOVE: statues at Jerpoint Abbey.
BELOW: Inistioge, a pretty Kilkenny town on the banks of the River Nore.

If you have time for a day-long drive around the Kilkenny area, explore one of the pretty villages on the rivers **Nore** and **Barrow**. The rivers meander through rich countryside with gently sloping wooded hills dotted with old villages of grey stone buildings, until they meet in New Ross and flow into the sea at Waterford.

Leave Kilkenny on the R700 south for **Bennettsbridge** ⓮. Some of Kilkenny's best craft makers live and work in this old-world village which straddles the River Nore, and have created their own craft trail. You can visit **Chesneau Leather Goods** (tel: 056-772 7456), makers of handbags, wallets etc., the **Nicholas Mosse Pottery** (tel: 056-772 7505), which makes painted spongeware and also has a pottery museum, and the **Stoneware Jackson Pottery** (tel: 056-772 7175). Another Kilkenny craft maker, **Jerpoint Glass** (tel: 056-772 4350), where you can watch heavy, uncut glass being shaped by hand into modern designs, can be visited in **Thomastown**. This is now a small market town (pop. 1,300) with a couple of good pubs, but in the 13th century it was walled and fortified. Its 18th-century stone-arched bridge over the Nore indicates its former importance.

Cross the bridge for a short (1½ miles/3 km) detour to **Jerpoint Abbey** (tel: 056-772 4623, admission fee), one of the most attractive monastic sites in Ireland. The ruined Cistercian monastery dates from the 12th century. The clois-

ters are especially fine, and there are many interesting carvings and effigies.

Return to Thomastown and cross the Nore again to reach **Inistioge**. The village is on a bend of the river and has a tree-lined square beside a 10-arched stone bridge. Its narrow, sloping streets of small stone houses make it a popular location for filming period movies such as the 1994 comedy-drama *Widow's Peak* with Mia Farrow and Joan Plowright. **Woodstock Estate Forest Park** which was laid out in the 19th century with interesting shrubs from the Far East, is open to the public, but the house itself was burnt down in 1922.

Seven miles (11 km) south of Inistioge, turn left off the N700 to **The Rower**. This little village marks the start of an especially scenic stretch of road, with views over the River Barrow on the right hand side, and the Blackstairs Mountains beyond the river.

Graiguenamanagh ("the hamlet of the monks") ⓯ was an important commercial centre in the 19th century, when the River Barrow was used to transport coal and grain. Nowadays herons fish along its weir, and one of its stone-built warehouses has been turned into a stylish waterside B&B and restaurant.

There is a genuinely nostalgic stretch of old-fashioned pubs on the hill to the west of the bridge, in whose dark interiors you can buy groceries as well as pints. At the top of this hill on the right is **Duiske Abbey**, a Cistercian Abbey founded in 1204, but much added to since. The exterior is pebble-dashed and does not look very promising. However, the main nave of the abbey was adapted in 1983 to serve as the parish church. Its combination of modern and ancient features is much praised by some, and lamented by others. Whatever your opinion, it is certainly worth a look at its light-filled interior. Look out for the **Knight Of Duiske**, an effigy in chain mail, the hammer-beam roof in Irish oak, and the

Map, page 170

Gráig na Manach, the Gaelic name for the town in which Duiske Abbey (above) was built, means The Hamlet of the Monks.

BELOW: the harbour, Graiguenamanagh.

magnificent Romanesque processional door in the south transept. Return to Thomastown on the R703, and from there to Kilkenny.

Clonmel and Cashel

From Kilkenny, follow the N76 south to **Clonmel** , a busy county Tipperary market town on the River Suir. The area to the north and east of the town is known for its apple orchards, and Clonmel is the centre of the Irish cider-making industry. However, travel to the south, and you will find another kind of scenery altogether.

The **Nire Valley Drive** is a sign-posted circular route of about 23 miles (37 km) that travels along the edge of the **Comeragh Mountains** to **Ballymacarbry**, and the **Nire Valley**, and returns to Clonmel through **Clogheen** and **Ballybeg**. This is not for the faint-hearted; the roads are narrow, sometimes steep, and there are several hair-pin bends. However, it is an extraordinary experience to leave the tranquil apple-growing plains of Clonmel and, after only a few miles, find yourself in a wilderness area consisting mainly of pine forest and, above the tree line, uninhabited boglands. If you are interested in walking, **Ballymacarbery** village is a good base from which to follow the various way-marked trails in the area.

From Clonmel, head northwest on the R688 to **Cashel** . A cluster of romantic-looking, grey, turreted buildings stands on a limestone outcrop rising 60 metres (200 ft) above the Tipperary plain, and absolutely every tour bus stops here. It will greatly enhance your visit if you can avoid the crowds by visiting the rock at lunch time or in the late afternoon.

The **Rock of Cashel** (tel: 062-61437, admission fee) was probably once a centre of Druidic worship. By the 4th century AD Cashel was the ceremonial

The reason so many Irish place-names start with Bally- is that the word Baile in Irish means "town". So Ballmacarbery means Town of the Mac Cairbre Family. It is estimated that over 5,000 Irish place names start with Bally-.

BELOW: the Rock of Cashel.

centre of the Kings of Munster. According to legend, it was here that St Patrick baptised King Aengus.

The largest building on the rock, the shell of **St Patrick's Cathedral**, built in the Hiberno-Romanesque style, was in use from the 13th to the mid-16th centuries when it was desecrated in Oliver Cromwell's campaign. The octagonal staircase leads to the top of the tower, and a wonderful view of the Tipperary plain. **Cormac's Chapel** is a simpler building dating from 1127, with a high, corbelled roof similar to those found in early saint's cells in Glendalough and Dingle.

Spend some time lingering among the carvings and stones of Cashel, absorbing its unique atmosphere. Rather than spending time and money on the various heritage centres in Cashel town, concentrate on the Rock. A bypass, opened in 2004, has improved the town's atmosphere. Take a quick look and maybe a light snack at the **Cashel Palace Hotel,** a red-brick, Queen Anne-style bishop's palace built in 1730. A path leads to the rock from its back garden. Note also the well-preserved wooden Victorian shop fronts across the road.

Cahir ⓲ (pronounced *Care*) has improved enormously since it was bypassed by the main Dublin-Cork road. **Cahir Castle** (tel: 052-41011, admission fee) is a massive limestone fortress dating from the mid-12th century set on a rock in the River Suir. There is an informative guided tour, but avoid the audio-visual display. Walk up the hill beside the castle to have a look at Cahir's main square which has some good Georgian buildings and several serious antique shops. About a mile outside Cahir on the Clonmel road is the **Swiss Cottage** (tel: 052-41144, admission fee, closed Dec–mid-March), a thatched *cottage orné* built in 1810 to amuse the Earls of Glengall.

Walkers might like to detour northwest on the N24 for 14 miles (22 km) to **Bansha**, and on to Tipperary town and the **Glen of Aherlow**, an excellent area for hiking with marked trails of various lengths. The Glen, which is partly wooded and runs alongside the Aherlow River, has great views of the Galtee mountains (sometimes spelt Galty), and is a good base for getting off the beaten track.

The Glen of Aherlow leads to **Kilfinane** ⓳, at the heart of the Galtee and Ballyhoura Mountains. Its main feature, the Kilfinane Moat, is an ancient, flat-top mound encircled by three ramparts. The 56-mile (90-km) **Ballyhoura Way** is a marked footpath that travels through north Cork and county Limerick to Tipperary town. More than 930 miles (1,500 km) of way-marked loop walks varying in length from 2 miles (3 km) to 12 miles (20 km) have been laid out in the Ballyhouras, with a map board at the starting point of each walk. This is beautiful, unspoilt country, a mixture of pasture and woodland, with several medieval and megalithic monuments, well worth exploring on foot.

You will see the south side of the Galtee mountains from the main N8 Cork road between Caher and **Mitchelstown**. If the open-air market is on, stop for a walk around Mitchelstown's main square. This will give you a taste of life as lived by the local farmers and their families, who travel perhaps once a week to this small market town.

From Mitchelstown it will take you less than an hour's driving to reach Cork city. ❏

Map, page 170

Stone carvings on Cashel's cathedral. When Henry VII asked Gerald, Earl of Kildare, why he had burned the cathedral in 1495, Gerald said he had thought the archbishop was inside. The king was amused.

BELOW: Cahir Castle.

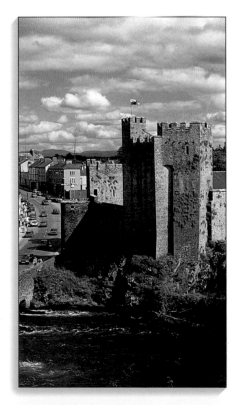

THE TRAVELLING PEOPLE

Ireland's 30,000 nomads belong to an ancient and romantic tradition – but the conditions under which they often live these days are far from romantic

Among the vacations on offer to tourists in Ireland are trips in horse-drawn caravans. It is something of a bad joke that, while tourists enjoy the freedom and leisure of a make-believe nomadic life, the country's real nomads subsist for the most part in poverty and squalor.

There are over 3,500 families of travelling people in Ireland, North and South, adding up to more than 30,000 people. About a third of these families are living in illegal campsites – by the road sides, on waste ground, on land cleared for development. They are a tiny minority: less than 1 per cent of the population. But even the casual visitor is likely to see some of them: bedraggled women and children begging in Dublin or a jumble of caravans, trailers, dogs and children glimpsed by the roadside.

PREJUDICE REMAINS

They are frequently moved on. Temporary sites provided by local councils often resemble refugee camps, and are resisted by communities, though a 1995 law forbade discrimination. Yet Travellers are no more drunken or lawless than other people.

"Tinkers", a word deriving from the days of the roving menders of tin kettles and pots, has become a term of abuse. "Itinerants" is intended to be polite but smacks of condescension. The travelling people hate it. "Travellers" is the word they prefer.

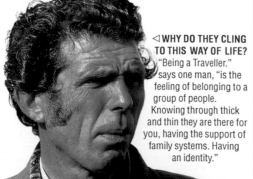

◁ **WHY DO THEY CLING TO THIS WAY OF LIFE?** "Being a Traveller." says one man, "is the feeling of belonging to a group of people. Knowing through thick and thin they are there for you, having the support of family systems. Having an identity."

◁ **LIFE ON THE OPEN ROAD**
Until the early 1960s, almost all travellers lived in brightly painted horse-drawn caravans or in tents. They dressed differently from other people – especially the women, with plaid shawls wrapped around their heads and shoulders. Then they began drifting to urban areas such as Dublin.

▽ **FAMILY LIFE**
Travellers traditionally have had large families, until recently averaging eight children. The birth rate has been falling, however, and many children are now more attracted to settled urban life than to the tradition of travelling. But it's not an easy tradition for families to make.

THEY'RE PART OF AN ANCIENT TRADITION

Although Ireland's Travellers share similar traditions to the 500,000 Gypsies in France and Spain and the 3 million in Romania, they are completely Irish in their ethnic origins. The true Romanies, like the Romans, never reached Ireland.

Like their counterparts in the rest of Europe, however, they have no tradition of written history and therefore it is hard to trace their origins with any degree of certainty. Some sociologists believe they are descended from various groups who took to the roads in the past few hundred years: families dispossessed or evicted from their homes, tradesmen who had to travel to make a living, individuals who "dropped out" from settled society, as some still do.

It has also been suggested that today's travellers may be descended from the roving bards referred to in Irish literature or from a particular caste in ancient Gaelic society.

The word *tynker* appears in 12th-century records as a term for an itinerant trades-man and Travellers are still occasionally called tinkers. In the days before recycling became fashionable, they were great recyclers of farm and household scrap metal. But the relentless erosion of Ireland's agrarian economy in the 20th century destroyed their economic base.

◁ **REDUNDANT SKILLS**
Travellers played a particular economic role for a society that was still mainly rural: mending utensils, making baskets and sieves, peddling ornaments and knick-knacks, dealing in horses and donkeys, and selling scrap.

△ **LIVING CONDITIONS**
The infant mortality rate for Travellers is twice that of the settled population. Most do not have electricity, and many do not have adequate toilet or washing facilities. But children have the security of having an extended family.

CORK CITY AND SURROUNDINGS

Map, page 194

After experiencing Cork's gentle charms, you can explore the port of Cobh, visit an innovative wildlife park and hope to acquire eloquence by kissing the Blarney Stone

The inhabitants of Cork, Ireland's second city with a population of 123,000, are known for their strong sense of civic pride. While visitors from Dublin and other European capitals might find Cork a small, drowsy city, to Corkonians it is a place of enormous importance.

The old city of Cork was founded by St Finbar in the 6th century. The name *Corcaigh* means "marshy place" in Irish. While the marshes are long gone, the city is still well-endowed with waterways. The city centre stands on an island between two branches of the River Lee. First impressions are of a confusing number of bridges and quays. Its medieval buildings have long gone, and the fabric of today's Cork dates mainly from the 18th and 19th centuries. The centre is flat, but to the north of the River Lee an escarpment rises up so steeply that many streets have steps cut into their pavements.

Cork was at its most affluent in the 18th century, when its butter market was a source of vast wealth. Much of the best domestic architecture as seen in the South Mall, Grand Parade and the North Mall dates from this period. Cork has retained the sober air of a merchants' city, and new industry in the form of multinational chemical plants and other high-tech industries have replaced heavier industries, such as car assembly and shipbuilding. An on-going programme of inner city regeneration was given a strong impetus by **Cork 2005**, a year-long programme in which Cork became the smallest city to receive official EU designation as European Capital of Culture. Over 250 projects and events featured the best in architecture, craft, dance, design, film, literature, music, sport, theatre and visual arts.

PRECEDING PAGES:
Blarney Castle.
LEFT: Cornmarket Street, Cork. **BELOW:** wall art in Cork.

Cork may lack the youthful energy that characterises Galway City and Dublin's Temple Bar, but it has a gentle, old-fashioned charm of its own.

A walking tour of the city centre

The centre of Cork is best explored by foot. The highlights can be comfortably covered in half a day. Start at the **Tourist Information Office Ⓐ** (tel: 021-425 5100, www.corkkerry.ie) on **Grand Parade**. Take a look across the street in front of the TIO at a terrace of three elegant Georgian houses with slate-hung, bow-fronted windows, typical of Cork's 18th-century prime. In the west, across the south channel of the River Lee, you can see the spires of **St Fin Barre's Cathedral Ⓑ**, where the city began as a monastic school in about AD650. Both the Gothic, late 19th-century cathedral, and the bridge across the Lee are built of characteristic white limestone.

Washington Street, which reaches Grand Parade in a T-junction opposite the multiplex cinema, leads, after

Pavement artists like this one in Cork are popular in Irish cities – surprisingly in view of the island's reputation for year-round rainfall.

a 10-minute walk, to the campus of **University College, Cork G** (tel: 021-427 6871). Known locally as UCC, the college has about 10,000 students. Guided tours of the campus, which has a 19th-century Tudor-Gothic style quadrangle and an interesting Hiberno-Romanesque chapel dating from 1916, are available on request. The campus has several interesting modern buildings, notably the Lewis Glucksman Gallery. Walk a few steps to the left of the TIO for a look at **South Mall**, Cork's most fashionable residential area in the city's 18th-century prime. It is now the legal and banking district.

Leaving the river to your back, walk along the Grand Parade to Cork's indoor food market, the **Princes Street Market D**, also known as the English Market, which extends across a whole city block. Recent refurbishment work has revealed an ornate Victorian cast-iron frame. At the far (Princes Street) end of the market there is a top-lit piazza with a central fountain. Some 150 stalls sell a wide variety of fresh food. Note the stall at the door with a display of tripe (cows' intestines) and drisheen (blood sausage). This, and more tempting local specialities can be sampled at the fountain end of the market in its first-floor **Farmgate Café** (inexpensive), one of the city's liveliest lunch spots.

European Capital of Culture

Follow Grand Parade into the graceful curve of **St Patrick Street**, Cork's main shopping street. The major department store, Brown Thomas, has a good stock of Irish crystal. Be sure to look up, because above the modern shop fronts many of the buildings on Patrick Street (as it is generally called in conversation) have retained 18th- and 19th-century features. After lunch you'll hear a unique Cork phenomenon – cries of "Eeeechooo!" from vendors of Cork's evening paper,

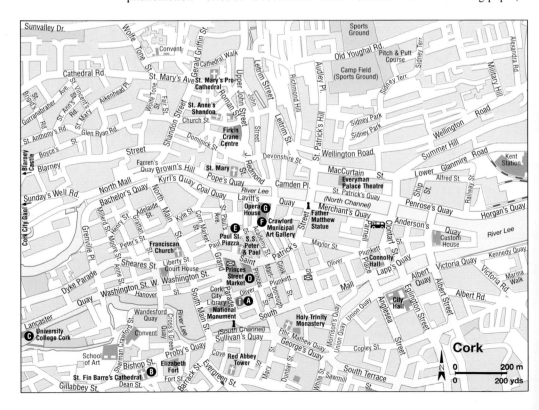

The Echo. A bronze statue of this quintessential Cork symbol, "the Echo boy", stands at the junction of Patrick Street and Cook Street. Patrick Street's distinctive paving, street furniture and lamp standards were designed by the Catalan architect Beth Galí and installed in 2004.

About 20 metres along St Patrick Street, on the left-hand side, a pedestrian alleyway next to the Body Shop leads to the **Rory Gallagher Piazza E**, a pedestrian square popular with buskers, named for the Cork-born rock and blues guitarist who died in 1995. This area is the closest Cork gets to a "left bank", with a cluster of antique shops, bookstores, art galleries, design conscious home furnishing stores, fashion boutiques and trendy cafés.

Turn right on to Paul Street for the **Crawford Municipal Gallery F** (tel: 021-427 3377). It has an unusually interesting permanent collection, in which most major 20th-century Irish artists are represented, and a good collection of topographical paintings of Cork in its 18th- and 19th-century prime. It also mounts and hosts touring exhibitions in an extension, built in 2001, which wraps around the existing red-brick building, using the same material, in an adventurous design by Dutch architect Eric van Egeraat.

Those interested in contemporary art should also check out the first floor **Vangard Gallery** in Carey's Lane (off Paul Street, tel: 021-427 8718), the **Fenton Gallery** at Wandesford Quay (off Washington Street, tel: 021-431 5294) and the **Triskel Gallery** (Tobin Street, off Grand Parade, tel: 021-427 2022), a government-subsidised arts centre for emerging artists.

The **Opera House G**, just around the corner in the direction of the river, dates from 1965, and was recently given a stylish new facade and a pedestrianised forecourt, to the great delight of local skateboarders. To your right is St Patrick's

Map, page 194

TIP

The Crawford Café in the Municipal Gallery is a popular meeting place, run by a team from the famous Ballymaloe House, serving light lunches and cakes*.

BELOW: Cork City.

The bells in St Anne's Church were made famous by the ballad:
'Tis the bells of Shandon
That sound so grand on
The pleasant waters of the River Lee.

BELOW: kissing the Blarney Stone.

Bridge, and straight ahead is the modern Christy Ring Bridge. Both lead from the central island of Cork to the northside.

Cross the Christy Ring Bridge, and climb the hill to the **Firkin Crane Centre**. Part of the Firkin Crane, a classical rotunda attractively built in cut limestone, is used for dance performances, and part of it houses the **Shandon Craft Market**. The Firkin Crane dates from the 18th century when much of Cork's wealth derived from the exporting of butter. Butter was packed in wooden barrels known as firkins, which were weighed here by a crane.

Across the road is **St Anne's Church**, whose Shandon Steeple is topped by a large salmon-shaped weather vane and has a four-sided clock. This is a famous landmark, that can be seen from most of the inner city. It is also known as the four-faced liar, as the clock often tells a different time on each side. For a small fee, you can climb the tower and attempt to ring a tune on the bells.

Blarney Castle

A visit to Blarney Castle makes a pleasant half-day outing. Don't be put off by Blarney's reputation as a tourist trap. The castle is surrounded by well-tended gardens, and is well worth seeing. **Blarney Castle ❷⓿** (tel: 021-438 5252, admission fee) is not furnished, but nor, like many castles of its age, is it a ruin. It is basically a 15th-century fortified home, and the staircase is narrow so that it can be defended by one man holding a sword.

Kissing the **Blarney Stone** is supposed to bestow the gift of eloquence. The word Blarney has entered the English language to mean "smoothly flattering or cajoling talk", but the origins of the tradition are obscure. The stone (which is actually the sill of an opening through which boiling liquids could be poured on

invaders in the old days) is located right at the top of the castle, on a parapet which is open to the sky. To kiss the stone you must lie on your back while an attendant holds on to you, and drop your head backwards and downwards. There is no charge, but most people who play along with this preposterous legend are so happy to survive the ordeal that they tip €1.

Map, page 170

Fota Wildlife Park and Arboretum

The east side of Cork Harbour is formed by three islands, **Little Island**, **Fota Island** and **Great Island**, all of which are connected by causeways. The road from Cork to Cobh brings you past the walls of the 780-acre (315-hectare) **Fota Estate**. **Fota Wildlife Park** ㉑ (tel: 021-481 2678, admission fee, closed Nov–mid-March) aims to breed certain species that are under threat in the wild. Giraffe, zebras, ostrich, oryx and antelope roam freely in grassland, monkeys swing through trees on lake islands, while kangaroos, wallabies, lemurs and peacocks have complete freedom of the park. Fota is the world's leading breeder of cheetahs, one of the few animals here that must be caged.

The **Fota Arboretum** (freely accessible) is beside the Wildlife Park, behind Fota House (tel: 021-481 5543, admission fee, www.fotahouse.com). The house, built as a shooting lodge, was enlarged in 1820 to a symmetrical neo-classical design. The arboretum has a beautiful collection of mature trees.

ABOVE: free-ranging in Fota Wildlife Park.
BELOW: Cobh Harbour, departure point for emigrants.

The Cove of Cork

Cobh ㉒ (pronounced *Cove*) was a small fishing village, referred to as the Cove of Cork. It grew in importance as a British naval base during the American War of Independence, thanks to its natural deep-water harbour. It grew again during the French Revolutionary and Napoleonic Wars (1792–1815). The fine cut-stone buildings on the two main islands in its harbour date from this period. In Victorian times it became Queenstown.

Cobh is attractively located on a steep slope with a Victorian-style promenade, and panoramic views of Cork harbour. While it is a popular commuter town, linked by rail to the city, commercially it is rather run-down, lacking attractive bars and restaurants. However, great efforts are being made to showcase Cobh's maritime history as the last – and first – European port of call for transatlantic shipping.

Between 1848 and 1950 about 2½ million adults and children emigrated through the port. Their transport ranged from convict transports and the notorious "coffin ships" of the famine years, overcrowded and unseaworthy, to the luxury of White Star and Cunard liners. Cobh was the last port of call of the *Titanic* in 1912, and it was to Cobh that most of the bodies recovered from the torpedoing of the *Lusitania* in 1915 were brought. Cobh's history is covered in **The Queenstown Story** (tel: 021-481 3591, daily, entry fee; www.cobhheritage.com), a lively and imaginative visitor centre at the entrance to Cobh. Allow at least an hour.

A large, Gothic-revival church, **St Colman's Cathedral**, was built in granite between 1868 and 1915. From its parapet you can see Roches Point in the south, which marks the harbour entrance, and the open sea beyond.❑

THE SOUTHWEST

Map, page 170

This is where the Atlantic first touches Europe, and the mild climate enhances the spectacular scenery of Bantry Bay, Killarney, the Ring of Kerry and the Dingle Peninsula

This is as far as you can get from Dublin, both physically and mentally. The pace of life really is slower, people have time to stop and talk, and a friendly informality prevails. Leave your formal clothes at home; bring strong walking shoes, waterproof jackets, casual evening wear, and buy a hand-knitted sweater at the first craft shop you visit. For many visitors Cork and Kerry are the essence of Ireland, combining wild, rugged landscape and, where the coastal waters are warmed by the Gulf Stream, a mild, frost-free climate.

The pleasures of the southwest are chiefly rural. Most people who visit the area are here for the outdoors and the scenery. The lakes and mountains of Killarney can compete with the best Europe has to offer, while the Ring of Kerry presents a succession of spectacular seascapes. The less-frequented Beara Peninsula is preferred by walkers and cyclists who enjoy the relative lack of traffic and the simple B&B accommodation. The coast of West Cork also has its champions, people who like the relatively small scale of its cliffs and hills, the miles of fuchsia hedges, dripping with dark red, honey-scented flowers, clashing exuberantly with great swathes of purple heather.

The most popular part of the west among visitors is the tip of the Dingle Peninsula, a largely Irish-speaking area rich in prehistoric and early Christian remains, with some of the world's best coastal scenery and arguably the country's best traditional music.

PRECEDING PAGES: west coast vista near Caherdaniel. **LEFT:** Slea Head, the Dingle Peninsula. **BELOW:** Old Head Lighthouse, Kinsale.

Kinsale – Ireland's gourmet capital

Kinsale ㉓, 12 miles (19 km) south of Cork Airport on the R600, is the big success story of Irish tourism. Once a run-down fishing port, it is now a wealthy resort with so many restaurants that it's known as "the gourmet capital of Ireland". It is situated at the top of a fjord-like harbour where the River Bandon runs into the sea. Craft shops, galleries, restaurants and antique shops abound.

The **Old Courthouse** in Market Square dates from 1600. In 1706 a Dutch-style gabled frontage and octagonal clock tower were added. The Courthouse contains the **Kinsale Regional Museum** (tel: 021-477 7930, entry fee), whose exhibits include mementoes of the *Lusitania*, sunk 14 miles (23 km) off the coast by a German submarine in 1915.

Also of interest nearby are the 12th-century **St Multose Church** and the 16th-century newly restored **Desmond Castle** which now houses a wine museum (tel: 021-477 4855, daily 10am–6pm Apr to mid-Oct).

Charles Fort (tel: 021-477 2263, daily 10am–5.15pm Mar–Oct, weekends 10am–5pm Nov–Mar), a five-minute drive down Kinsale Harbour, is a star-shaped fort enclosing 9 acres (3.5 hectares) of ground, and was built in 1677. Because it is overlooked by high ground, it was never a great success militarily, and its working

life as a recruit training centre ended in 1921 when the IRA burnt it down. There is good cut-stone work on many buildings, and wonderful sea views.

Leave Kinsale by crossing the River Bandon to the west. The land at the extremity of the **Old Head of Kinsale** became a private golf club in 1997 and you can no longer walk to the lighthouse, but there are good sea views from the road. The R600 then runs along the edge of the **Courtmacsherry Estuary** which in winter months is home to great flocks of plover, oyster catchers and curlew. In the summer cormorants, egrets and herons should be easy to spot.

The distant view of **Timoleague** ❷ is dominated by the grey stone ruins of a waterside 12th-century **Franciscan Friary**. Until the 16th century the monks were wine importers. The ruins are freely accessible. There are some garish modern graves inside, but the tall Gothic windows framing views of the estuary offer an irresistible photo-opportunity. The interior walls of Timoleague's tiny 19th-century **Church of Ireland** are entirely covered by a mosaic mural in the decorative style favoured by the Oxford Movement. The replica Hiberno-Romanesque-style **Church of Our Lady's Nativity** contains some fine stained-glass windows by the acclaimed Dublin artist, Harry Clarke (1889–1931).

Clonakilty and Environs

Turn left off the main road in **Clonakilty** ❷ at the large Catholic church and park. **Emmet Square** is lined by tall Georgian houses. The General Post Office is in a small 19th-century church. Note the hand-painted shop signs above wooden shop fronts which have been revived in recent years. The **West Cork Model Railway Village** (tel: 023-33224, admission fee) in the old railway station at the east end of town is a 1:24 scale model of the towns of Bandon, Kinsale,

BELOW:
Kinsale Harbour.

Clonakilty and Dunmanway, as they were in the 1940s – and the long closed West Cork Railway. Historians will like the eclectic **West Cork Regional Museum** which features memorabilia of the controversial patriot Michael Collins among its extensive collection. Collins's birthplace is signposted 4 miles (6.5 km) west of Clonakilty just beyond **Lissavaird**.

Continuing west on the N71, the road crosses a wide sea inlet at **Rosscarbery** ㉖. This was an important monastic centre from the 6th to the 12th centuries. The small Protestant Cathedral (1612) has been attractively renovated.

Turn left just beyond Rosscarbery on to the R597 Glandore road. From June to September this little road, and many others like it around west Cork, are lined by tall hedges of *fuchsia magellanica*, a shrub with bright red bell-shaped flowers imported from Chile in the 19th century. It has adapted so well to the climate that it grows wild in profusion.

About 2 miles (3.5 km) along is the road to the **Drombeg Stone Circle**, one of the most complete and most impressively situated of the region's early Iron Age remains. The circle is oriented to the winter solstice. If it's cloudless on 21 December, it's an impressive sight as the last rays of the sun travel through a cut in the distant mountains and land on the flat stone at the far side of the circle.

In winter **Glandore** ㉗, a tiny village built on the south-facing slope of a protected harbour, with a year-round population well below 100, will be virtually empty, while in summer it will be teeming with wealthy visitors and their yachts. This lovely spot is known locally as Millionaire's Row. **Union Hall**, on the opposite side of Glandore Harbour, is a small fishing village. Note the characteristic multi-coloured houses: it's said this tradition began when fishermen used whatever was left over from the annual painting of their boats to brighten up their houses.

Map, page 170

Michael Collins bust at his Pike Cross birthplace. He was gunned down on the Macroom to Bandon Road in Co. Cork in 1922 during Ireland's civil war.

BELOW: Drombeg Stone Circle.

ABOVE: Sailing on Lough Ine.

Castletownshend is signposted from Union Hall on an attractive back road which passes through **Rineen**. Castletownshend may be the prettiest village in west Cork, but it is also the least typical. Wander along its two streets, noting its large, well-designed three- and four-storey houses, often stone-built and neo-classical. These belonged to "planter" families – Protestant English ex-soldiers – who were given lands in the area in the late 17th century.

A wall plaque in **St Barrahane's Church** enlarges on their history. Behind the church are the graves of Edith Somerville (1858–1949) and her writing partner, Violet Martin (1862–1915). As Somerville and Ross, they are best known for a series of comic sketches of Irish country life, *Some Experiences of an Irish RM* (Resident Magistrate). They also wrote a well-received novel, *The Real Charlotte*. There's a wonderful view of the sheltered anchorage from their graves.

Skibbereen is a traffic-choked market town built in a solid bourgeois style in the 19th and early 20th centuries. **Lough Ine** (also spelt Hyne) is just off the Baltimore road. The land-locked salt water lake is a marine reserve with many unusual species. Its high wooded shores and sheltered location give it a very special atmosphere. Walk around the path on the west side of the lake to discover the narrow passage where sea water rushes in at high tide.

Baltimore, 13 km (8 miles) south of Skibbereen, is another popular sailing and holiday village, the most easily accessible port on **Roaringwater Bay**. Baltimore can be hectic in July and August. The bay covers an area between the Mizen Head in the west and Baltimore in the east which is known for its numerous rocks and islands. In good visibility, the **Fastnet Rock Lighthouse**, can be seen on the horizon some 14 miles (23 km) to the south.

BELOW: Skibbereen.

Baltimore is also the base for the mail boats and ferries servicing Roaring

Water Bay's two largest inhabited islands, Clear and Sherkin. **Sherkin Island** is only a quick hop (tel: 028-22001 for ferry details; regular services in summer 9am–8pm). There are two pubs, the Jolly Roger and Murphy's Bar, and the ruins of a 15th-century Franciscan friary.

Map, page 170

Birdwatching centre

Clear Island is reached by a thrilling 45-minute boat ride through the rocks of Roaringwater Bay (tel: 028-39153 for ferry details. There is usually a boat out at 11am, returning at 4pm, weather permitting). Cape Clear (pop. 170) is an Irish-speaking island about 3 miles (5 km) long by 1 mile (2 km). There are three pubs, a youth hostel, a bird observatory, a heritage centre and about 20 B&Bs. Because of its southerly position, Cape Clear's Bird Observatory often reports landings of rare migratory birds, and the appearance of large flocks.

The N71 west leaves Skibbereen beside the banks of the **River Ilen**. About 6 miles (9 km) out of town, keep an eye out to the left for your first panoramic view of Roaringwater Bay and its numerous islands.

Ballydehob ㉙ is a lively, brightly-painted village built on a hillside, apparently in the middle of nowhere. Although it appears to be inland, Ballydehob has a harbour. Before the harbour silted up, the village was the marketing centre for the islanders of Roaringwater Bay. Now it's a popular retreat for city folk – English, Dutch, German and even Irish – seeking a better quality of life.

Continue on the R592 towards Schull. In good weather you will see **Mount Gabriel** (1335 ft/407 metres) on your right. The two white balls on its summit guide transatlantic air traffic. If you wake early in west Cork, you can often hear a stream of jumbo jets high above, heading for the airports of Europe. While

Cape Clear is Ireland's most southerly point. The Fastnet Rock and lighthouse, 4 miles (6 km) to its southwest, are familiar navigation points to sailors.

BELOW: mermaid sculpture by the river at Ballydehob.

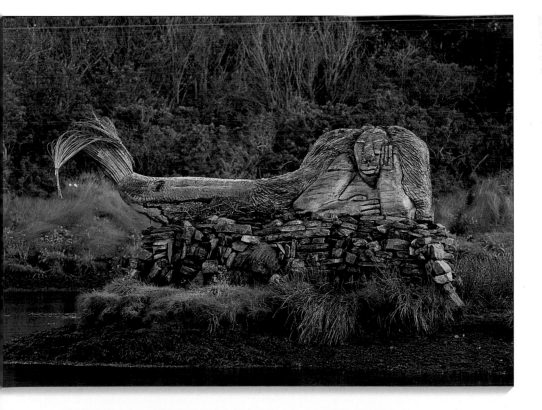

Altar Rock. For more
information about
megalithic tombs,
see page 227.

Ballydehob has a reputation for being arty, **Schull**, 3 miles (5 km) down the R592, is the heart of fashionable west Cork, a summer resort for wealthy Dubliners. Walk down to the pier for another look at Roaringwater Bay, then explore its one main street, checking out its restaurants, bookshops and craft boutiques.

Leave Schull on the R592 to travel to the tip of the **Mizen Peninsula**. The road passes rocky, rugged bits of low-lying coast. About 4 miles (7 km) west at **Altar**, there is a megalithic tomb on the left, known locally as the Altar Rock. The **Mizen Head** is a dramatic spot with wild Atlantic waves pounding the rocks even in the calmest weather. The lighthouse signal has been automatic, and the station unstaffed since 1993. The **Mizen Vision** (tel: 028-35591, www.mizenvision.com, admission fee) is located in the lighthouse keeper's house on an island at the tip of the peninsula. To reach it you must cross a concrete suspension bridge while the waves swirl around 150 ft (45 metres) below. It's worth bringing a camera.

The **Sheep's Head Peninsula** is a thin finger of land dividing Dunmanus Bay from Bantry Bay to the north. From Goleen or Schull follow the R591 to Durrus, and follow signs for the Sheep's Head Drive (50 miles/80 km) which leads to the N71, and Bantry town. The peninsula is small and sparsely populated, with most people living in scattered farmhouses. There is a timeless air about the gorse and heather of the heathland, and the rough green fields with grey stone walls. The views are superb, with the more sheltered south coast looking back across the narrow Dunmanus Bay to the Mizen Head, and the north coast overlooking the wide expanse of Bantry Bay, and the Beara peninsula. Even the villages – **Kilcrohane** and **Ahakista** – are on a smaller scale than elsewhere. Stop at the Tin Roof Pub in Ahakista to experience old-style hospitality.

The shores of Bantry Bay

The town of **Bantry** ❸⓪ is distinguished only by its setting on the shores of **Bantry Bay**. **Bantry House** (tel: 027-50047), a short walk from the town centre, is a large, mid-18th century mansion with a magnificent setting overlooking the famous bay (which is 4 miles/6.5 km wide), and the mountains on the opposite shore. The interior is either under-restored, verging on the shabby, or full of atmosphere depending on your taste.

There is a fine collection of treasures, including Aubusson carpets, Gobelin tapestries, Russian icons, Chinese lacquer and a mixture of French and Irish 18th-century furniture. In the yard the **Bantry 1796 French Armada Exhibition Centre** is a small museum commemorating the failed attempt by Wolfe Tone and his French allies to land 14,000 troops in Bantry Bay over 200 years ago. The landing was impeded by bad weather.

Head inland from Bantry via **Kealkil** to visit **Gougane Barra**, a deep tarn which is the source of the River Lee. The lake is walled in on three sides by steep precipices which run with cataracts after heavy rain. **St Finbar's Oratory**, a small stone-built chapel on an island in the lake, can be reached by a causeway. The existing building is a 20th-century replica, built on the site where St Finbar supposedly lived and prayed in the 6th century before founding his monastery downstream in the place that is now Cork city. A pilgrimage is still held on the first Sunday after St Finbar's Feast Day, 25

Map, page 170

September. There's certainly something special about the place, particularly if you arrive early, before the majority of day trippers.

The N71 climbs above Bantry Bay into open, more rugged country, offering ever-changing views across the bay. **Glengarriff** ⓷, a wooded glen with a sheltered harbour warmed by the Gulf Stream, has an especially mild climate, with an average annual temperature of 11°C (52°F). Azaleas, rhododendrons, magnolia, and camellias grow in abundance. Glengarriff village is teeming with craft shops and coach parks, but **Ilnacullin Gardens** (tel: 027-63040, admission fee, closed Nov–Feb) on Garinish Island, five minutes offshore, are well worth a visit. (Boat fare is in addition to fee). An added bonus in sunny weather is the sight of basking seals on the rocks between the mainland and the island. Allow about an hour and a half. Don't miss the Italian Garden, a formal garden with colonnades and a terrace from which the contrast between the classical man-made beauty of the garden, and the wild mountain scenery that surrounds it, is at its greatest.

TIP

There are good opportunities for bathing in the area around Allihies.

The Ring of Beara

The Ring of Beara is less well known than its neighbour to the north, the Ring of Kerry, yet it also offers impressive scenery. It is a favourite haunt of walkers, cyclists, bird watchers and people who enjoy natural beauty. Although the drive covers only about 68 miles (110 km), much of it is on narrow, winding roads, so allow a full day. The **Beara Peninsula** stretches for about 30 miles (48 km) southwest from Glengarriff, forming the north side of Bantry Bay. The **Caha** and **Slieve Miskish** mountains run down the centre of the peninsula, and the road around it is mainly on a narrow coastal plain.

A shorter route to Kenmare can be taken at Adrigole, about 12 miles (19 km)

BELOW: digging for sea urchins at Bantry Bay.

beyond Glengarriff. The R574 climbs north across the peninsula in a series of small but sharp hairpin bends, leading to the **Healy Pass** (1,083 ft/330 metres). Stop here to enjoy a panoramic view of Bantry Bay to the south, with the Kenmare river and the MacGilligcuddy Reeks in the north. Turn right at Lauragh on to the R571 Kenmare road.

Many would consider **Castletownbere ㉜**, with a population of about 850, little more than a village. However, it is a busy working port, home to Ireland's largest white fish trawling fleet. Large Russian factory ships are often anchored for months between the town and Bere Island. Get a feel for the place by walking along the quays and admiring the brightly coloured fishing fleet.

Leave town on the R575 for **Allihies**. This straggling line of brightly coloured cottages set between sea and hills, was originally built for the copper miners working in the hills behind it. The sandy beach at **Ballydonegan** was formed of spoil from the mines. Walk up to the abandoned mines (marked by tall brick chimneys) and enjoy the views of sea and wild hillside. You can walk from here to the next village, Eyeries (7 miles/11 km), on a footpath that forms part of the Beara Way. Even if you only walk a few miles of it, the peace and isolation will be unforgettable.

The road between Allihies and **Eyeries**, another village of small, brightly coloured houses, is one of the highlights of the Ring of Beara. In good weather the **Iveragh Peninsula** is clearly visible to the north, across the **Kenmare River**, as are the conical shaped **Skellig Rocks** off its tip. You will get a closer look at these rocky islands from the Ring of Kerry.

Derreen Gardens (tel: 064-83103) were planted 100 years ago beside Kilmakilloge Harbour, a sheltered inlet on the south shore of the Kenmare River. The woodland gardens run down to the water's edge and contain many azaleas

BELOW: jaunting cars are popular with tourists.

and rhododendrons, massive stands of bamboo and groves of New Zealand tree ferns – all of which thrive in the mild air warmed by the Gulf Stream.

The first Marquess of Lansdowne, the local landowner, was responsible for the layout of **Kenmare** ㉝, an attractive market town at the head of the Kenmare River (which is in fact a sea inlet). The two principal streets intersect each other to form an X. Kenmare, with its background of mountains, is a popular stop on the Ring of Kerry, and has a good selection of shops. Guided cruises of the Bay and Islands are run from Kenmare Pier (mid-April–Sept, tel: 064-83171). The **Kenmare Heritage Centre** (tel: 064-41233, admission fee, closed Oct–Mar) explores themes of local interest. There is a Kenmare lace showroom above it.

Killarney's lakes and mountains

Killarney ㉞ may be the most commercialised area in the Southwest, but it is still possible to avoid the crowds and enjoy the lakes and hills. The romantic scenery of boulder-strewn, heather-clad mountains, deep blue lakes dotted with wooded islands, and wild woodland has been preserved within a large National Park. Avoid the town by day. Killarney isn't a good place to shop for crafts in spite of (or because of) its large number of visitors. Kenmare and Blarney are better shopping destinations. The town is chiefly remarkable in high season for its traffic jams. However, there are several good restaurants open in the evening, and the singing bars can be enjoyable if you don't mind organised fun.

Enjoying a visit to Killarney is largely a matter of attitude. You won't appreciate Killarney from the inside of a car. One great pleasure here is the damp woodland aroma that permeates the mild air. As in the rest of Kerry, it is important not to be put off by rain. Any weather, good or bad, tends not to last long

Map, page 170

ABOVE:
Muckross House.

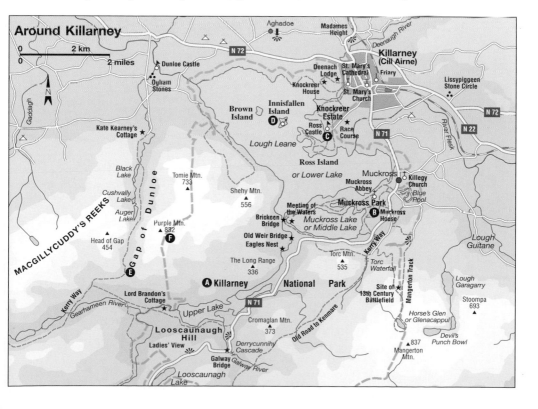

**Map,
page 209**

around here. In fact, the lakes of Killarney look especially good when seen through a light drizzle.

Rather than regarding Killarney as a series of sights to be ticked off a list, it is more satisfying to do only one or two things in a leisurely way. Arriving from Kenmare, you may decide to stop on the N71 and climb the path beside the **Torc Waterfall** to enjoy the view – and plan your next move.

A nice contrast to the wildness of Torc can be found across the road in **Muckross Park**, a neatly trimmed lakeside area with gravel paths that forms the nucleus of the **Killarney National Park Ⓐ**. This is a car-free zone, and it is a good place to take a ride on one of Killarney's famous jaunting cars (open horse-drawn carriages). The drivers, who are called jarveys, are traditionally great talkers. Don't be surprised if you hear a phone ring during your quaint jaunting car ride; most drivers carry mobile phones to help locate their next fare.

Muckross House ⒷB (tel: 064-31440, admission fee), built in the 19th century in the Elizabethan style, houses a folklore and farming museum. You can admire the rhododendrons and azaleas in the formal gardens free of charge.

Ross Castle ⒸC (tel: 064-35851, closed Nov–Mar) is a 14th-century castle keep that has recently been fully restored. You can hire a rowing boat here, and take a picnic over to **Innisfallen Island ⒹD** about 1 mile (1.5 km) offshore. The wooded island has the remains of an abbey founded about AD 600, which is famous for the *Annals of Innisfallen*, a chronicle of world and Irish history written in this remote and beautiful spot up to 1320 by a succession of monastic scribes.

Consider taking an organised half-day coach-horse-and-boat trip through the **Gap of Dunloe ⒺE**, a narrow mountain pass formed by glacial action. The organised trip has the advantage of allowing you to travel through the Gap on foot or

The Macgillicuddy's Reeks (peaks) include Carantuohill, Ireland's highest summit at 3,414 ft (1,041 metres).

BELOW: the alluring Ring of Kerry.

horseback and then go back to town by boat without having to retrieve your car. The Gap itself is an unpaved path that stretches for 4 miles (6.5 km) between the **Macgillicuddy's Reeks** and the **Purple Mountain** ❻, which gets its name from the heather that covers it in the autumn. There is no motor traffic, but in summer there is a constant stream of ponies, jaunting cars and pedestrians. The scenery is first-rate, with a chain of five small lakes beside the road, and massive glacial boulders, but don't expect solitude.

The Ring of Kerry

You can drive non-stop around the 112 miles (180 km) of the Ring of Kerry in about four hours, but allow a full day as you will want to make several stops. The Ring of Kerry is justifiably famous for its combination of lush, sub-tropical vegetation and rugged seascapes. In July and August the narrow two-lane road can be clogged by a slow procession of tour buses and RVs. If traffic and commercialism bother you, do the Ring of Beara instead, or go straight to Dingle.

Killorglin ❸❺ is a busy village which makes the most of its strategic position on the road between Killarney and Dingle. It is famous for Puck Fair – Ireland's oldest festival, dating back to pagan times – on 10–12 August. On the first day a mountain goat is crowned King Puck and installed on a tall throne overlooking the town, until the evening of the third day. There are various explanations of its origin, but nowadays it is chiefly a drinking festival, and can get rowdy. A short drive inland from the road to Glenbeigh, **Caragh Lake** is a delightful, sheltered spot, popular with game anglers. The lake shore is discreetly dotted with luxury hotels and holiday homes, mostly 19th-century.

Glenbeigh is a popular touring base, convenient for both sea and hills. Nearby

Maps: pages 170 & 209

The Barracks: destined, some say, for India and built in Ireland as a result of clerical error.

BELOW: horse for sale at Killorglin's Puck's Fair.

Rossbeigh is a 3-mile (5-km) long sandy beach facing west over Dingle Bay, backed by dunes. There are good walks here in **Glenbeigh Woods**.

Cahersiveen ❸⓿ (pronounced Cah-her-sigh-*veen*) is the chief market town for the Iveragh peninsula, but don't expect a buzzing metropolis. At its best it has a certain dilapidated charm. Don't miss the community-funded visitor centre, **The Barracks** (tel: 066-947 2777, admission fee.). This is an exotic-looking, white-turreted building. The story goes that it should have been built in India, on the Northwest Frontier, but the plans were mistakenly sent to Ireland. In fact its architect, Enoch Trevor Owen, habitually built in what he called the Schloss style, and looked at from another angle, his design suits the hill-backed location very well. But why spoil a good story? Nowadays it houses an amusing and informative series of exhibitions. Follow the sign outside The Barracks to the pier. The prettiest part of Cahersiveen is its backside which overlooks the wide estuary of the River Ferta and the green hills beyond.

Look out for signs to the Valentia Island car ferry about 3 miles (5km) west of Cahersiveen. This lands you in **Knightstown** at the eastern tip of **Valentia**, a sleepy place, eerily quiet, with a couple of bars. The island is 6¾ miles (11 km) long and 1¾ miles (3 km) broad, a quiet place with a population of about 700. The original transatlantic cable connecting Europe with Newfoundland was laid from here between 1857 and 1865. Valentia is connected to the mainland by a causeway at **Portmagee**.

The Skellig Experience (tel: 066-947 6306, admission fee, closed Dec–Mar), beside the causeway, is a dull and portentous visitor centre. Opt instead for a boat trip to the islands (tel: 066-947 7156). Bear in mind that all the boats are open, the water can be rough, and bad weather leads to cancellations.

Skellig Michael was popular for centuries with pilgrims, who performed penances on the island. Extra penances were to endure the rough seas and steep slopes.

BELOW: the lure of the Atlantic.

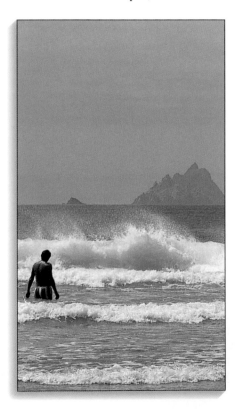

Skellig Michael, the largest of the three islands, was inhabited by monks from the 7th until the 12th centuries. It rises in a cone shape to a double peak 712 ft (217 metres) high. A flight of over 500 steps lead to the monastery which is built of dry stone with no mortar. It has undergone major restoration work to enable it to cope with increased visitor numbers. Enthusiastic guides, all trained archaeologists, live on the island from June to August, to supervise visitors and tell them the island's history.

A scenic drive

If the weather is good, take the scenic road from Portmagee to Waterville through **Ballynahow**. The road climbs the **Coomanaspig Pass**, revealing an impressive arc of coast and mountains. It then travels through **The Glen**, offering the best views so far of the Skelligs. Drive through **Ballinskelligs**, an Irish-speaking area, and rejoin the main Ring road just before Waterville. **Waterville** ❸⓿ is a popular base for golfers, who enjoy the famous links, and anglers who have a choice of deep-sea fishing in Ballinskelligs Bay or angling on Lough Currane.

The next stretch of road which winds along the edge of **Ballinskelligs Bay** through the **Commakesta Pass**, then crosses **Lamb's Head**, has some of the best views on the Ring, with rocky coastline backed by rugged green hills. **Derrynane House** (tel: 066-947 5113, admission fee) is a mile beyond **Caherdaniel**. The house belonged to Daniel O'Connell (1775–1847), also known as The Liberator, who is remembered chiefly for his campaign for Catholic emancipation (granting civil rights to Catholics), which was won in 1829. O'Connell is still a great hero in this part of the world, and the house contains a greatly respected collection of his personal possessions and furniture. These range from a magnificent throne-like carved chair, to the pistol with which O'Connell killed a man in a duel in 1815. The 320 acres (130 hectares) of woods surrounding the house have pleasant walks, and access to an attractive sandy beach.

Castlecove is a small, friendly place with several good sandy beaches. A narrow lane beyond the church climbs 1¾ miles (3 km) to **Staigue Fort**. This is a well-preserved example of a prehistoric stone fortress, dating from 1500 BC. It consists of a circular dry-stone wall, 115 ft (35 metres) in diameter, varying in thickness from 13 ft to 5 ft (4–1.5 metres). A series of steps in the walls lead to a platform with good sea views. A small donation is requested by the landowner.

Sneem ❸ is another pretty but untypical village, laid out English-style around a village green beneath a semi-circle of low mountains. A variety of indifferent modern sculpture is dotted around. Ignore this, and look for "the pyramids" as they are called locally, beside the Catholic parish church. These small stone-built beehive huts inlaid with stained-glass panels look ancient. In fact, they were built in 1990 with local labour, and designed by Cork artist James Scanlon.

Sneem marks the start of the most sheltered part of the Ring of Kerry's coast. Here you will see lush, subtropical growth – wild rhododendrons, azaleas, camellias and bamboo – evidence of the benign effect of the Gulf Stream.

The N70 continues on to Kenmare, where the N71 leads to either Killarney

Map, page 170

ABOVE: a kingly tree sculpture at Derrynane House.

BELOW: Sneem.

or Glengarriff. If you are heading for Dingle, turn left at **Blackwater Bridge** to drive through the **Ballaghbeama Gap** and **Glencar**, a popular base for climbers and walkers, to Killorglin. This is a narrow, twisty road, not recommended for nervous drivers, but it offers some wonderful unspoilt bogland scenery.

The Dingle Peninsula

The weather can make or break a visit to Dingle. If the sea mist is down, consider postponing your trip. At Killorglin take the N70 to Castlemaine, and in Castlemaine take the R561, which gives good views of the coast of the Iveragh peninsula. **Inch** has 4 miles (6.5 km) of sandy beach backed by dunes.

Dingle ❸❾, the chief town of the peninsula, has a population of about 1,500, which can treble in summer. Backed by mountains, it faces on to a sheltered harbour. Until the 16th century, Dingle was a walled town, and had regular trade with France and Spain. It is in an Irish-speaking area.

Dingle's tourism was boosted by the filming nearby of *Ryan's Daughter* in 1969. It was boosted again in 1985 with the arrival of Fungi, a bottle-nosed dolphin who will play with swimmers and follows boats in and out of the harbour. If you prefer to stay on dry land, you can see more than 100 different species of fish at **Oceanworld Mara Beo Aquarium** (tel: 066-915 2111, www.dingle-oceanworld.ie).

Dingle offers an appealing combination of the bucolic – farmers come to town on their tractors, perhaps with a few sheep in the trailer behind – and the sophisticated, with a choice of serious restaurants and craft shops. A triangular walk from the pier area, up Green Street, down Main Street and back along the Mall to the pier takes you past the best shops, pubs and restaurants.

Continue west on the R559. Between **Ventry** and Slea Head there are over 400 *clocháns* ("beehive" huts). The farmers may charge you a nominal sum to visit them. These small conical huts of unmortared stone are not in fact prehistoric, as the farmers claim; the oldest date from the early Christian period, the 5th to 8th centuries, and were used by hermit monks. Others were built as recently as the 19th century to house farm implements. The road climbs westward around Eagle Mountain to **Slea Head,** and has good panoramas.

The Blasket Islands

The group of seven rocky islands offshore are the **Blasket Islands**. **Great Blasket,** the largest one, is about 4 miles (7 km) long and ¾ mile (1.5 km) wide. It was inhabited until 1953. The islanders were great story-tellers and have made a lasting contribution to Irish literature. The **Great Blasket Centre** (tel: 066-915 6444, admission fee, closed Oct–Easter) tells their story using many old records and photographs. Below Mount Eagle is the village of **Dunquin**, a scattered settlement whose harbour was once the landing point for the islanders. Stop at Dunquin Pier, and walk down the steep, concrete path to a tiny landing place.

Boats go to the island regularly in the summer (Easter–Sept, tel: 066-915 6455). The crossing takes 20 minutes, but landing is by transfer to rubber dinghy, so you must be fit and agile. There are frequent crossings between 10am and 4pm, weather permitting.

ABOVE: one of Dingle's local crafts.

BELOW: on the road at Dingle in a self-drive caravan.

On towards Tralee

Gallarus Oratory (well signposted) is an extraordinary little building of unmortared "dry" stone, probably dating from the 8th century. It is in the shape of an inverted boat, with a door at the west and a window in the east wall. It remains as dry and solid as the day it was built, and is very dark inside.

Avoid the **Connor Pass** in bad weather – take the N78 through Anascaul instead. The drive is hair-raising in all weathers as you climb steeply to 1,496 ft (456 metres) above sea level. A section of the narrow-gauge **Tralee and Dingle Light Railway**, which closed in 1963, has been restored at **Blennerville** and is Europe's most westerly railway line; steam trains operate May–Sept (tel: 066 7121064). Beside the old ship canal is the Blennerville Windmill and visitor centre (tel: 066-712 1064, daily Apr–Oct 10am–5pm) and the adjoining Jeanie Johnston Visitor Shipyard (tel: 066-712 9999, daily 9am–6pm) where a replica of the Jeanie Johnson famine ship was built. A nostalgic half-hour steam journey can be taken into Tralee (tel: 066-712 1064, admission fee, closed Nov–Apr).

Tralee ⑩ (pop. 22,000) is the county town of Kerry, but don't expect a lot. While it may seem like a booming metropolis after a few days in Dingle, Tralee is a dull place. The exception is in August, when the whole town parties for a week during the **Rose of Tralee Festival**, a beauty and personality pageant, and then adjourns to the adjacent Ballybeggan racecourse for a six-day race meeting. The town's most attractive area is the Denny Street area near the museum, with its nicely proportioned Georgian houses. The enjoyable **Kerry County Museum** (tel: 066-712 7777, admission fee) is in a neo-classical building at the top of the street. Tralee is also the base for Siamsa Tire, Ireland's national folk theatre, which stages nightly performances of Irish folklore, music and dance during the summer. ❑

Map, page 170

ABOVE: Gallarus Oratory.

BELOW: the oddly shaped "Dead Man", one of the Blasket Islands off Slea Head.

THE SHANNON REGION

Within easy reach of Limerick is a region of ruined castles, a dramatic coastline, spectacular caves and the eerie moon-like landscape of the Burren

Map, page 170

Shannon Airport is on the estuary of the mighty River Shannon, the longest river in Britain or Ireland, which flows through Lough Derg, the last and the largest of its lakes, emerging into the Atlantic through a wide estuary. Limerick city, Ireland's fourth largest town, sits on a bend in the river. When Shannon Airport opened in 1945 it attracted many foreign companies to its surrounding estates, and revived a region that had been in decline. Since the 1960s, high-tech multinationals have been setting up bases in the area.

In the far west, the coast of County Clare is a popular holiday destination, offering a combination of Atlantic rollers, sandy beaches and imposing cliffs. The Cliffs of Moher rise almost vertically out of the sea to a height of 650 ft (200 metres). From the top you can see the Aran Islands and, to the north, across Galway Bay, the shores of Connemara. The Burren, in north Clare, consists of huge pavements of exposed grey limestone topped with massive boulders, and is often said to resemble a lunar landscape. An amazing variety of wild flowers, both Mediterranean and Alpine, grow in the crevices of the rocks.

PRECEDING PAGES: on the road to Limerick. **LEFT:** the mighty Cliffs of Moher. **BELOW:** a memorial in Limerick city to the 1916 Rising.

Limerick City

Limerick ⓪ (pop. 75,000) is probably Ireland's least loved city. It's a staunchly Roman Catholic and conservative place, with innumerable mainly Victorian churches. In the 17th century Limerick supported the Jacobite cause for a whole year after the defeat of James II at the Battle of the Boyne. When the Irish leader, Patrick Sarsfield, finally surrendered in 1691, the Treaty of Limerick marked the start of the denial of religious and property rights to Catholics which lasted until Daniel O'Connell's Catholic Emancipation Bill in 1829.

The bulk of the city lies to the east of the River Shannon, and until recently Limerick's city centre resolutely turned its back on the river, the wide, fast-flowing Shannon, its best asset. New developments have concentrated on putting the river back into the life of the city. The 17-storey, oval-shaped **Clarion Hotel** has become a symbol of the regeneration of Limerick's docklands, and of the city's new self-confidence. The **Tourist Information Office** at **Arthur's Quay** is another boldly-designed modern building near the riverbank. Ask here for details of Angela's Ashes walking tours of the locations described in Frank McCourt's memoir. The inland side of the TIO leads to **O'Connell Street,** Limerick's main shopping area, a mass of neon and plate glass. The liveliest part of the shopping district is the pedestrianised **Cruises Street** area.

Head north of Arthur's Quay for **The Custom House** to view the **Hunt Museum** (tel: 061-312 833, www.huntmuseum.com, admission fee). This magnifi-

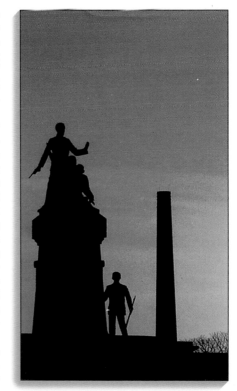

cent collection of treasures ranges from the 9th-century enamel Antrim Cross, to Egyptian, Roman and Etruscan pieces, Chinese porcelain, and even a drawing by Picasso. The collection was privately assembled by John Hunt, a medievalist, and his wife Gertrude, and left to the nation on his death in 1976.

Turn left out of the Hunt Musuem and cross the bridge to **St Mary's Cathedral**. It dates from the 12th century and was built in the form of a cross, incorporating both Romanesque and Gothic styles. Note the black oak seats of its misericords, which are carved with animal features.

North of the cathedral is the 13th-century **King John's Castle** (tel: 061-411 1201, admission fee), one of the most impressively sited Norman fortresses in Ireland, with curtain walls and drum towers surviving. Climb one of the round towers for a good view of both river and town. An audio-visual display recounts Limerick's history from its foundation by the Vikings in AD992.

Return past the Hunt Museum to **O'Connell Street**, which will lead you into Georgian Limerick, a district known as **Newtown**. The **Belltable Arts Centre** (tel: 061-319 709) at No. 69 has contemporary exhibitions and a theatre. The **Georgian Crescent** has been well restored. From here Barrington Street leads to **Pery Square** and the **People's Park**. The **Georgian House** at No. 2 (tel: 061-314 130, admission fee) has been restored and furnished in 18th-century style, and also has displays relating to the filming of *Angela's Ashes*. Opposite is the City Gallery (tel: 061-319 709), once a Carnegie Library, which has a small collection of Irish art and also mounts contemporary shows.

The best thing in Limerick's suburbs is the campus of the newly created (1989) **Limerick University** at **Plassey** which is a successful showcase for contemporary Irish architecture and sculpture.

Limerick claims the origin of the five-line verse, known worldwide as the limerick and all too often beginning "There was a young lady from..." The genre, originally oral, was most famously adopted by the English painter and humorist Edward Lear.

BELOW: King John's Castle, Limerick.

North of Limerick City

This is castle country, with ruined stumps of crumbling tower houses dotted around the place. There were once over 420 tower houses in the Limerick area. Few are as imposing nor as carefully restored as Bunratty, whose rectangular 15th-century keep is surrounded by four corner turrets, each topped with battlements and a set of flags.

Bunratty Castle and Folk Park ㊷ (tel: 061-360 788, open daily year-round, admission fee) is strategically placed on the road between Shannon Airport and Limerick City. It contains an interesting collection of furniture and paintings from the 15th and 16th centuries. The Folk Park behind it consists of 25 acres (10 hectares) of reconstructed and fully furnished farmhouses, cottages and shops, as they would have appeared to a visitor to mid-western Ireland in the late 19th century. There is even a village street with blacksmith, pub, drapery, print works and post office. It is aimed firmly at the first-time visitor, but is so carefully detailed that it is hard to resist getting involved. Don't miss **Durty Nelly's**, an old-world Irish pub next door to the village, which has been copied all over the world.

Another corny but enjoyable experience is the medieval Irish banquet, a purely tourist-oriented but good-natured event – essentially a meal with Irish cabaret in which the guests are serenaded by Irish colleens – which takes place twice nightly at Bunratty and also at the nearby **Knappogue Castle** (tel: 061-360 788, admission fee) at **Quin** to the north of Bunratty. Knappogue is a 15th-century Macnamara stronghold that has also been fully restored and furnished in period.

The **Craggaunowen Project** (tel: 061-367 178, admission fee) is built in the grounds of another castle, a 16th-century tower house. The project has recon-

Map, page 170

ABOVE: Bunratty Castle interior.
BELOW: by the River Shannon in the city.

structed authentic replicas of dwelling places in prehistoric and pre-Christian Ireland. On an island in the lake, reached by means of a footbridge, is a *cranndg*, a fortified dwelling of clay and wattle. A small ring fort which shows how a farmer would have lived in the 5th or 6th centuries has been built. Also at Craggaunowen is the traditionally-built boat in which the writer and adventurer Tim Severin sailed to Nova Scotia in 1976, retracing the legendary 6th-century voyage of St Brendan, and making a plausible case for its historical reality.

To escape from the beaten path of the castle trail, consider an outing to **Scarriff ㊸**, a quiet little town set on high ground overlooking Lough Derg. It is a true rural backwater, popular with visitors in summer and totally sleepy in the winter, which has a reputation for good traditional music. **Drewsborough House** near **Tuamgraney**, to the south of Scarriff, is the birthplace of the 20th-century novelist Edna O'Brien who has written scathing descriptions of the narrow-minded inhabitants of this area which was considered relatively remote 50 years ago.

Edna O'Brien's "The Country Girls" (1960) was the first of a trilogy of novels tracing the fortunes of two ex-convent girls as they escaped from rural Ireland to the bright lights of Dublin and later London.

Both Scarriff and Tuamgraney are on the scenic drive that goes all the way around **Lough Derg**, a wide, almost sea-like part of the Shannon River which is popular with watersports enthusiasts and other outdoor types. It is worth taking in at least the 5-mile (8-km) stretch northeast to **Mountshannon**, a neat 18th-century village. Offshore you can visit **Holy Island**, an uninhabited 49-acre (20-hectare) island which had a 7th-century Christian settlement. There are the remains of five churches and a 79-ft (24-metre) high round tower.

Ennis ㊹ is the county town of County Clare, a busy place with narrow streets. Its recently refurbished market area is a cheerful, brightly painted, partly pedestrianised area with numerous small shops. **Ennis Friary** (tel: 065-682 9100, admission fee) beside the fast-flowing **River Fergus**, was once next to an important school with 350 friars and over 600 pupils. The remains date chiefly from the 14th century and include cloisters and a roofless church with interesting medieval stone carvings.

BELOW: pasture near Lough Gur.

South of Limerick City

Lough Gur ㊺ (tel: 061-361 511, admission fee, closed Oct–Apr), 12 miles (19 km) due south of Limerick on the N24–R514, is one of Europe's most complete Stone Age and Bronze Age sites. It is a lovely quiet lake, rich in bird life. The **Grange Stone Circle** is 150 ft (45 metres) across and contains about 100 boulders. More than 20 other stone circles, tombs, hut foundations, lakeside dwellings and ring forts have been excavated beside Lough Gur. An interpretative centre built in the form of Neolithic huts houses a collection of artefacts and has an audio-visual presentation introducing the site.

Adare ㊻, 10½ miles (17 km) southwest of Limerick, is generally considered one of Ireland's prettiest villages. Several of its stone-built cottages are thatched, and they all have colourful front gardens. Adare is noted for its antique dealers, but don't expect great bargains. Opposite the Dunraven Arms Hotel is the entrance to **Adare Manor**. This was the seat of the Earls of Dunraven, who built the picturesque cottages that line the village for their workers. It is now an American-owned luxury hotel. The original 18th-century manor was enlarged in the Gothic Revival style in the mid-19th century. In its grounds are the ruins of the 14th-century **Desmond Castle** and of a **Franciscan Friary** dating from 1464. The latter are especially attractive, with an ancient yew growing in the centre of the cloisters. The **Adare Heritage Centre** (tel: 063-396 666, admission fee, closed Nov–Feb) has a helpful history display and a model of medieval Adare. The 14-arch bridge dates from medieval times and leads to the **Augustinian Friary**, built in 1315. The cloisters were converted into a mausoleum for the Earl of Dunraven in 1826 and the church was restored in 1852.

Rathkeale ㊼ is more of a typical Irish village – its long main street of small shops and bleak-looking houses straggling along the road. It is worth going there to visit **Castle Matrix** (tel: 069-64284, admission fee, May–Sept 10 until sunset, Oct–Apr by appointment), a 15th-century tower house. The castle is sumptuously furnished with interesting objects. It has a tiny chapel on its top floor, and a medieval bedroom. Its library contains a collection of documents relating to the Wild Geese, Irishmen who served in European armies in the 17th and 18th centuries. There is also a collection of weaponry from the Middle Ages and earlier. It is said that Sir Walter Raleigh and the poet Edmund Spenser met here while they were both serving in Ireland.

Situated on the south bank of the Shannon Estuary, **Foynes** ㊽ played an important part in aviation history. In the late 1930s flying boats would land on the sheltered stretch of the Shannon between Foynes Island and the shore, having made the transatlantic crossing from Newfoundland. **Foynes Museum** (tel: 069-65416, admission fee, closed Nov–Mar except by appointment)

Map, page 170

Rathkeale's ancient origins are underlined by its Gaelic name, Ráth Caola, meaning Caola's Ring-fort.

BELOW: slowly through the lanes of Limerick.

commemorates those days with models and photographs, and includes the original terminal building, radio room and weather forecasting equipment. It was at Foynes during the flying boat days that Irish Coffee – coffee and whiskey topped with whipped cream – was invented by an enterprising barman, Joe Sheridan, who wanted to cheer up a group of cold, travel-weary passengers who had been forced back by bad weather.

Glin derives from the Gaelic An Gleann, meaning The Valley. It is an important centre for the dairy industry.

There is a pleasant drive along the wooded shores of the estuary to **Glin Castle** ❹ (tel: 068-34173, admission fee. By appointment outside May and June). There has been a Fitzgerald castle on this site, right on the banks of the Shannon, for over 700 years. The present house, which is surrounded by formal gardens and parkland, is an 18th-century building. The crennelations and Gothic details which make it look like a fairy-tale castle were added in the mid-19th century. There is an amazing "flying staircase" in its entrance hall with delicate balustrades and a mahogany handrail. The hall also has a superb plaster work ceiling. The head of the Fitzgerald clan is known as the Knight of Glin. The present (29th) Knight, Desmond Fitzgerald, is a keen campaigner for Irish heritage, and an authority on Georgian furniture and Irish painting. The interior of the house is impeccable, and houses an impressive collection of 18th-century furniture, ceramic and paintings.

From Glin it is only 7 km (4 miles) to **Tarbert** where a car ferry will take you across the Shannon Estuary in 20 minutes to County Clare.

The coast of West Clare

BELOW: a fresh catch at Carrigaholt.

From Ennis take the N68 to Kilrush. Kilrush is 5½ miles (9 km) west of Killimer, where the car ferry from north Kerry docks. **Kilrush** ❺, with a population of 2740, is the biggest town, or village if you prefer, on the coast of west Clare. Like Adare, Kilrush was designed by a local landlord in the 18th century to complement his estate. Unlike Adare's cottagey English pastiche, the style chosen for Kilrush is pleasantly neo-classical, with wide streets and a main square big enough to accommodate horse fairs which are still held there regularly. Kilrush became popular as a holiday resort in the 19th century. The **Kilrush Heritage Centre** (tel: 065-905 1577, admission fee, closed Oct–Apr) in the main square expounds on local history.

The ruins of the Vandeleur family mansion, which was destroyed by fire in 1897, are at the centre of the 420-acre (170-hectare) **Kilrush Forest Park** (freely accessible). The Vandeleur Walled Garden (tel: 065-905 1760, admission fee) has been replanted and is slowly maturing. A 15-minute boat ride from Kilrush marina will take you to **Scattery Island** which has a 6th-century monastery founded by St Senan, the remains of five churches and a round tower. **Scattery Island Visitor Centre** (tel: 065-905 2139, closed mid-Sept to mid-June) explains the history of the island.

Kilkee, 8½ miles (13 km) to the west, is on the Atlantic coast of Clare, as opposed to the banks of the Shannon Estuary, and has a good sandy beach. There is a scenic drive from there south to **Loop Head** lighthouse, a round trip of about 34 miles (55km). At **Carrigaholt** there is a 16th-century tower house beside the pier with good views from its top floor across the Shannon Estuary to north Kerry. A **dolphin watching cruise** (tel: 065-905 1327, www.shannondolphins.ie, open Apr–Oct) operates from Carrigaholt daily in summer, weather permitting, to watch families of bottle-nosed dolphins playing in the estuary.

There are good sandy beaches, popular with surfers, wind surfers and families, all the way up the coast to Lahinch. **Lahinch** is chiefly famous for its golf links. **Ennistymon**, 2½ miles (4 km) inland is a charming, old-fashioned resort town on the **Cullenagh River** which has retained many original wooden shop fronts. The river has a series of waterfalls visible from its seven-arched bridge.

A short (5½-mile/9-km) drive inland from Ennistymon will allow you to visit the **Burren Centre** (tel: 065-708 8030, admission fee, closed Nov–mid-Mar except by appointment) at **Kilfenora** ❺. The small, low-tech visitor centre provides a good introduction to this unusual region and has an excellent video on the Burren landscape commentated by naturalist Eamonn De Buitléar. This tiny village also has the remains of a 12th-century cathedral and three 12th-century high crosses with weathered but still decipherable carvings.

All roads around here lead to the **Cliffs of Moher** ❺, or so it seems from the innumerable signposts. Park at the **Visitor Centre** (tel: 065-708 1565, open, year round) which will introduce you to the flora and fauna of the area, and explain the local bird life. Don't be put off by the crowds and the buskers at the bottom of the hill – the razzmatazz is easy to escape by simply walking up to the cliffs themselves. The great, dark shale and sandstone cliffs are magnificent, rising 650 ft (200 metres) sheer above the Atlantic and stretching for about 5 miles (8km). At their base the Atlantic waves throw white spume on to jagged stacks. In May–June you can spot comical-looking puffins

Map, page 170

ABOVE: the Sea Life Centre at Lahinch. **BELOW:** pitch and putt at Lahinch.

ABOVE:
fresh produce on
sale at Ailwee Cave.

nesting on the ledges, while other seabirds wheel around in the up-currents.

Doolin (also called Roadford on some maps) is a tiny village consisting of numerous B&Bs and hostels, several restaurants and three pubs. The pubs are renowned for traditional music. Some young musicians spend the whole summer camping here, learning from their elders.

There is an open-boat ferry from Doolin pier to the smallest of the bleak but romantic **Aran Islands**, which makes an interesting day trip *(see pages 253–4)*.

The Burren

You will have noticed an absence of trees on driving up the coast. The Atlantic wind means that trees grow very slowly here, and seldom reach any great height. Many were cut down for fuel in the past 150 years when times were hard, and there is no tradition of replacing them.

Beyond Doolin the deeply fissured limestone plateau of the **Burren** dominates. The limestone is revealed in great irregular slabs known as pavements, with deep cracks between them. Their geological name is karst, from an area in Yugoslavia with similar terrain. Turloughs, seasonal lakes which disappear underground in dry weather, appear at times on the plateau's surface. As far as the eye can see the landscape is grey, which comes as quite a shock after the predominant green of the rest of Ireland. So barren did it look to Oliver Cromwell's troops in the 17th century that they declared that here was neither wood to hang a man, water to drown him nor earth to bury him. The Burren is of immense botanical interest *(see feature on pages 226–7)*. Unfortunately some tourists have taken to building tiny dolmens, destroying the limestone pavement and stone walls in the search for building materials. You are advised to take nothing but photographs and leave nothing but footprints.

BELOW: a waterfall
in Ailwee Cave.

The best Burren drive goes inland through **Lisdoonvarna** ㊾, an odd little spa town with hot water springs, where Ireland's bachelor farmers congregate in September for the Matchmaking Festival at which they attempt, usually half-heartedly, to find a wife. Continue down the switchback **Corkscrew Hill** to **Ballyvaughan**, a lively little seaside village, and back to Lisdoonvarna around **Black Head**. Scattered throughout the region are tombs, chambers and dolmens of the Stone Age, notably near Corkscrew Hill, the Poulnabrone Dolmen, 2500BC. Beyond Black Head the three **Aran Islands**, are visible in the west. For more information see www.burrenbeo.com, which also has contact details of local guides.

If you are keen to see the Burren from the inside, stop at Ballyvaughan to visit **Ailwee Cave** (tel: 065-707 7036, admission fee). The guided tour takes you through a tunnel stretching for ¾ mile (1 km) into the Burren which contains stalactites and stalagmites, and ends at a waterfall which is floodlit from below.

There is a pleasant scenic drive from Ballyvaughan along the south shore of Galway Bay to **Kinvara**, a charming little fishing village at the head of Galway Bay, with a grassy quayside. Kinvara is increasingly popular with visitors, who enjoy its old-fashioned pubs and more up-to-the-minute restaurants. The highlight of the year is the annual *Cruinniú na mBád* in mid-August, literally "the gathering of the boats". This is a festive regatta in which traditional Connemara sailing craft – the famous brown-sailed Galway Hookers – which were once used to carry turf across the bay, race against each other in a grand spectacle.

The other sight to see in Kinvara is the floodlit **Dunguaire Castle** (tel: 061-360 788, admission fee, closed Nov–Apr), a four-storey tower house built by the shore in 1520. At night this lonely sentinel is used for medieval banqueting, hence the floodlighting.

The easiest way back to the N18 from Kinvara is the R347 Ardrahan road. Turn right at the N18 in the Gort direction to visit **Thoor Ballylee ⑤**, a 16th-century tower house which was the summer home of the Nobel prize-winning poet W. B. Yeats from 1917 to 1928. The tower is carefully restored and contains much of Yeats's original furniture, but the incessant audio commentary that follows you around the interior is unnecessarily intrusive. It is beautifully situated in a wooded area near a stream.

The tower house was discovered for the poet by his benefactor, Lady Gregory (1852–1932), herself a playwright and collector of folklore. Her house at **Coole Park ⑤** just off the Gort road was demolished in 1947, but its grounds are now a national park with a deer enclosure, forest walks and a lake whose petrified trees stick out of the water. In the walled garden is a great copper beech tree on which Lady Gregory's guests – Yeats, the playwrights George Bernard Shaw, J. M. Synge and Sean O'Casey, the poet John Masefield and the painter Augustus John – carved their initials.

The N18 continues south to Ennis and north to Galway. ❑

Map, page 170

ABOVE: the autograph tree at Coole Park.
BELOW: Dunguaire Castle, Kinvara.

THE BURREN

North Clare contains one of Ireland's strangest landscapes, a treeless limestone plateau which is a place of pilgrimage for botanists and geologists

A frustrated general serving Oliver Cromwell, one of the many ruthless invaders from across the Irish Sea, famously condemned this bleak place as having "not enough wood to hang a man, not enough water to drown him, not enough clay to cover his corpse." The view probably hasn't changed much in 350 years, but now the Burren (meaning great rock) is a national park. It covers 500 sq. km (200 sq. miles) of lunar-like limestone formation with delicate flora and fauna of Arctic, Alpine and Mediterranean origin, brought to the area by migrating birds. Here you will find, in seasonal abundance – but protected by the State – orchids, the purple bloody cranesbill and azaleas. The Burren is also an area of potholes, seasonal lakes, caves and streams.

THE VIEW FROM CORKSCREW HILL

Properly appreciating the extraordinary nature of the place requires some study. The Burren Experience, on the northside of Ballyvaughan village, on the Kinvara road, gives an introduction, but a finer overview can be had at the original Burren Centre, to the south in Kilfenora village. A good overall view of this "stony district" can be had from the so-called "Corkscrew" Hill on the road lining Ballyvaughan with Lisdoonvarna, but by far the best way to explore the fissured terrain is on foot.

Scattered throughout the region are tombs, chambers and dolmens of the Stone Age – notably, near Corkscrew Hill, the famous Poulnabrone Dolmen, 2500BC.

▽ OCEAN FURY
Co. Clare is very much part of the western seaboard, from its natural boundary of the Shannon estuary to its northern border with Galway. The full force of the Atlantic can be felt here and lighthouses played a vital part in warning ships clear of the treacherous coastline.

◁ A HARDY BREED
It is surprising to find, in such a stony landscape, pockets of small green fields. But sheep farmers need to be a determined breed to survive the bleak winters in the west of Ireland. Animal farming has always flourished, though, because of the Burren's natural mineral wealth, which has proved particularly beneficial for horse breeding.

THE TOMBS THAT HAVE DEFIED TIME

Poulnabrone Dolmen (above) dates from 2500BC and is a striking example of the many ancient monuments which are particularly common in this part of Ireland because of the ready availability of limestone slabs. Its name means "pool of sorrows". Because its massive cap-stone is set at an angle, it has been fancifully been called a launching-pad for a Stone Age missile.

Such single-chambered portal graves were originally covered with a mound of earth and stones, and are a testament to the great reverence the Neolithic people had for their dead.

Passage-graves, in which the burial chamber was reached through a passage, reveal sophisticated building techniques and often intricate abstract carvings. Some of Europe's most spectacular examples can be seen at Newgrange, west of Drogheda in Co. Louth.

Stone circles, which served as prehistoric temples, are probably related to the megalithic tombs. Some of the most impressive can be found at Lough Gur in Co. Limerick and near Hollywood in Co. Wicklow.

The commonest monument is the ring fort – about 30,000 survive. These were circular stone defences surrounding dwellings or royal seats.

◁ BRONZE AGE SECRETS

Carran, to the east of the Burren, means the Cairn and has yielded up some of the most useful archaeological evidence of Bronze Age life. The stones that today form walls to keep the wind at bay were then used to construct a great cairn of stones 8 ft high and 50 ft in diameter (2.4 by 15 metres) which protected the bodies in the burial mound. At Kilnaboy, in the upland part of the Burren, the magnificent stone fort of Cahercommaun, dating from the 7th to the 10th centuries. The outermost of its three massive walls was 450 ft (140 metres) in diameter.

△ AN ANCIENT RUIN

Lemaneagh Castle, on route R476 from Kilfenora through Killinaboy, dates from 1480. It was once owned by a formidable woman, Máire Rua McMahon (Red-haired Mary), who saw off two husbands, including one of Oliver Cromwell's officers, but she held on to Lemaneagh.

▽ PLETHORA OF PLANTS

Pictured below is bird's-foot trefoil (*Lotus corniculatus*), one of the many plants which flourish in the apparently inhospitable landscape of the Burren. They are nurtured by a unique combination of soil, heat and mositure.

◁ LUNAR LANDSCAPE

This bleak limestone terrain had its origins 70 million years ago when shells of marine animals were compacted on the seabed and later pushed above the waves by geological shifts. A soft rock, the limestone has been eroded by wind and rain, creating cracks and crevices which both drain off rainwater and provide shelter for the remarkable variety of fauna.

Midlands and Far West Region

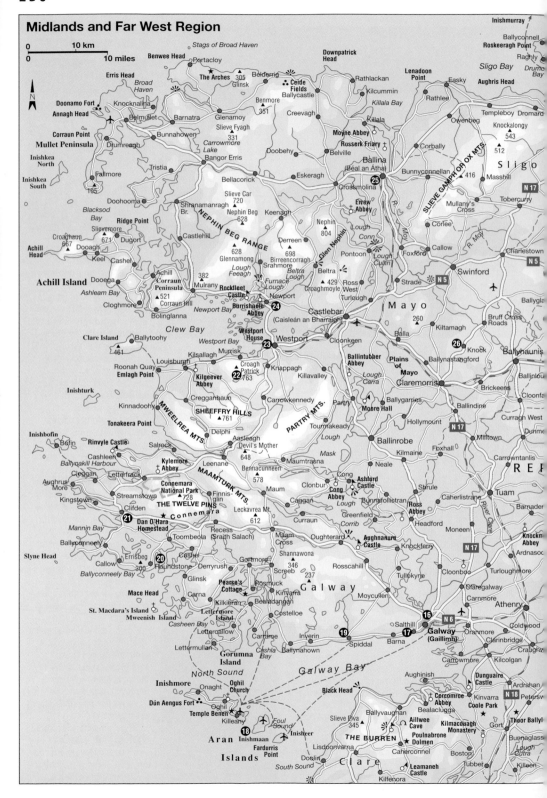

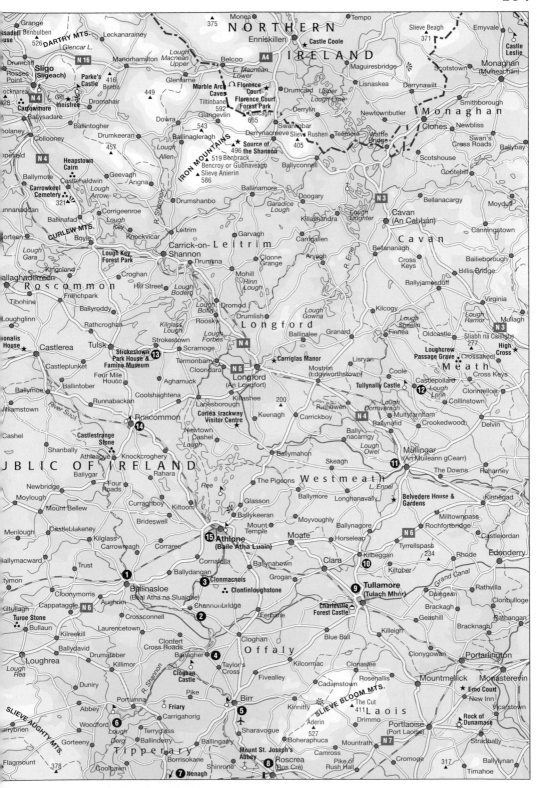

THE MIDLANDS

Water, in the form of bogs, lakes and rivers, dominates this often overlooked region. Fishing and boating are the big attractions, and the landscapes are seductive

Map, page 230

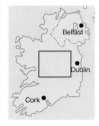

I rish schoolchildren used to be taught that Ireland could be visualised as a saucer, the raised rim standing for the hilly coastal regions, and the flat base representing the low-lying Midlands. Not only are the Midlands low-lying; a high proportion of the so-called land is in fact water of one kind or another, and if not water, then it is bog. The tract of country running north from County Laois through Offaly, Westmeath, Longford and Roscommon consists of bog pasture and water: canals, scores of rivers, hundreds of lakes and streams, thousands of ditches, all of them feeding into the River Shannon which bisects the region. Little wonder that many of the visitors to the region are keen anglers.

Most visitors to Ireland who venture beyond Dublin go either to the coastal areas or the mountain and wilderness areas. The Midlands of Ireland have to work harder to attract visitors than naturally spectacular places like Killarney or Connemara. Vast improvements have taken place over the past 10 years to ensure that visitors will be entertained and looked after. Hotels, restaurants and B&Bs have improved greatly, while major heritage attractions like Strokestown House and Famine Museum, Carriglas Manor, Birr Castle Gardens and Emo Court are being enthusiastically discovered by independent travellers, and are even tempting the occasional tour bus away from the beaten track.

The towns of the Midlands are not especially exciting. While it's one thing to pass through and admire their old-fashioned charm, most visitors are probably very glad that they don't have to live full-time in these small, architecturally undistinguished, often culturally dormant communities. Nevertheless, their shops and pubs can be enjoyable if you are susceptible to antiquated ways of doing things. Readers of William Trevor's Irish short stories will feel at home in the Midlands. "Time warp" is the expression that comes to mind. You are far more likely to find a bar with groceries on one side and tall stools, whiskey and Guinness on the other in the Midlands than you are in the more picturesque and fashionable Connemara or West Cork.

PRECEDING PAGES: Lough Key. **LEFT:** fresh fruit at the fete. **BELOW:** farmers confer at market.

Bog Rail Tour

Ballinasloe ❶, the chief town of east County Galway, has long been an important crossing place of the **River Suck**, and marks a kind of border, more psychological than physical between the west of Ireland and the Midlands. Every year during the first week of October the oldest horse fair in Europe takes place here.

Take the R357 to **Shannonbridge ❷**. This is the point where county Galway meets counties Offaly and Roscommon, and the River Suck flows into the River Shannon. You will see a lot of bog in the Midlands, in various stages of development, and the **Clonmacnoise and West Offaly Railway** (tel: 090 967 4114, admis-

The 13-ft (4-metre) Cross of the Scriptures at Clonmacnoise dates from the 10th century and has scenes from the Last Judgment and the Crucifixion.

BELOW: roadside sales; O'Rourke's Tower, Clonmacnoise, dating from 1124.

sion fee, closed Nov–Mar) just outside Shannonbridge on the R357, provides an excellent introduction to its flora and fauna. The narrow-gauge railway takes a slow 5-mile (8-km) circular tour across the **Blackwater Bog**. Ironically, it is run by **Bord na Mona**, the state-run Irish Peat Board, who also run the nearby **Blackwater Power Station**, which is powered by peat, as the brown smoke belching from its chimneys confirms. The tour includes a view of the various stages in harvesting the peat, and you can have a go yourself with a special sharp spade called a slane. The tour also gives you a close-up view of the plants that thrive in this intensely acid environment.

Clonmacnoise ❸ (tel: 090 967 4195, daily, admission fee) is one of Ireland's most important monastic sites, superbly located on a bend in the River Shannon. It was built on an esker, or natural gravel ridge, that overlooks a large marshy area. The monastery was founded in AD545 by St Kieran and was the burial place of the Kings of Connaught and Tara. While it may appear remote today, in earlier centuries transport for pilgrims was easier by water than over land.

The earliest of the surviving ruins dates from the 9th century. The monastery was regularly plundered from then onwards by the Irish, the Vikings and the Anglo-Normans until it was destroyed in the Elizabethan wars of the mid-16th century by the English garrison from Athlone. Nevertheless, there is still plenty to be seen. The Visitor Centre has a collection of carved grave slabs dating from the 9th to the 12th centuries, as well as a helpful audio-visual presentation.

Among the older surviving buildings of the complex are the shell of a small cathedral, two round towers, the remains of eight smaller churches and several high crosses. There are various doorways and chancel arches in the Irish

Map, page 230

Romanesque style. One of the churches, Temple Connor, was restored by the Church of Ireland in 1911 and is used for services.

Around Lough Derg

Head south for **Shannon Harbour**, the junction of the Grand Canal and the River Shannon which is a popular mooring place for river cruisers. About 5 miles (8 km) further south is **Banagher ❹**, another popular boating centre with a new marina. This pretty, one-street village will be eerie and empty in winter, and bustling with river enthusiasts in summer. Signposted from the centre of the village and lying a mile or so outside it is the lovingly restored **Cloghan Castle** (used for private functions only).

Birr ❺ is an attractive Georgian town, more or less in the centre of Ireland, dominated by **Birr Castle and Demesne** (tel: 0509-20336, admission fee). The gardens of Birr Castle cover 100 acres (40 hectares) and have more than 1,000 species of trees and shrubs with an especially strong Chinese and Himalayan collection. In spring, magnolias, crab apples and cherries will be in flower; in the autumn, maples, chestnut and weeping beech supply colour. The box hedges subdividing the formal gardens are the highest in the world.

The 17th-century castle is private, but its stable block now houses **Ireland's Historic Science Centre** (tel. as above). The owners of Birr Castle, the Parsons family, later ennobled as the Earls of Rosse, have manifested a scientific bent for several generations. In the 1840s the 3rd Earl of Rosse built the Great Telescope which enabled him to see further into space than any of his contemporaries. The telescope, which has a 56-ft (17-metre) tube and a 6-ft (1.8-metre) mirror, was in use until 1908 and has been restored to working order.

TIP

Fans of Georgian houses can find some good examples in Birr, in John's Mall and Oxmantown Mall.

BELOW: Birr Castle.

ABOVE: good country for walkers.

BELOW: Nenagh.

Walk into town along **Oxmanton Mall**, a tree-lined thoroughfare which leads from the castle gates past a row of elegant Georgian houses. **Emmet Square** in the town centre is the location of **Dooly's Hotel** (1740, www.doolyshotel.com) which gave its name to the Galway Blazers when they set fire to it after a Hunt Ball in 1809, almost but not quite destroying the building.

From Birr, head to **Borrisokane** and the western shores of **Lough Derg ❻**. At Lough Derg the Shannon widens into a 50 sq. mile (130 sq. km) lake that is about 10 miles (16km) across at its widest point. This side is in County Tipperary and the west of the lake is in County Clare. The circular **Lough Derg Drive** (about 50 miles/90km) passes through a succession of pretty villages, but the lake itself is not always visible. The villages on this side of Lough Derg are peaceful, out-of-the-way places to stay that have recently been gaining in popularity. Most visitors either have a boat of some kind or are interested in fishing – mainly coarse angling – on the lake. Others enjoy walking, both near the lake and on the other side of Birr in the way-marked trails of the **Slieve Bloom Mountains**.

Terryglass is one of the prettiest villages near Lough Derg, although you have to leave the main road to find the lake. **Dromineer** on the other hand is right on the water, and has a ruined castle on its pier. Many of the people you meet in the pubs will be temporarily living on river cruisers which they own or have hired.

Nenagh ❼ is a Tipperary market town with the disadvantage of being on the busy Dublin-Limerick main road. All that remains of the original Norman settlement is the **Nenagh Castle Keep**, or donjon, with walls 20 ft (6 metres) thick. It reaches to a height of 100 ft (30 metres). Across the road in the

Governor's House of the old town gaol is the **Nenagh Heritage Centre** (tel: 067-32633, admission fee) which includes the condemned cells and execution room of the gaol, and a museum of rural life

Map, page 230

Roscrea 8, further up the N7 in the Dublin direction, is also plagued by traffic. In fact, the Dublin–Limerick road actually cuts through the remains of the 12th-century **St Cronan's Abbey**. As you sit in a traffic jam on a bend in the road, you will probably see the west facade, which is all that remains, with a round-arched doorway containing a moulded figure of St Cronan. Roscrea is worth visiting to see its Norman castle which contains an 18th-century town house, Damer House, within its walls. The 13th-century castle is a polygonal structure with two D-shaped towers. The gate house is topped by 18th-century gables and chimneys. It now houses the **Roscrea Heritage Centre** (tel: 0505-21850, admission fee also includes Damer House) which has an interesting exhibit on Norman castles.

The 8th-century Book of Dimma, which once belonged to Roscrea monastery, can now be seen in Trinity College, Dublin. It includes a copy of the Gospels.

Damer House, which stands inside the castle walls, is an elegant, three-storied house dating from the 18th century with a plain, symmetrical facade and a handsome pine staircase. It was completed in the 1720s and became a Bishop's Palace before being converted to a military barracks in 1798. It was very nearly demolished in the 1970s to make room for a car park but was saved through the vigilance of the Irish Georgian Society.

Great Irish houses

Travel east again, by-passing **Portlaoise**, to visit **Emo Court** (tel: 0502-26573, admission fee; house closed Nov–Mar). This fine Georgian mansion was built in 1792 for the Earl of Portarlington in the Classical style by James

BELOW: tranquillity on the borders of Co. Meath and Co. Cavan.

Gandon, best known for Dublin's Four Courts and Custom House *(see pages 159 and 153 respectively)*. It was restored and donated to the nation in 1996 by a private benefactor. The interior has some fine examples of plaster work. The gardens were created in two parts. The Clucker, named because it was once the site of the nun's quarters of an ancient abbey, is planted with azaleas, rhododendrons and Japanese maples. The Grapery is planted with trees and shrubs and leads down to the peaceful lakeside walk.

Half a mile west of Tullamore is Shrah Castle, built in 1588. It is a good example of the small fortified house that Elizabethan settlers constructed.

There is another interesting recently restored house in an entirely different style to the north near **Tullamore ❾**, **Charleville Forest Castle** (tel: 0506-21279, May–Sept 10am–6pm daily, otherwise by appointment, admission fee). The house was designed by Francis Johnston in 1798 in the neo-Gothic style. It is built of grey limestone. An internal gallery extends the full length of the garden front, and is decorated with plaster work. The morning room, music room and dining room are also of impressive size and proportion, and are decorated in the William Morris style. Five avenues lined by Irish yew trees radiate from the house. The grounds include many impressive trees including an oak which is believed to be 700 years old. Tullamore is also where Irish Mist and Tullamore Dew liqueurs are made. The drinks' histories and traditional distilling methods are explained in the Tullamore Dew Heritage Centre (tel: 0506 25015, daily all year, admission fee).

Around Lough Ennel

Below: Lough Ennel; at play in Bantry Golf Club.

Follow the N52 from Tullamore for 7½ miles (12 km) north to **Kilbeggan ❿**. **Locke's Distillery** (tel: 0506-32134, admission fee), advertised for miles around, is on the banks of the River Brosna which is fed by springs from

nearby Lough Ennel. It is said that all good whiskey depends on the water that goes into the distillation process. The distillery was in use from 1757 to 1953, and much of the original equipment is still in place. There are enticing smells of malt and oak as you view the equipment, and a tasting before you leave rounds off the visit appropriately.

The low-lying **Lough Ennel** can be seen from the N52 between Kilbeggan and Mullingar. It is a popular place for swimming, boating and fishing. The recently restored **Belvedere House and Gardens** (tel: 044-49060, open daily, admission fee) is remarkable for its beautiful setting, with terraced gardens descending in three stages to the shores of the lake. The family history behind Belvedere House is far from edifying – the first Earl of Belvedere, who built the house as a fishing lodge in 1740, spent his life fighting with his younger brothers, and imprisoned his wife for 31 years in another house on suspicion of an adulterous affair with one of them. He actually built a ruin, in a part of the world where you will have noticed that ruins abound, in order to block his view of the house where his brother lived. This large and oddly attractive Gothic folly is known as the **Jealous Wall**.

Mullingar ⑪, the chief town of County Westmeath, is an important cattle-dealing centre which is also popular with anglers. If things military appeal to you, the **Military Museum** (tel: 044-48391, phone in advance for appointment) should not be missed. It contains weaponry from both world wars, uniforms and flags from all over the world and a section dedicated to the old IRA (as distinct from the more recent incarnation). The museum is run by the army, curated by an army captain who will show you around and is actually located in the **Columb Barracks**.

Map, page 230

Fishermen like Irish trout because most are wild – a rarity in Europe. Some lakes are stocked with fully grown fish, but fingerlings reared from wild stock are more usual. There are also some lakes stocked with rainbow trout.

BELOW: brown trout can be found in Lough Ennel.

Lady Antonia Fraser, part of the Longford clan, is famous as the biographer of Mary Queen of Scots and Oliver Cromwell. She is married to the playwright Harold Pinter.

BELOW: Lough Derravaragh.

Around Lough Derravaragh

Tullynally Castle (tel: 044-61159, admission fee; house closed Sept–Apr, admission fee), to the north of Mullingar, just beyond **Castlepollard** ⑫, used to be known as Pakenham Hall. This massive, grey stone, turreted house overlooking **Lough Derravaragh** is well worth a visit. It has been the seat of the Pakenham family, now the Earls of Longford, since 1655. The current family includes the Socialist peer, Lord Longford, his biographer wife Elizabeth, his historian son Thomas, and their daughters, biographer Antonia Fraser and novelist Rachel Billington. The castle is the home of Thomas Pakenham.

The original fort was converted into a two-storey house in the 18th century. A Gothic facade was added in the early 19th century, and in the mid-19th century Sir Richard Morrison designed the central tower and two wings. There is an entertaining upstairs-downstairs guided tour, which includes the Great Hall, the library (which is one of Ireland's largest private collections with over 8,000 volumes), the drawing room and also the kitchen and laundry, fully equipped as in Victorian times. The landscaped gardens, which include a grotto, have spectacular views of Lough Derravaragh.

Multyfarnham, a 2-mile (3-km) detour off the N4 Longford road, is a one-street town with some good old-fashioned pubs. Multyfarnham's **Cistercian monastery**, founded in 1306, has an attractive slender tower 88 ft (27 metres) high. The abbey was restored by the Franciscans in 1973. Its new stained-glass windows show the legend of the Children of Lir who were turned into swans and lived nearby on Lough Derravaragh. The Franciscans have built a life-size Stations of the Cross in a grove of evergreens beside a fast-flowing stream.

Just to the north of Longford is **Carrigglas Manor**. Oddly enough, its stables are considered more interesting architecturally than the grand house itself. They were designed by James Gandon, architect of the Dublin Custom House *(see page 153)*. To the south of Longford off the R397, the **Corlea Trackway Visitor Centre** at Kenagh (tel: 043-22386, open daily, Apr–Sept, admission fee) interprets an iron age Bog Road dating from 148 BC – the largest of its kind ever to be uncovered in Europe.

If you can only visit one stately home in the Midlands, then follow the N5 for 25 miles (40 km) west of Longford to **Strokestown Park House and Famine Museum** (tel: 078-33013, admission fee, closed Nov–Mar except for pre-booked tours). The village leads to an imposing Georgian-Gothic arch which leads to the house. The village, with its exceptionally broad main street, was laid out in the early 19th century to complement the new entrance. The house itself is a fine Palladian mansion designed by Sir Richard Cassels in the 1730s. The central block was the family's residence while the wings either side contained the stables and the kitchen areas. The kitchen is especially interesting. A gallery runs above it from which the lady of the house could oversee the staff without entering the kitchen itself. Each Monday morning she would drop a menu with instructions for the week's meals. Tunnels to hide the movements of tradesmen and servants link the main block of the house to the kitchens and stables. The walled garden has also been restored in line with horticultural practices of the 18th century.

The house, which is accessible by guided tour only (40 minutes) was at the centre of a large estate. It stayed in the Mahon family until 1979 when it was bought by a local businessman and restored. Allow another hour to do justice

The great period of country house building in Ireland began in the early 1720s. English architects who had studied in Italy introduced Palladianism and soon a diluted version of the style appeared everywhere, from village churches to farmhouses.

BELOW:
traditional piper.

Map, page 230

In Roscommon town itself, the ruins of a Dominican priory contain the tomb of the priory's 13th-century founder, Felim O Connor. The carved tomb vividly displays the clothes and armour worn at that time.

to the **Famine Museum**, which is housed in the stable yard. This presents a vivid and comprehensive display which traces the history of the family and the estate and links this to the national events in the mid-19th century which led to Ireland's Great Famine and the subsequent mass emigration to America, England and elsewhere. West of Strokestown where the N5 crosses the R367 lies **Tulsk** and the **Cruachan Visitors Centre** (tel: 071 963 9268, Mon–Sat all year and Sun June–Oct, admission fee), which explores the archaeological, historical and mythological aspects of Cruachan, burial place of the Kings of Connacht and a site rich in legend.

Roscommon ⓮, to the south of Tulsk, is a pleasant market town built on a low hill in the midst of rich cattle and sheep country. **Roscommon Castle** (freely accessible), to the north of the town, is an impressive ruin on a green field site. It was originally a 13th-century Norman stronghold. It has massive walls defended by round bastions at each corner, and the mullioned windows can still be seen in some of the remaining walls.

Around Lough Ree

Thanks to the new ring road around Athlone, it is possible to drive from Roscommon to **Glasson** which is about 6 miles (10 km) outside Athlone, without going through Athlone's often traffic-clogged centre. Glasson is one of a series of pretty villages on the eastern shore of **Lough Ree**, which is part of the **River Shannon**. There are good amenities for water sports, attractive country pubs and restaurants, and a series of lake shore and forest walks.

The poet and dramatist Oliver Goldsmith (1730–74), best known for his 1773 comedy *She Stoops to Conquer*, is associated with this area. The house where he grew up, now in ruins, **Lissoy Parsonage**, can be visited near the village called **The Pigeons**.

Athlone ⓯, which straddles the **River Shannon** at an important strategic point to the south of Lough Ree, has the distinction of being half in County Westmeath and half in County Roscommon. It is now an important commercial centre, and the busiest town in the Midlands. **Athlone Castle** (tel: 090 644 2100, admission fee, closed Oct–Apr) is a squat, 13th-century building, which was badly damaged in 1690 when the Irish made a stand here against the advance of Oliver Cromwell's forces. The castle keep now houses a **Folk Museum** which includes souvenirs of the tenor John McCormack, who was born in Athlone in 1884. The area behind the castle is being promoted as Athlone's "Left Bank". There are some nice old town houses dating from the 18th and 19th centuries, several good restaurants and bars, but the project has a way to go yet.

You will notice that even relatively modest restaurants in Athlone tend to have trilingual menus. This is because the town is very popular with holiday makers on Shannon cruisers, most of whom eat ashore as often as they can. The nicest thing to do in Athlone is to take a boat trip up the Shannon to Lough Ree. Boats leave regularly between June and August for a 90-minute cruise from the **Jolly Mariner Marina** (tel: 0902-72892) on the Shannon's Right (west) Bank. ❑

BELOW: an Athlone shopkeeper. **RIGHT:** where freedom is a cabin cruiser.

THE FAR WEST

Beyond Galway city lies a wild, romantic landscape at the very edge of Europe where Irish is still spoken. But can the increasing number of visitors still find solitude?

Map, page 230

Galway city ⓰ stands at the mouth of the salmon-filled river that flows between **Lough Corrib** and the sea. It began as a fishing village, but by the 13th century had become a walled and fortified town in the most sheltered corner of **Galway Bay**. The fishing village survived until the mid-1930s as a neat collection of picturesque thatched cottages. They were demolished, for sanitary reasons, and replaced by the present-day Claddagh, a cluster of grey, slated cottages. The place has given its name to the distinctive Claddagh finger-ring, carrying a crowned heart motif between two hands.

The city developed as a Norman-English settlement surrounded by hostile natives. Its governors were very loyal to the English crown and the city gained its Royal Charter, as an independent city state, from Richard III in 1484. This led to a long period of political stability, material prosperity and increased trade with England and the Continent. During this period the city was ruled by the representatives of the 14 most prominent families, or Tribes, and Galway is still known as the City of the Tribes.

The style in which they lived can be judged by what remains of their architecture. The **Church of St Nicholas**, on the market place, is the largest parish church of the medieval period in Ireland and has been the Anglican Cathedral since the Reformation. Lynch's Castle, town house of the premier Tribe, is now a bank on the main street, and **Browne's Gateway**, which was the entrance to the town house of another great merchant family, has been erected at **Eyre Square**, near the **John F. Kennedy Memorial Garden**.

Myth makers

In a country where myth is often as potent as history, and in a city much given to creative folklore, the visitor will hear much that must be taken with a grain of salt. One of the main tourist "sights" in Galway is **Lynch's Window** where, in 1493, Walter Lynch, mayor of the city, hanged his own son for the murder of a Spanish guest. It was a crime of passion and such was the son's popularity with the people that the mayor feared a mob would release him from jail. He then decided to perform the hangman's task himself. Some writers have speculated that this event originated the term "lynch law". However, historians have found no basis for the story in any of the contemporary records. But the window is worth seeing and is only around the corner from the Church of St Nicholas, where Christopher Columbus is reputed to have heard Mass before leaving to discover America. The "evidence" for this is that one of his crew was known as William of Galway.

Much more of the architectural excellence of this period in Galway's history would have survived had the

PRECEDING PAGES: Clifden, Connemara. **LEFT** and **BELOW:** turf is big business in the boggy Far West.

city fathers not backed the wrong political horse in the middle of the 17th century. But they staunchly backed England's Royalist forces against Cromwell's invading army and paid the price. When the city was forced to surrender in 1652, the Roundheads pillaged, plundered and burnt, destroying many of the finest stately homes. All that remains of the elaborate city walls is the portion known as the **Spanish Arch** across the river from Claddagh.

Although this military defeat resulted in the decline of Galway as a major port and commercial centre, it also began a new relationship between the city and its hinterland. Today, Galway is the only city or town in Ireland where two languages, English and Irish, can be heard spoken daily in the streets. In summer many other languages can be heard as the city has become one of the country's busiest tourist centres: the gateway to the Aran Islands, Connemara and Mayo.

Galway's gatherings

Galway today is a prosperous place. In 1986 it became Ireland's first newly created borough since independence was achieved, with a population of over 50,000. Alone among Irish cities it has managed to retain, virtually intact, the maze of narrow, winding streets that comprise its commercial centre. This extends from **Eyre Square**, through **Williamsgate Street**, **Shop Street** and **Mainguard Street** as far as **O'Brien's Bridge**, including the many streets that meander away toward the Corrib and the docks.

Although busier in summer than in winter, because of the influx of tourists, Galway is always a bustling place. It has a growing university (the original limestone building and quadrangle dates from 1849) as well as a College of Technology, two large hospitals, docks and a thriving industrial complex on the

ABOVE: Galway's slogan. **BELOW:** the city's High Street.

outskirts of the city. There are two theatres: **An Taibhdhearc** (pronounced *thive ark*), which stages plays in the Irish language; and the **Druid Theatre**, which has created a reputation that extends to the West End of London.

Kenny's bookshop (tel: 091-568544, 9am–6pm, Mon–Sat; www.kennys.ie) is on High Street. This four-storey cramped building, part of which dates from 1472, became a bookshop in 1942. It holds an unbelievable collection of books of antiquity as well as contemporary titles, old and new paintings and pieces of sculpture. It encourages browsing with a cup of tea and a chat with the Kenny family, who so obviously enjoy search, research and book queries.

The highlight of the year is the summer **Race Week**, which begins during the last week in July. The racecourse is situated on the slope of a hill at **Ballybrit**, about 4 miles (6 km) from the city centre and overlooking Galway Bay and the Aran Islands. It is as much a carnival as a race meeting and, although over £1 million is wagered daily, many of those attending remain in the popular enclosure and rarely see a horse, such is the variety of side-shows: hawkers, musicians, fortune-tellers, three-card-trick operators and travelling people who converge from all parts of Ireland. Such is the fun to be had at Ballybrit that the city closes down every afternoon to enable everyone to get there.

A breath of sea air

To recover from the excesses of a day at the races – not to mention the hectic nightlife that follows – victims would be well advised to head for the nearby seaside resort of **Salthill** ⑰ It is within pleasant walking distance from the city centre and, although it is not a particularly beautiful place – consisting mainly of functional tourist hotels, pubs, clubs and casinos, it has a magnificent 2-mile

Map, page 230

BELOW: Sunday lunchtime jazz in Galway's "Latin Quarter".

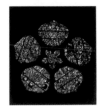

(3-km) stretch of promenade that skirts the sea, with an uninterrupted view of the bay and the Burren beyond. It is said locally that an early morning walk from one end of it to the other has the curative powers of two gins and tonics. **Leisure-land** (tel: 091-521455) has water-based amusement for the family with a 213-ft (65-metre) waterslide and tropical beach pool and treasure trove; an 80-ft (25-metre) swimming pool and an outdoor amusement park.

But gentler pleasures are also on hand. One could stand for hours on the **Salmon Weir Bridge**, which spans the river at the point where it flows out of Lough Corrib. Here the salmon lie in ever-shifting ranks waiting to assault the weir on their way upstream. The bridge leads to what was once Galway Jail, now the site of Ireland's newest cathedral. This is the **Catholic Cathedral of St Nicholas and Our Lady Assumed into Heaven**. Consecrated in 1965, it is constructed in an amazing variety of architectural styles in local limestone and Connemara marble. It also contains some unusual mosaics in its side-chapels; particularly the mortuary chapel where the lately-departed are presided over by images of John F. Kennedy and Pádraic Pearse, one of the leaders of the 1916 Easter Rising.

American connections

Above: a stained-glass window in the cathedral. **Below:** Pádraic O'Conaire's statue, Eyre Square.

President Reagan visited Galway during its quincentennial celebrations in 1984 and, like President Kennedy, who visited in 1963, is enrolled as a Free-man. The Kennedy visit is marked by a stone tablet in the garden named in his honour at **Eyre Square**.

At one of its corners stands a beautiful limestone statue of the writer, Pádraic O'Conaire. Although born in the city, he was reared in Connemara and wrote exclusively in Irish until his death at an early age in 1927. As he was as famous

for his nomadic life-style as he was for his writings and was very partial to the bottle when he had the price of it, some of the more respectable citizens were scandalised when it was proposed to erect this statue in his honour. It has long since become one of the country's showpieces, as most of the country's recently erected statuary is quite hideous, and Galway has the distinction of being the first town in Ireland to erect a memorial to a contemporary artist.

The striking fountain, with its triangular brown centrepieces, which stands behind **Browne's Gateway**, was erected to commemorate the city's quincentennial. The motif is the sails used on the traditional Claddagh fishing boats, known as hookers. They no longer exist in Claddagh but many of the surviving boats have been restored along the Connemara coast for use as pleasure craft.

Before venturing west from Galway it is necessary to know that without the benefit of a car (or a conducted coach tour) it is difficult, if not impossible, to explore Connemara and Mayo by public transport. Railways have almost vanished and buses are scarce. But the main roads are good and the secondary ones reasonably so, if only because most people who use them also travel by car.

Map, page 230

The Aran Islands

Before moving out of the city, though, it is worth casting an eye at the three **Aran Islands** ⑱ that straddle the mouth of the bay, like three limestone whales at rest on the surface of the Atlantic. Without the benefit of this natural breakwater, Galway Bay would be a very exposed harbour and it is from Galway that the regular ferry boats to Aran sail all through the year. A daily plane service to the three islands is run by Aer Arann (Aran Air, www.aerarannislands.ie) from Connemara Regional Airport, about a 40-minute drive from Galway City. The air

ABOVE: busking in the High Street.
BELOW: stone walls breaking the wind on the Aran Islands.

journey takes only 15 minutes; the sea journey three hours. However, the air journey costs much more. In summer (Jun–Sept) many small ferries run between **Ros a' Mhíl (Rossaveal)** on the Connemara coast and all three islands. The journey to Inisheer (the furthest island) takes approximately one hour.

The three Aran Islands, **Inishmore**, **Inishmaan** and **Inisheer**, have been inhabited long before recorded history and contain many pre-Christian and early-Christian remains. Most noteworthy is **Dún Aengus** stone fort on Inishmore, one of Europe's finest prehistoric monuments. Perched on the edge of a vertical 200-ft (60-metre) cliff, it consists of four semi-circular defensive walls.

The experts have failed to date Dún Aengus with any accuracy: some say 4,000BC and others 1,000 BC. But apart from its striking aspect and historic interest, the view from its ramparts is one of the most striking imaginable. On a clear day one can follow the sweep of coastline from Kerry and Clare to the south, as well as the length of Galway to the western extremity of Connemara.

The islands have long attracted artists, writers, philologists, antiquarians and film makers. Robert Flaherty's film *Man of Aran* (1934) made the islands known to a worldwide audience. The playwright John Millington Synge wrote his book *The Aran Islands* while living on Inishmaan, where he also heard the plot of his most famous play, *The Playboy of the Western World*. Inishmore has produced one internationally known writer, Liam O'Flaherty. Born in the shadow of Dún Aengus, he is famous for his nature stories and as author of the novel *The Informer* (filmed by John Ford in 1935).

Irish is the daily language of the people of Aran, but most are equally fluent in English. This is also true of the people living on the southern shore of the Connemara coast, across the bay. Both areas are part of what is known as the Gaeltacht. About 65,000 native speakers of Irish live in areas of varying sizes in Waterford, Cork, Kerry, Galway, Mayo and Donegal (though perhaps only 10,000 speak it regularly in the home).

The Gaeltacht

The Connemara Gaeltacht begins on the outskirts of Galway, on the coast road through **An Spidéal (Spiddal)** **⑲**. This is obvious to the tourist for, suddenly, the signposts are in Irish only instead of being bilingual. This is a recent innovation, brought about by public agitation in the 1970s as part of an effort to strengthen the role of Irish in everyday life. It also resulted in the setting-up of a special radio service for all the Gaeltacht areas with its headquarters in Connemara. (Because most existing road-maps still carry anglicised place-names, these forms are also given in brackets here).

Connemara is one of the most beautiful regions in Ireland and also one of the most barren. To travel through it is to understand why so many of its people are to be found in Boston, Birmingham and London. The amazing thing is that so many remained to eke out a precarious existence on the rugged, marshy land and on the sea. They are a hardy and resourceful people and one of the ways by which they supplement their income is through the illegal distillation of a white spirit called poteen: from the Irish *poitín*, a little pot. The tourist is bound to hear of it, and may even be offered some to

TIP

Avoid the Aran Islands during the summer peak. As many as 3,000 day-trippers can clog Inishmore's roads and overwhelm the population of 730.

BELOW: the Aran island of Inishmore.

drink or to buy, as it is now made in even greater quantities among the hills and on the remote lake and sea islands that abound in Connemara. It is made from a mixture of barley, sugar, yeast and water. The resulting liquid, or "wash", is then boiled over a constant flame and the steam run through a home-made still: usually a coil of narrow copper piping in a barrel through which cold water flows.

Before bottled gas was invented, the police were always on the look-out for the spiral of peat-smoke in isolated places. The pungent smell of the boiling "wash" made isolation necessary and the penalty for being caught in the act meant a heavy fine. Now the odds are in favour of the makers, and poteen costs about half the price of legal whiskey. If the liquid is run through the still three times the poteen is perfectly safe, if exceedingly fiery, to drink. One-run poteen, or poteen to which some unscrupulous distillers add commercial alcohol, can be very dangerous. Beware. For the benefit of those who like to live dangerously, the greatest centres of poteen-making in Connemara are **Leitir Móir (Lettermore)**, **Leitir Mealláin (Lettermullan)** and **Ros Muc (Rosmuck)**.

Bays and hills

By following the coast road to **Casla (Costelloe)**, then turning right to **Scrib (Screeb)** and then left again along the much-indented coast road through **Cill Chiaráin (Kilkieran)**, **Caiseal (Cashel)**, **Roundstone** ⓴ – where one re-enters the non-Gaeltacht part of Connemara – and on to Clifden, one sees all that typifies coastal Connemara. The land is painfully poor, with tracts of lake, mountain and moorland stretching as far as the eye can see to the north. To the south lie the deep, curling bays filled with islands and fringed by black, red and orange seaweed. Along the road, and away in the hills, are clusters of white-washed

Map, page 230

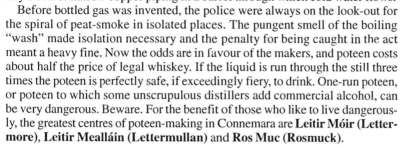

A cottage on Inisheer.

BELOW:
a tour by horse and trap on Inishmore.

cottages and modern bungalows. The village of Roundstone is outstanding, with a lovely bay and a lively harbour area. It contains no-frills restaurants and pubs and is a venue for deep-sea anglers. Here are small-scale craft industries, including a *bodhrán*-making business, open to visitors seven days a week. This one-sided drum is made of stretched goat skin and gives a variety of sounds, depending on the skill of the player.

A little-known gem is **St Macdara's Island**, lying a few miles off Connemara's coast near Roundstone. Although only 60 acres (24 hectares), it has an exquisite 6th-century oratory. It was named after St Macdara, a protector of sailors and the first recorded Irish saint to have a surname. There is no regular ferry service to the island, but local fishermen will transport visitors for a fee.

A lure for fishermen

Clifden ㉑ is the region's principal town and one of the best places to buy traditional tweed. Off the N59, 5 miles (8 km) outside Clifden on the Galway side is the **Dan O'Hara Homestead** which introduces the visitor to the life of a tenant farmer just prior to the Famine. The tour includes a visit to a neolithic site and a demonstration of turf cutting (tel: 095-21246, Apr–Oct daily 10am–6pm). If time permits, it would be worth continuing on this road towards Galway, through **Recess**, and **Oughterard**. This road affords a fine view of the **Twelve Pins** mountain range and the islands on Lough Corrib. Those who come to Ireland with a view to fishing for salmon, trout, and a variety of coarse fish would find an agreeable and rewarding base in any of the many hotels and guest-houses along this road. About 2 miles (3km) east of Oughterard is **Aughnanure Castle** (tel: 091-552214, May–Oct, admission fee). Built by an O'Flaherty in the 16th century, it

ABOVE: crosses made locally from Connemara marble.

BELOW: fresh lobsters on offer at the Oughterard House Hotel.

is picturesque and well preserved, an example of a tower house with two fortified enclosures and watch tower and a banqueting hall. It stands on a natural but drying-up moat on the shores of Lough Corrib.

From Clifden one can also enter **Mayo** by a pleasant route. It goes by **Kylemore Abbey**, one of Ireland's most-photographed buildings, which looks even better in reality. It is a late 19th-century limestone and granite building erected by a Liverpool merchant as a gift to his son, and is now run by the Benedictine nuns as a boarding-school for girls. The hall, Gothic chapel – a replica of Norwich Cathedral – and three reception rooms are open to visitors (tel: 095-41126, open daily). There's a visitor centre and a 6-acre (2.4-hectare) Victorian walled garden.

Mayo is Ireland's third largest county but most of its interesting features are in the western half, particularly along its varied coastline.

The road from Kylemore Abbey leads to **Leenane**, where the **Leenane Cultural Centre** (Mar–October), on the Clifden-Westport road, deals interestingly with sheep rearing, wool production and products. It is functioning with 20 breeds of sheep grazing locally. Further on is **Killary Harbour**, Ireland's only fjord – so deep and sheltered that it could accommodate the entire navy of any world power – and a left turn takes you to **Louisburgh**, a small town at the back of **Croagh Patrick** ㉒, Ireland's holy mountain. It is a place of pilgrimage for thousands on the last Sunday of July, but a climb to its summit, on a clear day, is rewarding for even the greatest unbeliever.

It affords one of the finest panoramic views in Ireland: out over the Atlantic and the offshore islands, to the west; south over the mountain fastnesses of Mayo and Connemara; the rolling plains of central Mayo to the east; the island-studded **Clew Bay** to the north with **Achill Island** looming in the distance. The English

Map, page 230

The bodhran, made locally, is a round goatskin tambourine or drum, and is played with a small stick.

BELOW: the much photographed Kylemore Abbey.

ABOVE: trying a fireman's hat for size at Westport.

BELOW: a typical quiet Mayo high street – this one is in Castlebar.

writer William Makepeace Thackeray, who visited the west in 1842, described the scenery around Clew Bay as the "most beautiful in the world".

Westport ㉓ (pop. 4,000) lies on an arm of Clew Bay and is unique among Irish towns in that it was designed to the plan of the well-known architect of the Georgian period, James Wyatt (1748–1813). The Mall, with its lime trees lining both sides of the **Carrowbeg River**, is one of the country's most charming thoroughfares. **Clare Island** is well worth visiting to learn the seafaring exploits of Grace O'Malley, a 16th-century pirate queen who preyed on cargo vessels. Clare Island has a population of about 350 and holds much interest for the botanist. It measures 3½ by 1½ miles (5.5km by 2.5km) and has a small hotel and B&Bs. There is a ferry service of 15 minutes from Roonagh Harbour, Louisburgh. **Westport House** (www.westporthouse.ie; closed Oct–Apr except Easter weekend), a stately home near the Quay, is home to the Altamont family. descendants of Grace O'Malley. The grounds have many amusements for children, including a zoo.

On the way from Westport to Achill Island the huge disused, arched railway bridge that dominates the little town of **Newport ㉔** is a sad comment on the social life of this area, and particularly Achill Island. It is all that remains of the railway that once linked the island and Westport but was closed in 1936.

Although Achill has been connected by a bridge to the mainland since 1888, it still retains many of the characteristics of an island. It is dominated by two mountains, skirted by wild moorland. The rest of the land is a dazzling combination of magnificent cliffs, golden strands, purple heather and scattered cottages that look even whiter than they are because of the dark background.

To the north lies one of the most desolate and depopulated areas in Ireland, the boglands of **Erris** that lead to the Erris Peninsula, where **Belmullet** is the

principal town. From Belmullet the coast road runs via Belderrig to Ballycastle. Between these two towns it passes the **Ceide Fields** (daily mid-Mar–Nov; tel: 096-43325 for winter opening) a Stone-Age excavation site which can hardly be missed thanks to its giant, pyramid-shaped visitor centre. Opposite the centre, the **Ceide Cliffs** attract geologists and birdwatchers.

The next town is **Killala**, which has a 10th-century round tower. It was here that the French forces landed during the 1798 Rising. Just outside the town is **Moyne Abbey**, founded by the Franciscans in 1460, and a little further to the south, near Ballina, is **Rosserk Friary**, a monastery from the same period. **Ballina** ㉕, Mayo's largest town (pop. 7,000), is good for shopping. Its cathedral is situated beside the ruins of a 15th-century Augustinian Friary. The more pleasant part of the town is along the river on the Sligo road.

Miracle at Knock

The journey coninues through wonderful scenery along the west coast of **Lough Conn** to arrive at **Castlebar**, County Mayo's capital. From here it is worth taking a detour to the village of **Knock** ㉖, where, on a wet evening in 1879, several local people supposedly saw the Blessed Virgin silhouetted on the gable of the local church. **Knock Folk Museum** (tel: 094-88100; May–Oct daily) documents the story of the apparition. A 15,000-seat basilica dominates the village and, although no great miracles have been claimed or verified by Catholic authorities, hundreds of thousands of pilgrims, many of them invalids, journey to Knock each year. It was to celebrate the shrine's centenary that the Pope came to Ireland in 1979 at the invitation of the local parish priest, Monsignor James Horan, whose political lobbying later led to the building of the local "international airport". ❏

Map, page 230

TIP

You can fly directly to Knock from England. Ryanair has daily flights from London Stansted, British Airways Express flies from Manchester, and Aer Lingus flies from Birmingham.

BELOW: a religious procession and selection of sacred souvenirs at Knock.

Northern Region

THE NORTHWEST

*The counties of Sligo, Leitrim and Donegal combine
Stone Age burial sites, a craggy coastline, quiet
fishing villages, and echoes of William Butler Yeats*

Map,
page 260

South-western Sligo, a land of bright lakes and dramatically carved valleys left behind when the last ice age retreated 10,000 years ago, wears its history on its sleeve. Huts from 2,000BC cluster on a plateau high in the **Bricklieve Mountains** west of Lough Arrow. To their west lie the passage tombs of **Carrowkeel Cemetery** where these Stone Age farmers buried their dead. Cairn K catches the rising sun on the year's longest day, yet the main road to Dublin, the N4, is just a mile west. Across it and across **Lough Arrow**, south of Riverstown, beside a modern bungalow, is the 200-ft (70-metre) unexcavated **Heapstown Cairn**. Almost every hilltop has a passage grave, every lake a defensive artificial island, a crannog, every river confluence a castle, a friary, a priory.

North-west, 5 miles (8 km) along the R295, Richard de Burgo, the Red Earl of Ulster, has left us the 10-ft (3-metre) walls and six towers of his castle, built in 1,300, in tiny **Ballymote ❶**. The ruins beside it are of a Franciscan friary where, in 1391, priests wrote the *Book of Ballymote* which enabled scholars to interpret Ireland's ancient Ogham script. At **Collooney**, north again 5 miles (8 km), stands a castle, site of a great battle between the English and the French who had come to support the Irish insurgents in the rebellion of 1798.

Travellers coming from the west, from **Ballina**, can follow the surfers' coast through **Easky** with its 15th-century Rosalee Castle and two Martello towers built to repel Napoleon in the early 19th century. One eclectic diversion is to visit the seaweed baths at **Inishcrone** (Kilcullen's Bath House, tel: 096-36238), another is to take the road south from Easky, past the sparkling waters of Easky Lough deep into the Ox Mountains before joining the N17 at Tobercurry.

Prehistoric sites

At **Carrowmore ❷**, 5 miles, (8 km) south-west of the eponymous county town, Sligo, the 6,000-year-old Bronze Age graves of Ireland's largest Megalithic cemetery (Visitor Centre, tel: 071-61534, daily 9.30am–6.30pm, admission fee, closed Oct–Easter, site open all year) are easily approached, scattered across the hussocky fields, whilst up above them, on the horizon, west, on top of 1,078-ft (328-metre) Knocknarea, is the vast cairn, 200ft (70 metres) long by 35ft (11 metres) high, consisting of 40,000 boulders. It is named **Mebh's** (pronounced *Maeve's*) **Cairn**, supposedly for the 1st-century AD Mebh of Connaught whose lust for glitz, baubles and fine clothes would put many a modern royal princess in the shade. Her fall, when, coveting the Brown Bull of Cooley, she sent her army north on a cattle raid "The Taín", is recorded in the Irish equivalent of the *Iliad*, the *Ulster Cycle*. The advised approach is from the south. In the National

PRECEDING PAGES:
Rosses Point,
Co. Sligo.
LEFT: Rathcormack
village, Co. Sligo.
BELOW: sheep
shearer at work.

Museum in Dublin is a splendid casket supposed to have held the tooth St Patrick lost the when he tripped over the entrance stone to 10th-century Killaspugabone Church on **Strandhill beach**, 5 miles (8km) west of Sligo by the R282 past Sligo Airport.

But **Sligo** town ❸, with its associations with the poet, playwright and Abbey Theatre co-founder William Butler Yeats, is the county's tourist magnet. It's a fair enough market town, with the river Garavogue cutting though it, with excellent pubs and delicatessens, diverting narrow streets, plus beaches to the west, mountains to the north, and the ruins of a Dominican friary.

"The best lack all conviction, while the worst Are full of passionate intensity."
—W. B. Yeats

But Yeats, who spent most of his childhood here, is the main attraction. In the **Municipal Art Gallery** (County Library, Stephen Street, 071-91-41405, Mon–Sat) hang drawings and painting by that excellent artist, his brother Jack B. Yeats, given to vigorous impressionist watercolours, oils and drawings of country fairs and horse races. There are also fine Paul Henrys and George (A.E.) Russells, the latter being one of Yeats's fellow mystics. The **Sligo Art Gallery** (Yeats Memorial Building, Hyde Bridge, 071-91-45847) houses changing exhibitions of touring contemporary works.

Next door is the **Sligo County Museum & Yeats Memorial Collection**, (071-7147190, Tues–Sat). There are many Yeats letters, a complete collection of his poems, photographs of his funeral, and his Nobel Prize citation. The **Yeats Memorial Building** (Yeats Society, Wine Street, Douglas Hyde Bridge, 071-91-42693) is the venue for the Yeats International Summer School in August. A bronze statue portraying the poet as half swan, half stern cobra, stands nearby.

BELOW: the dolmen at Carrowmore.

Seasoned travellers, after asking in the tourist office for directions to the

offices of the local solicitors **Argue and Phibbs**, checking out the Yeats connections, and fingering the finest of woollens and tweeds in Dooney's shop on
O'Connell Street will settle – with a volume of Yeats, or a copy of the local
paper, the *Sligo Champion*, to hand – into the dark recesses of a snug in
Hargadon's Pub almost opposite, for a pint of stout and a sandwich. The bar
could be the model for many another spirit-grocers in the west of Ireland. The
paper lists local pubs with traditional music and gives the programmes for the
adventurous **Hawk's Well Theatre** (Temple Street) and its nearby competitor
the **Blue Raincoat** theatre group. You can make your own sandwiches from
supplies at Cosgrove's Delicatessen (Market Street) and plan a Yeats picnic.

The elusive Innishfree

To the east, the L16/R288 follows the 24-mile (40-km) circuit of beautiful
Lough Gill ④, swinging south, just into county Leitrim, at the elegant
restored 17th-century lakeside **Parke's Castle** (Fivemile Bourne, 071-64149,
admission fee, open Apr–Oct) to Dromahair and the 15th-century **Creevylea**
abbey ruins. The final stage of the journey, a visit to Yeats's **Lake Isle of
Innishfree**, can be taken on the Wild Rose Waterbus (tel: 071-91-64266, daily
mid-Jun–Sept; Sundays only April, May and Oct).

The Yeats brothers spent their holidays at often windswept **Rosses Point**,
4 miles (6 km) north-west on the R291. The view across to Knocknarea is
inspiring; mid-channel is a seafarer's marker, the **Metal Man**, according to
the sour Yeats "the only Rosses Point man who never told a lie."

North of Sligo, 5½ miles (9 km) on the N15 is tiny **Drumcliff ⑤**, at the foot
of the majestic cliffs of Benbulben. Although he died in France, Yeats by his

**Map,
page 260**

ABOVE: Lough Gill.

BELOW: Drumcliff's
Church of Ireland
cemetery, resting
place of W.B. Yeats..

ABOVE: Lissadell House, which Yeats immortalised.

own request was re-interred here in the dour little Protestant Church of Ireland's graveyard, citing the spot in his poem which begins: *Under Ben Bulben's head"* and finishes with the celebrated words inscribed on his tomb: *"Cast a cold eye/ On life, on death, / Horseman, pass by!"* The church has been restored.

The adjoining round tower is evidence of St Columba's AD575 monastery, whilst on the 10th-century **high cross** it is *just* possible to make out the bible stories of Cain and Abel, Adam and Eve. **Glencar Lough**, east on the N16 and half in county Leitrim, has a most dramatic setting.

Literary haunts

Branching west, 4 miles (6 km) along the northern shore of Drumcliff Bay, is **Lissadell House** ❻ (071-63150, admission fee, closed Sun and Oct–May). It is languid, shabby even, and was built in 1832 for the Gore Booths, whose Arctic explorer son Henry mortgaged the house to help Famine victims in 1845–46. Even if the house were to crumble, Yeats has immortalised it: *"The light of evening, Lissadell, / Great windows open to the south, / Two girls in silk kimonos, both / Beautiful, one a gazelle."* The girls were poet Eva and her sister Constance, later to become Countess Markievicz, friend of Michael Collins. Constance, although sentenced to death for her heroic part in the 1916 Easter Rising, was the first woman to be elected to the British House of Commons. She never took the seat, preferring Ireland's equivalent, the Daíl.

Earlier literary diversions may be contemplated at **Cooldrumman**, half way between Drumcliff and Lisadell. Here, in the **Battle of the Books**, AD561, 2,000 monks of various factions, and their supporters, died in an argument as to whether St Finian was right in citing Derry's St Columba for breach of copyright. The story is told in Drumcliffe Visitors Centre.

BELOW: the harbour at Mullaghmore.

Further north off the N15, turn west at Grange for superb **Streedagh Strand** with Carriag na Spáinneach, Spaniard's Rock, where three ships of the Spanish Armada foundered in 1588. Most of the shipwrecked, cold and starving, were put to the sword. Some re-grouped, joined the *Gerona*, only to suffer similar fates at Port na Spániagh, Dunluce, county Antrim. The little road east from Grange leads up Benbulben.

Mullaghmore ❼ is a picture-postcard, holiday harbour village from some perfect childhood. The beach is golden, bright boats rock by the pier, waves splash on Mullaghmore Head. But Lord Mountbatten was assassinated here in his boat, with innocent youngsters, by the IRA in 1979. The fairytale Cassiebawn Castle was his holiday home.

On **Innishmurray**, 4 miles (6 km) offshore, there are the still stunning remains of St Molaise's 6th-century monastery, three churches within a 12-ft (4-metre) high dry-stone wall – just about the only survivors of Viking raids in the 9th century. If the crossing from Mullaghmore, or Rosses Point, was rough enough, travellers might seek out the island's other curiosity, its cursing stones.

Leitrim: Rescued by water

North of Mullaghmore, Leitrim is allowed to just dip its toes into 2½ miles (4 km) of the Atlantic, before the shore line reaches the **Drowes**, one of the best of salmon rivers and the boundary with Donegal. Ten miles (16 km) inland and Leitrim's border is with Fermanagh in Northern Ireland. Another 20 miles (32 km) east and its northern border is with Monaghan. At **Lough Allen**, its biggest lake, there are scarcely 5 miles (8km) of Leitrim soil between Monaghan north, and county Roscommon south.

Thus it has been too easy to dismiss this tiny county of lakes and rushes, meandering rivers, bumpy roads, crumbling farmhouses, low hills, neglected fields, as "Ireland's Cinderella". Sligo even takes credit – via Yeats – for Lough Gill and for **Glencar 8** with its waterfall immortalised in Yeats's poem *The Stolen Child*, though the two counties share them. Fermanagh is more associated with salmon-rich **Lough Melvin** than Leitrim on its southern shore, and the same can be said for the magic of **Lough Macnean Upper**, which is similarly divided.

The great famine of 1845–46 hit the county hard, and emigration has continued ever since. The unflinching novels of John McGahern, who lives at Mohill, catch the area's air of rural desperation. But as the attractions of the unspoilt environment begin to mean as much as the pull of the beaches, Leitrim has much going in its favour. A glance at the map shows a necklace of lakes linking the great rivers Shannon and Erne via the Ballinamore-Ballyconnell Canal – now more prosaically marketed as the **Erne Shannon Waterway.**

From spring to winter, the banks of the lakes and rivers – where cows drink hock-high amongst the flag irises – are dotted with the big green umbrellas of visiting fishermen after bream, eel, perch, pike, roach and rudd. Hired cruisers

Map, page 260

The county takes its name from the village of Leitrim, whose Gaelic name, Liatroim, means Grey Ridge.

BELOW: tranquillity in Leitrim's lanes.

flying Austrian, British, Dutch, French and German ensigns ply the canal, their crews clinking their gin 'n' tonic glasses, their skippers nautical in caps, binoculars at the ready. Heron poise in the reed mace, great crested grebe dive before the bow wave. Amid the uncut watermeadows, amateur botanists count sedges, birdwatchers tick off another species of warbler, cup their ear for the cry of corncrake and cuckoo.

Carrick-on-Shannon has developed into one of Ireland's major cruise boat centres.

Thus small villages such as **Drumshanbo** on the R280 to the south of Lough Allen, **Carrick-on-Shannon** ❾, the county town 8½ miles (13 km) south, **Drumsna**, just south, where Anthony Trollope wrote his first novel, *The McDermotts of Ballycloran*, and **Roosky** 9 miles (14 km) south again, have found prosperity. The new money has brought music back to the pubs, turned old market houses into heritage centres and tourist offices, and refurbished town piers and lake fishing stands.

The **Leitrim Heritage Centre and Museum** at **Ballinamore** shows that the original canal was a nonsense, built too late for the Canal Age; only a dozen or so boats ever traversed its original stone-built locks. Near the canal, fragments of the old Sligo Leitrim and Northern Counties Railway, whose initials were interpreted locally as the Slow Late and Never Completely Reliable, can be traced.

Dromahair's **Breffni Castle** ruins are the setting for the complex tale of Dervorgilla, Ireland's Helen of Troy, involving elopements, local chiefs, England's Henry II and Welsh barons. **Manorhamilton** has a ruined mansion and a Wild Rose Colleen beauty contest and **Carrigallen** has a flourishing theatre, the **Corn Mill**. A diversion from fishing could be **Lough Rinn House** (071-96-31427, admission fee, closed mid-Sept–May), once home to the Earl of Leitrim and now an open demesne 10 miles (16 km) east of Carrick-on-Shannon.

BELOW: wall mosaic, Carrick-on-Shannon.

Donegal

The Atlantic storms into Donegal's rocky coves, rumbling round white boulders up in banks beside the sheep cropped grass. Rusty winches, skeletal memories of long-lost fishing enterprises, paint red the stone of crumbling piers. Dreamers and poets, and stressed-out business persons from Continental Europe, put thatch back on the roofs of old stone cottages, whilst locals, seemingly with no planning constraints erect new bungalows higgledy piggeldy, despoiling (for the tourist) the silent landscape of empty valleys, purple mountains, rushing streams, towering sea-cliffs.

Donegal's people, like Leitrim's, will argue that they are hard done by. In Donegal, tenuously linked to the rest of the Republic by a slender isthmus, they say Dublin forgets them, and that only tourism generated by Northern Ireland's middle classes (and a handful of foreigners) keeps them going. Certainly much of the county harks back to another age: tiny fields bound by dry-stone walls, the hay cut by scythe then tossed in cocks; a scattering of sheep, woolly dots on a distant, bare, impossibly steep, mountainside.

Off pot-holed village streets, monosyllabic, big knuckled, red-faced solid farmers – mountainy men – suck on tobacco pipes, read the death notices in the *Donegal Democrat* in sepulchral pubs, their children off in Amerikay, or Glasgow, or the hotel bar across the square, swaying to country and Irish – a more lachrymose version of country and western. And the tourist season, though it packs pubs, hotels and rented cottages, is short enough with a winter such as Donegal's around the corner after harvest.

Bundoran  is a brash resort, kiss-me-quick and windy. Rossnowlagh, its smaller quieter cousin, is a base for surfers and – in the friary – the Donegal Historical Society Museum (071-98-51267, free). In the one-time garrison town of **Ballyshannon**, where the waters of the Erne are tamed to produce hydro-electricty, pretty Georgian houses survive and literary folk commemorate the town's most famous son, poet and bank official William Allingham, remembered for his verse *Up the airy mountain,/ Down the rushy glen,/ We daren't go a-hunting / For fear of little men.* The town's history can be traced in the Abbey Water Wheels visitors centre (tel: 071-98-51580, open Easter week and Jun–Aug daily 10.30am–6.30pm; Sept/Oct Sun only 12–6pm), which has a museum and audio-visual display.

The county town

Donegal , the lively county town, has a busy triangular "Diamond" market square, congested with tourist traffic all summer. The town's history has a familiar ring. Its **castle** (073-22405, admission fee, open Easter–Oct), once an O'Donnell stronghold, was redesigned, as was the town itself, by the Brookes, planters who took over the land after the O'Donnells were deported in the so-called "Flight of the Earls" at the turn of the 17th century. In the now ruined O'Donnell-financed Franciscan abbey, south on the estuary of the Eske, monks compiled, in the 1630s, *The Annals of the Four Masters*, tracing Ireland's history back to the time of Noah's granny.

ABOVE: a distinctive Donegal pub sign.

BELOW: gossip is the stuff of life in a Donegal village.

Complementary to tourism, the weaving and making up of tweeds is the town's main industry, and Magee's, the town's largest shop, is the industry's principal outlet. A mile south, Donegal Craft Village (Ballyshannon Road, 073-22225, closed Sun out of season) demonstrates weaving and other craftworks.

Three miles (5 km) south of Donegal town, at Laghy, the R232 runs southeast for Pettigoe from where the R233 bears north 3 miles (5 km) across desolate bogland to **Lough Derg** ⑫, with its tiny **Station Island**, focal point for a major act of pilgrimage, St Patrick's Purgatory. The island, now covered with buildings, looks from a distance like some Canaletto painting and the pilgrims commemorate the 40 days Ireland's saint spent on it, praying, fasting and expelling evil spirits. There can be few Irish Catholics over the age of 40 who have not spent, sometime between June and August, the required three days of ritual there, walking barefoot, repeating prayers, and consuming nothing but black tea and dry toast.

Craggy coastline

The road west from Donegal town runs past **Bruckless,** where there are live oysters and mussels for sale, then through the fishing port of **Killybegs** where hefty trawlermen, drinking amongst the Victorian villas, give the town a raffish, frontier air. **Kilcar** 7 miles (11 km) on along the craggy, beautiful coastline, is another vacation, traditional music and tweed centre somewhat overshadowed by **Ardara** 20 miles (33 km) north. However, it is rewarding to continue further west through quiet **Carrick**, then turning south for the precipitous drive past **Teelin** to Carrigan Head at the eastern end of 2,000-ft (650-

TIP

During the pilgrimage season, from 1 June to 15 August, only pilgrims are admitted to visit Station Island.

BELOW:
Donegal Castle.

metre) **Slieve League** whose sheer cliffs drop a scary 765ft (235 metres) into the indigo sea beyond. An alternative is to leave transport at Teelin, walking the signposted One Man's Pass in the same direction. The views from **Amharc Mór** are, when not shrouded in mists, spectacular – and vertiginous.

Glencolumbkille ⓭, further west in the lowlands at the head of Glen Bay, represents a landmark in the development of a particular kind of Irish tourism. The idea was devised here that the draughty, cold traditional thatched white-washed cottage could be up-graded, given central heating, pine furniture, shower, television and fridge and clustered into a marketable group. Purists dismiss it, while its protagonists argue that it sustains life and employment in distressed rural communities. Four cottages in the village's **Folk Village Museum** (073-30017, admission fee, closed Oct–Easter) present traditional life over the centuries; one cottage, the Shebeen, sells seaweed and fuschia wines – but no poteen.

Tiny **Port**, difficult to reach in the next valley north, demonstrates what happens when a village dies, but most travellers continue north-east the 16 miles (26 km) to **Ardara**, then **Glenties ⓮**, both awash in season with Belfast's holidaymakers buying Guinness, tweeds, Aran sweaters, salmon flies for the Owena and Owentocker rivers, and tapping their toes to fiddlers. Glenties' **St Conall's Heritage Centre** (075-51277, admission fee, closed Oct–May) is in its Georgian courthouse.

North, the N56 continues to Dungloe, capital of the **Rosses**, a raggedly charming peninsula of islands, trout lakes and inlets. From **Burtonport**, 4 miles (6 km) north-west, a 25-minute ferry service (075-20532) runs to **Aranmore** island 3 miles (5 km) offshore, with its 900 souls, dry stone walls and holiday

One of the village's buildings, the National School replica, has a display on Rockwell Kent, an American painter who captured many local scenes.

Map, page 260

BELOW: the harbour at Burtonport; peat digger, Horn Head.

ABOVE: the gardens at Glenveagh Castle.

cottages. Ferries for bare and windswept **Tory Island** , now a popular tourist destination, run the 15-mile (24-km) sea journey regularly from **Bunbeg** almost 15 miles (24 km) by the coast road north and from **Meenlaragh** round the **Bloody Foreland** near Gortahork. Home once to Balor, the one-eyed God of Darkness, Tory gave its name (meaning outlaw) to Britain's right-wing political party when it opposed James II in 1680. The island's main village, West Town, has a 51-ft (15-metre) round tower and the ruins of two churches. This area, like Gweedore to the north, is traditionally Irish-speaking.

The dramatic mountain north of Dunlewey is **Errigal**, Donegal's highest at 2,466ft (752 metres). The peak south is Slieve Snacht, 200ft (60 metres) less.

Twenty-one miles (37 km) north on the N56, **Dunfanaghy**'s fame rests on its popularity with Northern Ireland's golfers who take time off from the links to drive back south to Falcarragh, then east 8 miles (13 km) along the R255 to walk through the 10,000 acres (400 hectares) of always open **Glenveagh National Park** ⑯ (074-37090, admission fee visitor centre and castle, closed Nov–Easter). The park was given to the nation by Henry McIlhenny, who made his fortune from Tabasco Sauce.

With its castle and its formal French and Italian gardens mixing with the wild mountains, the park has a further surprise in the Regency-style **Glebe House Gallery** (074-37071, 11–19 April daily 11am–6pm; 16 May–28 Sept Sat–Thurs 11am–6.20pm), housing paintings by Degas, Renoir, Picasso and the primitive painters of Tory Island. **Gartan Lough,** 3 miles (5 km) south via a narrow bog road, is much photographed.

Letterkenny ⑰, the county town, situated on the River Swilly 10 miles (16 km) to the southwest, is useful as a base because it has ATMs, hole-in-the-wall

BELOW: Tory Island.

cash machines being pretty scarce in rural Donegal. A little restaurant (ask in the Tourist Office, because its name changes) is on the site of Laird's Hotel where Wolfe Tone, patriot of the 1798 rebellion, was arrested over breakfast. Its most prominent landmark is the Cathedral, built in modern Gothic style by local masons using Donegal stone.

Map, page 260

A choice of routes

The traveller could go north from Letterkenny, or follow the N56 south-east from Dunfanaghy, then taking the R245 north chasing the **Atlantic Drive** past the golfer's haven of **Rosapenna** around **Mulroy Bay** with its farmed mussel rafts and salmon cages, around windswept **Fanad Head**, then south again to **Rathmullan** ⓲, from whence, in 1607, the leading clan chiefs took flight by ship for Spain. Their story is recalled in the **Flight of the Earls Heritage Centre** (074-61817, closed Oct–Easter).

Beyond, 7 miles (11 km) is charming preserved, conserved, restrained, riverside Ramelton, in whose Heritage Centre you can find your local roots – should you have any – in **Donegal Ancestry** (open Mon–Fri, free, tel: 074-51266): thence to Letterkenny again.

From here it's a tempting run north, for 16 miles (26 km), to the 4,000-year-old **Grianán of Aileach**, a really spectacular circular stone enclosure atop a 800-ft (240-metre) mound. Its name is translated, controversially, as "sun-palace".

Even more tempting now is the drive 40 miles (64 km) north to Ireland's most northerly point, **Malin Head** on the Inishowen Peninsula. The great estuary south is that of the river Foyle, on which sits Northern Ireland's second (and most vibrant) city, Derry *(see page 280)*. ❑

The flight of the most powerful Irish clan princes in 1607 was more than just another setback for the Irish cause: it effectively marked the end of Gaelic supremacy.

BELOW: Malin Head; the ancient Grianán of Aileach.

THE NORTHEAST

*The evidence of Northern Ireland's civil strife is there to see,
but even more evident are gorgeous lakes and glens,
a stunning coastline and a wealth of golf courses*

Map,
page 260

Until the 1970s, it was hard to tell when you had crossed the border from the Republic into Northern Ireland. Perhaps you noticed that the post boxes and telephone booths were no longer green but red. Or that the road surface had suddenly improved and deduced that British rather than Irish taxes had financed it. But that was about all. No passports were required. A few crossings had Customs posts, but most people were casually waved through.

Then the differences became marked. Passports were still not required, but many lanes which used to weave across the border and back again, as unpredictably as a St Patrick's Day drunk, were blocked by wedges of reinforced concrete a metre thick. On authorised roads, the visitor's first glimpse of Northern Ireland was of a British Army checkpoint, a concrete bunker with bullet-proof glass and silver anti-sniper screens, manned by a soldier wearing a flak jacket and carrying an automatic rifle. It was an unsettling sight. At some crossings, as one soldier asked you for some means of identification, an unseen colleague inside the bunker tapped your car registration number into a terminal linked to a computer at police headquarters. This was programmed with details of all suspect vehicles and within seconds you were cleared – or arrested.

After the IRA ceasefires in 1994 and 1997, the security became much less obtrusive. Although many could not believe that peace was permanent, most barriers were removed from towns throughout Northern Ireland and efforts were made to make everything look as normal as possible. If things *looked* peaceful, it was reasoned, peace would be encouraged.

Where's the border?

One reason it is so difficult to be sure of the border's exact location is that it snakes its way along 18th-century county boundaries through farming land that is sometimes bleak, more often breathtakingly beautiful. It takes little account of natural boundaries, such as rivers, or of the cultural differences that separate Republican-minded Roman Catholics and British-oriented Protestants. A priest may find part of his parish on one side of the border, the rest on the other. Houses straddle it so that, as the joke has it, a man may sleep with his head in the United Kingdom and his heart in the Republic of Ireland.

Political expediency accounts for the absurdities. It had been intended to redraw the border rationally after partition in 1920, and a Boundary Commission was set up to advise. But in the end the British and Irish governments, both hoping to avoid further trouble, suppressed the commission's report and left things as they were. Had they decided differently, much of the subsequent conflict might have been averted.

PRECEDING PAGES:
the Giant's Causeway. **LEFT:** harbour
at Cushendun, Co.
Antrim. **BELOW:** a
long and winding
road through the
Mourne Mountains.

ABOVE: Derry's walls
were completed in
1618 at a cost of
£8,357.

Many confusions were created. Whereas the ancient Irish province of Ulster consisted of nine counties, the new state of Northern Ireland, popularly known as Ulster, consisted of only six: **Antrim**, **Down**, **Armagh**, **Derry**, **Fermanagh** and **Tyrone**. Yet the three counties which went to the Republic – **Donegal**, **Cavan** and **Monaghan** – are still bound to the other six by firm family and trading ties. To many locals, therefore, the border is an abstraction. And indeed it's hard to take it wholly seriously when the states it divides can't even agree about its length, the Republic claiming it is 280 miles (448 km) long and the Northern Ireland authorities adamant that it is 303 miles (485 km).

Since this book's concern is the convenience of travellers rather than tribal loyalties, we have included Donegal in the previous chapter and will here roam freely within the remaining eight counties of ancient Ulster. And it *is* possible to roam freely without seeing much evidence of sectarian conflict. As the Northern Ireland Tourist Board likes to point out, its bailiwick consists of 1,200 golf holes with a number of towns and villages scattered among them.

Old Derry's walls

Across the border from Donegal, is the county of **Londonderry** – whose chief city council, in a pointed rejection of the city's imperial links, changed its name from Londonderry Corporation to Derry City Council, ⑲ is famously friendly. Even in its sectarian squabbles, it is far less implacable than Belfast. The 19th-century Scottish historian Thomas Carlyle called it "the prettiest looking town I have seen in Ireland" and, though the Troubles seriously scarred it, recent refurbishment has restored its attractiveness. But the city, finely situated on the **River Foyle**, doesn't set out to be a calendar girl; it prefers to provide exhilarating com-

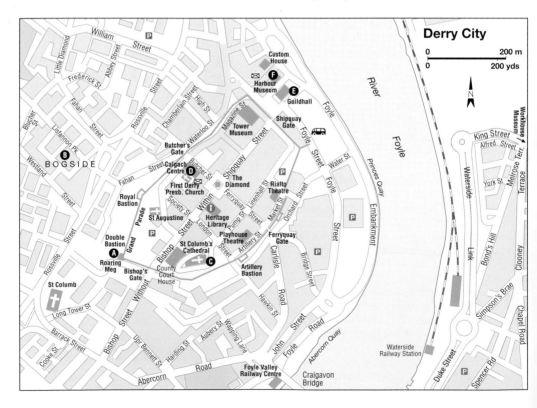

pany, and it succeeds. There has been a renaissance in community activity, especially in the arts, and enthusiasts will tell you that Derry is the first city in Western Europe to face up to the realities of the high-unemployment post-industrial age.

The city's growth was financed by London guilds, which in 1614 began creating the last walled city in Europe. Its purpose was mercantile success and you can still see traces of its former economic confidence in the ornamental facades of the old shirtmaking factories, which provided the city with its livelihood for generations. The walls, 20 ft (6 metres) thick and complete with watch-towers and cannon such as the 18-pounder **Roaring Meg Ⓐ** (dating from 1642), are marvellously intact. (Tours tel: 028-7126 7284 with fee, otherwise free access.)

Two 17th-century sieges failed to breach the walls, earning the sobriquet "maiden city". Some say the city still has a siege mentality, a theory reinforced by the IRA's daubed slogan "You are now entering Free Derry." This was the name given to the **Bogside Ⓑ**, a densely populated Roman Catholic housing estate, when its inhabitants barricaded it against the police in 1969. Their grievances were old ones. After Ireland's partition in 1920, the city's governing Unionists had fixed constituency boundaries to ensure a "permanent" majority for themselves in what was a mainly nationalist area – an artificial majority that wasn't overturned until the mid-1970s. Feeling isolated from the prosperous eastern counties, Derry's citizens built up both a wonderful community spirit and a resentment that finally boiled over.

The most famous siege – which is still commemorated by Protestant marches today – took place in 1689, when the Catholic forces of James II, the last of England's Stuart kings, blockaded the Protestant supporters of William of Orange for 15 weeks, almost forcing them into submission. About 7,000 of the 30,000 people packed within the city's walls died of disease or starvation. One member

Maps,
city 280
area 260

The famous "Londonderry Air" was based on an old folk melody. It became "Danny Boy" when an English songwriter, Frederic Edward Weatherly (1848–1929), added lyrics.

BELOW: the view from the walls; the statue to Peace.

of the besieged garrison chillingly recorded the selling prices of horseflesh, dogs' heads, cats, and rats "fattened by eating the bodies of the slain Irish." The city's eventual relief is depicted on the siege memorial window of **St Columb's Cathedral** ● (London Street, tel: 028-7126 7313, admission fee) a graceful 17th-century Anglican church built in "Planters' Gothic" style. The chapter house contains siege relics. Outside the walls, off Bishop Street Without, **St Columb's** (tel: 028-7126 2301, admission free), built 1784, known as the Long Tower Church, has a lavish interior.

For those interested in the city's turbulent history, the award-winning **Tower Museum** (Union Hall Place, tel: 028-7137 2411, free on Wed, closed Sun and Mon, except July–Aug, open daily) skilfully uses audio-visuals and photography to tell its story from both sides of the sectarian divide. The **Genealogy Centre** ● (14 Bishop Street, tel: 028-7126 9792, Mon–Fri) has genealogical research facilities.

Streets from the city's original four gates (Shipquay, Ferryquay, Bishop's and Butcher's) converge on **The Diamond**, a perversely square-shaped market place at the top of Shipquay Street, the steepest main thoroughfare in Ireland. At the bottom of the street, the **Guildhall** ● (Guildhall Place, tel: 028-7137 7335, admission free, closed weekends and bank holidays), one of those Tudor-Gothic structures popular in Northern Ireland, clearly shows the influence of the London merchants. Its grandeur has been stained by the Troubles too. A Republican entering as a newly elected councillor turned out to be the same man who had blown part of it up 13 years previously. He had made a political statement by carrying in the bomb, he explained, and he was making the same political statement now.

St Columb (c. 521–597), also called Columba and Columcille, founded Derry around 546 and later set up a community on Iona, off Scotland's west coast. His feast day is 9 June.

BELOW:
The Diamond.

Behind the Guildhall is **Derry Quay**, celebrated in song by hundreds of thousands of emigrants who sailed down the Foyle from here, bound for a new life in America. The city's maritime past is covered in the **Harbour Museum ⑥** (Harbour Square, tel: 028-7137 7331, admission free, closed weekends); displays include a replica of a 30-ft (9-metre) curragh in which St Columba sailed to Iona in AD563. Its railway past is explored in the **Foyle Valley Railway Centre** (Foyle Rd. tel: 028-7126 5234, fee for train ride, closed Sun–Mon).

The **Earhart Centre** 1½ miles north-west on B194 (Ballyarnet, tel: 028-7135 4040, admission free) focuses on one incident in aviation's past – the day Amelia Earhart, the first woman to fly solo across the Atlantic, landed here in 1932. On the other side of the river, the Workhouse Museum on Glendermott Road (tel: 028-7131 8328) has exhibitions on the Famine, Victorian poverty and a memorial exhibition on the role of the city in the battle of the Atlantic and the Second World War (admission fee).

Context (Artillery Street, tel: 028-7137 3538, closed Sun–Mon) and McGilloway (6 Shipquay Street, tel: 028-7136 6011) are fine contemporary art galleries, whilst touring and homespun ballet, drama and opera visit the Playhouse (Artillery Street, tel: 028-7126 8027), and Millennium Forum (Newmarket Street, tel: 028-7126 4455).

Small-town Tyrone

Thirteen miles (21 km) southwest of Derry City, in county Tyrone on the A5 is **Strabane ⑳**, a border town paired with Lifford on the Donegal side. John Dunlap, printer of America's Declaration of Independence, learned his trade in **Gray's Printing Press** (49 Main Street, tel: 028-7188 4094, museum free, Tues–Sat, all

Maps, city 280 area 260

The dramatist George Farquhar (1678–1707) was born in Derry. His best plays are The Recruiting Officer and The Beaux' Stratagem.

BELOW: echoes of the old working-class town.

year; admission fee to National Trust section, Apr–Sept Tues–Sat pm only). In Dergalt, 2 miles (3 km) to the southeast, signposted off the B47, is a whitewashed cottage, the ancestral home of US president Woodrow Wilson (tel: 028-71883735, admission fee, closed Oct–Mar).

Sion Mills, 3 miles (5 km) south of Strabane, is a village whose name betrays its origins. The linen-workers' old cottages are charming. The Parish Church of the Good Shepherd is a striking Italian-style edifice, contrasting sharply with the modern architecture of St Teresa's Catholic Church, whose facade displays a large image on slate of the Last Supper.

As you drive into **Omagh** ㉑, the county town of Tyrone, 16 miles (25 km) along the A5, the religious fragmentation of Northern Ireland is immediately apparent. On the right is the Presbyterian Church (Trinity); on the left, the Methodist Church; next, St Columba's Church of Ireland; then the Gothic spires of the Roman Catholic Church of the Sacred Heart, a poor man's Chartres Cathedral. There are many more. The joining of the Rivers Camowen and Drumragh to form the Strule make the location pleasant enough, but Omagh is more a town for living (and praying) in than for visiting. In its shops, alongside the usual linen souvenirs, are plaques and statuettes made of turf (peat). This is cut from the **Black Bog** between Omagh and Cookstown, 27 miles (43 km) to the east.

American connections

During tough times in the 1800s, the area's strong Scots-Presbyterian work ethic spurred many to seek their fortune in America. The results were remarkable and Northern Ireland claims that 11 US presidents have had roots in the province: Andrew Jackson, James Knox Polk, Andrew Johnson, James Buchanan, Ulysses S. Grant, Chester Alan Arthur, Grover Cleveland, Benjamin Harrison, William McKinley, Theodore Roosevelt and Woodrow Wilson. Genealogists pore over old documents, hoping to add more names, and many Americans visit to seek out ancestral homes.

The Mellon banking family of Pittsburgh, having traced their roots to 4 miles (6 km) north of Omagh, off the A5, endowed the **Ulster-American Folk Park** ㉒ on the site at Camphill (tel: 028-8224 3292, admission fee, Apr–Sept Mon–Sat 10.30am–4.30pm, Sun 11am–5pm; Oct–Mar Mon–Fri 10.30am–3.30pm). To illuminate the transition made by the 18th-century emigrants, craftsmen's cottages, a schoolhouse, a blacksmith's forge and a Presbyterian meeting-house from the Old World have been rebuilt on a peat bog alongside log cabins, a Pennsylvania farmstead and a covered wagon from the New World. Peat is kept burning in the cottages, and there are demonstrations of candle-making, fish-salting and horseshoeing. An indoor exhibit recreates the main street of an Ulster town 100 years ago, its hardware shop displaying foot warmers and lamp wicks, its medical hall containing Bishop's Granular Effervescent Citrate of Magnesia and Belladonna breast plasters. A replica of an emigrant ship links the continents. There's not a whiff of Disney, thanks to the attention to detail, though the American "half" looks more prosperous than the original settlers found it.

Also north of Omagh (7 miles/11 km on the B48) the outdoor **Ulster History Park** (Cullion, Lislap, Omagh, tel: 028-8164 8188, admission fee, closed Sat and Sun Oct–Mar), traces back 10.000 years by means of reasonably realistic recreations of the built environment, from Neolithic huts and ring-forts to round towers and planters' houses.

Map, page 260

Relics of old industries

There's nothing Northern Ireland likes better than history, and almost every village in Tyrone – **Castlederg**, **Creggan**, **Donaghmore**, **Fivemiletown, Newtownstewart** – has its heritage centre. The most interesting, a little further along the B48, near **Gortin**, is the **Sperrin Heritage Centre**  (274 Glenelly Rd., Cranagh, tel: 028-8164 8142, admission fee, closed Nov– Mar), which includes the history of local gold-mining and lets you try your luck panning in an iron pyrite stream.

Ireland's linen industry began in 1698 when Louis Crommelin brought over a group of Huguenots from France to escape the wars of religion during Louis XIV's reign.

With the eclipse of Ulster's once-flourishing linen industry, hard times have again come to villages such as **Draperstown** (built in 1618 by the London Company of Drapers) in the archaeologically rich, blue-tinged **Sperrin Mountains**. Near **Maghera**, a working linen mill (Wm. Clark and Sons, Upperlands, tel: 028-7954 7200) may be visited by arrangement. The fortunes of towns like **Dungannon**, 13 miles (21 km) south of Cookstown and once the seat of the great O'Neill clan, have faltered too.

Signposted from the M1 motorway, exit 13, 7 miles (11 km) east of Dungannon, is the always open **Peatlands Park** (Peatlands Park Centre and Railway, tel: 028-3885 1102, fee for railway which is closed Sept–Easter Sun), a unique preservation of the flora and fauna of an Irish bog which can be viewed from a miniature railway. Three miles (5 km) to the northeast, **Coalisland's Corn Mill Heritage Centre** (Lineside, 028-8774 8532, fee for tour, Sat and Sun by

BELOW: the Mellon Homestead at the Ulster-American Folk Park.

ABOVE: The poet
Seamus Heaney
grew up in Bellaghy.

BELOW: Lower
Lough Erne.

appointment only and limited hours Oct–May) commemorates coal-field and canals that never fulfilled their promise.

Twenty-five miles (40km) east of Omagh, **Cookstown** ㉔, the exact middle of Northern Ireland, is renowned for its main street, 2 miles (3 km) long and 160 ft (50 metres) wide, and can be located from miles away by the 200-ft (61-metre) spire of the Gothic-style Catholic church. The town (population 6,700) has a strong tradition of nationalism, often refined in its many old-fashioned pubs. Local livestock sales give a good insight into the rough amiability of the rural Ulster character. Four miles (4 km) west, the water-powered **Wellbrook Beetling Mill** (Wellbrook, 028-8674 8210, admission fee, closed Oct–Mar and Tuesdays) demonstrates arcane processes of linen polishing.

Just east of the town an 18-hole golf course (200 Killymoon Rd., tel: 028-8676 3762) occupies the grounds of **Killymoon Castle**, designed in 1803 by John Nash, architect of London's Regent Street. Some years ago, a farmer bought the castle, then derelict, for £100.

Many Neolithic graves and stone circles are sprinkled around both towns. The best are at **Beaghmore**, (free access) 10 miles (16 km) west of Cookstown, off the A53. Villages such as **Clogher** and **Coagh**, **Moneymore** and **Pomeroy** are noted for fine traditional musicians and a variety of ecclesiastical architecture. There's a run-down air about some, the result of chronic unemployment. But it's as well to remember writer John Broderick's advice in *The Pilgrimage*: "The city dweller who passes through a country town and imagines it sleepy and apathetic is very far from the truth: it is watchful as the jungle."

The poet Seamus Heaney, a Nobel Laureate, is celebrated near his native village (**Heaney Library**, Bellaghy Bawn, Bellaghy, tel: 028-7938 6812, open

Mon–Sat Easter–Sept 10am–6pm, admission fee, closed weekends am). Much of Heaney's poetry derives its imagery and colloquial language from his rural upbringing in this part of Northern Ireland.

Map, page 260

Ulster's lakeland

To the southwest, **Fermanagh**, adjacent to Monaghan and Cavan, has many things in common with them, particularly its tempo. Politically it is part of Northern Ireland and is the province's lakeland playground: a third of it is under water. But political divisions are less of a barrier these days: the restoration of the Ballinamore–Ballyconnell cross-border canal means that you can now travel all the way here from Limerick by inland waterway.

The county town, **Enniskillen** ㉕, a Protestant stronghold since Tudor times, is built on an island between two channels of the River Erne as it flows from **Upper** to **Lower Lough Erne**. In summer, pleasure boats ply (MV *Kestrel*, Round O Jetty, tel: 028-6632 2882, May and June Sun; July and Aug daily; Sept Tues and weekends) the lakes, and western Europeans cruise them in hired craft (Manor House Marine, Killadeas, tel: 028-6862 8100).

The town's strategic importance is shown by **Enniskillen Castle** (Castle Barracks, tel: 028-6632 5000, admission fee, closed Sat, Sun and Mon am, open May–Jun & Sept Mon–Sat; July and Aug daily; Oct–Apr Mon–Fri) the earliest parts dating from the 15th century and the imposing water gate from the late 16th century. The castle houses two museums, one specialising in prehistory, the other in military relics.

Enniskillen is rich in small bakeries and butcher's shops, and there's a gossipy atmosphere as farmers mix with townsfolk in Blakes of the Hollow, one of

One of the worst terrorist outrages in Ulster took place in Enniskillen when a bomb exploded during a Remembrance Day service at the war memorial in 1987, killing 11 people.

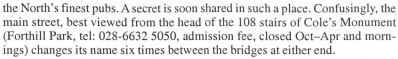

On the outskirts of Enniskillen, to the northwest, is Portora Royal School, founded in 1608. Its most famous pupils were Oscar Wilde and Samuel Beckett.

the North's finest pubs. A secret is soon shared in such a place. Confusingly, the main street, best viewed from the head of the 108 stairs of Cole's Monument (Forthill Park, tel: 028-6632 5050, admission fee, closed Oct–Apr and mornings) changes its name six times between the bridges at either end.

A true taste of the region's flavour can be gained by circling Lower Lough Erne by road or by boat. **Devenish Island** ㉖ is reached by ferry (boat fare and admission fee, accessible Apr–Sept, except Mondays) from Trory Point, signposted 3 miles (5 km) north of the town at the A32/B82 junction. It is the best known of the lough's 97 islands because of its elaborate and well-preserved round tower, which you can climb by internal ladders. Close by are the decorative ruins of the 12th-century Augustinian Abbey of St Mary. Three miles (5 km) south of Kesh on the B82, along the lough's north shore, a ferry departs (Castle Archdale Park Marina, tel: 028-6862 1156, ferry fare, admission free, Easter and June–Sept only except Mondays) for **White Island** with its 12th-century church along one wall of which are lined up eight mysterious pagan statues, discovered only in the 20th century. Their origins fox experts; some speculate that seven may represent the deadly sins.

Ancient monuments

A few miles further, past the village of **Kesh**, with its modern sailing school and fortified police station, is the strangest of all the ancient stone figures: the two-faced Janus statue on **Boa Island** ㉗, which is joined to the mainland by a bridge at each end. In most countries, such a find would have been turned into a major tourist attraction. Here, you have to watch for an easily missable road sign pointing to "Caldragh Cemetery" (free access), then tramp through cowpats down a farm lane until you come across a field full of overgrown, moss-covered gravestones, in the middle of which lurks the inscrutable Celtic figure. The lack of refurbishment makes the place feel splendidly eerie; you notice the figure's sexual arousal and the hollow in its head and wonder whether that hollow once held sacrificial blood.

A second Janus figure was discovered on the little island of **Lustybeg**, near Kesh. There are holiday chalets for hire on this island.

Following the lough's shoreline, you reach **Pettigo**, an old plantation town once the railhead for pilgrims visiting the holy sites at **Lough Derg,** across the border in Co. Donegal. The River Termon, running through Pettigo, marks the border and is said to be stuffed full of bilingual trout. It is also said that when a man had his skull fatally cracked during a fist fight in the middle of the bridge a surveyor had to be called to determine whether he had died within the jurisdiction of the Northern police or the Republic's gardai. An oak tree on one side of the bridge was planted in 1853 to mark the British victory at Sebastopol. A statue on the other side commemorates four IRA men who died fighting the British in 1922.

Castle Caldwell, on the A47 4 miles (6km) east of Belleek a ruined 16th-century castle by the loughside nearby, has become the centrepiece of a Forest Park (details tel: 028-6863 1253, free access, daily dawn to dusk), popular with picnickers and bird watchers. Worth

BELOW: an ancient two-faced Janus figure on Boa Island.

seeing is a "Fermanagh cot", a 30-ft (10-metre) wooden barge used for trans-
porting cattle and sheep to and from the islands of Upper and Lower Lough
Erne. A fiddler who, the worse for drink, fell off a barge and drowned is remembered on a fiddle-shaped monument with a cautionary verse that ends: *On firm
land only exercise your skill. There you may play and safely drink your fill.*

The border touches the River Erne again at **Belleek** ㉘, where anglers assure
you that you can hook a salmon in the Republic and land it in Northern Ireland.
You can sense how tightly knit the town is by reading the advertisements on a
restaurant's table-mats. On one, a local businessman offers to provide you with
souvenirs, confectionery, Sindy dolls, cigarettes, and his personal services, day
and night, as a funeral director. The village is famous for its lustrous **Belleek
pottery**, manufactured from felspar imported from Norway. Half-hour tours
(Belleek Pottery, tel: 028-6865 9300, www.belleek.ie, admission free, weekends
no tours; Sept–Apr Mon–Fri) of the working factory are available. The pottery's
Visitor Centre opens Mon–Fri all year and daily during summer.

You can take the scenic drive back to Enniskillen along the south side of the
lough, stopping 5 miles (8 km) north-west of Derrygonnelly on the A46 at
Lough Navar Forest Park (details 028-6864 1256, free access, daily, dawn
to dusk, restricted access for cars), where a lookout point offers a panorama of
five counties. At **Tully**, off the A46, 3 miles (5 km) north of the village, is one
well-preserved 17th-century castle (admission fee, open Tues–Sat, Apr–Sept)
whilst at **Monea**, 7 miles (11 km) north-west of Enniskillen on the B81, is
another with free access at all times.

"Over 300 million years of history" – impressive even by Irish standards – is
the slogan used to promote **Marble Arch Caves** ㉙ (Marlbank Scenic Loop,

**Map,
page 260**

ABOVE: home of
Belleek pottery.

BELOW: the ancient
Marble Arch Caves.

The Marble Arch Cave was first explored by E.A. Martel, a Frenchman, in 1895.

TIP

To telephone Cavan from Northern Ireland dial 00353 and omit the initial zero from the local code. To call Northern Ireland from Cavan, dial 0044 and omit the initial zero from the local code.

BELOW: Castle Coole, Co. Fermanagh.

Florencecourt, tel: 028-6634 8855, admission fee, accessible Mar–Sept, weather permitting), an extensive network of limestone chambers, containing remarkable stalactites. A 75-minute tour includes an underground boat journey. The "Moses Walk" is so called because the dammed walkway has been created through a lake, with more than a metre of water on either side. Twelve miles (20 km) south-west of Enniskillen, the caves are reached by following the A4 southwest for 3 miles (5 km), then following signposts after branching off on the A32 towards Swanlinbar.

Florence Court (National Trust, tel: 028-6634 8249, admission fee, closed Oct–Mar, as well as Tues and mornings all year; open weekends only during May), is a beautiful 18th-century mansion 4 miles (6 km) back. Contents include fine rococo plasterwork and 18th-century furniture. The grounds include an ice house, a water-powered sawmill and a walled garden.

Two miles (3 km) southeast of Enniskillen on the A4 is Ireland's finest classical mansion, **Castle Coole** (National Trust, tel: 028-6632 2690, admission fee, closed Oct–Mar; open Apr, May, Sept weekends and by appointment; Jun–Aug Fri–Wed). Completed in 1798, it is a perfect example of late 18th-century Hellenism and has furniture dating from before 1830. The park lake's flock of graylag geese was established here 300 years ago.

Cavan's cruising

Across the border to the south of Enniskillen, landlocked County Cavan, emptied by emigration, bridges the two Irelands by providing the source of two great rivers: the **Shannon,** which flows south to the Atlantic, and the **Erne,** which flows north into Fermanagh's magnificent lakes. Both rivers are ideal for cruising. Most of the county's scattered towns and villages have small hotels which cater for visiting

fishermen. The grandiose scheme to re-open the Ballinamore-Ballyconnell canal linking the two river systems has been completed. Pleasure trips along the canal are on demand (Shannon Erne Waterway office, tel: 071-96-44855 for info).

Cavan town ③⓪ is the site of a 14th-century Franciscan friary, of which only a belfry tower remains. The Roman Catholic Cathedral, in contrast, dates from 1942. Cavan Crystal (Dublin Road, 049-4331800, admission free) offers glass-blowing displays and a new visitor centre offers the comfort of a sofa and open fire while you examine the crafts. If you've ever wanted to know how to make perfect brown bread, visit to the Lifeforce Mill in Cavan town (tel: 049-4362722, fax: 4362923; May–Sept except by appointment), where you can mix the dough under instruction and collect your loaf hot from the oven at the end of a tour.

A tour going west and north from Cavan would take in **Arvagh**, a peaceful village 14 miles (22 km) south-west on the R198 by Lough Garty; **Cornafean**, north off the R198, 4 miles (6 km) from Cavan where Corr House has a fascinating collection of curios such as three-legged pots and cow bells housed in a converted pighouse; 17th-century **Cloughoughter Castle** on an island in Lough Oughter and nearby **Killeshandra**, a popular spot for anglers; **Dowra**, on the R200 near the Black Pig's Dyke, thought to be an ancient frontier earthwork; **Swanlinbar**, with its faded, once-a-spa charms, on the Border; **Blacklion**, on Lough Macnean 33 miles (52 km) north-west on the N3/R200, a hamlet surrounded by many prehistoric ringforts and cairns including a beehive-shaped sweat house, a Celtic form of Turkish bath; and **Butlersbridge**, 4 miles (6 km) north on the N3 near which Ballyhaise House, now an agricultural college, has a rare 1733 oval saloon and two storeys vaulted over in brick.

A tour going east and south would cover: **Cootehill**, 16 miles (26 km) east on

Map, page 260

Cavan's tourist office is on Farnham Street and is open Apr–Sept Mon–Sat 9am–6pm. Tel: (049) 4331942.

BELOW: Ballyconnell, Co. Cavan.

the R118 which has a splendid Palladian house, **Bellamont House**, built for the Coote family in 1730 in Bellamont Forest; south-east 13 miles (21 km) on the R192 to **Shercock**, where the playwright Richard Brinsley Sheridan once lived; **Kingscourt**, whose Catholic church has some renowned stained glass; **Bailieborough**, on the R165, which has a fine main street; **Virginia**, 19 miles (33 km) south-west on the N3, planned as a garrison town in 1610 and now a handsome, peaceful place with Cuilcagh House, owned by playwright Tom McIntyre (private), where Dean Swift began *Gulliver's Travels* 3 miles (5 km) east; and **Ballyjamesduff**, where the Cavan County Museum in Virginia Road (tel: 049-8544070 Tues–Sat all year Sun pm June–Sept) houses a collection of pre-Christian and medieval artefacts including the 1,000-year-old Lough Errol dug-out boat and Lavey Sheela-na-gigs.

Monaghan's mix of monotonous low hills and poor small farms was well captured by the novelist and poet Patrick Kavanagh (1905–67), who grew up here on a farm at Inishkeen.

Mild Monaghan

To the northeast, in Monaghan, is the small agricultural town of **Clones** ㉛ (pronounced *Clone-ess*), whose most famous son is Barry McGuigan, the "Clones cyclone" who became world featherweight boxing champion in 1985. The town's commercial centre is Fermanagh Street, signalling the town's former significance for the farmers of south Fermanagh. But, just as partition destroyed its role as an important railway hub, so the Troubles initially hit trade as northerners became reluctant to cross the border. But the two tills on most shop counters hint that the two different currencies – the British pound in Northern Ireland and the euro in the South – have encouraged a great deal of cross-border shopping as consumers seek out the better price, especially on fuel for their vehicles.

BELOW: making music in a Monaghan pub.

Clones has an ancient lineage. The remains of a 12th-century Augustinian abbey (known as **"the Wee Abbey"**) can be seen in Abbey Street. An ancient cross in the marketplace shows scenes from the Bible, such as the Fall of Adam and Eve and the Adoration of the Magi. The cemetery has a 9th-century **round tower**, 75 ft (23 metres) high and rather dilapidated, and an early Christian carved **sarcophagus**, thought to be the grave of the founder, St Tiarnoch; the key to which can be obtained from nearby Patton's pub. Several Georgian houses are a reminder of the town's greatest period of prosperity, in the 18th century. Another sign of the vanished "Ascendancy" era are the "big houses", once the homes of the well-to-do Anglo-Irish, many of which have fallen into disrepair.

Monaghan is a quiet, trim county of snug farmhouses and tranquil market towns, and lakes and rivers that draw fishermen. Its administrative centre, **Monaghan** ㉜, 12 miles (19 km) northeast of Clones, has a **Market House** dating from 1792, an imposing 19th-century Gothic Revival cathedral (**St Macartan's**) a good **County Museum** (047-82928, open Tues–Sat) highlighting prehistoric relics and local arts and crafts. The **Garage Theatre** (047-81597), located in a disused ward of a psychiatric hospital, mounts excellent touring productions. To the north, 5 miles (8 km) on the R185, by Glaslough, is the reputedly haunted **Castle Leslie** (047-88109), home of the literary Leslie family and now a hotel.

To the south, east of **Newbliss**, 10 miles (16 km) on the R188, at **Annamakerrig House** is the **Tyrone**

Guthrie Centre (tel: 047-54003, www.tyroneguthrie.ie), an international haven for professional writers. Six miles (10 km) east is Rockcorry where John Gregg invented Gregg's Shorthand, America's favourite. The poet and novelist Patrick Kavanagh grew up 10 miles (16 km) east of attractive **Carrickmacross**, at tiny Inishkeen, where a riverside museum, the **Patrick Kavanagh Centre** (tel: 042-9378560, Tues–Fri all year plus Sat–Sun in Jun–Sept), celebrates his work. Traditional local lace is sold in Carrickmacross. **Ballybay** and **Castleblayney** are unremarkable except for their proximity to **Lough Major** and **Muckno Lake**, both filled with a variety of coarse fish and surrounded by nature trails and picnic sites.

Bandit country

To the northeast and crossing the border again brings you to County Armagh, traditionally known as the Apple Orchard of Ireland, and more recently, its southern acres, thanks to terrorist activity near its border with the Republic, by the less inviting sobriquet of Bandit Country.

Its county town of **Armagh** ❸ (always called a city despite a population of just 15,000) symbolises many of Northern Ireland's problems. Its two striking cathedrals – one Protestant, one Catholic, both called **St Patrick's** – sit on opposite hills like, someone once said, the horns of a dilemma.The two communities live mostly in separate parts of the city, with little interaction.

Armagh is known for its dignified Georgian architecture. At one end of an oval **Mall** – where cricket is played in summer – is a classical courthouse, at the other a jailhouse. The Ionic-pillared **County Museum** (The Mall, tel: 028-3752 3070, admission free, closed Sun) contains many local artifacts, as well as records of Ireland's worst railway disaster, which happened in 1889 just outside Armagh; 80

Map, page 260

The Book of Armagh, a Latin manuscript of the Old Testament and two lives of St Patrick transcribed in 807, is kept in the library of Trinity College, Dublin.

BELOW: Armagh's two St Patrick's Cathedrals – one Catholic (left), the other Protestant.

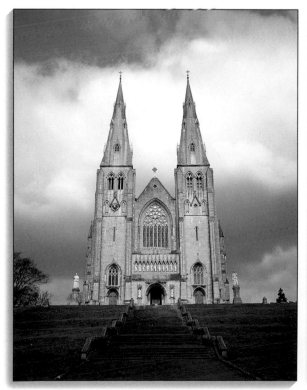

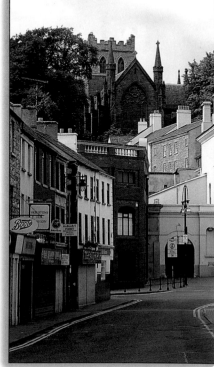

Above: the Navan Fort, an ancient site.

Below: Saturday afternoon cricket on Armagh's Mall.

Sunday School excursionists died when 10 uncoupled carriages ran down a steep incline into the path of a following train. Nearby, the **Royal Irish Fusiliers Museum** (Sovereign's House, The Mall, tel: 028-3752 2911, admission fee, open Mon–Fri, plus Sat in summer), exhibits regimental uniforms, medals and flags.

Access is free into the ordered gardens of the adjacent **Observatory** which also boast Ireland's only **Planetarium** (College Hill, tel: 028-3752 3689, reopening in 2006 after major refurbishment). Its Eartharium allows you to view cities in close-up via spy satellites and forecast the weather and its outdoor Astropark has a scale model of the solar system.

Two miles (3 km) west of the city, off the A28, is the high-tech **Navan Centre** (tel: 028-3752 5550, admission fee for exhibition, free into site), celebrating Emain Macha, Ulster's Camelot around 600BC. Until recent restorations, it was a neglected hilltop; now it comes complete with hands-on computers and audio-visual interpretation facilities. Access to the hilltop itself is free.

The **Palace Stables Heritage Centre** (tel: 028-3752 9629, Friary Road, admission fee, closed Sunday am in winter), past the ruins of a 13th-century friary, at the former archbishop's palace, recreates the building's daily life in 1786 and offers carriage rides. In the city centre **St Patrick's Trian** (tel: 028-3752 1801, English Street, admission fee for exhibition, closed Sun am all year) explains St Patrick's connections with the city and cashes in on Dean Swift's habit of holidaying nearby with a "Land of Lilliput" presentation aimed at children.

The city is surrounded by neat villages, reached through a network of pleasant lanes. Each May, the countryside around **Loughgall** is radiant with apple blossom. In the village the **Dan Winter Ancestral Home** (9 The Diamond, Derry-loughan Road, tel: 028-3885 1344, admission free, open daily Apr–Oct, Sun pm only) displays details of the founding of the Orange Order. Near **Markethill**, in **Gosford Forest Park** (tel: 028-3755 1277, admission fee, closes at dusk), Gosford Castle is a large turreted mock-Norman edifice built of local granite. **Bessbrook** is a model linen-making town, created by a Quaker and therefore lacking a pub.

Map, page 260

Bullet, a variant of Cork's road bowling, is played in summer and autumn in the winding lanes around Armagh. The idea is to propel an iron ball over a 4km distance in the least number of throws. Motorists should be vigilant.

Crossmaglen has a remarkably large market square, containing a bronze monument to the IRA; this village was in the front line of battles between the IRA and the security forces. Remarkably, after enduring many bloody sectarian murders, Crossmaglen has begun promoting tourism with some success in the 1990s. On the B30, 8 miles (13 km) towards Camlough, the thatched **Mullaghbawn Folk Museum** (tel: 028-3088 8278, admission fee, tours by appointment only) preserves a traditional farmhouse of past centuries. The village of **Tynan** has a 10th-century sculptured stone cross, 13 ft (4 metres) high.

Between Armagh and Belfast is a chain of towns built on commerce. **Portadown** ❹, 10 miles (16 km) to the northeast, has found its role scaled down from that of a major railway junction to a prosperous market town noted for rose growing and coarse fishing. Linen manufacturing has diminished, as it has in **Lurgan**, 6 miles (10 km) further along the A3. In the 1960s it was decided to link the two towns to form the "lineal city" of **Craigavon**, thereby reducing congestion in Belfast; but the new city's population never arrived and civic pride has kept the separate identities of Portadown and Lurgan very much alive despite the mushrooming between them of housing estates, schools and countless traffic circles. Lough Neagh's wildlife is well explained in the **Lough Neagh Discovery Centre** (Oxford Island, tel: 028-3832 2205, admission fee, Apr–Sept daily 10am–7pm; Oct–Mar Wed–Sun 10am–5pm). Lough trips on the *Master McGra'* (Marina, Oxford Island, tel: 028-3832 7573, not Oct–Easter) are available.

Seven miles (11 km) west of Portadown, off the B28, two National Trust mansions – 17th-century **Ardress House** (closed weekdays in Apr, May and Sept, all Tues and open Oct–Mar pm only; tel: 028 3885 1236) and 19th-century **The Argory** (open daily Jun–Aug and Easter holidays; tel: 028-87784753).

BELOW:
Kinnego Marina,
Lough Neagh.

Echoes of the Brontës

Banbridge ❸, 10 miles (16 km) south of Lurgan, has a peculiar main street, bisected by an underpass taking through traffic, with sections of road on either side serving a varied collection of small shops.

To its south-east, off the B10, is "**Brontë Homeland**", promoted from the Brontë Interpretive Centre (Drumballyroney, Rathfriland, 028-4063 1152, admission fee, closed Oct–17 Mar and Mon all year), a confusingly signposted trail invented by the tourist authorities to capitalise on the fact that Patrick Brontë (or Brunty or Prunty), father of the novelists Charlotte, Emily and Ann, was born in a cottage at Emdale, 3 miles (5 km) southeast of Loughbrickland. The family's fame was cemented in Yorkshire, not in Emdale, and there's nothing here to conjure up the claustrophobia of *Wuthering Heights* or *Jane Eyre*. But the drive through country lanes so narrow that the hedges almost meet is worth taking and, if you lose track of Patrick Brontë's trail on

Ballynaskeagh Road, or Ballynafern or Lisnacroppin, it doesn't much matter.

The river valleys are peppered with the tall chimneys of disused linen mills so for access to the history and impact of what was the province's major industry go north-west along the Lagan valley to the impressive **Irish Linen Centre and Lisburn Museum** (Market Square, **Lisburn**, tel: 028-9266 3377, admission free, closed Sun) with its hand-loom weaving workshop. Fascinating day and half-day summer tours, passing blue-flowered flax meadows and visiting linen processors modern and arcane, are available.

Newry ❸❻, 19 miles (10 km) to the south-west of Banbridge, is a bustling border town, disfigured by the Troubles but, thanks to the resilience of the Northern Irish, a cheery enough place. Its mercantile history is recalled by a canal, one of Britain's oldest, detailed in **Newry Museum** (Arts Centre, Bank Parade, tel: 028-3031 3180, admission free, Mon–Fri) and 12 miles (19 km) north on the A27 in **Scarva Visitor Centre** (Main Street, tel: 028-3883 2163, admission free, closed Nov–Feb and all Mondays except public holidays).

Four miles (6 km) west of Newry, on the A25, the thatched 18th-century **Derrymore House** (National Trust, tel: 028-9751 0721 for opening times) recalls a more sheltered world.

Seaside relaxations

The atmosphere lightens as you travel either 5 miles (8 km) southwest to **Slieve Gullion Forest Park** (tel: 028-9052 4480, admission fee for cars, summer dawn to dusk, closed winter), where a forest drive winds up to two mountain-top Stone Age cairns, or southeast to the respectable little resorts of Warrenpoint and Rostrevor, overlooking Carlingford Lough. **Warrenpoint** ❸❼ has two piers (good

for fishing), a spacious square and a half-mile promenade lined with trees. **Rostrevor**, a favoured retirement spot sheltered by high hills, can be a sun-trap in summer and has more of a Victorian atmosphere.

A steep half-mile walk up the slopes of **Slievemartin** (1,595 ft/486 metres) brings you to **Cloghmore**, a "Big Stone" supposedly hurled by the Irish giant Fionn MacCool at a rival Scot. The geological explanation for this misplaced piece of granite is more mundane, having to do with glacial drift.

Skirting round the **Mourne Mountains**, past 14th-century **Greencastle** takes you to the active fishing village of **Kilkeel**, capital of the so-called "Kingdom of Mourne." Its winding streets, stepped footpaths and old houses are alluring. There's a choice here: you can proceed along the coast via **Annalong**, a smaller fishing village with old cottages and a **cornmill** (Marine Park, tel: 028-4376 8736, admission fee, Feb–Nov Tues–Sat and bank holidays 11am–5pm) with waterwheel, or you can turn inland into the Mournes.

Meandering in the Mournes

The Mournes are "young" mountains (like the Alps) and their chameleon qualities attract walkers. One moment the granite is grey, the next pink. You walk by an isolated farmhouse, and within moments are in the middle of a wilderness. One minute, the Mournes justify all the songs written about them; the next, they become plain scrubland and unexceptional hills. The weather has a lot to do with it.

Off the B27 the remote **Silent Valley** (Head Road, tel: 028-9074 6581, admission fee) cradles a large dam which supplies Belfast and Co. Down with water. **Slieve Donard**, the highest peak at 2,796 ft (850 metres), has exhilarating views.

As you reach the foothills of the Mournes, turn right just before Hilltown

Map, page 260

Welcome to
MOURNE
Area Of Outstanding
Natural Beauty

BELOW: Royal County Down Golf Club.

towards **Newcastle** . This is east Down's main resort, with a fine, sandy beach, an inordinate number of cake shops, and the celebrated Royal County Down Golf Club. It tries for amusement arcade jollity, but is too small and picturesque to be truly vulgar.

Newcastle's tourist information office is at 10–14 Central Promenade. Hours: Mon–Sat 10am–5pm, Sun 2–6pm. Tel: 028-437 22222.

Several forest parks – **Donard**, **Tollymore**, **Castlewellan** (admission fees) – are good for riding (by pony or bicycle) or walking. This is an area that invites you to unwind, that doesn't understand people who are in a hurry.

Five miles (8 km) inland from Newcastle, **Castlewellan** is a picturesque village with a wide main street. Nine miles (14 km) to the west, **Rathfriland** is a steep-streeted plantation town with lively livestock sales and, as elsewhere in Ulster, kerbstones painted red, white and blue to show political allegiance.

As an alternative to heading into the Mournes from Newcastle, one can continue round the coast, via, at **Dundrum,** Ireland's finest Anglo-Norman castle to **Ardglass**, where several smaller, ruined castles hint at its strategic importance in the Middle Ages to unwelcome kings visiting from Britain. It is an important herring fishing centre.

Seven miles (11 km) inland to the northwest is **Downpatrick** ③, which has a Georgian air and a cathedral supposedly built on the site of St Patrick's first stone church. The saint himself is said by some to be buried here; **Down County Museum** (The Mall, tel: 028-4461 5218, free, closed Sat/Sun am; Sept–May and Sat/Sun am) explains the proposition. The Christian theme continues, off the A7 a mile north-west at placid riverside Cistercian **Inch Abbey** (admission fee). The **Struell Wells** (free access always), off the B1, 1½ miles (2.5 km) east of the town, are evidence of pagan worshippers long before Christianity.

BELOW:
Strangford Lough.

North of the town there begins a prosperous commuter belt, populated by well-spoken professional people who put their money into making their homes ever more comfortable. The source of their prosperity and the commercial magnet to which they are drawn each working day lies to the north: Belfast.

The Ards Peninsula

Comber ④, 17 miles (27 km) to the north at the head of Strangford Lough, was a linen town and still has a working mill. The town centre retains its old character, despite the developers, with single-storey cottage shops and a square. **Castle Espie** (Wildfowl and Wetlands Trust, 78 Ballydrain Road, tel: 028-9187 4146, admission fee) is base for Ireland's largest collection of ducks, geese and swans.

Strangford Lough, an environmental conservation area, is noted for its myriad islands, most of which are sunken drumlins, the smooth glacial hillocks which characterise the Co. Down rolling landscape. There are rocky shores on this side of the lough at places like **Whiterock Bay**. **Mahee Island**, accessible by a bridge, has a golf course and the remains of **Nendrum Abbey** (free access to site always, museum fee, closed Monday), an early monastery.

You can reach the **Ards Peninsula**, a 23-mile (37-km) long finger dotted with villages and beaches, by means of a regular car ferry which chugs a slanted course from **Strangford** ④, 8 miles (13 km) from Downpatrick, across to Portaferry. The Vikings are said to have had a trading post at Strangford in the 9th century. Nearby is **Castle Ward House** (tel: 028-4488 1204, admission fee, open daily Jul–Aug and weekends only Mar–Jun & Sept–Oct; closed Nov–early Mar), an 18th-century Georgian mansion, once the home of the Lord of Bangor. Overlooking the lough, the house has two "fronts" in differing styles (classical and gothic) because the Lord and his Lady had diverging tastes. There are wildfowl in the 700-acre (280-hectare) grounds and the **Strangford Lough Wildlife Centre** is located at the water's edge. There's also a Victorian laundry, two small 15th-century castles and an adventure playground for children.

The ferry across the mouth of the lough deposits you where the sunsets are as fine a sight as anywhere in the world and where the local lobster and the **Exploris** (Castle Street, tel: 028-4272 8062, admission fee, closed Sun am), Northern Ireland's only sea aquarium, are not to be missed.

Nine miles (14 km) north of Portaferry along the A20 is the one-street town of **Kircubbin**, a boating centre with a small pier jutting into Strangford Lough. Two miles (3 km) inland takes you to the **Kirkistown Circuit**, a wartime airport and the home of car racing in Northern Ireland. Motor sport has a keen following in Northern Ireland; motorcycle racing and rallying can take place on public roads closed by Act of Parliament for the events.

Four miles (6 km) further north on the A20 in the pretty village of **Greyabbey** is the site, with "physick garden", of a Cistercian abbey dated 1193, and one of the most complete of its type in Ireland (tel: 028-4278 8585, free admission, open Apr–Sep Tues–Sat 9am–6pm and Sun 2–7pm). Two miles north of the village is another National Trust treasure, **Mount Stewart** (tel: 028-4278 8387, admission fee; gardens open daily all year; house open Mar–Oct daily except

Map, page 260

Emulating England's Glyndebourne, Castle Ward mounts three weeks of opera each June. Picnic hampers welcome.

BELOW: Mount Stewart.

Tues). It is an 18th-century house which has several fine gardens and a mild microclimate which fosters delicate plants untypical of the area. The rhododendrons are particularly fine, and the gardens contain a variety of statues of griffins, satyrs, heraldic lions and the like. Mountstewart House was the birthplace of Lord Castlereagh, England's foreign secretary during the Napoleonic Wars. The **Temple of the Winds**, an 18th-century folly in the grounds, was built by James Stewart, a rival of Robert Adam, and is modelled on another in Athens. It offers a splendid view of the lough.

The First Battle of the Somme, in 1916, cost more than 1 million lives. Ulster regiments were heavily involved and their sacrifice is still cited by Unionist politicians wishing to demonstrate Northern Ireland's loyalty to Great Britain.

Newtownards ㊷, a sprawling commuter town at the head of Strangford Lough, belies its name; it's an old town, dating back to the 17th century. It was an old market town and still is a bustling shopping centre with a blend of traditional shops and a covered shopping centre. There is a fine sandstone town hall and other buildings of historical interest include **Movilla Abbey** on the site of a 6th-century monastery about 1 mile to the east of the town. The airfield, a centre for amateur fliers (Ulster Flying Club, tel: 028-9181 3327), stages a spectacular annual display of aerobatics. The **Somme Heritage Centre** (Bangor Road, tel: 028-9182 3202, admission fee, July and Aug daily; Apr, June–Sept daily except Fri; Jan–Mar and Oct–Dec Mon–Thurs), on Bangor Road, reconstructs elements of the 1916 battle in which many Ulstermen died.

Overlooking the town is **Scrabo Tower** (Scrabo Country Park, tel: 028-9181 1491, opening hours vary), a 19th-century memorial to the third Marquess of Londonderry, offering splendid vistas of the lough and the soft-hilled countryside and good walks in the nearby **Killynether Wood**.

BELOW: Donaghadee.

Donaghadee ㊸, 8 miles (13 km) to the east, is notable for its much-painted harbour and lighthouse, and summer boat trips (Nelson's Boats, 028-9188 3403) up

Belfast Lough and to **Copeland Island** (a bird sanctuary), just offshore. The twisting road passes 18th century **Ballycopeland Windmill** (Millisle, 028-9054 6552, Tues–Sat Jul–Aug) and quieter beaches at **Ballywalter** and **Ballyhalbert**, and the fishing port of **Portavogie**, which has occasional evening quayside fish auctions.

Map, page 260

Popular resort

Bangor ㊹ was orginally a small seaside resort, noted for its abbey. The expensively rejuvenated seafront still has to gentrify some of its collection of fast-food bars and souvenir shops to do justice to the spanking new marina packed with yachts and cruisers. Rowing around the bay in hired punts and fishing trips from the pier are evergreen attractions. The town has a leisure centre with heated swimming and diving pools. For some reason, perhaps the bracing sea air, Bangor is favoured by evangelists who trawl for souls along the sea wall by the little harbour. The **North Down Heritage Centre** (Castle Park Avenue, tel: 028-9127 1200, closed Sunday am always, Mon except public holidays) could provide a refuge.

One of Bangor's first mentions in history is linked to a Viking raid in AD 839.

The old Bangor has been overgrown by acres of new housing developments and shopping centres, many of them inhabited by people who work in Belfast. It is a busy shopping town with a weekly open-air market, plenty of pubs and eating places, and parkland. The best beach is nearby **Ballyholme Bay**, a sandy arc which becomes very crowded when the sun shines.

If you leave Bangor by the A2, a signposted detour to the right will take in the beaches of **Helen's Bay**, the nearby wooded **Crawfordsburn Country Park** (tel: 028: 9185 3621, free), and the picturesque village of **Crawfordsburn** with its charming **Old Inn**. Such havens are unusual so close to a city the size of Belfast.

BELOW: all the fun of the fair at Bangor.

The "Gold Coast"

The A2 from Bangor to Belfast runs through what locals enviously describe as the **"Gold Coast"**. This is stockbroker country, where lush lawns meet mature woodland. Hillside sites, overlooking the shipping lanes, have traditionally lured the well-heeled. **Cultra**, 6 miles (10 km) from Bangor, has leafy lanes, splendid houses, and the resplendent **Culloden Hotel**. They go in for yachting, golf and horse riding around here. Nowhere is more removed from the TV image of Northern Ireland. **Holywood**, an ancient religious settlement a mile further on, enjoys a quiet prosperity since it was bypassed. Nothing much happens here, apart from summer jazz and rumours of the odd dance around the Maypole, but it has pleasant shops, and good pubs and restaurants.

Nearby, at Cultra Manor is the award-winning **Ulster Folk and Transport Museum** ㊺ (tel: 028-9042 8428, www.uftm.org.uk, admission fee, open daily), which brings social history to life. Farm-houses, cottages, churches and mills have been painstakingly reconstructed – often brick by brick from their original locations. Freshly made soda bread, a local speciality, is sometimes baked over a traditional peat fire. On another part of the site the Transport Museum has its own fascination; exhibits range from horse-drawn chariots right up to a prototype of the ill-fated Belfast-built De Lorean sports car (the company crashed but the car, with its distinctive gull-wing doors, lived on in the *Back to the Future* movies). The brilliant Ulster engineer Harry Ferguson, a pioneer of flying, tractors and four-wheel-drive cars, is the prize example of the remarkable local contribution to air, sea and land transport.

From here it's a straight run into Belfast (*see next chapter*).

ABOVE: a plaque at Carrickfergus.
BELOW: exhibit at the Ulster Folk and Transport Museum.

(plaque text:)
TO COMMEMORATE THE LANDING OF KING WILLIAM III AT THIS PIER ON 14TH JUNE 1690

North of Belfast

If you aren't in the mood for city life, however, a good ring-road system will take you through the city to the north shore of Belfast Lough and the suburbs of **Whiteabbey** and **Greenisland**, with some opulent housing.

Carrickfergus ㊻, 12 miles (19 km) north from Belfast along the A2, is yet another market and dormitory town. Its big synthetic-fibre plants are empty now – a contemporary monument to its industrial past. The imposing 12th-century Norman **Castle** (The Harbour, tel: 028-9335 1273, admission fee, closed Sunday am) beside the harbour, scene of gun-running exploits early in the 20th century, still attracts attention for its authenticity. It is a real castle in every sense, with a portcullis, ramparts looking out over the sea, chilling dungeons, cannons and a regimental museum in the keep. Looking to the new age of leisure, the town's **marina** has 300 berths. The parish church of St Nicholas (with stained-glass windows to Santa Claus) is 12th-century.

In Antrim Street, **Carrickfergus Museum** (tel: 028-9335 8049, free admission, open Mon–Sat, also Sun in Jul–Aug) provides general historical information about the town. The preserved **Carrickfergus Gasworks** (Irish Quarter West, tel: 028-9336 9575, admission fee, open Sunday pm only, June-Aug) will fascinate the mechanically minded. A mile to the east, the **Andrew Jackson Centre** (Boneybefore, tel: 028-9335 8049, free admission, open Apr–Oct, closed Sat and Sun am) is a reconstruction of the thatched cottage home of Andrew Jackson, the seventh President of the United States.

The countryside north of Carrickfergus becomes rich meadow land, with the sleepy seaside town of **Whitehead,** base for the Railway Preservation Society of Ireland (Castleview Road, Whitehead, tel: 028-2826 0803, occasional steam excursions). The town nestles at the mouth of the lough, with a seashore walk to the Black Head lighthouse. Beyond this begins the peninsula of **Island Magee**, with unspoilt beaches and caves, which wraps around Larne Lough. From here, the road runs into unlovely **Larne ㊼**, a port with frequent ferries to and from Stranraer in Scotland (70 minutes away). The Larne and District Historical Centre at 2 Victoria Road (tel: 028-2827 9482, free, opening hours vary) has a historical centre featuring photographs from 100 years ago.

The Antrim Coast Road

The rewards of continuing along the coast are spectacular views of brown moorlands, white limestone, black basalt, red sandstone and blue sea along the **Antrim Coast Road**. A notable engineering achievement, it is explained in the Larne Interpretive Centre (Narrow Gauge Road, tel: 028-2826 0088, free; Oct–Easter Mon–Fri; Easter–Sept Mon–Sat). The road, designed in 1834 by Sir Charles Lanyon as a work of famine relief, opened up an area whose inhabitants had previously found it easier to travel by sea to Scotland than overland to the rest of Ireland.

At various points, you can turn into one or other of Antrim's celebrated nine glens – **Glenarm, Glencloy, Glenariff, Glenballyeamon, Glenaan, Glencorp, Glendun, Glenshesk** and **Glentaisie** – and into another world. It's a world of weather-beaten farmers in tweeds and baggy trousers; a world of sheep sales

Map, page 260

Ulster Unionists opposed to a Roman Catholic-dominated united Ireland unloaded a large consignment of German-made rifles in Larne harbour in 1914. World War I shelved the problem for a few years.

BELOW:
Carrickfergus Castle, recalling the Norman Conquest; a round tower overlooking Larne Lough.

conducted by auctioneers who talk like machine guns; a world with a baffling dialect that turns an ewe into a *yow* and "six" into *sex*; a world where poteen, the "mountain dew", is distilled in lonely places. It's not hard to track down this illicit (and potentially lethal) alcohol. "It's floating about," they'll tell you. "In fact it's practically running down the streets."

Ballygalley ⓬, at the start of the famous scenic drive, has a 1625 fortified manor house (now a hotel) and, inland from the coast road, a well-preserved old mill and pottery. **White Bay** is a picnic area around which small fossils can be found. **Glenarm** has a beautiful park adjoining a fussy castle, home of the Earls of Antrim. **Carnlough** has a fine harbour and, running over its main street, a white bridge built in 1854 to carry limestone from the quarries to waiting boats. The Londonderry Arms hotel (also 1854) retains the charms of an old coaching inn. An eponymous literary summer school at Garron Tower 5 miles (8 km) north celebrates John Hewitt, an acerbic dissenter poet.

An Irish song-and-dance festival is held each July in the village of **Waterfoot**. This is also the entrance to **Glenariff Glen**, a deep wooded gorge dubbed by Thackeray "Switzerland in miniature". Wild flowers carpet the upper glen in spring and early summer, and slippery rustic footbridges carry walkers over the Glenariff River, past postcard-pretty waterfalls.

About 1½ miles (2 km) to the north, **Cushendall**, "capital of the glens", was created largely by a wealthy 19th-century landowner, Francis Turnly. His most striking structure was the four-storey red sandstone **Curfew Tower**, built as "a place of confinement for idlers and rioters". The village has a good beach and is a popular sailing centre. Just to the north is **Layde Old Church**, dating back to the 13th century and containing some ancient vaults. Six miles (10 km) further

ABOVE: roaming the Glens of Antrim.

BELOW: Cushendun.

on, **Cushendun** ④ is a village of charming Cornish-style white cottages, graceful old houses and friendly pubs, has been captured on countless canvases and the entire place is protected by the National Trust.

Map, page 260

The northern coast

Crossing the towering **Glendun Viaduct** (1839), one passes the ruins of **Bonamargy Friary**, founded around 1500. A vault contains the massive coffins of several MacDonnell chieftains who stood out successfully against the forces of England's Queen Elizabeth I. Nearby, **Corrymeela Community House** is an inter-denominational conference and holiday centre, whose idealism shines out amid Northern Ireland's prevailing political cynicism.

The best time to visit **Ballycastle** ⑤ is during the **Auld Lammas Fair**, held on the last Monday and Tuesday of August. Then this unspoiled town turns into one throbbing market place as farmers with impenetrable accents bring their livestock in from the glens and hundreds of stalls sell souvenirs, bric-a-brac, dulse (dried, edible seaweed) and yellowman (a sweet confectionery). The big attraction is the *craic* – pronounced "crack" (a Scots-Irish word for talk, enlivened by a glass or two of Bushmills). It's great fun – an authentic folk event that owes nothing to the manipulations of tourist boards. The **Ballycastle Museum** (59 Castle Streeet, tel: 028-2076 2024, free, closed Oct–June) concentrates on the folk social history of the Glens.

The Auld Lammas Fair is Ireland's oldest, dating back to 1606, when a charter was first granted.

A sea-front memorial marks the spot where, in 1898, Guglielmo Marconi first seriously tested wireless telegraphy. He made his historic transmission between here and **Rathlin Island** ⑤, 8 miles (13 km) off the coast towards Scotland's Mull of Kintyre. The boomerang-shaped island, whose population has slumped from 2,000 to 100 since 1850, makes its living from farming and fishing and attracts geologists, botanists and birdwatchers; there is a reserve (tel: 028-2076 3948) managed by the Royal Society for the Protection of Birds, an estimated 250,000 birds of 175 species. With the new ferry (tel: 028-2076 9299) installed, uncertainties about the 50-minute sailings being affected by weather and high seas are hopefully over. But whether the decrease in isolation will benefit the island's environment is another matter. There is one pub a hotel, guesthouse and youth hostel – but no policeman, and no need for one. A minibus tours the island in summer. Advance booking required (tel: 028-2076 3909 or Raghery Tours 028-2076 3451).

BELOW: eating seaweed, a delicacy at Ballycastle's Auld Lammas Fair.

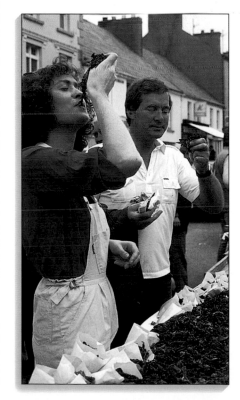

Five miles (8 km) west, off the A2, is the **Carrick-a-rede Rope Bridge** (May-Sept, 028-2073 2963, car park fee), 65 ft (20 metres) wide swinging over a 80-ft (24-metre) chasm to an island salmon fishery. Past Whitepark Bay is **Dunseverick Castle,** the slight remains of a 6th-century fortress perched on a high crag overlooking a fishing harbour.

The Giant's Causeway

The castle is at the eastern end of the **Giant's Causeway** ⑤, an astonishing assembly of more than 40,000 basalt columns, mostly perfect hexagonals formed by the cooling of molten lava. Dr Samuel Johnson, when asked by his biographer James Boswell whether this wonder of the world was worth seeing, gave the immortal reply: "Worth seeing? yes; but not worth going to see." It was a shrewd judgment in the 1770s when roads in the region were primitive enough to turn a journey into an expedition; indeed, the existence of the Causeway hadn't been known at all to the outside world until a gadabout Bishop of Derry stumbled upon them in 1692. Today this geological curiosity is accessible to the most monstrous tourist coaches, but it can still disappoint some visitors, who expect the columns to be bigger (the tallest, in the **Giant's Organ**, are about 12 metres) or who find that their regularity only diminishes their magnificence. It remains worth seeing, though. The formal approach is via the Causeway Centre (Causeway Head, tel: 028-2073 1855, car park fee) 2 miles (3 km) north of Bushmills on the B146.

The world's oldest distillery

The distillery at **Bushmills** ⓼ (Distillery Road, tel: 028-2073 3218. Guided tours, Apr–Oct daily; Nov–Mar Mon–Fri, www.whiskeytours.ie) a couple of miles away, boasts the world's oldest whiskey-making licence (1608). Old Bushmills, Black Bush and Bushmills Malt, made from local barley and the water that flows by in St Columb's Rill, can be tasted after a tour. Connoisseurs tend to prefer the classic Black Bush to the more touted (and expensive) malt. The main difference between Scotch whisky and Irish whiskey, apart from the spelling, is that Scotch is distilled twice and Irish three times.

About 2 miles (3 km) along the coast road are the romantic remains of **Dunluce Castle** (tel: 028-7073 1938, closed Mon and Sun am). Poised on a rocky headland besides sheer cliffs, the 14th-century stronghold is immense and dramatic. The novelist William Makepeace Thackeray wrote of "those grey tow-

BELOW: Dunluce Castle; the Giant's Causeway.

ers of Dunluce standing upon a leaden rock and looking as if some old old princess of old old fairy times were dragon guarded within." It was abandoned in 1641, two years after part of the kitchen collapsed into the sea during a storm, carrying many of the servants to their death. In the graveyard of the adjacent ruined church are buried sailors from the Spanish Armada galleass *Girona*, which was wrecked on nearby rocks in 1588 with 1,300 men on board and was located on the seabed in 1967. Many of the *Girona*'s treasures are in the Ulster Museum, Belfast.

Map, page 260

Next along the coast are two seaside resorts. **Portrush** ❺❹ is the brasher, tackier, offering amusement arcades, burger bars, karaoke pubs, souvenir shops, guesthouses, a children's adventure play park, boats trips for sea fishing and viewing the Causeway and two championship golf courses. The **Dunluce Centre** (028-7082 4444, admission fee, Apr–Sept daily; Mar–Oct weekends only; Nov–Feb closed, offers virtual-reality "myths and legends"). **Portrush Countryside Centre** (Landsdowne Crescent, tel: 028-7082 3600, free, closed Oct–Mar) has rock pool animals in a touch tank. **Portstewart** is the quieter, a tidy Victorian town with a huge strand, excellent for beach casting but plagued by speeding cars which, unaccountably, are allowed free access. Long-distance walkers can pick up the **North Antrim Coast Path** at Portstewart Strand; it forms part of the Ulster Way and extends eastwards for 40 miles (64 km) to **Murlough Bay**.

The Royal Portrush Golf Club is Northern Ireland's finest; it has one 9-hole and two 18-hole courses. Tel: 028-70822311.

Nearby **Coleraine** is a busy but unimaginative market town whose traffic schemes make little of its setting on the wide River Bann or of the fact that the earliest human settlement in Ireland was found at the 200-ft (60-metre) **Mount Sandel** in its southern suburbs. However, its university's **Riverside Theatre** (Colmore Road, tel: 028-7032 3232) imports interesting productions during term.

BELOW: Portstewart.

A choice of routes

Here, you can either continue westwards towards Derry City or proceed south towards Aldergrove Airport and Belfast.

Along the first choice, the A2 towards Derry City, on a windswept headland at **Downhill** ⑤, the massive roofless ruin of **Downhill Castle** (1780) dominates the skyline. Its **Mussenden Temple** (Mussenden Road, Castlerock, tel: 028-7084 8728, free; July–Aug daily; Apr, June and Sept weekends only; Oct–Mar closed), is perched precariously near a 200-ft (60-metre) cliff and housed an eccentric bishop's library and possibly his mistress; it was inspired by the temples of Vesta at Tivoli and Rome. **Downhill Forest** has lovely walks, a fish pond and waterfalls.

An inscription on Mussenden Temple reads: "It is agreeable to watch, from land, someone else involved in a great struggle while winds whip up the waves out at sea."

Beyond is **Magilligan Strand**, Ireland's longest beach. Along its magnificent 7 miles (11 km) of sand dunes can be found teal, tern, mallard, snipe, wild geese, and 120 different kinds of seashells. At the beginning of the strand is a **Martello Tower** with walls 10 ft (3 metres) thick, built during the Napoleonic wars. A ferry is proposed to Greencastle in Donegal.

The alternative route is southwards through the relatively prosperous farming country "east of the **Bann**". This long, under-used river, which flows from the southeast of the province through Lough Neagh and into the Atlantic near Portstewart, is a rough and ready political dividing line between the western counties of Londonderry and Tyrone, with their preponderance of nationalists and Roman Catholics, and the eastern counties of Antrim and Down, with their Unionist/Protestant majority. In a thriving market town like **Ballymoney** ⑤, 17 miles (27 km) southwest of Ballycastle, archaic words that would have been familiar to Shakespeare crop up in everyday conversation – a legacy of the Scots Presbyterians planted as settlers in the 1800s.

BELOW: the Mussenden Temple.

As elsewhere in Ulster, churches loom large. There's one on each of the four roads leading into a small village like **Dervock**, for instance, 4 miles (6 km) north of Ballymoney and ancestral home of America's President William McKinley (assassinated in 1901). Legend says that this strategic siting of churches keeps the Devil out. Locals suggest it probably keeps him in. Off the B96, 20 miles (33 km) south, the restored **Arthur Ancestral Home** (Dreen, Cullybackey, tel: 028-2588 0781, admission fee, closed Sun and Oct–Apr) commemorates Chester Alan Arthur, US president from 1881 to 1885, whose father emigrated from it in 1815.

Ballymena ⑤, 19 miles (30 km) southeast of Ballymoney, is the staunchly Protestant business centre of Antrim and, as a result perhaps of the traditionally strong Scottish influence, has been unkindly called the meanest town in Ireland.

Water sports on Lough Neagh

Antrim ⑤, the county town, 11 miles (18 km) to the southeast, offers a little more to see. **Pogue's Entry** (Church Street, tel: 028-9442 8000, open Thur–Sat) has several small 18th-century cottages, one of them the birthplace of Alexander Irvine who became a missionary on New York's Bowery. There's an almost perfectly preserved round tower, more than 1,000 years old, in Steeple Park. The **Antrim Castle Gardens,** (Randalstown Road, tel: 028-9442 8000, free admission) are laid out like a miniature Versailles and run down to the shore of Lough Neagh. The gardens, winner of a European Architectural Heritage Award, preserve the atmosphere and elegance of a formal 17th-century garden.

Lough Neagh (pronounced *Nay*), 17 miles long and 11 miles broad (27 by 18 km) is the largest inland sheet of water in the British Isles. Legend has it that the warrior giant Finn McCool created the lake by scooping up a mighty handful of earth to fling at a rival Scottish giant (he missed, and the rock and clay fell into the Irish Sea to create the Isle of Man). Because of the lough's marshy edges, it has surprisingly few access points – one reason, perhaps, why it has remained one of western Europe's most important bird habitats. The Lough Neagh Discovery Centre on Oxford Island (*for opening times, see page 295*) runs audio-visual shows about the wildlife and has a gift shop and café. Recreational facilities for sailing and water-skiing have been developed, with marinas at **Oxford Island** (south shore) and **Ballyronan** (west shore).

A large eel fishing industry is based at **Toome**. Until it became a fishermen's cooperative, gun battles used to take place on Lough Neagh between the police's patrol boats and the vessels of organised poachers.

Wonderfully atmospheric, **Patterson's Spade Mill** (751 Antrim Road, Templepatrick, tel: 028-9443 3619, admission fee, closed Oct–Mar and weekdays Apr, May and Sept; closed Tues July and Aug) is the last working water-powered spade mill in Ireland. And you can buy a spade, always remembering the Ulster saying about people who "dig with the other foot" – a reference from the days when the shapes of spades were very localised and a stranger's home and therefore, by inference, his religion could be told from the cut of his spade. Some obsessions in Ulster don't change much over the centuries. ❏

Map, page 260

TIP

To fish in Lough Neagh, you first need a rod licence from the Foyle Fisheries Commission (Tel: 028-713 42100). You may then need a further permit from an angling club.

BELOW: water sports on Lough Neagh, the largest lake in the British Isles.

MEN WHO MARCH

Parades and bunting, bands and bibles... it's hard
to escape these provocative rituals during July and
August. Just what is the marching season all about?

Northern Ireland is unique in its flourishing popular
culture: there are bands in every village and every
housing estate, and nowhere else in the UK do
normally discreet citizens sing and dance in the
streets. There are many processions throughout the
year, and some quiet church parades, but the
prolonged marching season in July and August can
heighten sectarian tensions.

The main Orange procession, which celebrates
the 1690 Battle of the Boyne in which William III
(William of Orange) cemented the Protestant
heritage, takes place on 12 July. On 13 July, the
Black Men (the Orange Order's elite) dress up in
period costume to re-enact King Billy's routing of
the Catholic King James II in the "Sham Fight" at
Scarva, County Down. On 12 August the
Apprentice Boys march through Derry City in
memory of 13 apprentices who closed the city's
gates against the forces of James II.

THE GREEN ORANGEMEN

Lady's Day, in honour of the Madonna, Mary
Mother of God, is held on 15 August by the Ancient
Order of Hibernians, who are
sometimes known as the
Green Orangemen.
(Green symbolises
Catholic Ireland,
orange Protestant
Ulster.) Like their
Orange counterparts,
the Hibernians mix
prayer with pageantry.

Before the current
Troubles began in
1969, many hoped
that such pageantry
would become less
political and more of
a tourist attraction.
Instead, it appears to
Catholics a sign of
"triumphalism" and to
Protestants as another
nationalist provocation.

◁ **THE BIG PARADE**
In Belfast, the main 12 July
Orange parade is a massive
affair that can take up to four
hours to pass any given point.
It attracts followers
from all over the
world, including
Glasgow, Liver-
pool, Canada,
Australia and
New Zealand.

△ **WEARING THE GREEN...**
The Ancient Order of
Hibernians dates its origins to
1565 when persecuted Irish
Catholics formed armed
bands to protect their priest.
The order united in its present
form in 1838. Its main march
takes place on 15 August.

◁ DRUMMING IT IN

The booming Lambeg drum, named after a village near Belfast, is often cited by nationalists as an obvious example of the Orangemen's triumphalist attitude towards Catholics. The "loyalists" say they march – or "walk" – simply to demonstrate their loyalty to the Protestant faith and to the British monarch.

▽ THE GREEN MACHINE

By rejecting the use of force to gain a united Ireland after World War I, the Hibernians lost ground to extremists, and today they number only about 20,000. There are probably five times as many Orangemen. Both Orders enjoy hymns and "blood and thunder" party tunes.

WHY THE BANDS ARE BIG BUSINESS

The world-famous flautist James Galway started his career in a Belfast band, and there can be few other parts of Europe where such a high percentage of the population plays a musical instrument.

Despite the years of conflict, enthusiasm for bands and music remains as jubilant now as it ever was. In late spring and early summer, motorists driving through the leafy lanes of the Ulster countryside must be prepared to round a corner and confront columns of men in bowler hats solemnly drumming and tootling their way to a local contest.

Scottish and Gaelic pipers compete with ecumenical harmony, at their own expense and "for the glory of it", in villages and small towns throughout summer. With a set of pipes costing around £1,500, that means there may be £2.5 million worth of pipes keening at a typical contest.

There are celebrated brass bands, like the Templemore and Britannia. Fife and drum, flute and even the tin whistle are favoured by the young, with accordians for girls. The musical range is colourful and varied: Irish or Scottish folk songs, "blood and thunder" party tunes (Orange or Green), military marches and hymns.

There are few places in the West where folk traditions remain so central to everyday life as in Ulster.

▽ CATCHING THEM WHEN THEY'RE YOUNG

Many Northern Irish children, who learn sectarian songs along with nursery rhymes, start marching at an early age. But fewer than 10 percent of Ulster schoolboys are lodge members today, compared with more than one-third 30 years ago.

△ ...AND THE ORANGE

The Orange Order dates back to the late 18th century when Protestant formed groups to defend their land from raids by its former Catholic owners. They celebrate the victory of William of Orange over the Catholic James II in 1690.

BELFAST

Forget the television coverage. This is a city of unexpected charms, mixing splendid Victorian architecture with a genuine hospitality

Map, page 316

Apart from one unique feature, Belfast is an unremarkable, medium-sized, post-industrial city on the western fringes of Europe. Its unique feature is that, as the capital of Northern Ireland, it has made world headlines for 30 years. Its setting, in a saucer of green hills and spanning the mouth of the **River Lagan** as it flows east into the Irish Sea, is charming. There are serried rows of red-brick terraces, a worthy, white stone and marble City Hall. The Linen Conservation Area attests to the source of its founding wealth and man-made fibre factories in surrounding towns continue textile's traditions. Massive cranes dominate the skyline where the Harland and Wolff shipyards produced the doomed *Titanic* and now, much reduced, maintain other traditional engineering skills. Short Brothers aerospace company remains a contender in the weapons race.

Belfast (pop. 400,000) looks little different from a provincial English city. Donegall Place, its "main street", is lined with UK multiple stores such as Marks & Spencer and Boots. And Britain's monarchy is well represented on the map. The first major bridge to link the city east and west was named Queen's for England's Victoria. The university is named Queen's for her too. Albert, her consort, gave his name to a monolithic, now leaning, clocktower. The Royal Botanic Gardens provide an island of calm. Windsor Park stages soccer internationals.

But 30 years of the "troubles" and 800 years of English colonial rule have set the city apart. In the blue-collar enclaves, the gable ends of red-brick houses are bright with murals. In one area, this "folk art" portrays hooded figures brandishing Kalashnikov rifles and the green, white and orange of the Irish Republic's tricolour flag; in another area, it features King Billy (England's William III) crossing the Boyne on his white horse.

A brief history of Belfast time

The city's history is brief, by European standards. When John de Courcy, an Anglo-Norman freebooter, marched north to take Ulster from Gaelic hands in 1177, the place was known for little more than its approach to the crossing point (*béal feirsde* in Gaelic) at the mouth of the Lagan. The 12th-century Irish horsemen, bareback, stirrup-less, were no match for de Courcy's mail-armoured lancers. De Courcy's aides built a strategic castle, fought over for centuries and remembered now only in a city crossroads, Castle Junction. In Elizabeth I's reign, Protestant Tudor England, at war with Spain, fought Catholic Ireland. The Virgin Queen's favourite, Lord Essex, built a fort at Fortwilliam and, in the fashion of the times, put to the sword the Irish he invited to dinner. Although he planned a corporate town here, Essex failed in this

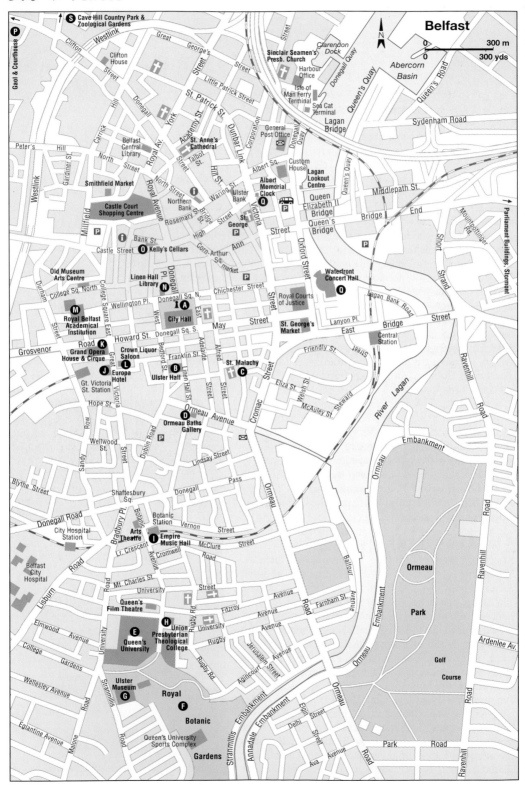

Belfast

300 m

300 yds

Cave Hill Country Park &
Zoological Gardens

Gaol & Courthouse

Clifton House

Clifton Street

Westlink

Great George's Street

Little Patrick Street

St. Patrick St.

Sinclair Seamen's
Presb. Church

Clarendon
Dock

Harbour
Office

Isle of
Man Ferry
Terminal

Sea Cat
Terminal

Donegall Quay

Queen's Quay

Sydenham Road

Peter's Hill

Carrick Hill

Donegall Street

Gardiner St.

North Street

York

Royal Av.

Academy St.

Talbot St.

St. Anne's
Cathedral

Belfast
Central
Library

Dunbar Link

Corporation

General
Post Office

Albert Sq.

Donegall

Custom
House

Lagan
Lookout
Centre

Queen's Quay

Lagan
Bridge

Queen Elizabeth II
Bridge

Queen's
Bridge

Middlepath St.

East End

Mountpottinger Rd.

Parliament Buildings, Stormont

Westlink

Millfield

Smithfield Market

Castle Court
Shopping Centre

North Street

Waring St.

High Street

Hill St.

Bridge St.

Rosemary

Northern
Bank

Ulster
Bank

St.
George

Albert
Memorial
Clock

Victoria Street

Ann Street

Corn-Arthur Sq. market

Oxford Street

Queen
Elizabeth II
Bridge

Waterfront
Concert Hall

Lagan Bank Road

Strand

Old Museum
Arts Centre

Durham

College Sq. North

College Square East

Bank St.

Castle Street

Kelly's Cellars

Linen Hall
Library

Donegall Pl.

Donegall Sq. N.

Wellington Pl.

Donegall Sq. N.

Chichester Street

City Hall

Royal Courts
of Justice

Royal Belfast
Academical
Institution

Grosvenor Road

Howard St.

Donegall Sq. West

May Street

Adelaide Street

Alfred Street

Linen Hall Street

St. George's
Market

Central
Station

East Bridge Street

River Lagan

Grand Opera
House & Cirque

Crown Liquor
Saloon

Europa
Hotel

Gt. Victoria
St. Station

Great Victoria Street

Bedford St.

Franklin St.

Ulster Hall

St. Malachy

Eliza St.

Eliza St.

Welsh St.

McAuley St.

Steward

Friendly St.

Hope St.

Ormeau Avenue

Ormeau Baths
Gallery

Cromac Street

Embankment

Dublin Road

Wellwood St.

Lindsay Street

Ormeau

Blythe Street

Sandy Row

Shaftesbury Sq.

Donegall Pass

Donegall Road

City Hospital
Station

Bradbury Pl.

Botanic Ave.

Botanic
Station

Vernon Street

Empire
Music Hall

McClure Street

Arts
Theatre

Lr. Crescent

Cromwell Road

Ormeau
Embankment

Ormeau

Park

Belfast
City
Hospital

Lisburn Road

Mt. Charles St.

University Street

Fitzroy Avenue

Farnham St.

Balfour Avenue

Golf

Course

Ardenlee Av.

Queen's Film
Theatre

Union
Presbyterian
Theological
College

Rugby Rd.

University Road

Rugby Avenue

Jerusalem Street

Agincourt Avenue

Elmwood Avenue

Queen's
University

Ulster
Museum

Royal

Botanic

Gardens

Queen's University
Sports Complex

Stranmillis Road

Eglantine Avenue

Wellesley Avenue

College Gardens

Malone Road

Delhi Street

Annadale Embankment

Stranmillis Embankment

Ava Street

Park Road

Ravenhill Road

Ravenhill

Abercorn
Basin

Queen's Road

venture and the task was left to Arthur Chichester, a robber of tax collectors, who was rewarded for deploying a scorched-earth policy against Irish resistance. He built a "towne of good forme" and it was all his, by its charter of incorporation, by 1613.

It was another Chichester of flawed character who made possible the modern city. For such were the extravagances of George Augustus Chichester, Lord Belfast – otherwise known as Gambling George – that he was in a debtors' prison before he succeeded to the title of 2nd Marquis of Donegall, and possession of the city, in 1799. Twenty years later much of his lands were leased in perpetuity, the rest sold on his death to meet massive debts.

Donegall Place, which was still shopless, a mix of mansions, orchards and falconries, was thus opened up to speculators who found their champion in architect Sir Charles Lanyon. A flamboyant ruthless and corrupt speculator, philanderer and Conservative MP, Lanyon made his first fortune marrying the boss's daughter and later became Mayor of Belfast.

At a time when financial services were less than regulated, banks which Lanyon designed had the solidity of an Italian merchant prince's palace. His County Gaol, County Courthouse and Custom House dignified authority. His Deaf and Dumb Institution glorified its benefactor, his Queen's College echoed Oxford's dreaming spires, and his Presbyterian College offered diligence and obedience. His Queen's Bridge underlined the monarch's majesty, his viaducts made permanent the railways of commerce, and his 14 churches beckoned God's blessing down upon the worthy. To understand what made Belfast what it is, a tour of his buildings is more than a useful aid, and it is possible to build a walking tour loosely around the Lanyon Trail.

The city centre

Belfast's imposing **City Hall** (Donegall Square, tel: 9027 0426, admission free; tours: summer Mon–Sat, winter Mon–Sat pm, call for times), with its imported marbled interior, isn't Lanyon's. It was designed by Brumwell Thomas, a Londoner, who had to sue the Corporation for his fees, and was built in the early years of the 20th century. The domes of its exterior and of its Council Chamber – laid out as to the manner of Westminster's House of Commons – pay tribute to the great English architect, Sir Christopher Wren. Northern Ireland's first House of Commons sat there in 1921–22, its Whispering Gallery has heard many a whisper, many a roar, and the assorted statuary speaks of a time when Britain's Empire ruled far and wide.

The best view of Thomas's work is not of the front with its dumpy statue of Queen Victoria, but rather of its rear, from down **Linen Hall Street** running parallel to **Bedford Street** in the **Linen Conservation Area,** still resonant with linen warehouses whose style is typified by Lanyon's work at number **35–37**. The nearby **Ulster Hall** (30 Bedford Street, tel: 9032 3900), once a music hall, hosts weekly Ulster Orchestra concerts, boxing matches, rock gigs and beerfests. Its annex, the **Group Theatre**, is the base for the province's amateur drama movement, but alternates their plays with avant garde professional

Map, page 316

TIP

If telephoning from other parts of the UK, prefix all numbers in this chapter with the code 028 (from outside the UK: 44-28).

BELOW:
Big Fish sculpture in Donegall Quay.

ABOVE: signs of the times as efforts increase to attract back tourists.

productions, bewildering senior citizen season ticket holders. East of Linen Hall Street runs **Alfred Street** with its wonderfully castellated red-brick Catholic **St Malachy's Church** . The creamy fan-vaulted ceiling, a wedding cake upturned, would have served well the cathedral it was intended to be. In 1886 the tolling of its bell was deemed to interfere with the maturing of whiskey in Dunville's then adjacent distillery. The bell was removed.

Where Linen Hall Street meets **Ormeau Avenue**, by the BBC building, Belfast's tiny red-light district operates at night on street corners by the city's newest modernist art space, the **Ormeau Baths Gallery** (18 Ormeau Avenue, tel: 9032 1402, admission free, closed Sun and Mon), which makes good use of an imaginative conversion of an 1887 public bath house.

The Golden Mile

No one knows where the city's much vaunted **"Golden Mile"** begins – or ends. Christened thus by a Tourist Board flaneur in the troubled tourist-free 1970s, it is an ever-changing 20-hour-a-day banlieu of bistros, restaurants, theme bars, ethnic eateries, pizza parlours, burger bars and design houses. It encompasses, roughly, a triangle whose base runs from Donegall Place's Linen Hall Library to College Square North's avant-garde, community-based **Old Museum Arts Centre** (7 College Square North, tel: 9023 5053, www.oldmuseumartscentre.org, closed Sun). Its east side is the Bedford Street–Dublin Road–Bradbury Place axis. Its apex is Queen's University. Its west side is definitely Great Victoria Street. By 3am the thoroughfare is impassable as disco clubs disgorge.

BELOW: festival time.

Although the Golden Mile may not rival London's Covent Garden, it does offer variety. **Morrison's**, on Bedford Street, was the first bar to market itself

as a recreation of the Edwardian rural spirit grocery store. **Dempsey's** opts for glitz and **Lavery's Gin Palace** in **Bradbury Place** melds 1960s drop-outs with '90s clubbers. Amongst the ethnics, crepuscular **Archana** does a firey balti and of the bistros, **La Belle Epoque** is a quiet haven of French provincial food. Its partner, **Frogities** in **Bradbury Place** dispenses with bookings, seeking younger customers. **Bishop's** dispenses fine fish and chips, mushy peas, pots of tea, slices of white bread, unselfconscious in its post-modernism.

The **Fenderesky** (2 University Road, tel: 9023 5245, admission free, closed Sun–Mon), in the enterprising Scots baronial-style granite **Crescent Arts Centre** (tel: 9024 2338), offers the best of contemporary Irish painting. The Centre itself, though obsessed with New Age-ery, runs a discerning line up of jazz, Latin American music, dance, cabaret and experimental theatre.

The university area

Queen's University , its blue-tinged red brick at its best near dusk, is one of Lanyon's delights, a pinnacle of Early Victorian, appropriating the Tudor of Oxford's Magdalen College. Its quad, open all hours, is rich in cherry trees and looks superb in May's blossom-time. The Visitor Centre (tel: 9033 5252) keeps office hours.

Across University Road, at 25 College Gardens, a gilded cockerel tops the spire of Italiante **Elmwood Hall**, a deconsecrated church, home to the Ulster Orchestra and a core venue for the University's adventurous autumnal Belfast Festival at Queen's (tel: 9097 2600 or www.belfastfestival.com for festival details, 9066 8798 or www.ulster-orchestra.org.uk for Ulster Orchestra details). The festival had become formulaic and middle-brow until it was re-born in 1997 under

Queen's College, named in honour of Queen Victoria, was established in 1849 and incorporated as a separate university in 1908. Pressed for space, it has taken over most of the houses in the vicinity.

BELOW: graduation, Queen's University.

director Sean Doran. Work by Robert Wilson, John Cage, Silviu Pucarete, Bill Viola and Hans Peter Kuhn is now common. The **Queen's Film Theatre** (7 University Mews, tel: 9097 2610) is an art-house cinema and the **Bell Gallery** (13 Adelaide Park, 9066 2998, Mon–Fri) deals in Irish landscapes.

South of the University, the **Royal Botanic Gardens** ❻ (tel: 9032 4902, admission free, closes at dusk) contain another Lanyon gem, his restored curvilinear **Palm House** (admission free, closed Sat, Sun and public holiday mornings). It dates from an era when the city's botanist clergymen preached to the far-flung Empire's corners, returning home with exotic plants sealed safe in micro-climate jars devised by a local inventor. In the **Tropical Ravine**, water drips from banana leaves in a miniature sunken rainforest.

On the park's Stranmillis Road boundary, north of the area's bistros, the excellent **Ulster Museum** ❼ (Botanic Gardens, tel: 9038 3000, admission free, open daily) houses well-presented displays of Irish art from the Bronze Age to today's, and explains the island's geological, biological, sociological and industrial histories. The natural science areas, plus the treasures rescued from the north coast wreck of the Spanish Armada galleas *Gerona*, are splendid. The museum shop sells replicas of these treasures, most poignant of which is a fine gold ring bearing the inscription *No tengo mas que dar te* – "I have nothing more to give you". Past the museum there are impressive views across the city of the white Portland stone of the Parliament Buildings at Stormont where the Northern Ireland Assembly meets when it isn't suspended.

East, past the Palm House, in College Park, is another Lanyon creation, **Union Presbyterian Theological College** ❽ (108 Botanic Avenue, tel: 9020 5080, admission by arrangement), fronted by Doric columns and built of beautiful, now neglected, Scrabo stone from County Down. The Corinthian-columned library and chapel housed Northern Ireland's first Parliament in the 1920s while the grandiloquent permanent buildings at Stormont were being completed.

ABOVE:
the Ulster Museum.

BELOW:
Botanic Gardens.

Evening entertainment

North again is raffish tree-lined **Botanic Avenue**, its café-bars, Eastern restaurants, bookshops, bookmakers, world trade bric-a-brac emporiums, charity shops, delicatessens and launderettes providing necessities of life for the chattering and student classes. Its **Empire Music Hall** ❿ (42 Botanic Avenue, tel: 9024 9276), another deconsecrated church, features Thursday night stand-up comedy during term time and from the participants' ironic patter visitors learn much about local politics. **Vincent's** is fine for espressos, **Madison's** has live music and an up-front decor worthy of Barcelona.

At the Avenue's northern extremity, those with a predilection for antique warehouses or biker shops can turn east down **Donegall Pass** which also boasts two of the city's most authentic Chinese restaurants, the up-market Cantonese **Manor House** and the budget **Sun Kee**.

As one crosses bleak, detritus-ridden **Shaftesbury Square**, glance up at the sculpture by Elizabeth Frink (1930–93), the city's finest alfresco artwork, on the south wall of the **Ulster Bank**. The well-heeled will stop off at Paul and Jeannie Rankin's award-winning **Roscoff**, its minimalist decor, exhilarating food, a contrast to its low-income surroundings. **Deane's** in Brunswick Street is a close rival, and **The Square** in Dublin Road is fast gaining a reputation as the current choice of journalists, politicians and "celebs".

Architectural gems

Great Victoria Street, which runs north off Shaftesbury Square, offers more eateries and also, near its northern end, several of Belfast's best-known tourist honey-pots. The first, the **Europa ❶**, a 179-room hotel of accepted international standards, is proud of its self-imposed sobriquet of "Europe's most bombed" (43 times). As well as 24-hour room service, there's 24-hour security.

The **Grand Opera House & Cirque ❿** (tel: 9024 1919), with its plush brass and velvet, its gilded elephant heads supporting the boxes, and its excellent acoustics, was designed by theatre architect Frank Matcham and opened in 1895 with a pantomime, *Bluebeard*. Pavlova, Beerbohm Tree, Orson Welles, Sarah Bernhardt, Donald Wolfit – and Laurel and Hardy – trod the boards until it fell victim to changing tastes. Rescued by conservationists in the 1970s and rendered sumptuous again, it re-opened with another pantomime, *Cinderella*.

It has occasionally been damaged by IRA bombs, as has the **Crown Liquor Saloon ❶**, across the road (46 Great Victoria Street, tel: 9027 9901, admission free, pub hours) with its magnificent tiled interior. Both delights are now fully restored. No visit to the city is complete without a pint (or pot of coffee), a plate of local oysters and a dish of champ (mashed potatoes) taken in one of the Crown's beautifully carved private snugs (where stage door Johnnies once

Map,
page 316

The Crown Liquor Saloon, described by the poet John Betjeman as a "many-coloured cavern", was built in 1885 by Banbridge-born Patrick Flanagan.

BELOW: the Grand Opera House.

propositioned chorus girls) before an evening of grand opera, rock, Shakespeare or contemporary drama at the Opera House. The Crown is classic enough to have been taken under the wing of the National Trust. **Robinson's**, **Flannagan's**, **Spinners'** and **Beaten Docket** are other local bars offering ersatz versions of this Victorian experience.

Another attraction, in Great Victoria Street's continuation, **College Square East**, is ignored by most tourist literature. Yet across its cricket square lawns, is the city's finest building, Sir John Soane's dignified dark red brick **Royal Belfast Academical Institution ⓜ**. The best view is from north-facing bedrooms in Jury's Inn hotel. The green statue facing the green sward, known locally as the "Black Man" since that was the colour of its predecessor, is of Henry Cooke, a rabble-raising 19th-century Presbyterian prebend. The baroque Portland stone building north, is, in local argot, the College of Knowledge – more correctly, the **College of Technology**.

A celebrated library

East along **Wellington Place**, the **Linen Hall Library ⓝ** (17 Donegall Square North, tel: 9032 1707, closed Sun) is all brass and mahogany, with its unique collection of printed "troubles" ephemera, is a must for visiting researchers. Its first librarian, Thomas Russell, was hanged for his part in the United Irishmen's revolution of 1798. Both Linen Hall Library and Marks & Spencer's frontage three blocks east were designed by Lanyon's firm.

To the north is **Donegall Place** with its street-scape of British chain stores. Off it, past **Castle Junction**, west down **Bank Street**, are **Kelly's Cellars ⓞ**, dating from 1780. Though considerably refurbished, the bars retain much of

Thomas Russell, the Linen Hall Library's first librarian and a prominent member of the United Irishmen, was hanged in 1803 for participating in an attempted uprising.

BELOW: the Crown Bar, preserved by the National Trust.

the charm which appealed to Henry Joy McCracken and other Protestant leaders of the United Irishmen as they caroused and plotted here in 1798.

East along Castle Lane towards Cornmarket is another essential of Ulster life, its street evangelists preaching round the bandstand in polygonal **Arthur Square** where the designs for the **Masonic Buildings, Nos 13-21,** came from Lanyon's office. And so east, along tacky **Ann Street**, dodging left into one of the entries which once made a warren of the area leading into **High Street**, where merchant ships tied up until the late 18th century. In **Pottinger's Entry,** at no 17, is the excellent **Morning Star** bar, the last of the many oyster houses which once thronged these narrow lanes, catering for sailors and thespians, for this was the city's theatrical district in times past.

Across **High Street**, north, is **Rosemary Street** where, at **No. 33, William Drennan**, founder of the United Irishmen was born and where, at No. 41, in the 1783 elliptical box-pewed interior of the **First Presbyterian (Non-Subscribing) Church**, the oldest place of worship within the city, lunchtime recitals provide lacunas of calm.

Lanyon's handsome 1845 makeover of what was the city's first public building, the 1769 **Exchange and Assembly Rooms**, now the **Northern Bank**, decorates the corner of **Bridge** and **Waring** Streets. The **Northern Ireland Tourist Board's** welcoming **Information Centre** is further up scruffy **North Street,** at no 59. Behind it, the landscaped **St Anne's Square** with sculpture by John Kindness, faces 1898 **St Anne's Church of Ireland (Protestant) Cathedral** in **Lower Donegall Street**, designated an urban conservation area for the detail on its houses and warehouses.

Catalyst Arts (5 Exchange Place, tel: 9031 3303), the most adventurous of

Map, page 316

BELOW: Castlecourt Shopping Centre.

the city's visual arts spaces, is housed in a converted shirt factory and empty shops in the surrounding area, particularly **North Street Arcade**, are frequently taken over by experimental visual artists. The **Duke of York**, in **Commercial Court**, is amongst the last of the journalists' pubs in the city's Fleet Street. The others are the **Front Page** opposite the Irish News building and the **A1** in Waring Street. The presses of the Catholic Nationalist *Irish News* (113–117 Upper Donegall Street, tel: 9032 2226) and the city's evening paper, the *Belfast Telegraph* (124 Royal Avenue, tel: 9026 4000), still unionist with a small 'u' although now owned by Dublin's Independent Newspapers, operates on a corner near **Belfast Central Library** (tel: 9050 9150, closed Sat pm and all Sun).

Lanyon enthusiasts will walk north-west up Clifton Street past spare elegant **Clifton House**, the Charitable Society's Poor House of 1771, to his **Gaol** and **Court House ❿**, facing each other across Crumlin Road.

Echoes of maritime history

Returning east from Donegall Street, cobbled **Hill Street** with its fashionable **Nick's Warehouse Wine Bar** points towards **Waring Street's** ornate **Ulster Bank,** rich in the extravagant carvings of Thomas Fitzpatrick whose stone work figures decorate so many of the city's buildings. **Skipper Street**, with the **Crow's Nest**, one of the city's two gay bars (the other, **The Parliament** is on nearby **Dunbar Link**) leads back to **High Street** with the **Albert Memorial Clock ❿**, a leaning tower that is Belfast's answer to London's Big Ben, and elegant Georgian **St George's Church** on the left, and Lanyon's Northern Bank (now **First Trust**) just beyond on **Victoria Street.** Lanyon's **Custom House**, is in **Custom House Square**, on the river bank, behind. His **Sinclair Seamen's Presbyterian Church, Corporation Square,** with its astonishing interior of ship's prow pulpit, binnacle font and lifeboat shape collection boxes, is worth the short stroll north through forbidding Tomb Street, Steam Mill Lane. A wee dram in Pilot Street's **Rotterdam Bar**, a prime music venue brushing shoulders with Lagan's re-gentrification, may also revive the soul. The ornate **Harbour Office** (Corporation Square, tel: 9055 4422, admission by arrangement) has unique reords of the city's maritime history.

From here, upstream, the Lagan's banks are witness to a declaration of confidence in the future, millions having been spent, via the state-sponsored Laganside Corporation, on gentrifying quays from **Clarendon Dock** southwards. A derelict docklands is becoming an area of stylish offices and designer street furniture. The **Lagan Lookout Centre** (Donegall Quay, tel: 9031 5444, admission fee, Oct–Mar closed Mon) relates the harbour's history. It bridges the river at **Queen's Square** where **McHugh's Bars**, once in the centre of the city's red-light district where painter Stanley Spencer's brother played piano, claim to be the city's oldest extant building. South is Victor Robinson's new, circular **Waterfront Hall ❿** (Lanyon Place, Oxford Street, tel: 9033 4455), the city's premier pop-to-classical concert hall and conference space, provides an astonishing vista from Chichester Street, past the imposing neoclassical bulk of the **Royal Courts of**

Justice, fashioned from near-white Portland stone. Across the River Lagan, the **Odyssey Pavilion** (Queen's Quay, tel: 9045 1055) is home to the Belfast giants ice hockey team and is a venue for sporting events and pop concerts. Under its transparent roof is a constantly changing mix of cinemas, shops, bars and restaurants, ten-pin bowling and exhibition areas.

Magennis's Whiskey Café, in May Street, almost faces Waterfront Hall. Belfast's Hilton and British Telecom's headquarters rise beside it, whilst the newly refurbished **St George's Market** is at the corner of Oxford Street and Cromac Square. Up river, on **Ormeau Road**, opposite **Ulster Television**, the huge **Gasworks** is also included in the plan.

However, walkers following the Lanyon Trail may return east to base via **Victoria Square**, for its two excellent old-fashioned pubs, **Bittle's** and the **Kitchen Bar**, or by **Chichester Street** with its occasional fine Georgian house and the **Garrick Bar**, favoured by barristers and such.

Around the city the carved heads above the ground-floor windows of one-time warehouses speak of its Victorian citizens' aspirations, no more so than in **Donegall Square South**, where the figures represent Columbus, Homer, Humboldt, Jacquard, Michelangelo, Newton, Shakespeare – and Peace.

On the outskirts of the city

A taxi (or bus) will be necessary to reach two areas of interest on the edge of the city. The first, **Cave Hill Country Park** ⑤, is where, by McArt's Fort United Irishmen planned the 1798 rebellion. In the park, there's a **Heritage Centre** inside the Scots Baronial-style **Belfast Castle** (Antrim Road, tel: 9077 6925, free access) designed in 1865 by Lanyon's son John, who borrowed freely from

Map, page 316

The Royal Courts of Justice were built in 1933 as a gift to the city by the British government, which had grudgingly accepted that the partition of Ireland wasn't going to be a short-lived affair.

BELOW:
Belfast Castle.

Prince Albert's sketches for the recently completed Balmoral Castle in Scotland. Beyond the castle, now a restaurant complex, is the **Zoological Gardens** (Antrim Road, tel: 9077 6277, admission fee). Set in a picturesque landscape, the zoo is praised for its breeding programmes and underwater sea lion viewing, but not everyone believes that caged tropical animals are entirely happy in Ireland's temperate climate. The **Cavehill Gallery** (18 Old Cavehill Road, tel: 9077 6784, opens only for shows: phone first) concentrates on living Irish painters.

The second area of interest is the much-televised **Parliament Buildings** at Stormont, 6 miles (10 km) to the east along the Newtownards Road. Echoing the pomp of Buckingham Palace, the seat of the new Northern Ireland Assembly is set in 300 acres (120 hectares) of lawns and trees and has a front drive a mile long. In the grounds is the smaller, baronial **Stormont Castle**, where the Ulster prime minister lived before Britain assumed direct control in 1972. For security reasons, it is not possible to visit either building. However, the public is admitted to the grounds Mon–Fri 9am–6pm.

Package up your Troubles

ABOVE: army patrol.
BELOW: Lord Carson guards the approach to Stormont; children in front of the "Peace Line" barricade.

Accepted wisdom insists that a visitor will never come to harm on the city's streets. Despite tribal animosities, the people have a natural warmth, a welcoming abrasive wit. In truth, Belfast is amongst Europe's safest cities, offences by what its long-suffering police force terms ODCs – ordinary decent criminals – being far below that for most English or American cities. This is partly because the terrorist organisations assumed responsibility for dispensing swift and vicious justice (such as knee-capping) to persistent offenders in the areas they controlled, and the visitor should tread tactfully in such working-class, headline-

grabbing enclaves of the Catholic Falls Road and the Protestant Shankill Road. For those keen to see the areas of greatest conflict, **Translink**, the State transport company, has afternoon **CityBus** tours which broaden the Belfast experience.

Belfast: A Living History takes in *all* the city's troubles, from the Viking long boats to the terrors of the past 35 years. This tour includes "Green" Falls and "Orange" Shankill plus the "Peace Line" in between. The commentary is admirably impartial. For the less adventurous, the **Belfast City Sightseeing Tour** (www.city-sightseeing.com) traces the history and development, with stops at Parliament Buildings.

Instructive, too, are the city's taxi-cabbies. Yellow Pages provide telephone numbers and there is hardly a driver who won't, for a negotiated price, lay on a tour of his favourite horrors, complete with a colourful commentary. The city's "**black taxis**" can also operate to the visitor's advantage. Whilst a small number of London-style cabs operate normally from ranks at City Hall, another system persists, a hangover from the 1970s when buses were terrorist targets. Fleets of second-hand London taxis were imported to serve, under paramilitary control, districts which had become no-go areas for buses. Now legal, they run regular routes into the ghettos, each cab departing only when jam-packed full.

Cabbies meeting the trains at the city's less than central **Central Station** on East Bridge Street try to pack 'em in too, and it takes a determined passenger to insist on solitude. Non-confrontational alternatives are: to telephone for a radio-controlled taxi which will look like an ordinary saloon car bearing the taxi firm's logo; to change trains and continue to the really central Great Victoria Street Station; or to take the York Street Station courtesy bus, but drop off in the city centre. And, yes, it is safe for a stranger to walk the streets. ❑

Map, page 316

TIP

If you're tempted to air your views on Ulster's future, don't. Debates become heated and an unbiased opinion is deemed not to exist.

BELOW: Republican mural hails Irish revolutionary leader James Connolly. **OVERPAGE:** the sun sets at Ferrycarrig, Co. Wexford.

✕ INSIGHT GUIDES

TRAVEL TIPS

CONTENTS

Getting Acquainted

The Place 330
Time Zones 330
Climate 330
The Economy 331
Language..............................331
Government 331

Planning the Trip

Visas and Passports..............331
What to Wear 331
Currency...............................331
Getting There 332
Public Holidays 332

Practical Tips

Emergencies..........................333
Media and Communications..334
Postal Services 334
Telephoning Abroad 334
Tourist Offices.......................335
Tracing Your Roots 335
Embassies 336

Getting Around

Public Transport 337
DART & suburban rail map....337
Driving & Car Rental 338
Horse-drawn Caravans 338
Dublin Literary Tours.............339

Where to Stay

Dublin...................................341
Southeast Region..................342
Southwest Region.................344
Midwest Region 345
Midlands Region 346
Far West Region....................347
Northwest Region 348
Northeast Region 349
Belfast 351

Eating Out

Dublin...................................352
Southeast Region.................354
Southwest Region................355
Midwest & Midlands 357
Far West 358
Northwest Region 358
Northeast Region 359
Belfast 361

Nightlife

Late Spots, Dublin................361
Late Spots, Belfast...............363

Culture

Theatre 363
Music, Art Galleries..............364

Festivals

Calendar of Events................366
Bloomsday............................367

Outdoor Attractions

Relics...................................368
Beauty Spots 368

Shopping

What to Buy..........................369
Shopping Hours 370

Sports

Spectator Sports...................370
Golf......................................370
Angling 371
Adventure Sports 371
Birdwatching........................372
Hill walking, climbing............372

Further Reading

General.................................373
Other Insight Guides.............373

Getting Acquainted

Note: The international dialling code for the Republic of Ireland is **353**. For Northern Ireland, it is **44**.

The Place

Ireland is a small country, just 170 miles (275 km) across at its widest point and 301 miles long (486 km). If you happen to be sailing single-handed across the Atlantic, look for it between 51½° and 55½° north latitude and 5½° and 10½° west longitude.

The warm drifting waters from the Gulf Stream ensure an equable climate and the winds from the Atlantic bring enough rain to guarantee that the proverbial 40 shades of green remain bright.

Six counties in the north-eastern sector, part of the ancient province of Ulster, are now Northern Ireland and come under the United Kingdom's jurisdiction; they occupy 17 percent of the island's landmass.

The island consists of a central plateau surrounded by isolated hills and mountains. The highest peak is Carrantuohill in Co. Kerry, at 3,412 ft (1,040 metres). The longest river is the Shannon, at 159 miles (256 km). The biggest lake is Lough Neagh in Northern Ireland, at 153 sq. miles (396 sq. km).

Although Ireland has a network of 57,000 miles (92,000 km) of roads, it has one of Europe's lowest traffic densities. Its population density is low, too, with just over 3.9 million people in the Republic (44 percent of them under 25) and 1.7 million in Northern Ireland.

The People

The Irish are a mixed race. Originally waves of settlers arrived over a period of 5,000 years from Britain and Europe. The predominant element consisted of Celts, tribes who came from central Europe by way of France, arriving in Ireland in the 7th or 8th centuries BC.

They are known to have been a combative people, their warriors high-spirited and boastful, and their strong story-telling abilities relied heavily on elements of the supernatural. These characteristics are still evident in Ireland, where Celtic culture survived after it was driven out of most of Europe by the Romans.

Another strong influence, especially in the east, was that of the Anglo-Normans. They first invaded in 1170, and were followed by settlers from England, Wales and Scotland.

The population, which expanded rapidly during the 18th and early 19th centuries, reached 8.1 million in 1841. The great potato famine, which began in 1845, led to mass starvation and emigration, particularly to North America. Ireland's population density is one of the lowest in Europe.

The Republic still has a distinctly rural orientation. Less than 59 percent of the population lives in towns of 1,000 inhabitants or more. More than one in five people live in the capital, Dublin, together with its seaport of Dun Laoghaire. The next biggest cities are all ports: Cork, Limerick, Waterford and Galway.

More than 90 percent of the Republic's citizens profess to Roman Catholicism. In Northern Ireland, two-thirds are Protestant, one-third Roman Catholic.

Time Zones

Ireland follows Greenwich Mean Time. In spring, the clock is moved one hour ahead for Summer Time to give extra daylight in the evening; in autumn it is moved back again to GMT.

At noon according to GMT, it is: **4am** in Los Angeles; **7am** in New York; **1pm** in western Europe; **8pm** in Singapore; **10pm** in Sydney; **midnight** in New Zealand.

Many visitors find that time passes more slowly in Ireland. A visitor once asked if the Irish attitude to time could be expressed by the word *mañana*. He was told: "Oh, we've nothing as urgent as that here."

The Four Provinces

Ireland consists of four ancient provinces – Ulster, Munster, Leinster and Connacht – but these are purely historical and have no administrative significance today. Since they're often referred to, though, it's useful to know which of the 32 administrative counties technically belong in which province:

Ulster: Cavan, Donegal, Monaghan (all in the Republic); Antrim, Armagh, Derry, Down, Fermanagh, Tyrone (all in Northern Ireland).
Munster: Clare, Cork, Kerry, Limerick, Tipperary, Waterford.
Leinster: Carlow, Dublin, Kildare, Kilkenny, Laois, Longford, Louth, Meath, Offaly, Westmeath, Wexford, Wicklow.
Connacht: Sligo, Mayo, Galway, Roscommon, Leitrim.

Climate

Although Ireland lies at roughly the same northerly latitude as Newfoundland, it has a mild, moist climate, because of the prevailing south-westerly winds and the influence of the warm Gulf Stream along its western coast. As no part of the island is more than 70 miles (110 km) from the sea, temperatures are fairly uniform over the whole country.

Average air temperatures in the coldest months, January and February, are mainly between 4°C and 7°C (39–45°F). The warmest months, July and August, have average temperatures between 14°C and 16°C (57–61°F), but occasionally reaching as high as 25°C (77°F). The sunniest months are May and June, with an average of between 5½ and 6½ hours a day over most of the country. The sunniest region is the extreme southeast.

Parts of the west of the country, with annual rainfall averaging 59 inches (1,500 mm), are twice as wet as the east because of the prevailing Atlantic winds.

The Economy

The Republic's gross domestic product is 90 billion euros (purchasing power parity) and its principal trading partner is Britain, followed by the United States, Germany and France. Racehorses, whiskey, handwoven tweed, handcut crystal glass, and agricultural products are among the best-known exports.

The country exports more goods than it buys, and is further buoyed by its substantial earnings from tourism and foreign investments. Tourism in particular continues to grow: the Republic's 3.9 million people welcome 5 million visitors a year.

Government

The Republic is a parliamentary democracy, with two Houses of Parliament, an elected president who is head of state and a prime minister (*Taoiseach*, literally "leader") who is head of government. In 1998 the Republic abandoned its constitutional claim to the six counties of Northern Ireland, which is part of the United Kingdom and is ruled by an elected assembly of unionists and nationalists, though political disputes often lead to direct rule from London being temporarily reimposed.

The national symbol is the shamrock, a three-leafed plant worn on the national holiday, 17 March, to honour Ireland's patron saint, St Patrick. This "wearing of the green" tradition has been successfully exported as thousands of sprigs of shamrock are despatched by Irish families each March to relatives all over the world.

The Language

The Republic of Ireland has two official languages, English and Irish (Gaelic). English is spoken everywhere, but while many people throughout the country know Irish, it is the everyday language of fewer than 100,000 people in remote areas known as Gaeltachts, mainly in the far west.

Intrepid linguists may wish to wrap their tongues round the following Gaelic phrases: *Dia dhuit*/God be with you. To which the reply is: *Dia 's Muire dhuit*/God and Mary be with you. *Conas atá tú*/How are you? To which the hoped-for reply is: *Tá mé go maith, go raibh maith agat*/I am well, thank you. *Slán leat*/Goodbye. To which the desirable reply is: *Slán leat agus go n-éirí an bóthar leat*/Goodbye and may the road rise to meet you.

Planning the Trip

Visas and Passports

Passports are required by everyone visiting the Republic except British citizens. Visas are not required by citizens of European Union countries, Australia, Canada or the US.

What To Wear

Casual clothing is acceptable almost everywhere in Ireland, including smart hotels and restaurants. Because of the unpredictability of the weather, pack an umbrella, some rainproof clothing and a warm sweater, even in summer.

But bring the suntan cream as well: when the summer sun shines, the ozone-laden winds from the Atlantic can intensify the burning effect of its rays.

Electricity

220 volts AC (50 cycles) is standard. Hotels usually have dual 220/110 voltage sockets for electric razors only. To use their own small appliances, visitors may need a plug adaptor (best purchased in their home country) to fit Ireland's 3-pin flat or 2-pin round wall sockets.

Currency

In 2002 Ireland became one of the first 12 countries to adopt the euro (€). It is divided into 100 cents. The coins used are 1¢, 2¢, 5¢, 10¢, 20¢, 50¢, €1, €2. The notes are €5, €10, €20, €50 and €100.

In Northern Ireland, the British pound is used. Exchange rates vary but many shops in border areas will accept either currency.

In the Irish Republic, banks are open 10am–4pm, Monday–Friday. Branches in small towns may close from 12.30pm to 1.30pm. Most Dublin banks are open until 5pm on Thursday. In Northern Ireland, bank opening hours are 10am–3.30pm, Monday–Friday.

British visitors to Northern Ireland can cash personal cheques with a bank card. Travellers cheques are accepted at all banks, money-change kiosks and many hotels.

MasterCard and Visa are the most commonly acceptable credit cards, followed by American Express and Diners Club. But many small guesthouses and bed-and-breakfast places will expect payment to be made in cash.

Getting There

BY AIR

Irish Republic

There are three major international airports in the Republic of Ireland, at Dublin, Cork and Shannon. The busiest by far is Dublin, with annual traffic of about 13.8 million passengers.

There is a regular bus service from Dublin Airport (tel: 814 1111 for general transport information) to the main bus station in the city centre, taking about 30 minutes. Aircoach (www.aircoach.ie) departs every 10–20 minutes for various city locations. The bus from Cork Airport (tel: 021-431 3131) to the city takes about 25 minutes. From Shannon Airport (tel: 061-471444) there is a regular bus service to Limerick city operating between 7am and midnight. It takes about 30 minutes.

Frequent flights from UK airports also arrive at regional airports such as Kerry, Waterford

and Knock. There are connections from Dublin and/or Shannon to many destinations in Britain and Europe, including London, Glasgow, Manchester, Liverpool, Amsterdam, Brussels, Copenhagen, Dusseldorf, Frankurt, Las Palmas, Madrid, Malaga, Milan, Moscow, Paris, Rome and Zurich, as well as to transatlantic destinations such as New York, Boston, Atlanta, Chicago and Havana.

Carriers serving Ireland from North America are Aer Lingus (www.aerlingus.com), Air Canada (www.aircanada.com), American Airlines (www.aa.com), Continental (www.continental.com), Delta (www.delta.com) and US Airways (www.usairways.com).

Aer Lingus flies direct from Boston, Chicago, Los Angeles and New York to Dublin and Shannon. **Air Canada** connects Toronto to Dublin and Shannon. **American Airlines** flies direct from Boston, Chicago, Los Angeles, New York to Dublin, with Boston flights also available to Shannon. **Continental** flies from Houston to Dublin and Newark to Dublin and Shannon. **Delta** flies from its hub in Atlanta to Dublin and

Public Holidays

- ● **January** New Year's Day (1)
- ● **March** St Patrick's Day (17)
- ● **March/April** Good Friday, Easter Monday
- ● **May** May Day (first Monday), Spring Bank Holiday (last Monday, *N. Ireland only*)
- ● **June** First Monday *(Republic of Ireland only)*
- ● **July** Orangeman's Day (12) *Northern Ireland only*
- ● **August** Summer Bank Holiday (First Monday in the Republic, last Monday in Northern Ireland)
- ● **October** Last Monday *(Republic of Ireland only)*
- ● **December** Christmas Day (25), St Stephen's Day (26)

Shannon and **US Airways** connects Philadelphia to Dublin and Shannon.

Aer Lingus can be contacted at the following numbers: US tel: 800 474 7424, UK tel: 0845 084 4444, Ireland tel: 0818 365 000. **American Airlines** can be reached via US tel: 800 433 7300, UK tel: 0845 778 9789, Ireland tel: 01-602 0550.

There is no shortage of flights to Ireland from the UK. Many of these flights depart and arrive at lesser known regional airports, can be easily purchased on-line and often beat the prices of major airlines which arrive at major airports. The leader in this market is **Ryanair** (www.ryanair.com) which flies to Dublin and Shannon. Cork has its own low-cost rival in **Aer Arann** (www.aerarann.com). Other key airlines include **Aer Lingus**, **British Airways** (www.ba.com), **BMI** (www.bmi.com) and **Easyjet** (www.easyjet.com).

Europe's main capitals and tourist destinations are also easily accessible from the Republic. **Ryanair** and **Aer Lingus** offer the most flights, but most countries' national airlines service Dublin if not Cork and Shannon.

Northern Ireland

Northern Ireland has two major airports, Belfast International (a 30-minute bus ride from town, 6am–11pm) and Belfast City, a short bus or taxi ride from the centre of town.

Belfast International (tel: 028-9442 2888) has recently started services to New York with Continental airlines, and to many UK cities and European capitals with **BMI** and **Easyjet**. Belfast City (tel: 028-9093 5076) serves the UK only via BMI, **Aer Arann** and **flybe** airlines.

Student/youth fares operate all year round between Britain and Ireland: contact STA Travel,

London (tel: 020 7361 6161). You may find that on-line bargains beat these discounted fares.

BY SEA

Many ferry services connect Ireland to Britain and France. Main routes include Dublin/Dun Laoghaire to Holyhead (Wales) or Liverpool (England); Rosslare to Pemborke or Fishguard (Wales), Roscoff and Cherbourg (France); Larne to Fleetwood, Cairnryan or Troon (Scotland), Belfast to Stranraer (Scotland) and Cork to Swansea or Pembroke (Wales). Many routes vary by season, as the Irish Sea is notoriously rough during the winter months.

Irish Ferries, www.irishferries.com. Tel: 0800 018 2211 *Services*: Holyhead – Dublin North Wall (3 hours 15 minutes) two crossings daily; Holyhead–Dublin fast service (1 hour 49 minutes) four crossings daily; Pembroke–Rosslare (3 hours 45 minutes). Also offers sailings every second day between Rosslare and the French ports of Roscoff and Cherbourg.

Stena Line, www.stenaline.ie. Tel: 01-204 7700 in Dublin; 08705 204 204 in the UK. *Services*: Holyhead–Dublin (3 hours 15 minutes); Holyhead–Dun Laoghaire (1 hour 39 minutes); Fishguard–Rosslare 3 hours 30 minutes or 1 hour 50 minutes); Stranraer–

Belfast (1 hour 45 minutes); Larne–Fleetwood (8 hours).

Swansea Cork Ferries, www.swansea-cork.ie. Tel: 021-427 1166 in Cork; 01792-456116 in the UK. *Services*: Swansea–Cork (10 hours) or Pembroke (8 hours).

P & O Irish Sea Ferries, www.poirishsea.com. Tel: 0870 24 24 777 in the UK. *Services*: Cairnryan–Larne (1 hour 45 minutes); Troon–Larne (1 hour 49 minutes, mid-Mar–mid-Oct); Liverpool–Dublin (8 hours).

BY BUS

Bus companies run through services from various points in England and Wales via the ferries. The ride to Galway from London, for example, takes around 17 hours by **National Express/Bus Eireann**, tel: 01-836 6111 in Dublin or 08705 80 80 80, www.nationalexpress.com.

Practical Tips

Emergencies

MEDICAL SERVICES

Medical insurance is highly advisable for all visitors. However, visitors from EU countries are entitled to medical treatment in Ireland, North and South, under a reciprocal arrangement.

With the exception of UK citizens, visitors for EU states should obtain form E111 from their own national social security office. These forms entitle the holders to free treatment by a doctor and free medicines on prescription. If hospital treatment is necessary, this will be given free in a public ward. UK visitors need only go to a doctor (or, in an emergency, a hospital), present some proof of identity (e.g. driving licence) and request treatment under EU health agreement.

For **emergency services**, such as police, ambulance, fire service, lifeboat and coastal rescue, tel: 999 in Northern Ireland and either 999 or 112 in the Republic and ask for the service you need.

The **Samaritans**, who help lonely, depressed and suicidal people, can be contacted on 01-872 7700 and in Northern Ireland on 028-9066 4422.

Other Useful Numbers

Poisons Information Service, Dublin, tel: 837 9964, 837 9966.

Alcoholics Anonymous, Dublin, tel: 01-453 8998; Belfast, tel: 028-9043 4848.

Factfile on the Irish Sea

The Irish Sea (*Muir Éireann* in Irish) is 130 miles (210 km) long and 150 miles (240 km) wide. Its total area is roughly 40,000 sq. miles (100,000 sq. km) and its deepest point is 576 ft (175 metres). It connects with Atlantic waters through St George's Channel in the south (between Ireland and Wales), where tidal currents reach up to 4 knots, and the North Channel in the north (between Northern Ireland and Scotland). Many geologists believe it was created by rifts at least 70 million years ago and could be as old as 1.6 million years.

The principal fish caught are herring in summer and whiting in winter, and there is some trawling for cod.

Rape Crisis Centre, Dublin, tel: 01-800 778 888 and Belfast, tel: 028-9024 9696.
Aids Helpline Dublin, tel: 1800 459 459. Mon–Fri 7–9pm, Sat 3–5pm.

Media

NEWSPAPERS

The Irish devour newspapers, and have no fewer than five morning newspapers to serve the island's population of 5 million. The *Irish Times* and the *Irish Independent* are published in Dublin. The *Examiner* is published in Cork.

The *Times*, the most serious and comprehensive, is best for foreign news, arts and business, and has a great letters page. It avoids political affiliations, but has a broadly liberal bias, and is part of a syndicating group that includes the *Guardian* in the UK, *Le Monde* in France and *El País* in Spain. The *Independent* broadly supports the Fine Gael party and aims for a hard-hitting style. The *Examiner* is the staple diet of business and farming people in the southwest. Two morning papers are published in Belfast: the Unionist/Protestant *Newsletter* and the nationalist/Catholic *Irish News*; it can be fascinating and instructive to compare their treatments of a controversial story.

There are three evening papers: the *Evening Herald* (from the Independent stable in Dublin), the *Echo* (Cork) and the *Belfast Telegraph*, which also publishes a tabloid Saturday morning edition. All contain lots of sport, gossip and showbiz.

The *Independent* has a Sunday version; also published from Dublin are the *Sunday Tribune*, which aims to be a serious paper of political analysis, arts review, etc., the *Sunday World*, a lurid tabloid (pin-ups, shocks, scares, scandals, etc) and the

Sunday Business Post, which concentrates on business and politics. The London *Sunday Times* Irish edition is published in Cork and distributed nationally. From Belfast, there is *Sunday Life* from the Telegraph stable.

Since all the British dailies and Sundays are readily obtainable on both sides of the border, even the most news-hungry visitor should be satisfied in this newsprint-mad country. However, UK readers can expect an "Irish edition" of their favourite paper, with a focus on Irish topics.

There are nearly 100 local papers, which may be entertaining and informative if you are interested in a particular region, or interested in newspapers.

MAGAZINES

Hot Press is a lively local pop culture paper. *In Dublin* is useful for telling you what's on at the theatre, cinema, etc.

RADIO AND TELEVISION

The national broadcasting service, Radio Telefís Éireann (RTÉ) has three TV channels (one of them, TG4, broadcasting exclusively In the Irish language) and three radio stations. Ireland's first independent television network TV3, was launched in 1998 to provide an alternative to RTÉ – "a middle-of-the-road service aimed at Middle Ireland".

In addition, the British TV channels (both BBC and commercial channels) can be received over much of the country – which accounts for the unsightly height of television aerials. Several satellite channels, including Sky and Screensport, are widely available via cable.

On Radio, RTÉ1 is the main station for news, current affairs and drama; RTÉ2 has a staple

output of pop music and the recently launched Lyric FM is for lovers of classical music. There are also a number of independent local radio stations.

Northern Ireland has full BBC radio and TV coverage with many local programmes. Ulster Television provides a commercial service, as does Downtown Radio (MW) and Cool FM.

Postal Services

At the time of writing, letters, postcards and airmail weighing less than 25 grammes (approximately the weight of an envelope containing up to three regular A4 sheets of paper) cost €0.48 within Ireland, €0.60 to the UK and €0.65 to all European Union countries and the rest of the world.

Philatelists may obtain information on Irish stamps from the Controller, Philatelic Section, GPO, Dublin 1.

In Northern Ireland, British postal rates apply: 30p for a letter sent first-class to anywhere in the British Isles. 42p for letters of less than 20 grammes within the EU), and 21p for letters sent second-class. Air-mail letters to destinations outside Europe cost 47p or 68p, depending on weight.

Telecommunications

The international dialling code for the Republic of Ireland is **353**. Northern Ireland's is **44**.

There are several telecommunications companies operating in Ireland – the largest one being Eircom (formerly a state owned company). A local call from a public telephone costs 30¢. Longer-distance calls to most places within Ireland can be dialled direct; area codes are listed in the front of the telephone directories. Have plenty of coins ready. About 50 percent of public phones are card phones.

Phone Cards are widely available from post offices, newsagents and supermarkets and are sold in denominations of 10, 20 and 50 units.

International calls can be dialled direct from private phones, or dial 114 for the international operator. To contact the local operator, dial 10. The long-distance services of AT&T, Sprint and MCI are also available.

Telephone services in Northern Ireland are operated by British Telecom; dial 100 for the operator. Local calls from public booths cost 20p.

Tourist Offices

IRISH TOURIST BOARD (BORD FÁILTE)

General postal enquiries: Fáilte Ireland, Baggot Street Bridge, Dublin 2, Ireland. Tel: 01-602 4000.

The following are the principal offices for the various regions and most are open throughout the year. A full list is available from any tourist information office, or look up the **website** on: www.ireland.ie.

Dublin and Environs
Dublin City: Dublin Tourism, Suffolk Street, Dublin 2. www.visitdublin.com.
Dublin Airport, Arrivals Hall.
Dun Laoghaire: Ferry Terminal, St Michael's Wharf.

For information in Ireland,

Tracing your Roots

The number of visitors to Ireland who want to uncover half-forgotten roots in the "ould sod" has mushroomed. The Irish Genealogy Centre, the country's largest genealogical agency, says it receives 150–200 enquiries a week. It gives free advice on how to go about tracing your own ancestry, but most people prefer to hire one of its panel of trained genealogists to do the time-consuming research. There is no fixed charge – clients pay for time, not results – but expect to pay €200 and upwards for a proper research to be conducted; initial assesments are available from €10 (tel: 01-882 8006; www.irishgenealogycentre.com).

Whether you intend to do your own research or hire a professional, it is important to gather as much information as possible in your home country. Try to find out the name of your emigrant ancestor; his or her place of origin in Ireland, as precisely as possible; approximate dates of birth, marriage and death; religion; occupation and social background; names of children. Look for old diaries, letters or family bibles.

In the US National Archives, Irish-Americans can often find their ancestor date and port of arrival in the New World. Immigrant records and shipping lists show the country, age and trade of the immigrant and the port of departure. Australian records are helpful because many immigrants arrived on state "assisted passage" schemes.

In Ireland, all centralised records for the 26 counties of the Republic are stored in Dublin. The main sources are as follows:
The National Library, Kildare Street, has an extensive collection of journals of local historical societies, trade directories, old newspapers, private papers and letters. Patient, helpful staff.
The National Archives (the old Public Record Office), in the Four Courts, was damaged badly in a fire in 1922 during the Civil War and many invaluable documents were lost (but not all).

The General Register Office, Joyce House, Lombard Street, has the civil registrations of all births, marriages and deaths since 1864.
The Register of Deeds, Henrietta Street, has deeds relating to property and marriage settlements dating from 1708. Most of these concern the gentry of the time.
The Genealogical Office, in Kildare Street, includes the State Heraldic Museum. The office records and designs coats of arms and will carry out research for a fee.
The State Paper Office, Dublin Castle, is of special interest to Australians because it houses records of people sentenced to be transported there. There is not necessarily any great stigma attached to this, since the crime concerned was often petty or notional, or simply that of supporting the rebel cause.

Many individual counties have now set up local genealogy companies. Initial assessments tend to cost around €20 and you can track them down through local libraries.

In **Northern Ireland**, records are held at the Public Record Office, 66 Balmoral Avenue, Belfast 9. Derry has opened a genealogy centre in Butcher Street called The Fifth Province, with records from 1642 to 1922. The Ulster American Folk Park in Omagh holds thousands of documents in its Centre for Migration Studies (tel: 02882-256 315; fax: 02882-242 241; www.qub.ac.uk/cms).

In both North and South, records are often kept at parish level, some going back over 200 years. For a list of approved research agencies, contact the Genealogical Office, 2 Kildare Street, Dublin 2 (tel: 01-603 0200). An annual Family History Conference focusing on practical research in Ireland's main archives takes place in September in Belfast. For details tel: 02890-332 288; fax: 02890-239 885; email: enquiry@uhf.org.uk; www.ancestryireland.co.uk.

tel: 1850 230 230; from the UK tel: 0800 039 7000; from anywhere else, tel: 00 353 669 792 083. For accommodation reservations in Ireland, tel: 1800 363 626; from the UK, tel: 00800 2580 2580; from anywhere else, tel: 00353 669 792 707.

Southeast
www.southeastireland.ie
Carlow: tel: 059 913 1554.
Wexford: Crescent Quay. Tel: 053-23111; fax: 053-41743.
Clonmel: Sarsfield Street. Tel: 052-22960.
Kilkenny: Rose Inn Street. Tel: 056-775 1500; fax: 056-776 3955.
Waterford: 41 The Quay. Tel: 051-875 823; fax: 051-876 720.

Southwest
www.corkkerry.ie
Cork City: Áras Fáilte, Grand Parade. Tel: 021-425 5100; fax: 425 5199.
Skibbereen: The Square. Tel: 028-21766; fax: 028-21353.
Killarney: Beech Road. Tel: 064-31633; fax: 064-34506
Blarney: Blarney. Tel: 021-438 1624.

Mid West
www.shannonregiontourism.ie
Limerick City: Arthur's Quay. Tel: 061-317 522; fax: 061-317 939.
Ennis: Arthur's Row. Tel: 065-

682 8366; fax: 065-682 8350.
Shannon: Airport. Tel: 061-471 664; fax: 061-471 661.

Midlands
www.eastcoastmidlandsireland.ie
Mullingar: Market Square. Tel: 044-48650; fax: 044-40413.
Glendalough: Tel: 0404-45688.
Athlone: Athlone Castle. Tel: 090 649 4630. (No fax; open April–Nov.)

Far West
www.irelandwest.ie
Galway City: Forster St. Tel: 091-537 700; fax: 091-537 733.
Westport: James' Street. Tel: 098-25711; fax: 098-26709.

Northwest
www.irelandnorthwest.ie
Sligo: Áras Reddan, Temple Street. Tel: 071-916 1201; fax: 071-916 0360.
Letterkenny: Neil T. Blaney Road. Tel: 074-912 1160; fax: 074-912 5180.

Northern Ireland
Belfast: 53 Castle Street, Belfast, BT1 1GH. Tel: 028-9032 7888, fax: 265 615.
Derry: 44 Foyle Street, Derry. BT48 6AT, tel/fax: 028-7136 9501.

Abroad
Britain: Nations House, 103 Wigmore Street, London W1U 1QS. Tel: 0800-039 7000.

US and Canada: 345 Park Avenue, New York, NY 10154. Tel: 212-418 0800, fax: 212-371 9052.
Australia and New Zealand: Sydney: 5th level, 36 Carrington Street, Sydney 2000, NSW, tel: 02-9299 6177, fax: 9299 6323.
Auckland: 6th floor, 18 Shortland St, Private Bag 92136, Auckland. Tel: 9-379 8720, fax: 9-3091 0735.
South Africa: Everite House, 20 de Korte Street, Braamfontein 20017. PO Box 30615 Johannesburg 2000. Tel: 011-339 4865, fax: 011-339 2474.

NORTHERN IRELAND TOURIST INFORMATION

www.discovernorthernireland.com
Belfast: 47 Donegal Place, Belfast BT1 5AD. Tel: 028-9024 6609, fax: 312 424.
Dublin: 16 Nassau Street, Dublin 2. Tel: 01-679 1977, fax: 677 1587.
Britain: Nations House, 103 Wigmore Street, London W1U 1QS. Tel: 0800-039 7000, fax: 020-7493 9065.
US: 345 Park Avenue, New York, NY 10154. Tel: 212-418 0800, fax: 212-371 9052.
Canada: 111 Avenue Road, Suite 450, Toronto. Tel: 416-925 6368, fax: 925 6033

Embassies

Dublin
Australia: Fitzwilton House, Wilton Terrace, Dublin 2. Tel: 664 5307.
Britain: 29 Merrion Rd, Dublin 4. Tel: 01-205 3700.
Canada: 65 St Stephen's Green, Dublin 2. Tel: 478 1988.
United States: 42 Elgin Rd, Dublin 4. Tel: 01-668 8777.

Belfast
American Consulate General, 223 Stranmillis Road, Belfast. Tel: 028-9038 6100.

Travellers with Disabilities

A lot of progress has been made in recent years to provide more facilities for visitors with disabilities. Ramps have been provided, giving access to many community buildings, the more modern city buses in Dublin have facilities for wheelchair users to board the bus, and trains have level entry access. Airlines are also friendly towards passengers with disabilities.

For advice and information, contact the **National Council for the Blind in Dublin**, tel: 01-830 7033, the **National Chaplaincy for the Deaf**, also in Dublin, tel: 01-830 5744, the **Irish Wheelchair Association**, tel: 01-818 6400, www.iwa.ie, the **National Disability Association**, tel: 01-608 0400, and **Bord Fàilte** (the Irish Tourist Board, see above). **Orchard Tours**, Gort, Co. Galway (tel: 091-632 416) organise holiday breaks specifically for the disabled.

Getting Around

Public Transport

In the Republic, the State transport authority, CIE, is the umbrella body for three companies: Dublin Bus (serving the city), Bus Éireann (serving provincial areas from Dublin) and Iarnród Éireann (operating inter-city trains as well as the DART, the Dublin Area Rapid Transit system).

Timetables for bus and train services, including details of various money-saving commuter and tourist tickets, are sold in newsagents. The public transport network caters adequately for travel between major centres, but plan ahead with care if your itinerary takes you to smaller towns. Once off the main routes, small towns and villages may only be served by a couple of buses a week. For

information, tel: 01-873 4222 (Dublin Bus, www.dublinbus.ie); 01-836 6111 (Bus Eireann, www.buseireann.ie); or 01-836 6222 (Iarnród Éireann, www.irishrail.ie). You can dial a recorded timetable for most mainline rail destinations (look in the telephone directory under Iarnród Éireann).

In Dublin city, the DART rail service is the most efficient way to travel, but it runs, alas, only along the coastal strip from Howth to Bray. The city's bus service can be maddeningly unpredictable, so try to be philosophical. The LUAS tram system (tel: 1 800 300 604; www.luas.ie) was introduced in late 2004. It offers a handy connection between Connolly and Heuston train stations, but its two lines mostly serve outlying suburbs not served by DART and are of little interest to tourists.

Bus Éireann city buses also serve Cork, Galway, Limerick and Waterford.

Eurailpasses are valid for bus and train travel in the Republic, excluding city services.

Reduced-rate Rambler passes are available providing unlimited travel on buses and/or trains, excluding city services, for

either 8 or 15 days. Tickets can be bought from any bus or train station in the Republic, or through a travel agent abroad.

In Northern Ireland, trains run from Belfast northwest to Derry via Ballymena and Coleraine; east to Bangor; and south to

Taxis

There are metered taxis at railway stations, ports and airports in Dublin, Belfast, Cork, Limerick and Galway. Elsewhere, fares are by arrangement with the driver in advance. In cities and towns you can book a taxi by telephone. Look in the *Golden Pages* classified telephone directory under "Taxis".

In Dublin taxis can be hailed in the street provided you are not near a taxi rank. At peak times it can be difficult to find one. There are taxi ranks at St Stephen's Green, College Green, O'Connell Street, and Westland Row, among other places.

Radio cab firms include **Blue Cabs**, 41 Westland Row, Dublin 2, tel: 676 1111; **Checkers Cabs**, tel: 834 3434; **City Group**, Noel Ebb's Taxis, City House, New Market, Dublin 8, tel: 872 7272; **National Radio Cabs**, Citywide, tel: 836 5555; **Pony Cabs**, tel: 836 0144 North City, 496 6777 Ranelagh, 269 1000 Donnybrook; **Southside Cabs**, Stillorgan, tel: 280 5545; **Swords Cabs**, Main Street, Swords, tel: 840 6600; and **Taxi Radio Link**, 1 Whitefriar Place, Dublin 8, tel: 478 1111.

DART and Suburban Rail Network

Dundalk
Drogheda
Laytown
Mosney
Gormanston
Balbriggan
Skerries
Rush-Lusk
Donabate
Malahide
Portmarnock
Bayside
Sutton
Howth Junction
Howth
Kilbarrack
Raheny
Harmonstown
Connolly Station
Killester
Clontarf Road
Tara St
Pearse Station
Grand Canal Dock
Lansdowne Road
Sandymount
Sydney Parade
Booterstown
Blackrock
Seapoint
Salthill & Monkstown
Dún Laoghaire
Sandycove & Glasthule
Glenageary
Dalkey
Killiney
Shankill
Bray
Greystones
Kilcoole
Wicklow
Rathdrum
Arklow

- DART
- SE Suburban
- N Suburban
- interchange station

Dublin via Newry. Information concerning rail and bus services throughout Northern Ireland is available from the Translink call centre, Belfast, tel: 028-9066 6630.

Private Transport

DRIVING

Outside the cities the roads are still amongst the least congested in Europe, although it's hard to believe this when stuck in a traffic jam in Dublin's ever-expanding suburbs. Drive on the left is the rule on both sides of the border, although there is a predilection in some rural areas for the middle of the road. Drivers and front-seat passengers must wear seat belts as must back seat passengers when belts are fitted.

In the Republic, the speed limit is 45 kmh, 60 kmh or 80 kmh (28 mph, 37 mph or 50 mph) in urban areas, and 80 kmh or 100 kmh (50 mph or 62 mph) on country roads, with 120 kmh (75 mph) permitted on motorways. On-the-spot fines can be issued for speeding offences. Drink driving laws are strict. It is an offence to drive with a concentration of alcohol exceeding 80 mg per 100 ml of blood.

In Northern Ireland, the limit for country roads is 60 mph (96 kmh), and 70 mph (113 kmh) is allowed on motorways and dual-carriageway trunk roads.

CAR RENTALS

Irish Republic

At the height of summer, hire cars can be harder to find than gold at the end of the rainbow, so book in advance. If you're heading west, the smaller the car, the better – the most alluring lanes are the narrowest. It pays to shop around – a recent survey revealed that rental prices were significantly lower outside the Dublin area. You must be over 23 with two years' full licence and under 76 to hire a car in the Irish Republic.

All the companies listed here are members of the Car Rental Council and operate a code of practice drawn up by the council and the Irish Tourist Board.

Note that all Dublin area telephone numbers need an 01-prefix if dialled from outside the area.

Alamo/National Car Rental, Arrivals hall, Dublin Airport, tel: 844 4162; Shannon Airport, tel: 061-472 633; Cork Airport, tel: 021-431 8623; Knock Airport, tel: 094-936 7252; Kerry Airport, tel: 066-976 4433; Galway Airport, tel: 091-771 929. Central reservations, tel: 021-432 0755. www.carhire.ie.

Argus Rent A Car, 59 Terenure Road East, Dublin 6, tel: 490 6173. www.argusrentals.com. Deliveries to Dublin airport, ferry ports and hotels.

Atlas Car Rentals, Arrivals hall, Dublin Airport, tel: 862 0306. www.atlascarhire.com.

Avis, Dublin Airport, tel: 605 7500; Shannon Airport, tel: 061-715 600; Cork Airport, tel: 021-432 7460; Killarney, tel: 064-36655; Galway, tel: 091-786 440. www.avis.ie.

Budget Rent-a-Car, Dublin City, tel: 837 9611; Dublin Airport, tel: 844 5150; Shannon Airport, tel: 061-471 361; Killarney, tel: 064-34341; Galway, tel: 091-566 376. www.budgetcarrental.ie.

Dan Dooley Rent-a-Car, Knocklong, Co. Limerick, tel: 062-53103. www.dan-dooley.ie.

Hamill's Rent-a-Car, Mullingar, tel: 044-48682. Delivery to Dublin, Shannon and Knock airports and Dublin ferry terminals. www.hamills.com.

Hertz Rent-a-Car, Dun Laoghaire Pier, Dublin, tel: 230 1769; Dublin Airport, tel: 844 5466; Shannon Airport, tel: 061-471 369; Cork Airport, tel: 021-496 5849. www.hertz.ie.

Murrays Europcar Rent-a-Car, Baggot Street Bridge, Dublin, tel: 614 2840; Dublin Airport, tel: 812 0410; Shannon Airport, tel: 061-701 200; Cork Airport, tel: 021-491 7300; Kerry Airport, tel: 064-30177. Killarney, tel: 064-30177. Galway Airport, tel: 091-562 222; Knock Airport, tel: 094-936 7221; Rosslare Harbour, tel: 053-33634. www.europcar.ie.

Hiring a Horse-drawn Caravan

Horses and caravans are available for hire in Counties Cork, Kerry and Wicklow. Expect to cover only about 10 miles (16 km) a day – but going slowly is just the point, giving you time to appreciate the countryside, meet and talk to passers-by and let your inner rhythms settle down to a more sensible pace. Feeding, grooming and harnessing the horse is time-consuming too, and quite hard work.

The caravans, which have gas cookers, are mostly for four people, with berths that convert into seating for daytime. Utensils, crockery, etc are provided. Fastidious people should note that caravans do not have toilets (well, didn't you want the real thing?). In high season, expect to pay from €508 to €635 a week; allow about €9 a night for overnight parking.

Operators include **Clissman's Horse-Drawn Caravans** in Co. Wicklow (tel: 0404-48188; fax: 48288), **Mayo Horse-Drawn Caravan Holidays** in Co. Mayo (tel: 094-903 2054), and **Into the West** in Co. Galway (tel: 090-974 5211, fax: 974 5987). Further details from the Irish Tourist Board.

Northern Ireland

Avis Rent-a-Car, Great Victoria Street, Belfast, tel: 028-9024 0404; Belfast International Airport, tel: 028-9442 2333; Belfast City Airport, tel: 028-9045 2017; City of Derry Airport, tel: 028-7181 1708; Larne, tel: 028-2826 0799. www.avis.co.uk.

Budget Rentacar, Belfast, tel: 028-90230 700; Belfast City Airport, tel: 028-9045 1111; Belfast International Airport, tel: 028-9442 3332. www.budget-uk.com.

Europcar, Belfast City Airport, tel: 028-90450 904; Belfast International Airport, tel: 028-9442 3444. www.europcar.co.uk

Hertz Rent-a-Car, Belfast International Airport, tel: 028-9442 2533; Belfast City Airport, tel: 028-9073 2451. www.hertz.co.uk.

CYCLING

This is an excellent way to see the countryside at a leisurely pace, provided you aren't anxious to cover too much ground (the modern disease). Throughout the Republic, specially appointed Rent-a-Bike dealers hire out sturdy Raleigh Tourer bicycles: a list of them is available from the Irish Tourist Board and the bikes can sometimes be delivered to airports. Expect to pay upwards of €70 a week for rental.

In Dublin, you can also hire a bicycle from **Track Cycles**, 8 Botanic Road, Glasnevin, Dublin. Tel: 01-850 0252.

Irish Cycling Safaris organise guided tours throughout Ireland. Tel: 01-260 0749. www.cyclingsafaris.com.

HORSE RIDING

Equestrian Holidays Ireland have details of residential and non-residential riding holidays around the country. Choose between post to post trail riding staying in a different guest house every evening, or equestrian centres with on-site accommodation and indoor and outdoor riding facilities.

For a detailed brochure, contact *Bord Fáilte* or look at the equestrian Holidays Ireland website (www.ehi.ie) with information on equestrian centres around Ireland.

INLAND WATERWAYS

The three main waterways for cruising are the River Shannon, navigable for 150 miles (240 km) downstream from Lough Key, Co Roscommon; the Grand Canal, which runs westward from Dublin across the central plain to the Shannon, and is joined in Co Kildare by a branch line running south to the River Barrow; and the River Erne, navigable for 50 miles (80 km) from Belturbet, Co Cavan through Upper and Lower Lough Erne to Belleek, near Enniskillen, Co Fermanagh. All three waterways are marvellous for fishing, birdwatching, rowing, photography, or just pottering peacefully along.

In the Republic, several companies offer cabin cruisers for hire on the River Shannon and the Grand Canal. Make sure they are affiliated to the Irish Boat Rental Association. Full details are included in Bord Fáilte's *Cruising Ireland* brochure. In Northern Ireland, several companies approved by the Erne Charter Boat Association operate on Lough Erne; ask for the *Holidays Afloat* brochure from the Northern Ireland Tourist Board.

Cruisers range in size from two berths to eight; all have refrigerators and gas cookers; most have heating, hot water and showers; dinghies, charts and safety equipment are included. Experience in handling a boat is an advantage, but instruction or guided cruises are provided for novices.

DUBLIN LITERARY TOURS

A **Bloomsday Walking Tour** based on James Joyce's *Ulysses* starts from the Post Office every 16 June. Contact Beatrice Healy on 01-454 5943.

A **Bloomstime Ulysses Bus Tour** is led by experts and staff of the James Joyce Centre on 16 June. They also do Joycean walking tours year round (tel: 01-878 8547).

Historical walking tours of Dublin are conducted by History graduates of Trinity College (tel: 01-878 0227). Meeting point Trinity College front Gate. www.historicalinsights.ie

A general **Literary Pub Crawl** starts at the Duke Pub nightly during the summer and Thur–Sun during the winter. Contact tel: 01-670 5602 for more information. Tickets available at the pub from 7pm (tours begin at 7.30pm) or from Dublin Tourism on Suffolk Street.

Where to Stay

The Choice

It is possible to pay as much as €300 or more for a room in a top-rated hotel, or as little as €20 for "bed and breakfast" in a family home which takes visitors. Dearer is not necessarily better, of course, but generally speaking the more you pay, the more facilities are on offer.

Apart from what you can afford to pay, you may decide that you don't need a hotel with suites available, night service, two restaurants, a health complex and uniformed attendants at every turn. Or you may simply dislike large, grand hotels and prefer small, family-run places with a bit more character, even if the bathroom is down the hall and the menu is pot luck. And a remarkable number of B & Bs now have rooms with "en-suite" shower or bath and some – especially farmhouses – offer first-class food. B & Bs are not necessarily budget options: large rooms decorated with antiques in stately homes like Bantry House may cost the same as a good hotel, but the experience will be much more memorable.

Both the Irish Republic and Northern Ireland classify hotels on broadly the same grading system, as follows:
★★★★★ Top-grade hotels, some in former castles; all rooms have private bathrooms and suites are available. High-quality restaurant.
★★★★ Hotels, ranging from modern, purpose-built premises to converted period houses, offering a high standard of comfort and service. With few exceptions all rooms have private bathrooms.
★★★ Medium-priced hotels, ranging from small, family-run places to larger, more commercial operations. Most rooms have private bathrooms.
★★ Mostly family-run hotels, with a limited but satisfactory range of food and comfort. Some rooms have private bathrooms.
★ Simple but acceptable accommodation and services.

Guesthouses

This is a category for B & Bs with over five rooms. Some but not all guesthouses have restaurant facilities, and those public facilities that you would expect in a hotel, such as residents' lounge, may be limited or non existent. Guesthouses are not licensed to sell beer and spirits (unless the guesthouse is also a pub), but some have wine licences.

When to Plan Ahead

Accommodation is seasonal in the more remote areas. Many places close from October or November to mid-March or Easter in the smaller villages of the southwest, far west and northwest areas. It is advisable to book ahead in July and August, especially in scenic and coastal areas.

Bed and Breakfast

B & B accommodation is offered in many private family houses, both in towns and in the countryside. Evening meals are normally provided if notice is given before noon. The newer B & Bs have often been designed for that purpose, and will have bathrooms en suite, and, in major towns, direct dial phones and TV.

What Prices Include

Prices indicated for Dublin are based on the rate per double room. Single rooms can be hard to find, and usually carry a premium. Guesthouses and B & Bs are both listed under the B & B category.

Hostels

The Irish Youth Hostel Association (An Oige) 61 Mountjoy Street, Dublin 7, tel: 01-830 4555; fax: 01-830 5808; email: mailbox@anoige.ie; www.irelandyha.org, has 23 hostels in the Republic, with fees varying from €10 to €20 per person per night. Hostels in Northern Ireland are run by Hostelling international Northern Ireland (ww.hini.org.uk). Members of the International Youth Hostel Federation can use any of these.

Independent Holiday Hostels of Ireland is an umbrella organisation for about 125 privately owned hostels. These are relaxed places, with none of the rules and curfews imposed by An Oige. As well as traditional dormitory accommodation, many also have private double and family rooms, and offer cooked breakfast as an optional extra, as well as kitchen facilities. For a brochure contact the IHH Office, 57 Lower Gardiner Street, Dublin 1. Tel: 01-836 4700; fax: 836 4710; www.hostels-ireland.com.

Some hostels prefer not to belong to any organisation. All independent hostels are privately owned, and can vary from scenic organic farms to a tiny townhouse stacked with bunk beds. The atmosphere is generally friendly, and you will soon learn about the best places by talking to fellow travellers. The one drawback is a tendency to over-crowding in July and August and at festival times.

Budget Accommodation

The Irish student and youth travel company USIT (www.kinlayhouse.ie) runs Kinlay House year-round centres in Dublin (tel: 01-679 6644), Galway (091-565 244) and Cork (021-450 8966). Prices start at below €15. During the long vacation from mid-June to mid-September, they also offer self-catering apartments in UCD Village, Belfield Campus, Dublin 4 (01-269 7111). Brookfield Holiday Village, also offer apartments at College Road, Cork (021-434 4032) with prices starting at under €30.

Self-catering Accommodation

This is available throughout Ireland in houses, cottages (some thatched), apartments, caravans and even a few castles (suitable for groups). If you are looking for a "traditional Irish cottage" be warned that many on offer are newly built in artificial "clusters", and used solely for holiday rentals. Be sure you are getting what you want when you book. There are also many caravan and camping parks for those who like to take their accommodation with them.

If touring the Republic, you can ask one of the local tourist information offices to book ahead for you. A small charge is made for telephone costs.

Dublin

€€€€
(over €200 a night for a double room)
Berkeley Court Hotel, Lansdowne Road, Dublin 4. Tel: 665 3200, fax: 661 7238. www.jurysdoyle.com. Ugly, concrete-shoebox exterior, but luxurious inside. Sited in Ballsbridge near the famous Lansdowne Road international rugby ground.
The Burlington, Upper Leeson Street, Dublin 4. Tel: 660 5222, fax: 660 8496. www.jurysdoyle.com. Ireland's largest hotel and confer-

ence centre. Located near "The Strip", although the number of nightclubs on the once legendary Leeson Street is now dwindling. The bar is a popular spot for *après*-rugby match knees-ups.
The Clarence, 6–8 Wellington Quay, Dublin 2. Tel: 407 0800, fax: 407 0820. www.theclarence.ie. City-centre, riverside location, backing onto Temple Bar. Recently refurbished and redesigned with stylish restraint, this place delights the eye as well as the stomach (the restaurant is first-class). Owners include members of the U2 rock group, clientele is self-consciously hip.
Conrad Dublin, Earlsfort Terrace, Dublin 2. Tel: 602 8900, fax: 676 5424. www.conrad-international.ie. Recently-built, American-style, gleaming five-star hotel across the street from the National Concert Hall and just a few metres from St Stephen's Green. Telephones even in the bathrooms.
The Morgan Hotel, 10 Fleet Street, Temple Bar, Dublin 2. Tel: 679 3939, fax: 679 3946. www.themorgan.com. New hotel in the heart of Temple Bar. High-tech facilities; all rooms have hi-fi systems and video players, ISDN lines and Internet access.
Shelbourne Hotel, 27 St Stephen's Green, Dublin 2. Tel: 663 4500, fax: 661 6006. www.shelbourne.ie. Long established as Dublin's most prestigious hotel, with plenty of old-world atmosphere. The lounge is a great place for afternoon tea, the Horseshoe Bar is popular with some of the city's "heavy hitters".
Westbury Hotel, Balfe Street, off Grafton Street, Dublin 2. Tel: 679 1122, fax: 679 7078. www.jurysdoyle.com. Modern, luxury hotel right in the city centre with

Tip: Book Ahead

It can be difficult to find a bed in Dublin at high season, so advance booking is advised. Check prices before booking.

a shopping mall next door. First-class food.

€€€
(over €100 a night double)
Buswell's Hotel, 23–7 Molesworth Street, Dublin 2. Tel: 614 6500, fax: 676 2090. www.quinnhotels.com. Former Georgian townhouses used as a hotel since the 1920s. A haunt of politicians because of its proximity to Leinster House.
Camden Court Hotel, Camden Street, Dublin 2. Tel: 475 9666, fax: 475 9677. www.camdencourt hotel.com. Large new hotel located 10 minutes' walk from the city centre. Modern interior and planned facilities include a leisure centre.
Central Hotel, 1–5 Exchequer Street, Dublin 2. Tel: 679 7302, fax: 679 7303. www.centralhotel.ie. Arguably has more character than some of the bigger, pricier places, with interesting paintings on the walls. Close to Grafton Street.
Gresham Hotel, 23 Upper O'Connell Street, Dublin 1. Tel: 874 6881, fax: 878 7175. www.gresham-hotels.com. Once rivalled the Shelbourne as Dublin's grandest hotel, but has suffered somewhat from the decline of O'Connell Street. Still characterful and atmospheric.
Longfield's Hotel, 9–10 Lower Fitzwilliam Street, Dublin 2. Tel: 676 1367, fax: 676 1542. www.longfields.ie. Charming small hotel in heart of southside Georgian Dublin. Good food in basement restaurant.
Mount Herbert Hotel, Herbert Road, Lansdowne Road, Dublin 4. Tel: 668 4321, fax: 660 7077. www.mountherberthotel.ie. Family-run guesthouse in an extended Victorian house near Lansdowne Road stadium. Children's playground.
Number 31, Leeson Close, Dublin 2. Tel: 676 5011, fax: 676 2929. www.number31.ie. Interesting, friendly guesthouse based in two houses, one modern, one Georgian. Just off Leeson Street. Delicious breakfasts.

Temple Bar Hotel, Fleet Street, Dublin 2. Tel: 677 3333, fax: 677 3088. www.templebarhotel.com. Sited in trendy Temple Bar area with its bustling night-life. Great location if you're not a light sleeper.

€€

(over €60 a night double)

Aberdeen Lodge, 53 Park Avenue, Dublin 4. Tel: 283 8155, fax: 283 7877. www.halpinsprivatehotels.com. Well-equipped guesthouse in pair of Edwardian houses on elegant road.

Bewley's Principal Hotel, 19–20 Fleet Street, Temple Bar, Dublin 2. Tel: 670 8122, fax: 670 8103. www.principalhotel.com. The legendary café group has branched into the accommodation market. An old-fashioned intimate hotel with every modern facility plus fresh Bewley's coffee.

The Davenport Hotel, Merrion Square, Dublin 2. Tel: 607 3500, fax: 661 5663. www.ocallaghanhotels.com. Luxurious hotel in the heart of Georgian Dublin. Sited near the National Gallery of Ireland, Trinity College and Grafton Street.

Hotel Isaacs, Store Street, Dublin 1. Tel: 855 0067, fax: 836 5390. www.isaacs.ie. Small, efficient, friendly place handily situated close to Connolly Station and Busaras (central bus stations).

Hotel St George, 7 Parnell Square, Dublin 1. Tel: 874 5611, fax: 874 5582. Email: hotelstgeorge@eircom.net. Comfortable hotel in two converted Georgian houses. Close to the Hugh Lane Municipal Art Gallery, Gate Theatre, and O'Connell Street.

King Sitric, East Pier, Howth. Tel: 832 5235, fax: 839 2442. www.kingsitric.ie. This is one of Howth's finest fish restaurants but it also has 8 seaside rooms. The gourmet breakfast is just as impressive as the evening meals.

Merrion Hall, 54 Merrion Road, Ballsbridge, Dublin 4. Tel: 668 1426, fax: 668 4280.

www.halpinsprivatehotels.com. Rambling, cosy Victorian guesthouse near the Royal Dublin Society grounds. Good breakfasts.

Mont Clare Hotel, Clare Street, Merrion Square, Dublin 2. Tel: 607 3800, fax: 661 5663. www.ocallaghanhotels.ie. Excellent location on the corner of Merrion Square, near National Gallery and main southside shops.

St Aiden's Guesthouse, 32 Brighton Road, Rathgar, Dublin 6. Tel: 490 2011, fax: 492 0234. Email: staidens@eircom.net. Good guesthouse in a pleasant south-side suburb of Rathgar.

€

(under €60 a night double)

Abraham House, 82–3 Lower Gardiner Street, Dublin 1. Tel: 855 0600, fax: 855 0598. www.abraham-house.ie. Hostel in two large Georgian houses. Double rooms, dormitories, parking. Cheap.

Anglesea Town House, Anglesea Road, Ballsbridge, Dublin 4. Tel: 668 3877, fax: 668 3461. Privately run guesthouse in Edwardian villa in Ballsbridge. Famous for its breakfasts.

Avalon House, 55 Aungier Street, Dublin 2. Tel: 475 0001, fax: 475 0303. www.avalon-house.ie. Well-located hostel near Grafton Street and Temple Bar. Single rooms, double rooms, family rooms, dorms. Cheap.

Carraige House Guesthouse, Lusk, Co. Dublin. Tel: 843 8857, fax: 843 8933. www.iol.ie/~carrhous. Cosy and welcoming, with extensive award-winning

gardens. Leisure centre free to guests.

Kinlay House, Lower Edward Street, Dublin 2. Tel: 679 6644, fax: 679 7437. www.kinlayhouse.ie. Close to Christ Church Cathedral, backing onto Temple Bar. Singles, doubles, 4–6 bedded rooms, dorms. Cheap.

The Oliver St John Gogarty, 58–9 Fleet Street, Temple Bar, Dublin 2. Tel: 671 1822, fax: 671 7637. www.olivergogartys.com. Recent addition to the budget end of the accommodation market, and offering bright and airy rooms in the heart of trendy Temple Bar. Hostel accommodation is cheap but the penthouse apartments cost about €200 per night.

Othello House, 74 Lower Gardiner Street, Dublin 1. Tel: 855 4271, fax: 855 7460. Email: othello@eircom.net. Handy, inner north-city location near the principal rail and bus stations. Well equipped.

Southeast Region

Cahir, Co. Tipperary

Kilcoran Lodge, Cahir. Tel: 052-41288, fax: 41994. www.tipp.ie/kilcoran.htm. Former hunting lodge in its own grounds on the main N8 with views over the Knockmealdown Mountains. €€

Cashel, Co. Tipperary

Cashel Palace Hotel, Main Street, Cashel. Tel: 062-62707, fax: 61521. www.cashel-palace.ie. Queen Anne-style Bishop's palace sumptuously converted into fine hotel. View of the Rock from back rooms. €€€

What the Tourist Boards Offer

In most places, prices vary according to season. Full details of current rates are given in Bord Fáilte's accommodation brochure, which can be purchased at any Irish Tourist Board office. The Northern Ireland Tourist Board publishes *Where to Stay*, also on sale at any of its branches. The *Hidden Ireland* brochure lists large and often grand family homes throughout Ireland which take visitors. In these, you are paying for ambience as well as accommodation.

Glen of Aherlow, Co. Tipperary

Aherlow House Hotel. Tel: 062-56153, fax: 56212. www.aherlow house.ie. Hunting lodge surrounded by pine forest and overlooking the Galtee mountains. Good base for walking/climbing. €€

Gorey, Co. Wexford

Courtown Hotel, Courtown Harbour, near Gorey. Tel: 055-25210, fax: 055-25304. www.courtownhotel.com. Small hotel run by owner-manager, with indoor heated pool in family-oriented seaside resort. €€
Marlfield House, Gorey. Tel: 055-21124, fax: 21572. www.marlfieldhouse.com. Grand Regency house with first-class restaurant in large conservatory. €€€

Hook Peninsula, Co. Wexford

Dunbrody Country House Hotel, Arthurstown. Tel: 051-389 600, fax: 389 601. www.dunbrodyhouse .com. A rambling Georgian manor in 8 hectares (20 acres) of parkland has been sensitively converted to an elegant but informal hotel and restaurant by the owner-chef and his wife. €€

Kilkenny, Co. Kilkenny

Hotel Kilkenny, College Road, Kilkenny. Tel: 056-7762000. www.griffingroup.ie. Modern hotel and leisure complex built around old home. Conservatory, indoor pool, jacuzzi. €€
Zuni Townhouse, 26 Patrick Street. Tel: 056-772 3999, fax: 775 6400. www.zuni.ie. Town-centre hip-hotel with minimalist decor and a popular Asian-themed restaurant. €

Rosslare, Co. Wexford

Hotel Rosslare, Rosslare Harbour. Tel: 053-33110; fax: 33386. www.hotelrosslare.ie. Modern cliff-top hotel overlooking Rosslare Bay and ferryport. €€
Kelly's Resort Hotel, Rosslare Village, Co. Wexford. Tel: 053-32114, fax: 32222. www.kellys.ie. Beachfront resort hotel estab-

---

Price Categories

For a standard double room in High season:
€ = under €60 each
€€ = €60–€100 each
€€€ = €100–€150 each
€€€€ = over €150 each

---

lished 1895, and run by the Kelly family ever since. Outstanding sports facilities and excellent food. €€

Thomastown, Co. Kilkenny

Mount Juliet Conrad, Thomastown. Tel: 056-73000, fax: 73019. www.conradhotels.com. Elegant 18th-century house on its own sporting estate which includes a Jack Nicklaus golf course, equestrian centre and tennis centre. €€€€

Waterford, Co. Waterford

Dooley's Hotel, The Quay, Waterford. Tel: 051 873531, fax: 870262. www.dooleys-hotel.ie. Family-run hotel with good food and lively bar in centre of town on the quays of River Suir. €€

Wexford, Co. Wexford

Ferrycarrig Hotel, Ferrycarrig Bridge, near Wexford. Tel: 053 20999, fax: 20982. www.griffingroup.ie. Stylish modern hotel in attractive setting by Slaney River 3 miles (5 km) outside town on the Enniscorthy road. €€€

BED AND BREAKFAST

Annestown, Co. Waterford

Annestown House, Annestown. Tel: 051-396160, fax: 396474. www.annestown.com. Cliff top house on coastal road between Tramore and Dungarvan with private paths to the beach. Tennis and billiards. €

Graiguenamanagh, Co. Kilkenny

Waterside, The Quay. Tel: 059-972 4246, fax: 972 4733.

---

www.watersideguesthouse.com. These simple but comfortable rooms above a popular restaurant are in a converted stone-built corn mill overlooking the River Barrow, and are popular with outdoor types. The quiet little village has some interesting old fashioned pubs. €

Kilkenny Town, Co. Kilkenny

Butler House, Patrick Street. Tel: 056-7765707, fax: 7765626. www.butler.ie. Once the Dower House of Kilkenny Castle, this town-centre Georgian house overlooking extensive gardens combines period elegance with contemporary design. €€
Lacken House, Dublin Road, Kilkenny. Tel: 056-776 1085, fax: 776 2435. www.lackenhouse.ie. Award winning restaurant with owner-chef offers comfortable, well-equipped rooms in small Georgian house. Restaurant is closed Sunday and Monday. €

Nire Valley, Co. Waterford

Hanorah's Cottage, Ballymacarbry. Tel: 052-36134, fax: 36540. www.hanorascottage.com. Hikers in Waterford's Comeragh mountains appreciate the comfort of this award-winning riverside retreat, and the imaginative home cooking at its restaurant. €

Waterford, Co. Waterford

Foxmount Farm and Country House, Passage East Road. Tel: 051-874 308, fax: 854 906. www.foxmountcountryhouse.com. This working dairy farm, only 15 minutes from Waterford city centre, has a 17th-century house, which offers simple, relaxing rooms, home-baking at breakfast, and a home-cooked evening meal on request. €

Wexford Town, Co. Wexford

Faythe Guest House, Swan View, Wexford. Tel: 053-22249, fax: 21680. www.faytheguesthouse.ie. Simple town house with views over Wexford Harbour. €

Southwest Region

Ballylickey, Co. Cork
Seaview House Hotel, Ballylickey, Bantry. Tel: 027-50073, fax: 51555. www.seaviewhousehotel.com. Elegant but relaxed country house hotel set in wooded grounds on the edge of Bantry Bay. €€

Clonakilty, Co. Cork
The Lodge & Spa at Inchydoney Island, Inchydoney Island. Tel: 023-33143, fax: 21164. www.inchydoneyisland.com. A relaxing modern hotel with great views across two vast beaches to the open sea. The main attraction is the Thalassotherapy (seawater) spa offering a wide range of treatments. €€€

Cork City
Ambassador Hotel, Military Hill, St Lukes. Tel: 021-455 1996, fax: 455 1997. www.ambassador hotel.ie. An imposing Victorian building has been converted into a stylish, hill-top hotel with great views of the city and harbour. €€
Hayfield Manor Hotel, Perrott Avenue, College Road. Tel: 021-484 5900, fax: 431 6839. www.hayfieldmanor.ie. This modern luxury hotel is built in the country house-style on carefully landscaped grounds near University College. A haven of tranquillity five minutes' drive from the centre. €€€
Hotel Isaac's, 48 MacCurtan Street. Tel: 021-450 0011, fax: 450 6355. www.isaacs.ie. Cheerful budget hotel and hostel in boldly converted warehouse. Handy for both bus and train stations. €€
Rochestown Park, Rochestown Road, Douglas, Co. Cork. Tel: 021-489 0800, fax: 489 2178. www.rochestownpark.com. Situated in the south suburbs, convenient for airport and ferry port this is a pleasant modern hotel with indoor pool built around an old manor house in lovely wooded grounds. €€

Dingle, Co. Kerry
Dingle Skellig, Co. Kerry. Tel: 066-915 0200, fax: 066-915 1501. www.dingleskellig.com. Well designed modern hotel on the water's edge. Sea view on request. Indoor pool. €€€

Killarney, Co. Kerry
Cahernane Hotel, Muckross Road. Tel: 064 31895, fax: 34340. www.cahernane.com. Once the shooting lodge of the Earl of Pembroke, this characterful old house has a lakeside location 1 km outside town. Most bedrooms are in a modern wing. €€
Great Southern Hotel, Killarney. Tel: 064-31262, fax: 35300. www.gshotels.com. Monumental Victorian railway hotel adjacent to town centre. Swimming, tennis, sauna and Irish entertainment nightly May–Sept. €€€

Kinsale, Co. Cork
Blue Haven Hotel, Kinsale. Tel: 021-477 2209, fax: 477 4268. Email: bluhaven@iol.ie. Small, family-run hotel in town centre noted for its seafood restaurant. €€€

Mallow, Co. Cork
Longueville House, Co. Cork. Tel: 022-47156, fax: 47459. www.longuevillehouse.ie. Relaxed family-run country house in a magnificent classical-style 18th-century house overlooking the Blackwater River midway between Cork and Killarney. The restaurant is renowned. €€€

Ring of Kerry, Co. Kerry
Ard-na-Sidhe, Caragh Lake, Killorglin. Tel: 066-976 9105, fax: 976 9282. www.iol.ie/khl.

Price Categories

For a standard double room in High season:
€ = under €60 each
€€ = €60–€100 each
€€€ = €100–€150 each
€€€€ = over €150 each

Luxurious lakeside Victorian mansion with antiques, open fires and extensive gardens. €€€
Butler Arms Hotel, Waterville. Tel: 066-947 4144, fax: 066-947 4520. www.butlerarms.com. Well-established, informal family-run hotel overlooking the sea. Golf, tennis, fishing, horse riding. €€
Parknasilla Great Southern Hotel, Sneem. Tel: 064-45122, fax: 45323. www.greatsouthernhotels.com. An imposing 19th-century mansion with extensive semi-tropical gardens. Private golf-course, swimming, riding, tennis, fishing, water-skiing. €€€€
Park Hotel, Kenmare. Tel: 064-41200, fax: 41402. www.parkkenmare.com. Luxurious, impeccably decorated hotel in grand 1897 greystone building with 11 acres of gardens. Excellent food. €€€€
Sheen Falls Lodge, Kenmare. Tel: 064-41600, fax: 41386. www.sheenfallslodge.ie. Kenmare's newest luxury hotel is in a rambling lodge on a 300-acre waterside estate. Award-winning restaurant. €€€€

BED AND BREAKFAST

Cork City
Garnish House, Western Road. Tel: 021-427 5111, fax: 427 3872. www.garnish.ie. Sample real Irish hospitality at this comfortable Victorian house near the university, a short walk from the city centre. €
Lancaster Lodge, Lancaster Quay, Western Road. Tel: 021-425 1125, fax: 425 1126. www.lancasterlodge.com. This four-storey modern building near the city centre was designed as a guesthouse, and offers free parking, hotel-standard bedrooms, lifts to all floors and an extensive breakfast menu. €€

Dingle, Co. Kerry
Cleevaun Country House, Lady's Cross, Milltown. Tel:

066-915 1108 fax: 066-915 2228. www.cleevaun.com. Modern house a mile outside town on Slea Head road with views over Dingle Bay. Extensive breakfast menu. €

Kanturk, Co. Cork
Assolas Country House, Kanturk. Tel: 029-50015, fax: 50795. www.assolas.com. Romantic 17th-century house with sweeping riverside gardens owned and managed by the Bourke family. Idyllic. Imaginative cuisine. €€

Killarney, Co. Kerry
Kathleen's Country House, Tralee Road, Killarney. Tel: 064-32810, fax: 32340. www.kathleens.net. This well-appointed modern guesthouse run by energetic owner-manager Kathleen O'Regan Sheppard is five minutes drive from town on the Tralee road. Dinner by arrangement. €
Earls Court House, Woodlawn Junction, Muckross Road. Tel: 064-34009, fax: 34366. www.killarney-earlscourt.ie. A purpose-built modern guesthouse near the town centre, this is also a comfortable family home, with antique furniture, and an open fire in the foyer, where tea and scones are served on arrival.€

Kinsale, Co. Cork
Kilcaw Lodge, Pewter Hole Cross. Tel: 021-477 4155, fax: 477 4755. www.kilcawhouse.com. Situated just outside town on the main road from Cork Airport this newly built guest house offers private parking, a welcoming open fire and country pine bedrooms. €
Old Bank House, Pearse Street, Co. Cork. Tel: 021-477 4075, fax: 477 4296. www.oldbankhousekinsale.com.Very comfortable, boldly converted Georgian town house. €€
Friar's Lodge, Friar Street. Tel: 021-477 3445, fax: 477 4363. www.friars-lodge.com. Sumptuously converted Georgian town house

with large rooms offering excellent value bed and breakfast. €

Midleton, Co. Cork
Ballymaloe House, Shangarry, Midleton. Tel: 021-465 2531, fax: 465 2021. One of Ireland's leading guest houses, virtually indistinguishable from a luxury hotel, Ballymaloe is a large, impeccably run and stylishly decorated Georgian house, owned by farming family. Renowned for its kitchen which pioneered imaginative use of fresh local produce. €€€

Ring of Kerry
Caragh Lodge, Caragh Lake, near Glenbeigh. Open April – October only. Tel: 066-976 9115, fax: 976 9316. caraghlodge.com. Secluded fishing lodge in lovely lakeside gardens. Boating, tennis, fishing. Dinner can be pre-booked. €€
Sallyport House, Glengarriff Road, Kenmare. Tel: 064-42066, fax: 42067. www.sallyporthouse.com. Exceptionally comfortable family home on the edge of town overlooking Kenmare harbour. Interesting antique furniture. €€
Tahilla Cove Country House, near Sneem. Tel: 064-45204, fax: 45104. www.tahillacove.com Secluded waterside retreat with 14-acre estate, run by the friendly Waterhouse family. Fully licensed. Home-cooked dinner. €€

Mid West Region

Adare, Co. Limerick
Dunraven Arms Hotel, Adare. Tel: 061-396 633, fax: 396 541. www.dunravenhotel.com Historic old inn in beautiful village. Equestrian and golf holidays a speciality. €€€
Woodlands House Hotel, Knockanes, Adare. Tel: 061-396118, fax: 396073. www.woodlands-hotel.ie. This is a friendly, family-run modern hotel with a lively bar and a busy local trade. A good base for touring. €€

Ballyvaughan, Co. Clare
Gregan's Castle, Co. Clare. Tel: 065-707 7005, fax: 707 7111. www.gregans.ie. An elegant country house hotel in extensive gardens at the base of the Burren's famous Corkscrew Hill with breathtaking views over Galway Bay. A little formal for some tastes, for others it is an oasis of sophistication. €€
Hyland's Burren Hotel, Co. Clare. Tel: 065-707 7037, fax: 707 7131. www.hylandsburren.com. Rambling, much extended family-run hotel in village centre with a lively bar and busy restaurant. €

Doolin, Co. Clare
Ballinalacken Castle, Doolin, Co. Clare. Tel and fax: 065-707 4025. www.ballinalackencastle.com. A converted shooting lodge with a modern bedroom wing, located beside the ruined castle for which it is named, on the coast road outside town. Superb views of the Atlantic and the Aran islands. €€

Ennis, Co. Clare
Old Ground Hotel, Ennis. Tel: 065-682 8127, fax: 682 8112. www.flynnhotels.com. Spacious, ivy-clad hotel partly 17th-century, with a quiet but central location 30 minutes from Shannon Airport. Lots of golfers. €€

Ennistymon, Co. Clare
Falls Hotel, Ennistymon. Tel: 065-707 1004, fax: 707 1367. www.fallshotel.net. Family-owned and managed large spa hotel near waterfalls on River Inagh on the edge of a quietly attractive old world village. Retains charm and atmosphere in spite of its relatively large size (130 rooms). €

Kinvara, Co. Galway
Merriman Inn, Main Street Kinvara. Tel: 091-638 222, fax: 637686. www.merrimanhotel.com. A large thatched building dating from 1997 in the centre of this attractive little fishing village, the

Merriman shows modern Irish design at its best. €

Limerick City

Castletroy Park, Dublin Road. Tel: 061-335 566, fax: 061-331 117. www.castletroy–park.ie This well-designed modern red brick hotel is on the edge of town near the university campus. While catering admirably for the business traveller, the hotel also has superb leisure facilities and a lively pub-bistro. €€
Clarion Hotel, Steamboat Quay. Tel: 061-444 100, fax: 444 101. This 17-storey oval-shaped hotel on the banks of the Shannon, Limerick's only landmark modern building, has panoramic views, uncluttered, modern design and good leisure facilities. €€

Lisdoonvarna, Co. Clare

Carrigann, Carigann Road. Tel: 065-707 4036, fax: 707 4567. www.gateway-to-the-burren.com. This quiet, family-run hotel in its own pretty gardens on the edge of town specialises in walking holidays on the Burren, either self-guided or escorted. The restaurant is excellent. €
Sheedy's Country House Hotel, Lisdoonvarna. Tel: 065-707 4026, fax: 707 4555. Small family-run hotel with turf fires. The main attraction is the exceptional food cooked by the owner's son and served in the restaurant. €

Newmarket on Fergus, Co. Clare

Dromoland Castle Hotel, Newmarket on Fergus. Tel: 061-368 144, fax: 363 355. www.dromoland.ie. Former seat of the O'Briens of Thomond, direct descendants of the High King of Ireland, Brian Boru, Dromoland is now an American-owned luxury hotel. Private golf course and lake, clay shooting, and horse riding on the estate. Interior decor is atmospheric and stylish. €€€€

BED AND BREAKFAST

Ballyvaughan, Co. Clare

Cappabhaile House. Ballyvaughan. Tel: 065-707 7260, fax: 707 7300. www.cappabhaile.com. Large, unpretentious stone-faced bungalow on the edge of the Burren purpose-built for the B & B business. Family-run restaurant. Walking distance to lively village pubs.Free use of pitch and putt course and full sized pool table for guests. €

Kilrush, Co. Clare

Old Parochial House, Cooraclare. Tel: 065-9059059, fax: 9051006. Spacious, informal period house on the edge of small seaside village. €

Lahinch

Berry Lodge, Annagh, Milltown Malbay. Tel: 065-708 7022, fax: 708 7011. www.berrylodge.com. Home cooking and simple country decor (old pine, patchwork quilts) are the main attractions at this substantial slate-roofed farmhouse. It's way out in the countryside midway between Lahinch and Milltown Malbay, with views of the sea at nearby Spanish Point, a 10-minute walk away. Owner Rita Meade is a well-known local chef. €€
Moy House, Milltown Malbay Road. Tel: 065-708 2800, fax: 708 2500. www.moyhouse.com. This is the ultimate romantic retreat, an 18th-century country house with 15 acres of grounds, on a spectacular clifftop overlooking the wild Atlantic. It's a three minute drive from the busy surfing-and-golfing

village, but a world apart, with an atmosphere more like a private country house than a guesthouse. €€

Midlands Region

Athlone, Co. Westmeath

Hodson Bay Hotel, Athlone. Tel: 090 644 2000, fax: 090 644 2020. www.hodsonbayhotel.com. Large, nicely modernised hotel with a superb location on the water's edge at Lough Ree just west of Athlone on the N61 Roscommon road. €€

Banagher-on-the-Shannon, Co. Offaly

Brosna Lodge Hotel, Banagher-on-the-Shannon. Tel: 0509-51350, fax: 0509-51521. www.brosnalodge.com. Simple hospitality in a lively Shannonside village. €

Birr, Co. Offaly

County Arms Hotel, Railway Road, Birr. Tel: 0509-20791, fax: 21234. Email: countyarmshotel @eircom.net. Small, owner-managed hotel in converted Georgian mansion. €€
Kinnitty Castle Demesne, Kinnitty, Birr. Tel: 0509-37318, fax: 37284. www.kinnittycastle.com. Exuberant, turreted Gothic castle about 9 miles (15 km) outside Birr in the foothills of the Slieve Bloom mountains, this is a genuine Irish castle experience with everything on a vast scale. €€€

Mullingar, Co. Westmeath

Bloomfield House Hotel, Belvedere, Tullamore Road, Mullingar. Tel: 044-40894, fax: 43767. www.bloomfieldhouse.com. Friendly hotel in old, castellated house on the shores of Lough Ennell that once served as a convent boarding school. Good value in unspoilt countryside. €€

Roscommon, Co. Roscommon

Abbey Hotel, Galway Road. Tel: 0966-26240, fax: 26021. www.abbeyhotel.ie. Modern hotel in venerable castellated shell parts of which date from the 18th century. Peaceful location surrounded by lawns. €€

BED AND BREAKFAST

Borrisokane, Co. Tipperary
Ballycormac House, Aglish. Tel: 067-21129. Pretty country cottage run by John and Cherylyn Lang. Dinner, bookable in advance, is made using home-grown and local produce. horses on site are available for riding. €

Mountrath, Co. Laois
Roundwood House, Mountrath. Tel: 0502-32120, fax: 32711. www.hiddenireland.com/roundwood. Informal hospitality in an 18th-century Palladian villa close to the Slieve Bloom mountains. Popular with walkers. Dinner by arrangement. €€

Nenagh, Co. Tipperary
Saint David's Country House, Puckane. Tel: 067-24145, fax: 24388. Picture-book pretty Victorian lakeside lodge refurbished to unusually high standard. Restaurant, bar. Fishing and horse riding are available locally. €€€

Terryglass, Co. Tipperary
Tír na Fiúise (Land of Fuchsia), Borrisokane. Tel/fax: 067-22041. www.countrycottages.ie. Quiet farmhouse well off the beaten track popular with those seeking rural solitude. Good walking country near scenic Lough Derg. Offers self-catering accommodation in restored old-style farm cottages. Price per week is €300 during high season. €

Far West Region

Achill, Co. Mayo
Ostan Ghob A'Choire (Achill Sound Hotel), Achill Island. Tel: 098-45245, fax: 45621. This splendidly scenic island is connected to mainland Mayo by

a causeway. Accommodation is simple, but you can expect some form of traditional entertainment most evenings in July and August. €

Aran Islands, Co. Galway
Ostan Inis Oirr, Lurgan Village, Inisheer. Tel: 099-75020, fax: 75099. www.ostaninisoirr.com. Whether you fly or take the ferry, this simple modern hotel makes a comfortable base for exploring the smallest of the Aran Islands. Traditional music nightly in the bar. €

Cashel Bay, Co. Galway
Cashel House Hotel, Cashel Bay. Tel: 095-31001, fax: 31077. www.cashel-house-hotel.com. Elegant, antique-filled country hideaway in lovely gardens overlooking bay and backed by the hills of Connemara. €€€

Clifden, Co. Galway
Abbeyglen Castle, Sky Road, Clifden. Tel: 095-21201, fax: 21797. www.abbeyglen.ie. Turreted mock castle on beautiful site on outskirts of "capital of Connemara." Good sports facilities including an outdoor heated swimming pool. €€€
Erriseask House Hotel, Ballyconneely. Tel: 095-23553, fax: 23639. www.erriseask. connemara-ireland.com. This small modern country hotel set amidst some of Connemara's best coastal scenery is impeccably run by Swiss brothers Christian and Stefan Matz. Stefan's cooking has a high reputation. €
Rock Glen Country House, Clifden. Tel: 095-21035, fax: 21737. www.connemara.net/rockglen-hotel. Elegant shooting lodge in quiet location 1.6 km outside Clifden on the shores of Ardbear Bay. Cosy. Good food. €€

Cong, Co. Mayo
Ashford Castle, Cong. Tel: 092-46003, fax: 46260.

www.ashford.ie. A castellated fairytale castle, standing on the isthmus between Lough Corrib and Lough Mask. American-owned with high very standards of comfort and decor. Private golf course, tennis, fishing, boating, horse riding and shooting are part of the "total resort" experience. Ronald and Nancy Reagan stayed here during their presidential visit to Ireland in 1984. €€€€

Furbo, Co. Galway
Connemara Coast Hotel, Furbo. Tel: 091-592 108, fax: 592 065. www.connemaracoasthotel.com. Well-run, imaginatively designed modern hotel. Swimming, tennis. €€

Galway City
Ardilaun House Hotel, Taylor's Hill. Tel: 091-521 433, fax: 521 546. www.ardilaunhousehotel.ie. Charming old world hotel is quiet, leafy location midway between Galway city and Salthill. €€
Brennan's Yard Hotel, Lower Merchant's Road. Tel: 091-568 166, fax: 568 262. Interesting warehouse conversion in city centre's newly revitalised dock area. €€
Glenlo Abbey Hotel, Bushy Park. Tel: 091-526 666, fax: 527 800. www.glenlo.com. Luxuriously converted monastery on the banks of Lough Corrib 4 km from city centre, surrounded by its own golf course. €€€€
Great Southern Hotel, Eyre Square, Galway. Tel: 091-564 041, fax: 566 704. www.gsh.ie. Grand old railway hotel on city's main square, still a major landmark and social centre. Indoor pool, health complex. €€€

Letterfrack, Co. Galway
Rosleague Manor Hotel, Letterfrack, Connemara. Tel: 095-41101, fax: 41168. www.rosleague.com. Beautifully situated Georgian house in

scenic Connemara with grounds running down to the sea. Relaxed country house hotel atmosphere. €€

Oughterard, Co. Galway
Sweeney's Oughterard House, Oughterard. Tel: 091-552 207, fax: 552 161. www.sweeneys-hotel.com. In spite of its main road location, this 200-year-old country house hotel retains an attractive, slightly faded, old world charm. Tea can be taken in the pretty gardens while a beautiful stretch of the Owenriff River runs in front of the hotel. €€

Recess, Co. Galway
Ballynahinch Castle Hotel, Ballynahinch. Tel: 095-31006, fax: 31085. www.ballynahinch-castle.com. Historic house full of character, splendidly sited in the wilds of Connemara at the foot of one of the "Twelve Bens", overlooking the Owenmore River. Private salmon fishing. €€

Westport, Co. Mayo
Hotel Westport, The Demense, Newport Road, Westport. Tel: 098-25122, fax: 26739. www.hotelwestport.ie. Comfortable, modern two-storey hotel with spacious rooms near the town centre. Surrounded by gardens with pleasant rural views. Good sports facilities. €€€
Olde Railway Hotel, The Mall, Westport. Tel: 098-25166, fax: 25090. www.anu.ie/railwayhotel Family-run hotel on a tree-lined riverside mall in town centre, more than 200 years old. Thackeray called it "one of the prettiest and comfortablest inns in Ireland". €€

BED AND BREAKFAST

Aran Islands, Co. Galway
Mainistír House, Inis Mór. Tel: 099-61169, fax: 61351. www.mainistirhousearan.com. B & Bs abound on all three Aran Islands, and you can book a room when booking your ferry or flight. This one is different – a hostel with private double or twin rooms where cook Joël d'Anjou has built up a reputation for imaginative cooking both at breakfast and dinner. €

Clifden, Co. Galway
Maldua Guesthouse, Galway Road. Tel: 095-21171, fax: 21739. www.maldua.com. Modern family-run guest house in peaceful surroundings ¾ mile (1.25 km) outside Clifden. €
The Quay House, Beach Road, Clifden. Tel: 095-21369, fax: 21608. www.thequayhouse.com. Beautifully located on a tranquil quay below the busy town, the large harbourmaster's house (1829) has been converted into a stylish and characterful country house and restaurant. €€

Galway City
Adare Guest House, 9 Father Griffin Place. Tel: 091-582638, fax: 583963. www.adarebedandbreakfast.com. Well-located, unpretentious accommodation with private parking three minutes' walk from city centre. €

Leenane, Co. Galway
Delphi Lodge, Leenane. Tel: 095-42222, fax: 42296. www.delphilodge.ie. Romantic Georgian country house in

remote Connemara valley. Lovely lakeside setting, private fly fishing, elegant but informal atmosphere. Freshly prepared gourmet dinner daily at 8pm. €€

Northwest Region

Bruckless, Co. Donegal
Bruckless House, Bruckless. Tel: 074-973 7071, fax: 973 7070. www.iol.ie/~bruc/bruckless.html. An 18th-century farmhouse with gardens, woods. Sea views. Home cooked breakfast. €

Carrick-on-Shannon, Co. Leitrim
Bush Hotel, Carrick-on-Shannon. Tel: 071-967 1000, fax: 071-962 1180. www.bushhotel.com. One of Ireland's oldest country town hotels. €€

Carrigart, Co. Donegal
Hotel Carrigart, Carrigart. Tel: 074-915 5114, fax: 074-915 5250. carrigart@ireland.com. Roadside hotel in French Mansard style offering excellent value. Heated pool, squash, sauna, solarium and 18 hole links. €

Dunfanaghy, Co. Donegal
Arnolds Hotel, Dunfanaghy. Tel: 074-913 6208, fax: 074-913 6352. www.arnoldshotel.com. Family-run since 1922. Excellent traditional cooking. Painting tuition, photography weekends and creative writing. €€

Dunkineely, Co. Donegal
Castlemurray House, St John's Point, Dunkineely. Tel: 074-973 7022, fax: 973 7330. Stylish restaurant with rooms. €

Killybegs, Co. Donegal
Bayview Hotel, Main Street, Killybegs. Tel: 074-973 1950, fax: 074-973 1856. www.bayviewhotel.ie. Overlooking busy harbour. Swimming pool. €€

The Lowdown on High Tea

This is a concept, common in hotel restaurants, which foxes many visitors. High tea is served between 5pm and 7pm and typically consists of sausages or a lamb cutlet, with a plate of cakes and scones. There's often a choice of freshly baked bread. High tea is different from afternoon tea, which is served between 3pm and 5pm and consists of a pot of tea plus sandwiches or cakes.

Letterkenny, Co. Donegal
Mount Errigal Hotel, Ballyraine, Letterkenny. Tel: 074-912 2700, fax: 074-912 5085. www.mounterrigal.com. Modern facilities include sauna, leisure centre. €€

Lough Arrow, Co. Sligo
Rock View Hotel, Lough Arrow, Ballindoon, Riverstown. Tel/fax: 079-66073. Popular with anglers, who get good tips from owners. €

Lough Eske, Co. Donegal
Ardnamona, Lough Eske, Donegal Town. Tel: 074-972 2650, fax: 075-972 2819. www.ardnamona.com. Famed for its wild rhododendron gardens. An 18th-century house with south-facing bedrooms. €€
Harvey's Point Country Hotel, Lough Eske. Donegal Town. Tel: 074-972 2208, fax: 074-972 2352. www.harveyspoint.com. Modern luxurious lakeside complex. Sports facilities. Recommended restaurant with rooms, Tennis courts. €€

Malin, Co. Donegal
Malin Hotel, Malin, Inishowen. Tel: 074-937 0606, fax: 074-937 0770. This is Ireland's most northerly hotel, family owned and run in rural location. €

Mohill, Co. Leitrim
Glebe House, Ballinamore Road, Mohill. Tel: 071-963 1086, fax: 071-963 1886. In 40 acres (16 hectares) of farmland, a splendid guest-house. €

Rathmullan, Co. Donegal
Pier Hotel, Rathmullan. Tel: 074-915 8115, fax: 074-915 8458. Family-run, home cooking. €
Rathmullan House, Lough Swilly, Rathmullan, Letterkenny. Tel: 074-915 8188, fax: 074-915 8200. www.rathmullanhouse.com. Country house on shores of Lough Swilly. Beautiful gardens. Period-style bedrooms. €€€

Rossnowlagh, Co. Donegal
Sand House Hotel Rossnowlagh. Tel: 071-985 1777, fax: 071-985 2100. www.sandhouse-hotel.ie. The way seaside hotels used to be. €€

St Ernan's Island, Co. Donegal
St Ernan's Hotel St Ernan's Island, near Donegal Town. Tel: 074-972 1065, fax: 074-972 2640. Email: res@sainternans.com. This hotel is beautifully situated on a small, wooded island reached via a causeway. €€

Sligo Town, Co. Sligo
Sligo Park Hotel, Pearse Road, Sligo. Tel: 071-916 0291, fax: 071-916 9556. www.leehotels.ie. Modern hotel, formerly part of the Jury's chain. Reasonably priced. €€

BED AND BREAKFAST

Ardara, Co. Donegal
The Green Gate, Ardvally. Tel: 074-954 1546. Traditional cottage with ocean views and a charming French host. €

The Northeast

Because this is a sizeable area, entries are grouped according to county.

Counties Cavan, Sligo, Monaghan
Coopershill, Riverstown, Co. Sligo. Tel: 071-916 5108, fax: 916 5466. www.coopershill.com. Handsome Georgian country house. Period fittings. Woodland settings. Family-run. €

Cromleach Lodge Country House Hotel, Castlebaldwin, Boyle, Co. Sligo. Tel: 071-916 5155, fax: 071-916 5455. www.cromleach.com. Restaurant with spacious airy bedrooms. Purpose-built. €€
Hilton Park, Clones, Co. Monaghan. Tel: 047-56007, fax: 047-56033. www.hiltonpark.ie. In the Madden family since Samuel, a friend of Dr Samuel Johnson, bought it in 1734, €
Markree Castle, Coolooney, Co. Sligo. Tel: 071-916 7800, fax: 071-916 7840. www.markree castle.ie. Eclectically run castellated mansion in gardens and parkland. €€
Slieve Russell Hotel and Country Club, Ballyconnell, Co. Cavan. Tel: 049-952 6444, fax: 049-952 6046. www.quinn hotels.com. A phenomenon. Luxury interior contrasting with hilltop convent-like exterior. Swimming pool, jacuzzi. Fine food. €€€
Temple House, Ballymote, Co. Sligo. Tel: 071-918 3329, fax: 071-918 3808. www.templehouse.ie. Victorian restyling of lakeside Georgian mansion overlooking 13th-century Templar castle in 1,000-acre (400-hectare) grounds. €€

County Antrim
Adair Arms Hotel, Ballymoney Road, Ballymena. Tel: 02825-653 674, fax: 028-25-64 0436, www.adairarms.com. Traditional town-centre hotel. €€
Bushmills Inn, Dunluce Road, Bushmills. Tel: 028-2073 3000, fax: 732 048. www.bushmills.com. Conveniently near the world's oldest whiskey distillery. €€€
Dunadry Hotel and Country Club, 2 Islandreagh Drive, Dunadry. Tel: 028-9443 4343, fax: 433 389. www.mooneyhotelgroup.com. Attractive old building. Close to airport. €€
Fullerton Arms, 22 Main Street, Ballintoy. Tel/fax: 028-2076 9613. www.fullertonarms.co.uk.

Modernised coaching inn.
B & B. €
Galgorm Manor, 136 Fenaghy Road, Ballymena. Tel: 02825-881 001, fax: 028-2588 0080. www.galgorm.com. Riverside gentleman's residence, converted. €€€€
Glens Hotel, 6 Coast Road, Cushendall. Tel: 02821-771 223, fax: 028-2177 2655. Comfortable hotel in the "capital of the glens". €€
Leighinmohr House Hotel, Ballymena. Tel: 028-2565 2313, fax: 028-2565 6669. www.leighinmohrhotel.com. Suburban hotel specialising in parties and weddings. €€
Londonderry Arms Hotel, Harbour Road, Carnlough. Tel: 028-2888 5255, fax: 028-2888 5263. www.glensofantrim.com. Old coaching inn that once belonged to Sir Winston Churchill. The present proprietor was a devotee of the great steeplechaser, Arkle, and set up a miniature museum in his honour. It includes a portrait of the horse by the Glens of Antrim painter, Charles McAuley. €€
Magherabuoy House, 41 Magherabuoy Road, Portrush. Tel: 028-70-82 3507, fax: 028-7082 4687. www.magherabuoy.co.uk. Near resorts with fine beaches. €€
Marine Hotel, 1–3 North Street, Ballycastle. Tel: 028-2076 2222, fax: 028-2076 9507. www.marinehotel.net. Lacking in personality, but excellent views. Popular for weddings. €
Rathlin Guest House, Rathlin

Island. Tel: 028-2076 3917. Reached by boat from Ballycastle, weather permitting. €
Rosspark Hotel, Kells. Tel: 028-2589 1663, fax: 028-2589 1477. City standards in heart of country. €€
Templeton Hotel, 882 Antrim Road, Templepatrick, Ballyclare Tel: 028-9443 2984, fax: 028-9443 3406. www.templetonhotel.com. New lodge-style hotel en route to airport. €€

County Armagh

Dean's Hill, 34 College Hill, Armagh. Tel: 028-3752 4923. Guesthouse calm as the deanery it once was. €
Seagoe Hotel, Upper Church Lane, Portadown. Tel: 028-3833 3076, fax: 028-3835 0210. www.seagoe.com. Good food. €€

County Down

Burrendale Hotel and Country Club, 51 Castlewellan Road, Newcastle. Tel: 028-4372 2599, fax: 028-4372 2328. www.burrendale.com. Good food. €€
Dufferin Arms Coaching Inn, 35 High Street, Killyleagh. Tel: 028-4482 8229, fax: 028-4482 8755. Email: dufferin@

dial.pipex.com. Stout walls, log fires and village gossip. €
Enniskeen House Hotel, 98 Bryansford Road, Newcastle. Tel: 028-4372 2392, fax: 028-4372 4084. Good food. €€
Glassdrumman Lodge, 85 Mill Road, Annalong. Tel: 028-4376 8451, fax: 028-4376 7041. Exquisite small hotel on edge of Mournes. €€€
La Mon House, 41 Gransha Road, Castlereagh, Belfast. Tel: 028-9044 8631, fax: 028-9044 8026. www.lamon.co.uk. Country hotel with pool quite close to Belfast. €€
Marine Court Hotel, The Marina Bangor. Tel: 028-9145 1100, fax: 028-9145 1200. www.mova.co.uk/nova/marine. Overlooking new marina. €€
Portaferry Hotel. 10 The Strand. Tel: 028-4272 8231, fax: 028-4272 8999. www.portaferryhotel.com. Overlooks Strangford narrows. Good seafood. €€
Old Inn, 15 Main Street, Crawfordsburn. Tel: 028-9185 3255, fax: 028-9185 2775. www.theoldinn.com. Pleasant hotel, good food. €
Slieve Donard Hotel, Downs Road, Newcastle. Tel: 028-4372 1066, fax: 028-4372 4830. www.hastingshotels.com. Mansion on beach with pool and superb view of Mourne Mountains. €€
Strangford Arms, 92 Church Street, Newtownards. Tel: 028-9181 4141, fax: 028-9181 1010. Country town hotel. €€

County Fermanagh

Killyhevlin Hotel, Dublin Road, Enniskillen. Tel: 028-6632 3481, fax: 028-66-32 4726. www.killyhevlin.com. Good food. Lakeland setting. €€
Lough Erne Hotel, Main Street, Kesh. Tel: 028-6863 1275, fax: 6863 1921. www.loughernehotel.com. Good food. €
Mahon's Hotel, Enniskillen Rd, Irvinestown. Tel: 028-6862 1656, fax: 6862 8344. www.mahonshotel.co.uk. Good food. €
Donn Carragh Hotel, Main

How to Make an Official Complaint

Your first move, of course, should be to complain to the manager of the offending establishment. If this fails to give satisfaction, turn to your nearest tourist office.

Complaints in writing may be directed to the Customer Relations Section, Irish Tourist Board, Baggot Street Bridge, Dublin 2, tel: (1890) 525 525, or the Northern Ireland Tourist Board, 59 North Street, Belfast BT1 1NB, tel: 028-9024 6609.

You could also contact the Consumers Association of Ireland Ltd., 43–4 Chelmsford Road, Dublin 6, tel: 01-497 8600; web site www.consumerassociation.ie.

Street, Lisnaskea. Tel: 028-6772 1206, fax: 6772 1223. B & B in village location. €

County Derry
Ardtara Country House, 8 Gortead Road, Upperlands, Maghera. Tel: 028-7964 4490, fax: 028-79-64 5080. www.ardtara.com. Deep in Seamus Heaney country. House of distinction with distinctive cuisine. €€
Beech Hill Country House Hotel, 32 Ardmore Road, Derry. Tel: 028-7134 9279, fax: 028-7134 5366. www.beech-hill.com. Four-poster beds, elegant grounds, fine kitchen. €€
Camus House, 27 Curragh Road, Coleraine. Tel: 028-7034 2982. B & B that will appeal to salmon fishers, €
City of Derry Travelodge, 22 Strand Road, Derry. Tel: 028-7127 1271, fax: 028-7127 1277. www.travelodge.co.uk. One of three city-centre business-orientated hotels. €€
Radisson Roe Park Hotel and Golf Resort, Roe Park, Limavady. Tel: 028-7772 2222, fax: 028-7772 2313. www.radissonroepark.com. Spacious conversion of Charles Lanyon mansion. €€

County Tyrone
Blessingbourne, Fivemiletown. Tel: 028-8952 1188. www.blessingbourne.com. Self-catering apartments and courtyard adjacent to Elizabethan lakeside manor, with mullioned windows and carriage museum. €
Grange Lodge, 7 Grange Road, Dungannon. Tel: 028-8778 4212, fax: 028-8778 4313. A charming guesthouse famed for its food. €€
Valley Hotel, 60 Main Street, Fivemiletown. Tel: 028-8952 1505, fax: 521 688. www.thevalleyhotel.com. Good food. €€

Belfast

Ash-Rowan Town House, 12 Windsor Avenue. Tel: 028-9066 1758, fax: 028-9066 3227.

Guesthouse with Irish linen sheets. Victorian furniture. Has character. €€
Belfast Central Travelodge, 15 Brunswick Street. Tel: 028-9033 3555, fax: 028-9023 2999. Bright renamed hotel (was the Plaza), aimed at the middle market, and right in the centre of it all. €€
The Crescent Town House, 13 Lower Crescent. Tel: 028-9032 3349, fax: 028-9032 0646. www.crescenttownhouse.com. Inexpensive busy hotel within easy walking distance of restaurants and nightlife. €€
Culloden Hotel, 142 Bangor Road, Holywood. Tel: 028-9042 1066, fax: 028-9042 6777. www.hastingshotels.com. Plush hideaway for top people in baronial-style mansion with wooded grounds outside the city on Belfast Lough shore. €€
Duke's Hotel, 65 University Street. Tel: 028-9023 6666, fax: 028-9023 7177. www.welcome-group.co.uk. Mid-market hotel in university area, 10-minute walk to city centre. €
Europa Hotel, Great Victoria Street. Tel: 028-9027 1066, fax: 028-9026 6099. www.hastingshotels.com. Large hotel with conference suites in heart of city. Once a popular target for bombers, now a watering hole for expense-account executives and pressmen. €€€
Holiday Inn Belfast, 22 Ormeau Avenue. Tel: 0870-400 9005, fax: 028-9062 6546. www.holiday-inn.co.uk. €
Holiday Inn Express, 106 University Street. Tel: 028-9031 1909, fax: 028-9031 1910. www.exhi-belfast.com. At the lower end of the Holiday Inn range. Impersonal, but fills a gap in the university area. €
Madison's, 59–63 Botanic Avenue. Tel: 028-9050 9800, fax: 028-9050 9808. www.madisonshotel.com. A stylish café-restaurant and bright rooms are the attractions of

this new venture in an off-campus milieu. €€
Old Rectory, 148 Malone Road. Tel: 028-9066 7882, fax: 028-9068 3759. Former rectory B & B, handy for South Belfast. Off-street parking. €
Renshaws Hotel, 75 University Street. Tel: 028-9033 3366, fax: 028-9033 3399. www.renshawshotel.com. Another new hotel in studentland, with bistro bar. Small but handily placed. €€
Stormont Hotel, 587 Upper Newtownards Road. Tel: 028-9065 1066, fax: 028-9048 0240. www.hastingshotels.com. Smart hotel beside former Parliament buildings and government offices. €€
Wellington Park Hotel, 21 Malone Road. Tel: 028-9038 1111, fax: 028-9066 5410. www.mooneyhotelgroup.com. Smart suburban hotel, with disco, close to university. €€

GUESTHOUSES

Botanic Lodge, 87 Botanic Avenue. Tel and fax: 028-9032 7682. Handy location in busy area. €
Helga Lodge, 7 Cromwell Road. Tel: 028-9032 4820, fax: 028-9032 0653. www.helgalodge.co.uk. Terraced house B & B conveniently close to the action. €
Windermere House, 60 Wellington Park. Tel: 028-9066 2693, fax: 9068 2218. Short walk from university area. €

Where to Eat

The Choice

You will find many superb natural ingredients on offer in Irish restaurants – fresh and smoked salmon, trout, prawns, oysters, succulent beef, pork and lamb – above all, perhaps, delicious and chewy wholemeal and soda bread. But you will find few dishes that are specifically Irish, partly because the country has no tradition of *haute cuisine* and partly because the people tend to associate traditional fare such as Irish stew of boiled bacon and cabbage with the poor old days. These may be humble dishes, but they are also wholesome and delicious. Keep an eye out, too, for the ever-growing range of Irish cheeses, many of which are first-class.

Eating out in Ireland is not cheap, though it is getting cheaper. In the cities and towns there is no shortage of fast-food places offering everything from hamburgers to fish-and-chips or sweet-and-sour chicken. At the other end of the scale there are plush, expensive restaurants, often attached to hotels or pubs. A welcome new development is the increasing trend towards bar food at lunch time and in the early evening. The meal will be served at your bar room table featuring a substantial but moderately priced main course (around €8) and a limited choice of starters and desserts.

The restaurant scene has undergone a revolution for the better in the past decade. Many young cooks who have trained in the best kitchens of Europe and America have returned home determined to make the best of Ireland's wonderful raw ingredients. They have opened restaurants – often small, un-prepossessing establishments – where you will eat succulent, fresh produce cooked simply and well, and you will find that the fresh Irish air gives you the appetite of a lifetime.

But you can still be unlucky enough to pay inflated prices to eat overcooked and over-dressed food (probably from a menu with misspelt French names) in pretentious surroundings. If this happens, please complain. Many Irish people hate to make a fuss, and bad restaurants survive as a result.

The Prices

Irish Republic

The symbols at the end of each entry provide a rough guide to prices, based on the average cost of a three-course evening meal, excluding wine, € = less than €25 per head; €€ = between €25 and €30 per head; €€€ = more than €30 per head. Lunch is usually cheaper. Prices for restaurants in Northern Ireland are given on page 359.

Dublin

Where no area code is given, the telephone number is in the Dublin exchange (01- prefix when dialling from another area). Numbers are given only where booking is possible.

EXPENSIVE

Eden, Meeting House Square, Temple Bar, Dublin 2. Tel: 670 5372. www.edenrestaurant.ie. Minimalist decor and well-defined flavours combine to make this restaurant a very sophisticated experience. €€€

Ernies, Mulberry Gardens, Donnybrook, Dublin 4. Tel: 269 3300. A restaurant beloved of socialites and name-droppers. But don't hold that against this dining institution whose reputation is also built on magnificent food. Intimate atmosphere. €€€

King Sitric, East Pier, Howth, Co. Dublin. Tel: 832 5235. www.kingsitric.ie. Seafood restaurant with no excuse for not having fresh fish. It's positioned beside one of the most scenic harbours in Dublin, with a view of Ireland's Eye. €€€

Les Frères Jacques, 74 Dame Street, Dublin 2. Tel: 679 4555. www.lesfreresjacques.com. Quality French food at affordable prices – provided you don't go mad with the tempting wine list – ensure that this restaurant has an enduring appeal to locals who keep going back. €€€

Lobster Pot, 9 Ballsbridge Terrace, Dublin 4. Tel: 668 0025. Long-established seafood restaurant near the city centre in which you'll feel immediately at home. Fresh seafood served in mouth-watering sauces. €€€

Locks Restaurant, 1 Windsor Terrace, Portabello, Dublin 8. Tel: 454 3391. Full of atmosphere – excellent food. Haunt of theatre goers. €€€

Mermaid Café, 69–70 Dame Street, Dublin 2. Tel: 670 8236. www.mermaid.ie. Recent arrival which is fast becoming the hippest place in town. A stylish restaurant with nothing in common with a truckers' stop-over. €€€

Old Mill, 14 Temple Bar Square Merchant's Arch, Dublin 2. Tel: 671 9262. One of the first restaurants to open in the trendy Temple Bar area of Dublin. Has succeeded in fighting off new and stylish rivals Eden and Trastevere. €€€

Patrick Guilbaud, 21 Upper Merrion Street, Dublin 2. Tel: 676 4192. Dublin's best-known

French restaurant, producing classic cuisine with immense attention to detail. The prices are commensurately high. €€€

Siam Thai Restaurant, 8a The Crescent, Monkstown. Tel: 284 3309. Popular restaurant in a pretty seaside village. Excellent Thai food. €€€

Tea Rooms, The Clarence Hotel, Wellington Quay, Dublin 2. Tel: 407 0813. www.theclarence.ie. International celebrities head to this restaurant part-owned by members of the U2 pop group. You can expect a lot of gossip columnists to turn up in tow. More refined than rock 'n' roll, this restaurant was awarded the Beck's Taste of Temple Bar Award. €€€

Trocadero, 3–4 St Andrew Street, Dublin 2. Tel: 677 5545. A Dublin institution with thespians and late-night revellers. A constant buzz and air of excitement sometimes make food irrelevant in this culinary hotspot. €€€

Wongs, 436 Clontarf Road, Dublin 3. Tel: 833 4400. Also at 7 Sandford Road, Ranelagh, Dublin 6. Tel: 496 7722. Good Chinese food in restaurants with an emphasis on relaxation and good service. €€€

MODERATE

Cafe En Seine, 40 Dawson Street, Dublin 2. Tel: 677 4369. Where anyone with any ideas about being someone goes. In other words, a stylish hangout for wannabees. €€

Cedar Tree, 11A St Andrew Street, Dublin 2. Tel: 677 2121. Lebanese restaurant popular with serious foodies and late-night revellers. Ultra-relaxed atmosphere – don't be surprised if the diners start dancing on the tables. €€

Chandni, 174 Pembroke Road, Dublin 4. Tel: 668 1458. Cosy Italian place where dependably good food is reflected in dependably good prices. €€

Cooke's Café, 14 South William Street, Dublin 2. Tel: 679 0536. Atmospheric restaurant serving Mediterranean/Californian cuisine. Pleasantly close to a range of good pubs around Grafton Street. €€

Da Vincenzo, 133 Upper Leeson Street, Dublin 4. Tel: 660 9906. Highly regarded Italian restaurant offering a standard tomato and olive oil-inspired menu. €€

Fitzer's Café, 51 Dawson Street, Dublin 2, tel: 677 1155; 40 Temple Bar Square, Dublin 2, tel: 679 0440; National Gallery of Ireland, Merrion Square, Dublin 2, tel: 663 3500. This restaurant chain offers a variety of attractive locations, each serving the same cosmopolitan and delicious dishes. €€

101 Talbot, 100–102 Talbot Street, Dublin 1. Tel: 874 5011. Italian/Continental fare in a convivial restaurant. The pre-theatre dinner menu is great value if you are heading to the Abbey Theatre, located around the corner. €€

Mao, 2–3 Chatham Row, Dublin 2. Tel: 670 4899. www.cafemao.com. Favourite among top models who have made something of a second home out of this groovy Indonesian restaurant. Great green curry and Indonesian beer. €€

Mongolian Barbeque, 7 Anglesea Street, Dublin 2. Tel: 670 4154. www.mongolianbbq.ie. Groovy American franchise in trendy Temple Bar. Choose your own stirfry ingredients which are cooked on a public hot plate. A boisterous, "cool" restaurant. Not for the self-conscious. €€

Nico's, 53 Dame Street, Dublin 2. Tel: 677 3062. Old-fashioned romantic restaurant for when you've proposed marriage on the Ha'penny Bridge. Tasty Italian dishes by candlelight. Plush setting. €€

Pizza Stop, 6–10 Chatham Lane, Dublin 2. Tel: 679 6712. Authentic Italian restaurant located in the heart of the shopping district. Popular any time of the day or night. €€

Rajdoot Tandoori, 26–8 Clarendon Street, Dublin 2. Tel: 679 4274. www.rajdoot.co.uk. Excellent Tandoori dishes in the restaurant which set the standard for authentic Indian cooking in Dublin. Good atmosphere. €€

Shalimar, 17 South Great Georges Street, Dublin 2. Tel: 671 0738. Relaxed and inexpensive Balti House downstairs; upstairs offers a more upmarket and extensive Indian menu. Very reliable. €€

Yamamori Noodles, 71 South Great Georges Street, Dublin 2. Tel: 475 5001. Japanese restaurant, and probably the best place for noodles in Dublin. Predominantly cool clientele. €€

INEXPENSIVE

Bad Ass Café, 9–11 Crown Alley, Dublin 2. Tel: 671 2596. www.

Pick of the Pubs in Dublin

The Brazen Head, 20 Lower Bridge Street, Dublin 8. The city's oldest pub, recently revamped and a popular venue for live music.
Davy Byrne's, 21 Duke Street, Dublin 2. James Joyce immortalised this city-centre pub in *Ulysses*. Good lunches, art deco surroundings.
Doheny & Nesbitt's, 5 Lower Baggot Street, Dublin 2. Atmospheric interior, dark and faded. Popular with politicians and journalists.
McDaid's, 3 Harry Street, Dublin 2. Gothic pub, once a morgue. Small but very lively, favoured by youngish clientele.
Neary's, 1 Chatham Street, Dublin 2. Faded Victorian elegance and genteel ambience. Liked by theatrical and showbiz types.

badasscafe.com. Sinead O'Connor worked here as a waitress before finding fame. Not as cool as it used to be but still serving good pizzas, pasta, and salads. €

Cornucopia, 19 Wicklow Street, Dublin 2. Tel: 677 7583. Vegetarian restaurant which makes the best use of fresh produce. Arrive early for lunch to guarantee a seat. €

Juice, South Great George's Street, Dublin 2. Tel: 475 7856. Tasty vegetarian dishes, organic wines, juice bar. €

Kilkenny Design Shop, 6 Nassau Street, Dublin 2. Tel: 677 7066. American tourists arrive here by the tour bus load for the Irish-made crafts and clothes as well as the tasty food dishes. Locals favour the freshly prepared stews and cakes. €

La Med, 22 East Essex Street, Dublin 2. Tel: 670 7358. Cafe/restaurant serving Mediterranean meals and snacks. €

The Winding Stair Bookshop and Cafe, 40 Lower Ormond Quay, Dublin 1. Tel: 873 3292. Cheap wholesome food, books to browse through, and soothing jazz sounds. Perfect. Lunchtime. €

DELICATESSENS

Magill's, 14 Clarendon Street, Dublin 2. Tel: 671 3830. Offering produce from every corner of Ireland including cheese, meats, and freshly prepared salads. Reflects the growing interest in international cuisine among locals in its interesting selection of imported goods.

Caviston's, 59 Glasthule Road, Sandycove, Dublin 6. Tel: 280 9120. Visit this seafood deli on an empty stomach and you'll end up in a state of dizzy confusion; the overwhelming temptations include a fresh fish and seafood counter, a cheese display, and any type of cooked meat you'd like to devour.

The Douglas Food Company, 53 Main Street, Donnybrook, Dublin

4. Tel: 269 4066. Swanky deli offering freshly prepared meals to fit any occasion.

Sheridans Cheesemongers, 11 South Anne Street, Dublin 2, tel: 679 3143; 7 Pembroke Lane, Ballsbridge, Dublin 4, tel: 660 8231; 14–16 Churchyard Street, Galway, tel: 091-564 829. www.sheridanscheesemongers.com. The brothers who own this chain of shops started out by selling Irish farmhouse cheeses in Galway's Saturday market. They still champion quality Irish cheeses but now also sell European varieties.

Southeast Region

Cashel, Co. Tipperary

Chez Hans, Rockside, Cashel. Tel: 062-61177. Serious continental cuisine is served by owner-chef Hans-Peter Matthias in a converted Wesleyan chapel right under the famous Rock. (Café Hans next door serves light meals from noon to 5.30pm.) €€€

The Spearman Bakery & Tea Room, 97 Main Street, Cashel. Tel: 062-61143. Bread, pastries and cakes are baked daily on the premises by the owners. Also offering home-made soup and sandwiches, and conveniently located behind the Town

Hall, this makes a wholesome lunchtime stop-over. €

Dungarvan, Co Waterford

The Tannery, 10 Quay St, Dungarvan. Tel: 058 45420. Ambitous owner-chef Paul Flynn, working in the open kitchen of a spacious converted tannery, has built up a big reputation for imaginatively cooked local produce with a Mediterranean twist, served with flair in striking modern surroundings. €€€

Gorey, Co. Wexford

Marlfield House, Gorey. Tel: 055-21124. Regency house in 35 acres of woodland and gardens. Award-winning restaurant in splendid, spacious conservatory. Must book. €€€

Kilkenny Town

Cafe Sol, William Street. Tel: 056-776 4987. Cheap and cheerful cafe-style restaurant opposite the town hall with plenty of healthy options including home baking, warm salads, fresh pasta and fish of the day. €

Lacken House, Dublin Road. Tel: 056-776 1085. Dedicated owner-chef serves freshly prepared food using seasonal local ingredients in elegant Georgian cellar restaurant. €€

Ristorante Rinuccini, 1 The Parade. Tel: 056-776 1575. The basement of a Georgian town house opposite Kilkenny Castle is an Irish-Italian venture, the chef being Italian. Classic veal, seafood and pasta dishes are given an Irish accent. €

The Drink of Choice

The most famous Irish drink is Guinness, that dark stout first produced by the 34-year-old Arthur Guinness in 1759. Ask for "a pint" in a Dublin pub and Guinness is what you'll get, black to within an inch and a half of the rim, creamy topped and served with ceremony.

Now owned by the London-based conglomerate Diageo, Guinness is brewed in 50 countries and sold in another 100. But nowhere does it taste better than in Ireland where it is stored in carefully controlled conditions. The slogan "Guinness is good for you" was killed by advertising regulators, but the toast is still *"Slainte!"* ("Health").

Kilmore Quay, Co. Wexford
The Silver Fox, Kilmore Quay. Tel: 053-29888. Unpretentious seafood restaurant with a reputation for the freshness of its locally-landed catch which may include crab, oysters and prawns. Non-fish eaters also catered for. €

New Ross, Co. Wexford
Galley Cruising Restaurant, New Ross. Tel: 051-421 723. Dine while cruising on the scenic River Barrow. Emphasis on seafood and fresh local produce. €€

Waterford City
Dwyer's, 8 Mary Street. Tel: 051-877 478. Talented owner-chef offers imaginative dishes in a cosily converted police barracks in the town centre. €€
The Wine Vault, High Street. Tel: 051-853 444. www.waterfordwinevault.com. Informal, bistro-style cooking in old townhouse noted for its wine list. Seafood, steak and chicken, game in season. Basement wine shop. €€
Waterford Castle, The Island, Ballinakill. Tel: 051-878 203. www.waterfordcastle.com. Luxury hotel restaurant in restored Fitzgerald castle, reached by winch ferry across estuary of River Suir. Oak -panelled dining room hung with oil paintings and suitably impressive haute cuisine. €€€

Wexford Town
La Riva, 2 Henrietta Street, Crescent Quay. Tel: 053-24330. Fresh organic local produce, cooked in a modern, Mediterranean-influenced style has made this pleasant, town centre restaurant a popular spot. Choose between views of the harbour, or of the busy, open-plan kitchen.
Oak Tavern, Enniscorthy Road. Tel: 053-20922. About 1 mile (1.6 km) outside town on the road to Enniscorthy, this tradi-tional pub-restaurant on the banks of the River Slaney serves freshly prepared food, including local steaks, salmon and seafood. €

Southwest Region

Ballydehob, Co. Cork
Annie's, near Skibbereen, Co. Cork. Tel: 028-37292. Now a West Cork institution, this tiny restaurant in popular mountain village uses the bar across the road as a reception area. Fresh local ingredients simply but tastily prepared, and served with hearty home-made brown bread and unusually tempting desserts. €€€

Baltimore, Co. Cork
Rolf's Café Art. Tel: 028-20289. www.rolfsholidays.com. A converted farmyard just outside the village is home to this rustic, family-run restaurant as well as self-catering and hostel accommodation. The ambience is friendly, informal, and mildly alternative/artistic. The views of the bay are great, and the café is good value. €–€€

Cork City
Café Paradiso, Lancaster Quay, Western Road. Tel: 021-427 7939. A lively vegetarian restaurant, with a great buzz, where owner-chef Dennis Cotter serves imaginative seasonal combinations on giant platters to his devoted clientele – many of whom are carnivores the rest of the time. €€€
Crawford Gallery Café, Emmet Place. Tel: 021-427 4415. www.crawfordartgallery.com. Convivial dining on Ballymaloe-style food (see below) in atmospheric art gallery setting. €€
Isaac's, 48 MacCurtain Street. Tel: 021-4503805. Young owner-chef has created Cork's most buzzing eating place in a high-ceilinged old warehouse. Eclectic menu combining Far Eastern and Mediterranean influences. €
Ivory Tower, Exchange Buildings, Princes Street. Tel: 021-427 4665. Home base of Seamus O'Connell, TV cook (Soul Food), culinary polymath and one of Ireland's most creative chefs. The first-floor, city centre room is plain, enlivened only by some original art, but the highly imaginative cuisine (carpaccio of wood pigeon, hot smoked sea trout, Roquefort soufflé in a globe artichoke) more than compensates. €€€
Jacob's on the Mall, South Mall. Tel: 021-425 1530. This relaxing city centre restaurant is one of the best in town. Imaginative cooking in a light, contemporary style is served with impeccable attention to detail in a room converted from a Victorian Turkish baths. €€€

Bantry, Co. Cork
O'Connor's Seafood Restaurant, Wolfe Tone Square. Tel: 027-50221. Simple restaurant with fishing nets and floats hung in the window which serves the local product, Bantry Bay mussels, in various guises. Also does leaping fresh "fish and chips". €

Castletownbere, Co. Cork (Beara Peninsula)
McCarthy's Bar, The Square, Castletownbere. Tel: 027-70014. If you've read Pete McCarthy's book, *McCarthy's Bar*, you'll want to visit this traditional pub, supplier of groceries to the local trawler fleet, and sample its famous hospitality. Even if you haven't read the book, you'll enjoy the friendly atmosphere. Simple soup-and-sandwich-style bar food is served up to 6pm, and they will recommend a local restaurant to suit your taste. €

Castletownshend, Co. Cork (nr Skibbereen)
Mary Ann's Bar and Restaurant, Main Street. Tel: 028-36146. A

small, low-ceilinged pub, at the bottom of the hill in this tiny fishing village, this is one of Ireland's oldest bars and one of its most famous. These days it is known for its superb bar food, served in its large garden as well as its restaurant. It specialises in local seafood including crab, langoustines and locally-smoked wild salmon. Bar food €, restaurant €€€

Dingle, Co. Kerry

Beginish Restaurant, Green Street. Tel: 066-915 1588. www.beginish-restaurant.com. Small, elegant town house with talented owner-chef in the kitchen. Outstanding seafood dishes featuring freshly-landed fish and lobster, lightly sauced, plus a choice of meat and fowl. €€€
Doyle's Seafood Bar, 5 John Street. Tel: 066-915 1174. Bright red exterior, cosy kitchen restaurant within. Speciality lobster, chosen live from tank in the bar. Menu chosen daily from catches landed by the Dingle fishermen and simply prepared. €€€

Kenmare, Co. Kerry

An Leath Phingin Restaurant, 35 Main Street. Tel: 064-41559. Chic, minimalist-designed modern restaurant

serving North Italian cuisine including excellent home-made pasta and crispy pizzas using unusual combinations of fresh local produce. €
Park Hotel, Kenmare. Tel: 064-41200. First-class modern Irish cuisine in spacious dining room overlooking the rolling lawns of one of Ireland's premier country house hotels. €€€
La Cascade, Sheen Falls Lodge.Tel: 064-41600. Classic French cuisine in airy modern restaurant overlooking natural waterfalls. €€€
Lime Tree, Shelbourne Street. Tel: 064-41225. An old schoolhouse near the Park Hotel is now a busy restaurant with an imaginative, up-to-the-minute menu. €€
Packie's, Henry Street. Tel: 064-41508. Ingenious bistro-style menu based on traditional Irish cooking combined with continental influences. Small town centre venue with open fire and local artists' work on display. €€

Killarney, Co. Kerry

Gaby's Seafood Restaurant, 27 High Street. Tel: 064-32519. Gert and Marie Maes run one of Ireland's oldest seafood restaurants, a popular landmark in the town centre. The atmosphere is informal with red

checked table cloths, and the seafood is the freshest. €€
Foley's, 23 High Street. Tel: 064-31217. Busy restaurant behind a quiet bar. Plush art nouveau-style decor and pleasantly old-fashioned menu featuring classic French seafood and local steaks, lamb and duckling. €€€
Old Presbytery, Cathedral Place. Tel: 064-30555. Across the road from Killarney's cathedral and once the home of its clergy, this is a spacious, candle-lit restaurant, with a friendly, unfussy atmosphere. Fresh local produce is prepared with style and imagination by owner-chef Simon Regan. €€

Kinsale, Co. Cork

Blue Haven, Pearse Street. Tel: 021-477 2209. Renowned seafood restaurant in quiet, elegant room overlooking a tiny garden and fountain. Busy bar food trade until 9pm. €€€
Casino House, Coolmain Bay, Kilbrittain. Tel: 023-49944. Not a casino, but an attractively converted farmhouse on the R600 midway between Kinsale and Timoleague. Light, tasty menu in relaxing surroundings freshly prepared by German-Yugoslav owner-chef Michael Relja and served by his wife Kerrin. €€
Crackpots, 3 Cork Street. Tel: 021-477 2847. Open fires and a lively atmosphere are complemented by a pleasantly eclectic menu. Owner Carol Norman also makes and sells ceramics, hence the name. €
Jim Edwards, Market Quay. Tel: 021-477 2541. Busy town centre pub restaurant renowned for generous portions of steak and seafood. Bar food (€) also available. €€€
Man Friday, Scilly. Tel: 021-477 2260. Popular. Short walk uphill from town centre serving popular food – steaks, sole on the bone, prawn cocktail – well cooked, generous portions. €€€

A Who's Who of Irish Whiskies

The comparative affluence and sophisticated tastes of recent years have stimulated the demand for Ireland's more traditional whiskies as well as Scotland's rarer malts. There are 15 or so different whiskies on sale in Ireland. John Power's Gold Label is by far the most popular. Next come Jameson, Bushmills, Coleraine (which sells in Northern Ireland), Paddy, Hewitt's and Dunphy's. Murphy's sells mainly in the United States, and Tullamore Dew, a particularly light brand, does well in Europe.

Two popular premium brands are Black Bush (from Bushmills in County Antrim, the world's oldest distillery) and Crested Ten, matured for 10 years in the Jameson stable. At the top of the range are liqueur whiskies, among the most exceptional drinks on earth. Bushmills Malt is a single 10-year-old; Jameson 1780 is aged for 12 years; and Redbreast, also 12 years old, is matured in wood by the house of Gilbey, renowned for its wines, ports and sherries. To put ice in these last three whiskies is an act of sacrilege to an Irishman.

The Vintage, Main Street. Tel: 021-477 2502. One of the original "front parlour restaurants" now under Swiss management with a rather hushed ambience and a seriously luxurious five course set menu featuring local seafood and game in season. €€€

Mallow, Co. Cork
President's Restaurant, Longueville House, near Mallow. Tel: 022-47156. Impressive 1720 Georgian mansion overlooking the Blackwater River with restaurant in large Victorian conservatory. Food mainly from farm, garden and river. Wine from Ireland's only vineyard. €€€

Midleton, Co. Cork
Ballymaloe House, Shanagarry. Tel: 021-465 2531. The farming Allen family pioneered the use of fresh local produce including herbs and vegetables from their own garden, local meat, and fish from nearby Ballycotton, and continue to serve delicious, simply prepared food in restful country house surroundings. Trade secrets are passed on at the neighbouring Ballymaloe Cookery School (Kinoith House, Shanagarry, tel: 021-464 6785). €€€

Tralee, Co. Kerry
Restaurant David Norris, Ivy Terrace. Tel: 066-718 5654. Tralee has plenty of hotels and pubs but very few restaurants, so chef David Norris's establishment has a loyal clientele. It is on the first floor of a modern building near the town park, and is furnished in an uncluttered art deco style. The menu is based on seasonal produce and everything is made on the premises inlcuding bread, pasta and ice cream. €€

Youghal, Co. Cork
Aherne's Seafood Bar and Restaurant, 163 North Main

Price Categories

€ = up to €20 per head
€€ = €20–€25 per head
€€€ = over €25 per head

Street. Tel: 024-92424. Long-established family-run bar and restaurant serving delicious fish dishes. Use the bar for a quick meal from the all-day menu (€), such as their famous seafood pie, or linger in the more formal restaurant over classically prepared seafood. €€€

Mid West Region

Adare, Co Limerick
The Wild Geese, Rose Cottage, Adare. Tel: 061-396 451. Quaint thatched cottage in village centre previously known as the Mustard Seed (see Ballingarry) uses fresh local produce in classical French cuisine. €€€

Ballingarry, Co Limerick
The Mustard Seed at Echo Lodge, Ballingarry. Tel: 069-68508. Two elegant dining rooms in a flamboyantly decorated country house 8 miles (13 km) west of Adare are presided over by owner Dan Mullane whose attention to detail is legendary. Traditional Irish food of the area. Have their own sherry. €€€

Ballyvaughan, Co. Clare (The Burren)
Monk's Pub, Quayside. Tel: 065-707 7059. This traditional pub on the water's edge serves hearty plates of bar food, including seafood chowder, mussels in white wine, and Irish (lamb) stew. Warm yourself by the open fire, and if you're lucky there might be a live music session underway. €
Gregan's Castle Hotel, Corkscrew Hill. Tel: 065-707 7005. On the N67, midway between Ballyvaughan and

Lisdoonvarna, the restaurant of this luxurious country house hotel is a relatively formal (jacket and tie), special-occasion place. Modern French cuisine is served amid Georgian antiques in a spacious dining room with vibrant red walls. €€€
Trí na Chéile Restaurant, Main Street. Tel: 065-707 7103. A small shop in the centre of the village connects to an attractive extension, furnished with rush-seated chairs and oil-cloth covered tables, to make a pleasant, café-style restaurant. Service is cheerful and efficient, and the food is good value, ranging from pasta dishes to steaks, warm salads and traditional Irish fare, including Irish bacon (ham) and cabbage, and salmon and potato gratin. €

Doolin, Co. Clare
Cullinan's Seafood Restaurant, Tel: 065-7074 1183. www. cullinansdoolin.com. A simple, cottage restaurant attached to a small guesthouse a short walk from the village centre, Cullinan's serves an interesting menu prepared by the owner-chef from fresh local produce. Burren smoked salmon, Doolin crabmeat, Aran Island scallops, locally-raised lamb and beef, and Irish farmhouse cheeses are prepared in a Mediterranean-influenced contemporary style. €€
O'Connor's Pub. Tel: 065-682 1547. Famed for traditional music sessions after 9pm, by day O'Connor's serves hearty home-cooked bar food including wild Doolin salmon and a great Irish stew. €

Kinvara, Co. Galway
Moran's of the Weir, Kilcolgan, Clarinbridge. Tel: 091-796 113. A plate of fresh oysters beside the weir outside this picturesque thatched cottage is a quintessential West of Ireland experience. Crab, prawns, smoked salmon and mussels. €€

Lahinch

Barrtra Seafood Restaurant, Liscannor Road. Tel: 065-708 1280. The traditional white-washed cottage on the cliffs outside Lahinch is a popular destination for good value seafood – and has the bonus of wonderful views. Local seafood, including lobster when available, is prepared in a light, unfussy style – the freshest of Atlantic fish is served with the lightest of sauces, or can be prepared as sushi. All bread is home-made, and vegetarian options are also available. €€

Limerick City

Brûlées, 8 Lower Mallow Street. Tel: 061-319 931. A redbrick Georgian town house in the city centre has dining areas on several levels, furnished in simple, classical style. The intimate ambience is enhanced by an imaginative menu in which fresh local produce and imported Mediterranean ingredients are prepared with imagination and attractively presented. €€€
Green Onion Café, Rutland Street. Tel: 061-400710. There's always a good buzz at this dimly-lit town centre restaurant (opposite the Hunt Museum) where the ground floor is overlooked by the mezzanine area. Salads, pasta dishes, tacos and steaks are served from noon to late against a background of muted jazz, while the locals table-hop and network. €€

Lisdoonvarna, Co. Clare

Sheedy's Hotel and Restaurant, Sheedy's Spa View. Tel: 065-707 4026. Chef John Sheedy trained at Ashford Castle and serves a surprisingly elaborate, robustly flavoured menu of contemporary Irish cooking in the refurbished dining room of this family-run hotel. Daily specials feature local seafood. €€

Midlands Region

Abbeyleix, Co. Laois

Preston House Café, Main Street. Tel: 0502-31432. Attractive creeper-clad Victorian town house on the main Cork-Dublin road, the restaurant has a country-style pine decor. Wholesome and appetising home-cooking including home-baked bread. €€

Athlone, Co. Westmeath

Wineport Restaurant, Glasson. Tel: 090-648 5466. Informal waterside restaurant in wooden chalet beautifully situated on Lough Ree just outside town. Good choice for vegetarians. Game tasting menu in season. €€
Restaurant Le Chateau, St Peter's Port, the Docks. Tel: 090-649 4517. First floor restaurant run by a husband-and-wife team in a renovated old church on banks of the river Shannon. Le Chateau has a good reputation for imaginative cooking of fresh local produce. €€

Birr, Co. Offaly

Emmet Room Restaurant, Dooly's Hotel, Emmet Square. Tel: 0509-20032. Above-average hotel restaurant in nicely preserved Georgian coaching inn. €€
The Thatch, Crinkle, Co. Offaly. Tel: 0509-20682. Restaurant in thatched pub just outside Birr, offering five-course dinner menu with hearty local produce and lighter à la carte choices. €€

Longford, Co. Longford

The Vintage, Moydow, near Longford town. Tel: 043-22122. Bar restaurant where owner-chef serves freshly prepared local

Price Categories

€ = less than €20 per head
€€ = €20–€25 per head
€€€ = over €25 per head

produce for Sunday lunch and dinner. Interesting use of herbs and vegetables. €€

Mullingar, Co. Westmeath

Crookedwood House, Mullingar. Tel: 044-72165. www.crookedwood house.com. Large country house well off the beaten track 8 miles (13 km) north of Mullingar with outstanding family-run cellar restaurant. Game a specialty in winter. Rooms available. €€€

Far West Region

Clifden, Co. Galway

Erriseask House, Ballyconeely. Tel: 095-23553. Swiss-run waterside hotel and restaurant 7 miles (11 km) south of Clifden where owner-chef has gained a fine reputation for well-judged, imaginative cooking. €€€

Galway

Kirwan's Lane Creative Cuisine, Kirwan's Lane, off Quay Street. Tel: 091-568 266. Trendy bistro cuisine with an Irish accent in a sharply designed modern restaurant that will make urban sophisticates feel at home. €€
McDonagh's Seafood House. 22 Quay Street. Tel: 091-565 001. www.mcdonaghs.net. For many years a wet fish shop with a few tables serving cooked seafood, McDonagh's is now a classic seafood restaurant, and the best place to try Galway oysters. Also renowned for their seafood platter of hot lobster, scallops, crab claws and prawns. €€€ (Adjacent fish and chip bar serves a wide choice of battered fish. €)
The Malt House, Olde Malte Arcade, High Street. Tel: 091-567 866. www.malt-house.com. Chintzy pub restaurant with white rough cast walls tucked away in an alley in the town centre. A place for old reliables like duckling à l'orange, steak

or fresh prawns pan fried in garlic butter. €€

Moycullen, Co. Galway
Drimcong House Restaurant, Moycullen. Tel: 091-555 115. Gerry and Marie Galvin's stylish country house restaurant 12 miles (19 km) from town on the N59 will be a high point of any gastronomic tour of Ireland. Gerry is an inventive chef with a light touch and the gift of making it all look – and taste – incredibly simple. Marie tends front of house and grows the many herbs and fresh vegetables that help to make Drimcong so different. Book well in advance. €€€
White Gables Restaurant, Moycullen. Tel: 091-555 744. www.whitegables.com. Cottage restaurant on main road but well insulated from traffic by thick stone walls. Owner-chef Kevin Dunne serves light, tasty menus with fresh local produce. Home-made bread and imaginative vegetables. €€

Spiddal, Co. Galway
Boluisce Seafood Bar, Spiddal. Tel: 091 553 286. Bar food and first floor restaurant in lively pub in the centre of Irish-speaking village in Connemara. Cheerful service and generous portions. Steaks, stir fries and local seafood. €–€€

Westport, Co. Mayo
Asgard Tavern and Restaurant, The Quay. Tel: 098-25319. Quayside bar with nautical decor offering simple bar food downstairs and a more formal and wide-ranging menu upstairs with emphasis on fresh ingredients and good value. €–€€
Quay Cottage, The Harbour. Tel: 098-26412. Small, always busy waterside cottage with scrubbed pine tables and a maritime theme. Lashings of excellent seafood plus vegetarian options and plenty of meat choices. €€

The Northwest

Ballybofey, Co. Donegal
The Looking Glass, Kee's Hotel, Ballybofey. Tel: 074-913 1018. Seasonal menus have local game and seafood. €€

Bruckless, Co. Donegal
Castlemurray House, St John's Point, Dunkineely. Tel: 074-973 7022. French provincial. Recommended. €€€

Bundoran, Co. Donegal
Le Chateaubrianne, Sligo Road. Tel: 071-984 2160. Traditional fare, good local produce. €€

Lough Eske, Co. Donegal
Ardnamona House, Lough Eske. Tel: 074-972 2650. Reliable general menu. €€€

Moville, Co. Donegal
McNamaras, Foyle Street. Tel: 077-82010. Old-world style, fresh fish a speciality.

Rossnowlagh, Co. Donegal
Smugglers Creek, Rossnowlagh. Tel: 071-985 2366. In 1845 building overlooking Donegal Bay. Specialises in fresh seafood. €€

The Northeast

Most of these entries are in Northern Ireland, where prices are in sterling. The symbols provide a rough price guide, based on the average cost of a three-course evening meal including a 10 percent service charge and VAT, but not wine.

Annalong, Co. Down
Halfway House, 138 Glassdrumman Road. Tel: 028-4376 8224. Scampi, plaice. £

Armagh City, Co. Armagh
Charlemont Arms, 63 English Street. Tel: 028-3752 2028. Country cooking. £

Ballygalley, Co. Antrim
Ballygalley Castle. 274 Coast Road. Tel: 028-2858 1066. Hotel-style general menu. ££

Price Categories
£ = up to £12 per head
££ = £12–£16 per head
£££ = over £16 per head

Ballymena, Co. Antrim
Galgorm Manor, 136 Fenaghy Road. Tel: 028-2588 1001. Oysters and halibut. ££
Leighinmohr Hotel, Leighinmohr Avenue. Tel: 028-2565 2313. Country cooking. ££

Bangor, Co. Down
Jenny Watts, 41 High Street. Tel: 028-9146 0682. Good bistro atmosphere. ££
Shanks, Blackwood Golf Club, Crawfordsburn Road. Tel: 028-9185 3313. Excellent. Recommended. £££

Bellanaleck, Co. Fermanagh
The Sheelin. Tel: 028-6634 8232. Thatched. Buffet £, gourmet evenings. £££

What "Country Cooking" Means

Traditionally Northern Ireland, even more than the Republic, wielded the frying pan with vigour. The "Ulster fry" – consisting of beef or pork, sausages and bacon, often with fried potato cakes thrown in – was a recipe for an early heart attack. The approach these days is healthier, but outside Belfast and a number of chef-driven restaurants around the province, the emphasis is still on plain cooking. The term "country cooking" in these listings implies that you can expect standard meat, chicken and fish dishes, reliably cooked.
● For a fuller discussion, see "A Fresh Approach to Food", page 125.

Bushmills, Co. Antrim
Bushmills Inn, 9 Dunluce Road.
Tel: 028-2073 2339. Good local
flavour. ££

Carnlough, Co. Antrim
Londonderry Arms. 20 Harbour
Road. Tel: 028-2888 5255.
Charming surroundings on
Antrim Coast Road. £

Carrickfergus, Co. Antrim
Dobbins Inn, 6 High Street. Tel:
028-9335 1905. Country cooking. £

Coleraine, Co. Londonderry
Salmon Leap, 53 Castleroe
Road. Tel: 028-7034 2992.
Game, smoked fish. ££

Cookstown, Co. Tyrone
Otter Lodge, 26 Dungannon
Road. Tel: 028-8676 5427.
Carvery, à la carte,
Recommended. ££

Crawfordsburn, Co. Down
Old Inn, 15 Main Street. Tel:
028-9185 3255. Thatched inn
with 18th-century minstrels'
gallery. ££

Cultra, Co. Down
Culloden Hotel. 142 Bangor
Road, Hollywood. Tel: 028-9042
1066. Reliable cooking in the
grand hotel style. £££
Cultra Inn. 142 Bangor Road,
Hollywood (part of the Culloden
Hotel). Tel: 028-9042 5840.
Country cooking. £

Derry City, Co. Derry
Badger's, 16 Orchard Street.
Tel: 028-7136 0736. Standard
pub grub. £
Beech Hill House, 32 Ardmore
Road, Ardmore. Tel: 028-7134
9279. £££
Brown's, 1 Bond's Hill. Tel:
028-7134 5180. Modern
European cuisine, Kilkeel fish.
£££
Everglades, Prehen Road. Tel:
028-7132 1066. Set meals, à
la carte. ££
White Horse Hotel, 68 Clooney

Road. Tel: 028-7186 0606.
Carvery, salmon, steaks. £££

Donaghadee, Co. Down
Grace Neill's, 33 High Street.
Tel: 028-9188 4595.
www.graceneills.co-uk. Claims
Daniel Defoe and Franz Liszt as
previous customers. ££

Downpatrick, Co. Down
Hogan's Bar & Restaurant, 78
Market Street. Tel: 028-4461
2017. Old-fashioned bar. ££
Justine's, English Street. Tel:
028-4461 7886. Ireland's oldest hunt club meets here. £££

Dromara, Co. Down
O'Reilly's, 7 Rathfriland Road.
Tel: 028-9753 2209. Seafood.
££

Dungannon, Co. Tyrone
Grange Lodge, 7 Grange Road.
Tel: 028-8778 4212. Home
cooking in country house. Highly
recommended. £££

Enniskillen, Co. Fermanagh
Franco's, 32 Queen Elizabeth
Road. Tel: 028-6632 4185. Fun
place for fish. ££
Scoffs, 17 Belmore Street.
Tel: 028-6634 2622. Situated
in the **Bug** pub. Excellent à la
carte dinner menu. £££

Giant's Causeway, Co. Antrim
Causeway Hotel. 40 Causeway
Road, Bushmills. Tel: 028-20-73
1226. Standard hotel menu. £

Hillsborough, Co. Down
Plough Inn, 3 The Square. Tel:
028-9268 2985. Great fish. £££

Holywood, Co. Down
Sullivan's, Sullivan Place. Tel:
028-9042 1000. Bistro seafood.
Restaurant at night. ££

Killinchy, Co. Down
Balloo House, 1 Cumber
Road. Tel: 028-9754 1210.
Fresh fish and game.
Recommended.
Daft Eddy's, Sketrick Island.
Tel: 028-9754 1615. Good food
with a view. A la carte at week-
ends. £

Killyleagh, Co. Down
Dufferin Arms, 35 High Street.
Tel: 028-4482 1182. Comfort
food in coaching inn. ££

Larne, Co. Antrim
Magheramorne House, 59
Shore Road. Tel: 028-2827
9444. Country cooking. ££

Limavady, Co. Londonderry
Radisson Roe Park Hotel, Roe
Park. Tel: 028-7775 2222.
Good-quality hotel food. £££

Maghera, Co. Londonderry
Ardtara Country House, 8
Gorteade Road, Upperlands.
Tel: 028-7964 4490. Chef
trained at Belfast's Michelin-
starred Roscoff. Elegant rooms.
Recommended. £££

Newtownabbey, Co. Antrim
Ginger Tree, 29 Ballyrobert
Road. Tel: 028-9084 8176.
Japanese. £££
McMillan's, 15 Kiln Road.
Tel: 028-9083 7144. Two
restaurants and lounge. Serves
modern international cuisine.
£/£££

Newtownards, Co. Down
Ganges, 69 Court Street. Tel:
028-9181 1426. Indian. ££
Cafe Amber. 47 Court Street.
Tel: 028-9181 5005. Wide
range of dishes. £

Portaferry, Co. Down
Portaferry Hotel, 10 The
Strand. Tel: 028-4272 8231.
Recommended. ££

Portrush, Co. Antrim
**Ramore Restaurant and Wine
Bar**, The Harbour. Tel: 028-

7082 4313. Noted for its excellent seafood. ££

Strangford, Co. Down
Lobster Pot, 11 The Square. Tel: 02844-881 288. Good fish. ££

Belfast

Alden's, 229 Upper Newtownards Road. Tel: 028-9065 0079. Famous for seafood. Good wine list. ££
Archana, 53 Dublin Road. Tel: 028-9032 3713. Belfast's authentic balti house. ££
Belfast Castle, Antrim Road. Tel: 028-9077 6925. In restored hall overlooking lough. Serves reliable traditional food. £££
Bengal Brasserie, 339 Ormeau Road. Tel: 028-9064 7516. Stylish Bangladeshi. £££
Capers, 313 Upper Newtownards Road. Tel: 028 9080 5600. Pizza specialists. £
Cayenne, 7 Ascot House, Shaftesbury Square. Tel: 028-9033 1532. Modern European cuisine. £££
Deanes, 38–40 Howard Street. Tel: 028-9033 1134. www.michaeldeane.co.uk. Its chef rated a Michelin star in his previous out-of-town restaurant and the food lives up to these standards. £££
Grill Room & Bar, 10 Donegall Square. Tel: 028-9024 1001. Handy location. Open seven days a week for breakfast, lunch and dinner. £££
Jeffers, 3 Skipper Street. Tel:

028-9023 2448. Gastropub with premium organic beers and great local produce. £££
Jharna Tandoori, 133 Lisburn Road. Tel: 028-9038 1299. Elaborately Indian. ££
Nick's Warehouse, 35 Hill Street. Tel: 028-9043 9690. www.nickswarehouse.co.uk. Trendy wine bar and restaurant near city centre. ££
Opus One 1 University Street. Tel: 028-9059 0101. Ingredients include sun-dried tomato, goat's cheese and ravioli. ££
Red Panda, 60 Great Victoria Street. Tel: 028-9080 8700. Hong Kong-style Chinese restaurant with wide-ranging menu. ££
Shu, 253 Lisburn Road. Tel: 028-9038 1655. A restaurant bar serving modern cuisine. Early evening "specials". £££
Speranza, 16 Shaftesbury Square. Tel: 028-9023 0213. Real Italian pizzeria. ££
Sun Kee, 38 Donegall Pass. Tel: 028-9031 2016. Good Chinese food. ££
Villa Italia, 39 University Road. Tel: 028-9032 8356. Italian family restaurant, no lunches, no bookings, but it's good. ££
Welcome, 22 Stranmillis Road. Tel: 028-9038 1359. Another good Cantonese place. ££

Nightlife

Dublin

Late Spots
If you're under 30 years old and believe in having a good time, the chances are you've heard of Dublin's club scene. Much has been written internationally about how the city has begun to rival fashionable European cities for exciting clubs. The reality behind the hype is improving all the time.

You don't have to dance till dawn. Those more sophisticated in years can enjoy late-night bars, cabarets, or smart nightclubs where tables positioned away from the dance floor allow for meaningful conversations.

A word about smoking: it doesn't matter where you go or how late you stay out – if you're indoors, all Irish pubs and clubs are smoke-free and smokers spend much of their time keeping bouncers from getting lonely.

Nightclubs
Club Anabel, Burlington Hotel, Upper Leeson Street, Dublin 4. Tel: 660 5222. This Leeson Street club is one of the oldest in town and remains unfailingly popular with the older, sophisticated crowd. Smart dress essential.
Gaiety Theatre, South King Street. Tel: 677 1717. At night the theatre opens its doors to the after-hours crowd. The atmosphere is relaxed and spacious as the punters are spread out over three floors – one with a DJ, one with a live act and one left with only the sound of conversation.

Pick of the Pubs in Belfast

The Crown Liquor Saloon, 46 Great Victoria Street. Stained glass, ornate decor, cosy snugs – all preserved by the National Trust.
Kelly's Cellars, 30 Bank Street. Founded in 1720. There's a stone-floored bar downstairs and a beamed restaurant upstairs.
The Front Page, 108 Donegall Street. The church-like upstairs bar is popular with journalists. Live music at night.
The Garrick, 11 Montgomery Street. Another authentic Victorian-style pub, named after the actor David Garrick.
The Morning Star, 17 Pottinger's Entry. Fine old-fashioned bar with good food, especially fish and steaks. Less crowded in the evenings.

The George, 89 South Great Georges Street, Dublin 2. Tel: 478 2983. Probably the city's most popular gay club. The George pub from which the club gets it name is a favourite meeting place among gay men. Stylish dress.

La Cave, 28 South Anne Street, Dublin 2. Tel: 679 4409. Cosy and compelling late-night venue which falls somewhere between a restaurant, wine bar, and nightclub, although there's no dance floor as such. The soothing Latino sounds and intimate atmosphere mean this is a winner with thirty-somethings wanting to kick back. Smart dress.

Lillies Bordello, Adam Court, Grafton Street, Dublin 2. Tel: 679 9204. www.lilliesbordello.ie. One of the most exclusive clubs in town, and one which prides itself on its VIP lounge where high-profile party animals rub shoulders with fellow celebrities. Non-members are not guaranteed entry, but looking like a celeb can work wonders on the bouncers. Stylish clothes essential.

Club M, Blooms Hotel, 6 Anglesea Street, Dublin 2. Tel: 671 5408. www.clubm.ie. If you don't feel like posing and just want to bop the night away. City centre disco playing classic '70s and '80s sounds. Smart dress preferred.

The POD, Harcourt Street, Dublin 2. Tel: 478 0225. www.pod.ie. Ultra-hip club where everyone who's anyone in rock music, the media, and the world of modelling congregate. The dance floor is home to the young and beautiful. You probably already know to wear hip clothes.

Ri-Ra, Exchequer Street, Dublin 2. Tel: 677 4835. www.rira.ie. Groovy club for babes with attitude and cool dudes. Funk, hip-hop, and audio-visual shows. As for clothes, the hipper the better.

Renards, 35–7 South Frederick Street, Dublin 2. Tel: 677 5876. www.renards.ie. The trendiest club in town when it was called the Pink Elephant, this new version tries hard to live up to its past reputation with particular doormen and a fashion-conscious clientele. Style is all.

Sugar Club, 8 Lower Leeson Street, Dublin 2. Tel: 678 7188. www.thesugarclub.com. Live bands most nights are followed by DJ dancing. The bar has one of the city's most extensive cocktail menus *(see also page 362)*.

Late Bars

Late-night bars are a new phenomenon in Dublin thanks to revised – though still not exactly liberal – licensing laws. The following pubs are open on various nights, mainly weekends, until the crazy hour of 1.30am.

Bleeding Horse, 24 Upper Camden Street, Dublin 2. Tel: 475 2705.

Fitzsimmons, East Essex Street, Dublin 2. Tel: 677 0014.

Foggy Dew, 1 Upper Fowne's Street, Dublin 2. Tel: 677 9328.

The Globe, Georges Street, Dublin 2. Tel: 671 1220.

Hogans, 35 Great South Georges Street, Dublin 2. Tel: 677 5904.

Market Bar, Fade Street, Dublin 2. Tel: 613 9094.

Mercantile Bar, Dame Street, Dublin 2. Tel: 670 7100.

Sinnotts, South King Street, Dublin 2. Tel: 478 4698.

Turks Head Chop House, 27–30 Parliament Street, Temple Bar, Dublin 2. Tel: 417 9900.

Whelans, 25 Wexford Street, Dublin 2. Tel: 478 0766.

Cabaret

Doyles Cabaret, Burlington Hotel, Upper Leeson Street, Dublin 4. Tel: 660 5222. Cabaret inspired by the postcard image of Ireland; lots of pretty *cailíns* doing Irish jigs and handsome men singing Celtic songs. A show with a certain charm for the mature and sentimental. Dinner can be included if you wish. Summer season, Monday to Saturday.

Fonntraí: *Cultúrlann na hÉireann*, Belgrave Square, Monkstown, Co. Dublin. Tel: 280 0295. Show with a strong Irish flavour. Musician, singers, storytellers and dancers entertain in the comfortable folk theatre. Runs during the summer months Monday to Thursday. Also a *ceilidh* on Friday nights and an informal session on Saturdays.

Jurys Cabaret, Jurys Hotel, Ballsbridge, Dublin 4. Tel: 660 5000. This cabaret has a strong accent on traditional Irish culture with dancers, singers and comedians. Likely to offer a good performance of *Danny Boy* before the night is over. Dinner included. Summer season, Tuesday to Sunday.

The Sugar Club, 8 Lower Leeson Street, Dublin 2. Tel: 678 7188. www.thesugarclub.com. A new multimedia theatre geared towards the over-25s with a vast range of entertainment from classic and cult cinema screening to international live music, comedy, live theatre, cabaret, burlesque, etc. Check the programme before you go. Open 7 nights a week with a bar licensed until 2.30am.

Comedy

Exchequer Bar, Exchequer Street, Dublin 2. Every Tuesday night the Exchequer becomes the home of Dublin's only free stand-up night. You get what you pay for.

International Bar, Wicklow Street, Dublin 2. Tel: 677 9250. Home to various comedy acts upstairs.

City Arts Centre, 23 Moss Street, Dublin 2. Tel: 677 0643. The occasional comedy slots at this multi-purpose arts venue allow emerging comics to cut their teeth while established comedians warm up for the Edinburgh Festival.

Belfast

Clubs

Fashions change, but constants on the club beat include:

The Elephant Room (Europa Hotel), 25 Glengall Street. Tel: 028-9026 6060. Easy listening, brassy.

Kube, 2 Dunbar Street. Tel: 028-9023 4520. Gay.

La Lea, 43 Franklin Street. Tel: 028- 9023 0200. www.lalea.com. Belfast's most prestigious club. Open Wed–Sat from 9pm.

M-Club, Bradbury Place. Tel: 028-9023 3131. www.mclub.co.uk. Commercial dance, a provincial obsession with B-list celebrities.

Mezza(nine), 38–42 Great Victoria Street. Tel: 028-9024 7447. two levels, two DJs and the hottest live bands. Dance and chart music.

Storm (a.k.a. Bob's), Lisburn Road. Tel: 028-9033 2526. Chart music, no sports wear.

Thompson's Garage, Patterson's Place. Tel: 028 9032 3762. House and garage music with a glam or scam dress code.

Jazz

Belfast Boat Club, Lockview Road. Jazz every couple of months. Tel: 028-9066 5012.

Cutter's Wharf, Lockview Road. Tel: 028-9066 3388. Sunday jazz brunch.

Auntie Annie's, 44 Dublin Road. Tel: 028-9050 1660. Ireland's biggest promoter of bands also showcases jazz and blues artists. Live music four nights a week.

Traditional Music

The John Hewitt, 51 Donegall Street. Tel: 028-9023 3768. Sessions on Tues & Wed.

Kitchen Bar, 16 Victoria Square. Tel: 028-9032 4901. Also authentic.

Kelly's Cellars, 30 Bank Street. Tel: 028-9032 4835. Wed, Fri, Sat and Sun. Less purist.

McHugh's. 29–31 Queen Street. Tel: 028-9050 9990. Music Tues–Sat.

Culture

Theatres

DUBLIN

Abbey Theatre, Lower Abbey Street, Dublin. Tel: 878 7222. Ireland's national theatre. Founded in the early years of the century by Yeats, Lady Gregory and their collaborators, it quickly won a world reputation with some outstanding plays and a unique style of acting. Many Irish classics feature in its programme. The Abbey's sister theatre, the **Peacock**, is used to try out new, experimental work.

Andrews Lane Theatre, 9–13 Andrews Lane, Dublin 2. Tel: 679 5720. Opened in September 1989 in a converted warehouse and is a popular smaller venue.

Gaiety Theatre, South King Street. Tel: 677 1717. A fine Victorian building, recently restored. The programme includes opera, ballet, pantomime, variety concerts and serious drama.

Gate Theatre, 1 Cavendish Row, Parnell Square. Tel: 874 4045. Founded by the actor Micheál MacLiammoir. The programme includes opera, ballet, pantomime, variety concerts and serious drama.

Lambert Puppet Theatre, Clifton Lane, Monkstown, Co. Dublin. Tel: 280 0974. www.lambertpuppet theatre.com. Where the country's only permanent professional puppet theatre company performs.

New Theatre, 43 East Essex Street, Temple Bar, Dublin 2. Tel: 670 3381. www.newtheatre.com. The New Theatre provides a stage for new works and classics – especially those which deal with modern Irish society's social issues.

Olympia Theatre, 72 Dame Street. Tel: 679 3323. Similar shows to the Gaiety. Once a Victorian music hall.

Samuel Beckett Theatre, Trinity College. Tel: 608 2461. Based in the university that produced such dramatists as Goldsmith, Synge and Beckett, and run in association with the university's Samuel Beckett Centre.

OTHER THEATRES

Belfast: Grand Opera House, Great Victoria Street. Tel: 028-9024 1919. www.goh.co.uk. Lyric Theatre, Ridgeway Street. Tel: 028-90381 081. www.lyrictheatre.co.uk.

Cork: Opera House, Emmet Place, tel: 021-427 0022; www.corkoperahouse.ie. Everyman Palace, 15 MacCurtain Street, tel: 021-450 1673; www.everyman palace.com. Both mix touring productions, popular entertainment and local productions.

Derry: Riverside Theatre, University of Ulster, Coleraine, Co. Derry. Tel: 028 7032 3232. New auditorium.

Fermanagh: Ardhowen Theatre, Dublin Road, Enniskillen, Co. Fermanagh. Tel: 028-6632 5440. www.ardhowentheatre.com.

Galway: Druid Theatre Company, Druid Lane Theatre, Chapel Lane, off Quay Street. Tel: 091-568 660. www.druidtheatre.com. One of Ireland's most successful repertory theatre companies presenting a mix of new work and revivals. Galway's other professional companies, Punchbag and Macnas, share the new Town Hall Theatre with the Druid.

Limerick: Belltable Arts Centre, 69 O'Connell Street. Tel: 061-319 866. www.belltable.ie. Small auditorium.

Sligo: Hawk's Well Theatre,

Temple Street. Tel: 071-916 1526/1518. www.hawkswell.com. Modern theatre hosting touring and local shows.

Tralee: Siamsa Tíre: National Folk Theatre of Ireland. Tel: 066-712 3055. www.siamsatire.com. Evokes Irish rural tradition in song, dance and mime.

Music

Ireland has some of the most vital traditional music in the world. You can hear it in pubs almost everywhere in the country, but visitors who want to be sure of hearing some good stuff are best advised to attend an organised session, such as one of those presented in summer on Wednesdays and Thursdays at Culturlann na hEireann, the headquarters of Comhaltas Ceoltoiri Eireann (the traditional music association). The address is Belgrave Square, Monkstown, Co. Dublin, tel: 280 0295. Buses No. 7 and 8 from Dublin city centre stop nearby and the Monkstown and Seapoint DART station is only a short walk away.

The biggest change in Irish popular music over the past few years, particularly among the younger people, is how "club" music has become the new and dominant means of musical expression. In European terms, Dublin is seen as a "clubbing capital" and venues like pod (Place of Dance) and The Sugar Club are two of the best places in the city in which to experience the modern musical sound of youthful Ireland. Local DJs are bringing out their own records on their own labels and dabbling in the contemporary genres of music known as Garage, Drum 'n' Bass and Trance.

Dublin's leading folk music club is at Slattery's of Chapel Street. Details of sessions there and at other venues appear in *In Dublin* magazine.

In Dublin (www.indublin.ie)

also carries details of jazz, rock and classical music events. The top venue for the latter is the National Concert Hall in Earlsfort Terrace, off St Stephen's Green, Dublin.

Art Galleries

DUBLIN AREA

Anyone interested in the visual arts should visit the **National Gallery**, the **Hugh Lane Municipal Gallery**, the **Irish Museum of Modern Art** and the **Chester Beatty Library**. There are also many smaller exhibition centres and commercial galleries which often contain interesting work.

Bank of Ireland Arts Centre, Foster Place. Tel: 671 1488. Tues–Fri, 10am–4pm. Puts on both modern Irish and international exhibitions.

Chester Beatty Library. Tel: 407 0750. www.cbl.ie. Oct–Apr, Tues–Fri 10am–5pm; May–Sept, Mon–Fri 10am–5pm; Sat, 11am–5pm; Sun 1–5pm. This superb collection of oriental art and manuscripts is housed in the Clocktower Building at Dublin Castle.

Combridge Fine Arts, 17 South William St. Tel: 677 4652. www.cfa.ie. Mon–Sat 9.30am–5.30pm. Conventional landscapes in oil and watercolour.

Douglas Hyde Gallery, Trinity College. Tel: 608 1116. www.douglashydegallery.com. Mon–Fri 11am–6pm (7pm on Thur), Sat 11am–4.45pm. Contemporary Irish and international painting, sculpture and photography.

Gallery of Photography, Meeting House Square, Dublin 2. Tel: 671 4654. www.irish-photography.com. Tues–Sat 11am–6pm, Sun 1–6pm. Irish and international exhibitions; postcards, prints and posters.

Green on Red Gallery, 26 Lombard Street East, Dublin 2. Tel: 671 3414. www.greenonred gallery.com. Mon–Fri 10am–6pm,

Sat 11am–5pm. Cutting-edge contemporary art.

5th@Guinness Storehouse, St James' Gate. Tel: 408 4800. www.5th.ie. Paintings and installations, at regular intervals, mainly spring and autumn.

Hugh Lane Municipal Gallery of Modern Art, Parnell Square, tel: 874 1903. www.hughlane.ie. Tues–Thur 9.30am–6pm, Fri–Sat 9.30–5pm, Sun 11am–5pm.

Irish Museum of Modern Art, Royal Hospital, Kilmainham. Tel: 612 9900. www.modernart.ie. Tues–Sat 10am–5.30pm, Sun noon–5.30pm. Irish and international art of the 20th century.

Kerlin Gallery, Ann's Lane, South Ann Street, Dublin 2. Tel: 670 9093. www.kerlin.ie. Mon–Fri 10am–5.45pm, Sat 11am–4.30pm. Contemporary European, Irish artists.

Malahide Castle, Malahide, Co. Dublin. Tel: 846 2516. Mon–Sat 10am–5pm, Sun and bank holidays 11am–6pm, closed for lunch (Apr–Oct); weekends and bank holidays 2–5pm (Nov–Mar). Houses a selection from the National Portrait Gallery.

National Gallery of Ireland, Merrion Square West. Tel: 661 5133. www.nationalgallery.ie. Mon–Sat 9.30am–5.30pm (8.30pm on Thur), Sun noon–5.30pm. Old masters, Irish and international art from the 16th to the 19th centuries. New permanent Yeats exhibition, mainly dedicated to the work of Jack B Yeats.

Oriel Gallery, 17 Clare Street. Tel: 676 3410. Mon–Fri 10am–5.30pm, Sat 10am–1pm. Has 19th- and 20th-century Irish paintings, mostly landscapes. Established names such as Paul Henry, Jack B. Yeats, "AE".

RHA Gallagher Gallery, 15 Ely Place, Dublin 2. Tel: 661 2558. www.royalhibernianacademy.ie. Tues–Sat 11am–5pm (8pm on Thur), Sun 2–5pm. Exhibitions by Irish and international artists in spacious modern gallery.

Rubicon Gallery, 10 St

Stephen's Green, Dublin 2. Tel: 670 8055. www.rubicongallery.ie. Mon–Fri 11am–5.30pm, Sat 11am–4.30pm. Contemporary Irish and international art.

Solomon Gallery, Powerscourt Townhouse Centre, Dublin 2. Tel: 679 4237. www.solomon gallery.com. Mon–Sat 10am–5.30pm. Contemporary Irish and international art.

Temple Bar Studios, 5–9 Temple Bar, Dublin 2. Tel: 671 0073. www.templebargallery.com. Tues, Wed, Fri, Sat 11am–6pm, Thur 10am–7pm, Sun 2–6pm. Avant garde contemporary Irish and international art.

SOUTHEAST

Butler Gallery, Kilkenny Castle, Kilkenny. Tel: 056-776 1106. www.butlergallery.com. Daily 10am–7pm. Late 19th-century and 20th-century Irish art.

Garter Lane Arts Centre, O'Connell Street, Waterford. Tel: 051-877 153. Daily 10am–6pm. Exhibitions by lively young artists.

Kilcock Art Gallery, School Street, Kilcock, Co. Kildare. Tel: 01-628 7619. www.kilcockart gallery.com. Mon–Fri 10am–5pm, Sat 2–5pm.

Wexford Arts Centre, Cornmarket, Wexford. Tel: 053-23764. www.wexfordartscentre.ie. Mon–Sat 10am–6pm. General purpose arts centre in 18th-century market house which hosts touring exhibitions.

SOUTHWEST

Crawford Municipal Art Gallery, Emmet Place, Cork. Tel: 021-427 3377. www.crawfordartgallery.com. Mon–Sat, 10am–4.45pm. Irish and European paintings, sculpture, silver, glass.

Frank Lewis, 6 Bridewell Lane, Killarney. Tel: 064-31108. www.franklewis.com. Commercial gallery hosting regular shows by

artists living or temporarily working in the south west.

Keane on Ceramics, Pier Road, Kinsale. Tel: 021-477 4553. Open daily. Represents a number of major Irish ceramic artists.

Kent Gallery, Town Park, Kinsale. Tel: 021-477 4956. www.kentgal.com. Wed–Sat and Mon 11am–6pm; Sun 2–6pm. Sells work by both up-and-coming and well established local artists.

Lavit Gallery, Father Matthew Street, Cork. Tel: 021-427 7749. Mon–Sat 10am–6pm. Fortnightly exhibitions by Irish artists.

Triskel Arts Centre, Tobin Street, Cork. Tel: 021-427 2022. www.triskelart.com. Mon–Sat 10am–5.30pm. Exhibitions, plays, poetry readings and music.

West Cork Arts Centre, Old Bank House, North Street, Skibbereen, Co. Cork. Tel: 028-22090. Mon–Sat 10am–6pm. Community arts centre with exhibitions of contemporary paintings, sculpture, ceramics. Directory of local artist and craft makers on request. Interesting shop.

MID WEST

Belltable Arts Centre, 69 O'Connell Street, Limerick. Tel: 061-319 866. www.belltable.ie. Mon–Sat 10am–9pm. Community arts centre hosting travelling exhibitions and shows by local artists.

Limerick City Gallery of Art, Pery Square, Limerick. Tel: 061-310 633. Mon–Fri 10am–1pm, 2.30–8pm, Sat 10am–1pm. Collection of 18th- to 20th-century oils and watercolours. Local and touring exhibitions.

FAR WEST

Clifden Art Gallery, Main Street, Clifden, Connemara. Tel:

095-21788. Daily. Landscape and other work by local artists.

Education Centre, Castlebar. Tel: 094-902 3159. Mon–Fri 10.30am–5pm. Irish art and crafts.

Galway Arts Centre, 47 Dominick Street, Galway. Tel: 091-565 886. www.galwayarts centre.ie. Mon–Sat 10am–6pm. Regular exhibitions by younger artists. Information centre for the lively Galway arts scene.

Kenny Bookshop and Art Gallery, Middle Street, Galway. Tel: 091-562 739. www.kennys.ie. Mon–Sat 9am–6pm. Commercial gallery showing original work chiefly by local artists.

Linenhall Arts Centre, Linenhall Street, Castlebar. Tel: 094-902 3733. www.thelinenhall.com. Mon–Fri 10am–5.30pm, Sat 11am–5pm. Community centre for all kinds of artistic activity including shows of local work.

NORTHWEST REGION

Glebe Gallery, Churchill, Co. Donegal. Tel: 074-913 7071. Tours 11.30am–5.30pm. Derek Hill collection; English-born artist associated particularly with paintings of Tory Island.

County Sligo Yeats Art Gallery, Stephen Street, Sligo. Tel: 071-914 2212. Tues–Sat 10–11.50am, 2–4.45pm. Over 100 paintings 20 of which are exhibited at a time. Includes work by John Butler Yeats and Jack B. Yeats.

Model Arts Centre, The Mall, Sligo. Tel: 071-914 1405. www.modelart.ie. Tues–Sat 10am–5.30pm, Sun 11am–4pm. Housed in a recently renovated model school dating back to 1862, the Model Arts and Niland Gallery maintains an extensive programme of visual arts.

Taylor's Art Gallery, Castlebaldwin. Co. Sligo. Tel: 071-916 5138. Mon–Sat 9am–6pm. Original work by local artists.

The Gallery, Dunfanaghy, Co.

Donegal. Tel: 074-913 6224. Mon–Sat 10am–5pm. Modern work by local artists and others.

NORTHERN IRELAND

Arts Council of Northern Ireland, 77 Malone Road, Belfast. Tel: 028-9038 5200. www.artscouncil-ni.org. Exhibitions, bookshop.
Bradbury Gallery, 1 Lyndon Court, College Street, Belfast. Tel: 028-9023 3535. Irish and international artists.
Bell Gallery, 13 Adelaide Park, Belfast. Tel: 028-9066 2998. www.bellgallery.com. 19th-century and 20th-century Irish artists, Victorian paintings.
Davison Art Gallery, 53 High Street, Holywood. Tel: 028-9042 5982. www.davisongallery.com. Traditional and modern work by well-known Irish artists.
Eakin Gallery, 237 Lisburn Road, Belfast. Tel: 028-9066 8522. www.eakingallery.co.uk. Traditional and modern Irish paintings.
Fenderesky Gallery, 2–4 University Road, Belfast. Tel: 028-9023 5245. Tues–Sat 11.30am–5pm. Contemporary and avant-garde Irish painting.
Malone House, Barnetts Park, Belfast. Tel: 028-9068 1246. www.malonehouse.co.uk. Early 19th-century house with permanent exhibition on Belfast parks and first floor art gallery.
Ormeau Baths Gallery, 18a Ormeau Road, Belfast. Tel: 028-9032 1402. Free public gallery in converted public baths. Contemporary exhibitions, often of conceptual art.
Tom Caldwell Gallery, 429 Lisburn Road, Belfast. Tel: 028-9066 1890. www.tomcaldwellgallery.com. Living Irish artists.
Ulster Museum, Botanic Gardens, Belfast. Tel: 028-9038 3000. www.ulstermuseum.org.uk. Ulster and Irish artists such as Sir John Lavery, Paul Henry, Jack B. Yeats, Colin Middleton.

Festivals

The number of events and festivals, big and small, seems to increase every year. There are folk festivals, music festivals, oyster festivals, potato festivals, regattas, angling competitions, drama festivals, chess congresses, sporting competitions of all kinds, beauty contests, song contests, parades, car rallies, boat rallies, literary festivals, jazz festivals, exhibitions, agricultural shows, horse shows, dog shows, cat shows, commemorations, celebrations, hunt meetings, marathons, summer schools, community festivals, *ceilidhs*... the list seems endless.

In many cases, dates and venues are variable and some festivals – particularly the smaller, local ones – may appear and disappear from year to year according to the availability of funds, enthusiasm or organisers.

Here is a small selection, listed in calendar order. Exact dates often vary, and local tourist boards can provide precise dates and details.

Calendar of Events

January Races, Leopardstown, Dublin: top-class National Hunt (jumping) meeting. Opening of Point-to-Point season: races run at different venues every Sunday over unfenced courses.
Aer Lingus Young Scientists Exhibition, RDS, Ballsbridge, Dublin. January.
Holiday and Leisure Fair, RDS,

Ballsbridge, Dublin. January.
Six Nations Rugby Championship (Ireland versus England, Wales, Scotland, France, Italy). Home matches at Lansdowne Road, Dublin. February/March.
Ulster Harp National, Downpatrick: steeplechase. Late February/early March.
Ulster Motor Show, King's Hall, Belfast. February annual.
Limerick Theatre and Music Festivals. Early March.
Irish Dancing Championships. February/March.
Dublin Film Festival. March/April. Irish premieres of a selection of Irish and international cinema.
St Patrick's Day (17 March): Festival of Ireland's national saint. Celebrated throughout Ireland and much of the world, notably in New York city.
World Irish Dancing Championships: venue variable. March/April (Easter).
Pan-Celtic week. Gathering of Celts from Brittany, Cornwall, Wales, Scotland and the home turf. Always around Easter. Venue changes every year.
Irish Grand National (steeplechase), Fairyhouse. Easter Monday.
Circuit of Ireland Car Rally. Easter weekend.
Dublin Grand Opera Society Spring Season, Gaiety Theatre. Late March/April.
Belfast Civic Festival and Lord Mayor's Show. May.
Belfast City Marathon road race. Mass masochism. May.
Northwest 200: fastest motorcycle road race in Britain or Ireland. Starts from Portstewart, Co. Derry. May.
Bantry Mussel Fair. Homage is paid to Bantry Bay's most succulent product. Early May.
Irish 2,000 Guineas (for 3-year-old colts) and 1,000 Guineas (for fillies), both run over one mile. First classics of the flat-racing season, staged on consecutive Saturdays at the Curragh in May.
Ulster Classic Fishing Festival,

Fermanagh Lakeland. Anglers' cornucopia. May.

Royal Ulster Agricultural Show, Belfast. May.

Sligo Arts Festival. Street entertainment, fireworks, theatre, readings, comedy and music. Late May.

Writers' Week, Listowel, Co. Clare. Late May/June.

Music in Great Irish Houses Festival: held in various mansions near Dublin. Early June.

Bloomsday Literary Festival, 16 June, Dublin. Held on the date on which Joyce's *Ulysses* takes place. Principally for Joyce buffs, but there is no shortage of those *(see below)*.

Ballybunion International Bachelor Festival, Ballybunion, Co. Kerry. Irish manhood's answer to the Miss World contest. Seeing is believing. Late June.

Irish Derby (1½-mile flat-race for 3-year-old colts). Most glamorous day in the Irish racing calendar. Held at the Curragh. Late June.

Westport Sea Angling Festival, Westport, Co. Mayo. Late June.

Irish Oaks, the Curragh, Equivalent of the Derby for fillies. Early July.

Willie Clancy Summer School, Miltown Malbay, Co. Clare (uillean piping). July.

Ulster Harp Derby, Downpatrick, Co. Down. July.

Orangeman's Day, all over Northern Ireland. 12 July.

International Rose Trials, Sir Thomas and Lady Dixon Park, Belfast. July–September.

Galway Races – heady, often hilarious, holiday horse-racing. Late July/August.

Galway Arts Festival. Massive celebration of international and Irish theatre, film, art, literature and music overlaps with the races *(see above)* to create a mighty buzz. Late July/August.

Ulster Steam Traction Rally, Shane's Castle, Antrim. July, huffing and puffing.

Stradbally Steam Rally, Stradbally, Co. Laois. Early

August, more huffing and puffing.

Yeats International Summer School. Sligo. Academics, writers and poetry enthusiasts from all over the world assemble to listen and learn. The biggest and oldest of many summer schools taking place in August.

Dublin Horse Show, RDS, Ballsbridge. Greatest event in the show-jumping calendar. August.

Puck Fair, Killorglin, Co. Kerry. Ancient pagan festival at which a goat is crowned. August.

Ulster Flying Club International Rally, Newtownards, Co. Down. Third weekend in June.

The Ould Lammas Fair, Ballycastle, Co. Antrim. The North of Ireland's most popular old fair, at which you traditionally "treat your Mary Ann to some dulse and Yellow Man." For elucidation, go to Ballycastle. Last Monday and Tuesday in August.

All-Ireland Amateur Drama Festival. August.

Ulster Grand Prix (motorcycling), Dundrod, near Belfast. August.

Merriman Summer School, Lisdoonvarna, Co. Clare. A week in August of intense intellectual debate about the nation's culture, liberally laced with drinking and partying.

Rose of Tralee International Festival, Tralee, Co. Kerry. Late August.

Fleadh Ceoil na Eireann (All-Ireland festival of Irish music, with competitions therein). Venue variable. August.

Matching Festival of Ireland, Lisdoonvarna, Co. Clare. More fun than computer dating. August-September.

Hurling and Gaelic Football: All-Ireland finals, Croke Park, Dublin. September.

Galway Oyster Festival, Galway city. Late September.

Irish Hot-Air Balloon Championships, Ballymahon, Co. Longford. Late September.

Dublin Theatre Festival. Late September/October.

Dublin Cat Show, RDS, Ballsbridge. October.

Wexford Opera Festival, Wexford town. October.

Cork Jazz Festival, Cork City. October.

Dublin City Marathon, More self-inflicted punishment. Late October.

Belfast Festival, Queen's University, Belfast. Ambitious, event-packed two weeks of music, drama, folksong, cinema, etc. November.

Dublin Grand Opera Society Winter Season, Gaiety Theatre, Dublin. December.

Bloomsday Turns Back the Clock

James Joyce's masterpiece, *Ulysses*, thematically based on Homer's *Odyssey*, documents a 24-hour period in the lives of an Irish Jew, Leopold Bloom, and a budding writer, Stephen Dedalus, as they move around Dublin; the story reaches its climax when they meet. Since 1954, the 50th anniversary of the events depicted in the novel, Joyce fans have recreated the day's events each 16 June and the Bloomsday celebrations are now rivalled only by St Patrick's Day. Participants, wearing what approximates to 1904 garb, trace the paths of the book's characters. After a Bloomsday breakfast in Sandycove, they can listen to readings delivered by costumed actors, lunch on Gorgonzola sandwiches and Burgundy in Davy Byrne's pub, walk through the northside, taking in Hardwicke Street, Eccles Street, Gardiner Street and Mountjoy Square, enjoy more readings at the Joyce Centre, and then discuss the book's finer points over a few pints.

Outdoor Attractions

Relics

Ireland is rich in relics of its fascinating, troubled past. From prehistoric times, there are monuments such as the extraordinary burial chamber at **Newgrange**, Co. Meath; the stone fort, **Grianán Ailigh** (Sunpalace of Aileach), Co. Donegal; the megalithic tomb of **Creevykeel Court Cairn**, Co. Sligo; or the strange carved stone figures on **White Island**, Lough Erne, Co. Fermanagh.

From the golden age of Celtic Christianity, there are the ruins of great monastic settlements such as **Glendalough**, Co. Wicklow; **Clonmacnoise**, Co. Offaly; **The Rock of Cashel** and **Holycross Abbey**, Co. Tipperary; **Mellifont Abbey** and **Monasterboice**, Co. Louth; and **Boyle Abbey**, Co. Roscommon.

From the times when Gaelic chieftains and Norman barons struggled for supremacy, there are hundreds of castles and fortresses: **Kilkenny Castle**, **Blarney Castle**, **Bunratty Castle**, **Cahir Castle**, **Knappogue Castle**, **Dunluce Castle**, to mention only a few.

From the centuries of Anglo-Irish Ascendancy, there are many historic and beautiful houses and gardens, such as **Castletown**, in Co. Kildare; **Strokestown House**, Co. Roscommon; **Carriglas Manor**, Co. Longford; **Damer House**, Co. Tipperary; the **State Apartments of Dublin Castle**; **Lissadell House**, Co. Sligo, celebrated in a great poem by Yeats; **Russborough**, Co. Wicklow, which houses a splendid art collection; **Birr Castle Demesne**, Co. Offaly, with over 1,000 catalogued species of trees and shrubs; **Howth Castle Gardens**, Co. Dublin; **The Japanese Gardens**, Tully, Co. Kildare; and **Mount Usher** and **Powerscourt** gardens, Co. Wicklow.

Then there are splendid national and civic parks and nature gardens, such as **Phoenix Park** and the **National Botanic Gardens** in Dublin city; **Glenveagh National Park**, Co. Donegal; **Killarney National Park**, Co. Kerry; **Fota Estate**, Co. Cork; **Lough Key Forest Park**, Co. Roscommon; **Tollymore Forest Park** and **Castlewellan Forest Park**, Co. Down; and **Gortin Forest Park**, Co. Tyrone.

Beauty Spots

Ireland is renowned above all else for its scenery: often lush, sometimes bleak, always memorable. Here is a handy checklist of places of scenic interest, county by county. (Many have little to offer except beauty or tranquillity and may not be mentioned in the main text.)

Antrim: Ballintoy, Ballycastle, Carnlough, Cushendall, Cushendun, Giant's Causeway, Glenariff, Portballintrae, Portrush, Waterfoot, Whitehead.
Armagh: Jonesborough, Newtownhamilton.
Carlow: Bunclody, Hacketstown, St Mullins, Tullow.
Cavan: Cootehill, Glengavlen, Shannon Pot, Swanlinbar, Virginia.
Clare: Aillwee Cave (Ballyvaughan), The Burren, Feakle, Kilkee, Lahinch, Lisdoonvarna, Cliffs of Moher, Mountshannon, Scarriff.
Cork: Adrigole, Allihies, Ballylickey, Ballymacoda, Barley Lake (Glengarriff), Blackwater drive, Castletownshend, Dunworley Strand, Glandore, Hungry Hill (Beara Peninsula), Glanworth, Gougane Barra, Keimaneigh Pass, Lough Ine (Skibbereen).
Derry: Castlerock, Draperstown, Glenshane Pass, Magilligan, Portstewart.
Donegal: Buncrana, Bundoran, Clonmany, Dunfanaghy, Dunlewy, Glen, Glencolumbkille, Glenveagh, Gweedore, Lough Swilly, Malin More, Rosapenna, St Patrick's Purgatory, Slieve League.
Down: Annalong, Bangor, Bryansford, Crawfordsburn, Donaghadee, Hilltown, Kilkeel, Newcastle, Portaferry, Rostrevor, Silent Valley, Warrenpoint.
Dublin: Dalkey, Dun Laoghaire, Howth, Killiney, Kilternan, Phoenix Park.
Fermanagh: Belcoo, Boho, Florencecourt (near Enniskillen), Marble Arch Caves, Tempo, Tully Bay.
Galway: Aran Islands, Ballynahinch Lake, Carna, Cashel Harbour, Clifden, Killary Harbour, Kylemore, Leenane, Lough Corrib, Lough Inagh, Lough Mask, Lough Nafooey, Oughterard, Recess, Roundstone.

What the Tourist Boards Offer

Bord Fáilte, the Irish Tourist Board, lists a selection of places to visit in its *Christian Ireland* and *Historic Houses, Castles and Gardens* brochures. The Office of Public Works has produced a lavishly illustrated and highly praised publication, *Heritage – A Visitor's Guide*, edited by Eilís Brennan.

The Northern Ireland Tourist Board will also supply details of visitor attractions in its area. **Contact addresses: page 335–6.**

Kerry: Ballydavid, Banna Strand, Caragh Lake, Connor Pass, Dingle, Glenbeigh, Glencar, Healy Pass, Kenmare, Killarney, Parknasilla, Valentia Island, Ventry, Waterville.
Kildare: Celbridge, Leixlip, Robertstown, Monasterevin.
Kilkenny: Graiguenamanagh, Inistioge, Thomastown.
Laois: Abbeyleix, Dunamase, Mountmellick, Rosenallis.
Leitrim: Dromahair, Glenade, Kinlough, Lough Allen, Lough Gill, Lurganboy, Manorhamilton.
Limerick: Ardpatrick, Bally-landers, Kilfinane, Montpelier.
Longford: Ardagh, Drumlish, Granard.
Louth: Carlingford, Omeath, Ravensdale.
Mayo: Achill Island, Ballycastle, Belderg, Clare Island, Croagh Patrick, Delphi, Inishbofin, Killary Harbour, Lough Conn, Lough Corrib, Louisburgh, Mulrany, Moyne Castle, Westport.
Meath: Oldcastle, Slane.
Monaghan: Carrickmacross, Castleblayney, Rockcorry.
Offaly: Clareen, Kinnitty, Slieve Bloom mountains.
Roscommon: Boyle, Lough Key, Strokestown.
Sligo: Benbulben, Cliffony, Drumcliff, Easky, Lough Gill, Rosses Point.
Tipperary: Aherlow, Clogheen, The Gap, Mitchelstown Caves.
Tyrone: Gortin, Newtown-stewart, Plumbridge.
Waterfold: Ballymacarbry, Cheekpoint, Kilmacthomas, Lismore, Tramore.
Westmeath: Castlepollard, Fore, Glassan, Mullingar.
Wexford: Ballyahck, Bunclody, Curracloe, Kilmore Quay, Rosslare, Scullogue Gap.
Wicklow: Annamoe, Aughrim, Avoca, Bray, Dunmore East, Enniskerry, Glendalough, Glenmalure, New Ross, Poulaphouca, Rathdrum, Roundwood, Sally Gap, Woodenbridge.

Shopping

What to Buy

Traditional crafts still flourish, partly as a source of merchandise but partly out of a very Irish sense that the excellence cultivated by past generations is worth nurturing. Cut crystal, a craft which had just about died out, was resurrected in the 1960s and today flourishes in Waterford and elsewhere.

Ireland's internationally renowned wool textile industry has moved its emphasis from the old homespun, handwoven tweed to very finely-woven scarves, stoles and dress fabrics. Linen and lace remain remarkably delicate.

Pottery has developed fast as a craft industry, and new studios are opening all the time. Basket-weaving remains wide-spread and provides such souvenirs as table mats and St Brigid crosses.

While Irish crafts have always been well-made, they haven't always been fashionable. This is changing, with designs much improved. Whether buying for the wardrobe or for the home, the fashion-conscious will be pleasantly surprised at the variety of styles available nowadays in Irish tweeds, knitwear and linen.

Dublin
The two main areas for shopping in Dublin are Grafton Street and its tributaries; and – less stylish but often better value – the Henry Street area, off O'Connell Street. Recent years have seen a major invasion of the city by British-based multiples such as Marks and Spencer, Boots, Habitat and Debenhams, and Dublin now retains only three indigenous department stores: Brown Thomas, on Grafton Street; Arnott's, on Henry Street; and Clery's, on O'Connell Street.

Don't miss the Powerscourt Townhouse Centre, just off Grafton Street, an 18th-century mansion and courtyard converted into a stylish shopping complex with many crafts and antiques shops and several restaurants. The Kilkenny Shop on Nassau Street, a showcase for Irish crafts and clothes, is also worth a browse. On the same street, the Celtic Note record shop specialises in Irish music. Blarney Woollen Mills and Kevin and Howlin stock classic Irish knitwear and tweeds. Just on the north side of the Ha'penny Bridge, Dublin Woollen Mills, stocks similar items at more reasonable prices.

There's an excellent range of Irish cheeses at Sheridans on St Anne Street; hard cheeses travel best. The Kilkenny Shop in Nassau Street has a selection of Irish-made jams, chutneys, cakes, biscuits and confectionery. Bewley's cafés sell attractive gift-packs of cakes, brack (a fruity loaf traditionally eaten around Hallowe'en), fudge, tea and coffee. Butler's Irish Chocolates in Grafton Street offers many delights for the sweet-toothed.

If you're interested in taking some Irish food home with you, smoked salmon is a good bet (but be sure it's labelled "smoked Irish salmon" as opposed to "Irish smoked salmon"). Air travellers can buy some at the Wrights of Howth shop in Dublin Airport

Belfast
The city's main shopping area stretches from Donegall Place,

opposite the City Hall, down the wide Royal Avenue, where you'll find most of the big British chain stores such as Marks and Spencer. There's a concentration of such stores in the vast Castlecourt Shopping Centre, located just off Royal Avenue and with a car park attached.

The distinctive Northern Irish gift is linen, which once accounted for much of the province's prosperity. One city-centre outlet is Smyth's Irish Linen at 65 Royal Avenue. For those wanting to know more, the Irish Linen Centre at Lisburn Museum (028-9266 3377) has displays and demonstrations. (Lisburn is to the southwest of Belfast, down the M1 motorway.)

Shopping Hours

Most shops are open from 9am to 5.30pm. Shopping centres stay open until 9pm on Thur and Fri. Many small grocery stores are open until late at night and there are a few 24-hour shops in Dublin.

Outside the large cities, there is often an all-day or early-closing (1pm) day once a week. This is usually on Wed or Thur.

Sport

Spectator

Gaelic Football

Cumann Luthchleas Gael, Croke Park, Dublin 3. Tel: 836 3222. www.gaa.ie. This now houses a museum devoted to the history of this uniquely Irish sport. For further information, tel: 819 2323, fax: 819 2324.

Rugby

Irish Rugby Football Union, 62 Landsdowne Road, Ballsbridge, Dublin 4. Tel: 647 3800. www.irishrugby.ie.

Soccer

Soccer Football Assocation of Ireland, 80 Merrion Square, Dublin 2. Tel: 703 7500. www.fai.ie.

Participant

Golf

Visitors are welcome to play at about 180 golf courses in the Irish Republic. Green fees range from about €20 to €75 a day (the charge is usually per day, not per round as in many countries). Reductions are available for weekly and monthly rates. Most clubs offer discounts to groups and societies. Some courses have sets of clubs for hire. Caddies are not usually available, except by prior booking. Most clubs hire out pull-carts, but not electric or petrol-driven carts. Visitors are advised to bring only light golf-bags, as they may have to carry their own.

For full details of golf courses,

holiday offers, or individual golf itineraries, contact the Golf Promotion Executive, Irish Tourist Board, Dublin 2. *Golfing* is a new publication available from Irish Tourist Board offices in Ireland and overseas. It includes details of golf accommodation offers, tour operators, golf clubs, access travel and golfing fixtures. There is also a useful website, www.golfireland.ie. The Northern Ireland Tourist Board publishes a leaflet listing the 80 golf courses in Northern Ireland.

Sea Angling

Shore fishing (from rocks, piers, beaches and promontories), inshore fishing (in bays and inlets) and deep sea fishing are popular in Ireland all the year round. No permits are required. There are over 250 competitions organised throughout the country from February to November.

Boats can be hired from more than 700 operators around the country. Expect to pay between €20 and €40 per angler per day, or between €225 and €400 for a daily charter. Full details of events and of boats for hire are contained in the free Irish Tourist Board publication, *Angling in Ireland,* which covers both coarse and sea angling or go to their designated website www.angling.ireland.ie.

Coarse Angling

The species of freshwater fish in this category are pike, arch, bream, rudd, tench, dace and various hybrids. The main area for coarse fishing is the Midlands, stretching from the River Erne system in the North southwards through the Shannon basin, the Monaghan and Westmeath lakes, the Grand and Royal Canals, to the Barrow River and Canal and the Munster Blackwater. There is no legal closed season, but a conservation order on pike was introduced in 1990. No licence is required in the Irish Republic.

In Northern Ireland, anglers require an annual general coarse fishing permit and a coarse fishing rod licence (for 15 days or a season) – available from local tackle shops, local hotels, handling agents or the tourist board.

Tackle can be bought but seldom hired in Ireland. Boat hire works out at around €30 per head per day based on six sharing. Pre-packed bait, such as pure breadcrumbs, white maggots and worms can be bought from a number of stock-lists, but it is best to pre-order from Irish Angling Services, Ardlougher, Co. Cavan. Tel: 049-952 6258. If you are bringing your own bait into Ireland, do not pack it in soil or vegetable material, the importation of which is illegal.

Game Angling
The species are salmon, sea trout and brown trout. The season for salmon fishing is from 1 January to 30 September, depending on district. A licence is essential, and usually a fishery permit also – though some loughs, for example Corrib and Conn, are free of permit charge. (Permits are not the same as licences and are paid to individual fishery owners.)

An annual licence costs €62, a 21-day licence €23, a district licence €29 and juvenile and one-day licences €10 and €16 respectively.

A salmon licence and permit also covers fishing for sea trout, which is in season from June to 30 September (12 October in some areas). For brown trout, a licence is required in Northern Ireland only and much of the fishing is free.

Full details are in Bord Fáilte's brochure Game Angling.

Under new laws governing brown trout and coarse fishing,

a system of co-operatives administers and funds the development of these fisheries through share certificates. The matter is complex and visiting anglers should seek clarification from local tourist offices and angling clubs.

Books and Guides on Angling
The Angler in Ireland: Game, Coarse and Sea, by Ken Whelan. Country House.
Trout and Salmon Loughs of Ireland, by Peter O'Reilly. Unwin Hyman.
Trout and Salmon Rivers of Ireland, by Peter O'Reilly. Unwin Hyman.
Coarse Fishing in Ireland, by Hugh Gough. Unwin Hyman.
Fly-fishing for Irish Trout, by Niall Fallon. Poolbeg.
Guides on game, coarse and sea angling are published annually by the Irish Tourist Board.

Adventure Sports
Canoeing, boardsailing, caving, hang-gliding, mountaineering, orienteering, parachuting, scuba diving, sailing, and water-skiing

are among the main activities provided for in a growing number of adventure centres located in suitably stunning locations from Cork to Galway to Donegal to Wicklow and beyond. The reputable centres are affiliated to the Association for Adventure Sports (AFAS); contact: Secretary Centre Standards Board, Carrowcashel, Ramelton, Co. Donegal. Tel: 074-915 2800. www.adventuresports.ie. Full details are also listed in Bord Fáilte and Northern Ireland Tourist Board brochures.

Surfing
Notable venues with Atlantic swells, stimulating breezes and foaming surf are at Strandhill and Easkey, Co. Sligo, Lahinch, Kilkee, Doolin Point, along the coast of Co. Clare. Coaching, including surf-board and wet-suit, costs about €15 per hour. These specialists operate all year round: Co. Sligo Surf Club, Strandhill, Easkey Surf Club, Easkey, Co. Sligo; West Coast Surf Club, Lahinch, Co. Clare. The Irish Surfing Association is

Useful Contacts for Anglers

Bord Fáilte (Irish Tourist Board), Baggot Street Bridge, Dublin 2 (tel: 01-602 4000, fax: 01-602 4100), and tourist offices in main cities and towns throughout country will provide up-to-date information on every aspect of angling.

Department of Marine and Fisheries Board, Fisheries Administration, Leeson Lane, Dublin 2. Tel: 01-678 5444.

Central Fisheries Board, Balnagowan House, Glasnevin, Dublin 9. Tel: 01-884 2600.

Eastern Regional Fisheries Board Blackrock, Dublin. Tel: 01-278 7022. www.fishingireland.net.

Southern Regional Fisheries Board, Anglesea Street, Clonmel, Co. Tipperary. Tel: 052-80055. www.srfb.ie.

Southwestern Regional Fisheries Board, Neville Terrace, Massey Town, Macroom, Co. Cork. Tel: 026-41221.

Shannon Regional Fisheries Board, Ashbourne Business Park, Dock Road, Limerick. Tel: 061-300 238. www.shannon-fishery-board.ie

Western Regional Fisheries Board, Weir Lodge, Earls Island, Galway. Tel: 091-563 110. www.wrfb.ie.

Northwestern Regional Fisheries Board, Abbey Street, Ballina, Co. Mayo. Tel: 096-22623.

Northern Regional Fisheries Board, Station Road, Ballyshannon, Co. Donegal. Tel: 071-985 1435.

at Easkey House, Easkey, Co. Sligo. Tel: 096-49428. www.isasurf.ie.

Bird-Watching
There are more than 55 recognised birdwatching sites in Ireland. For details of these, and of the various species to be seen at different times of year, contact Birdwatch Ireland, Rockingham House, Newcastle, Co. Wicklow. Tel: 01-281 9878. www.birdwatchireland.ie. There are two bird observatories at which visitors can stay. These are Cape Clear Bird Observatory (bookings via Mr Steve wing, Cape Clear Bird Observatory, Cape Clear, West Cork); and Copeland Bird Observatory, Co. Down (bookings Secretary is Mr N. McKee, 67 Temple Rise, Templepatrick, Co. Antrim, tel: 028-9443 3068. www.cbo.org.uk).

Hill-Walking, Rambling, Climbing
There is surely no need for further propaganda about the unspoilt beauty of Ireland's hills and mountains. Few of them rise above 3,000 ft (1,000 metres), but they have great character and variety, from the soft, bogcovered domes of Wicklow to the jagged peaks of Connemara, the ridges of Cork and Kerry, the strange, basalt outcrops of the Antrim plateau or the sweeping Mountains of Mourne. Most of Ireland's mountains command marvellous views of the sea.

The best-known long-distance walking path in the Republic is the "Wicklow Way," which extends for about 79 miles

Climbing Contacts
For further information and advice on mountaineering, rock-climbing and hill walking, contact the Association for Adventure Sports (AFAS), Carrowcashel, Ramelton, Co. Donegal. Tel: 074-915 2800.

(126 km) southwards from Marlay Park, Co. Dublin to Clonegal, Co. Carlow. The route switchbacks along the eastern flanks of the Dublin and Wicklow mountains, the largest unbroken area of high ground in Ireland, very sparsely inhabited. For information on the route and accommodation, and on hillwalking in other mountain regions of the Republic, contact Cospoir (The Irish Sports Council), 21 Fitzwilliam Square, Dublin 2. Tel: 240 7700. www.irishsportscouncil.ie.

The *Walking Ireland* brochure produced by Cospoir and Bord Fáilte, which is available from both organisations, gives full details of the marked long distance walking routes such as the Cavan Way, the Tain Trail around the Cooley mountains and Carlingford in the northeast, the Ulster Way, the Slieve Bloom Way, the Aran Island ways, the Kerry Way, Munster Way, Dingle Way and many more. It also lists Irish walking holiday specialists.

One of Europe's great long-distance paths, the "Ulster Way", virtually encircles Northern Ireland, stretching for 500 miles (800 km). For information, contact the Sports Council for Northern Ireland, House of Sport, Malone Road, Belfast 9. Tel: 028-9038 1222, fax: 028-9068 2757. Email: sportscouncil-ni.org.uk. www.sportni.net.

Further Reading

General

Aalen, F.H.A., Whelan, Kevin, Stout, Matthew (eds.) *Atlas of the Rural Irish Landscape* Cork University Press
Ardagh, John. *Ireland and the Irish*. Hamish Hamilton/Penguin.
Arnold, Bruce. *A Concise History of Irish Art*. Thames & Hudson.
Bardon, Jonathan. *Belfast*. Blackstaff Press.
Beckett, J.C. *The Making of Modern Ireland*. Faber.
Bell, Brian and McAuley, Liam (ed.) *Insight Guide: Dublin*. APA Publications.
Boylan, Henry. *A Dictionary of Irish Biography*. Gill & Macmillan.
Brennan, Eílis (ed.) *Heritage – a visitor's guide*. Office of Public Works.
Brown, Terence. *Ireland: A Social and Cultural History 1922–1985*. Fontana Press/Cornell University.
Cahill, Thomas. *How the Irish Saved Civilization*. Doubleday.
Catto, Mike. *Art in Ulster*, vol 2. Blackstaff Press.
Craig, Maurice. *The Architecture of Ireland*. Batsford.
Danaher, Kevin. *In Ireland Long Ago*. Mercier Press.
Seamus Deane. *Short History of Irish Literature* Hutchinson
Deane, Seamus (ed.) *Field Day Anthology of Irish Writing* Field Day publications, Derry.
Delaney, Frank. *James Joyce's Odyssey – A Guide to the Dublin of Ulysses*. Hodder & Stoughton.
Evans, Estyn. *Irish Folk Ways*. Routledge and Kegan Paul.
Fitzgibbon, Theodora. *A Taste of Ireland*. Pan.
FitzSimon, Christopher. *The*

Arts in Ireland. Gill & Macmillan.

FitzSimon, Christopher. *The Irish Theatre*. Thames & Hudson.

Gogarty, Oliver St John. *As I Was Going Down Sackville Street*. Sphere.

Guinness, Desmond. *Georgian Dublin*, Batsford.

Healy, Elizabeth (ed.) *The Book of the Liffey from source to the sea*. Wolfhound Press.

Kearney, Richard (ed.) *The Irish Mind*. Wolfhound.

Kee, Robert. *Ireland – A History*. Weidenfeld.

Lydon, James and MacCurtain, Margaret (eds.). *The Gill History of Ireland* (12 vols.). Gill & Macmillan.

Lyons, F.S.L. *Ireland Since the Famine*. Collins.

MacLysaght, Edward. *Irish Families and their Names and Origins*. Figgis.

MacLysaght, Edward. *Surnames of Ireland*. Irish Academic Press.

McDonald, Frank. *The Destruction of Dublin*. Gill & Macmillan.

Mahon, Derek and Fallon. Peter (eds.). *Penguin Book of Contemporary Irish Poetry* Penguin

Mitchell, Frank. *The Shell Guide to Reading the Irish Landscape* Town House & Country House.

Murphy, Dervla. *A Place Apart*.

Murray.

Murphy, Matt & Susan (ed). *Ireland's Bird Life* Sherkin Island Marine Station publications.

Murphy, John. *Irish Shopfronts*. Appletree Press, Belfast.

O'Brien, Maire and Conor Cruise. *Concise History of Ireland*. Thames & Hudson.

O'Canainn, Tomas. *Traditional Music in Ireland*. Routledge & Kegan Paul.

O'Connor, Frank. *A Book of Ireland*. Collins.

O'Connor, Nuala. *Bringing It all Back Home – the Influence of Irish Music* BBC Books.

O'Connor, Ulick, illus. Bewick, Pauline. *Irish Tales and Sagas*. Granada.

O'Faolain, Sean. *The Irish*. Penguin.

O'Riada, Sean. *Our Musical Heritage*. Dolmen.

Potterton, Homan. *The National Gallery of Ireland*.

Prendergast, Mark. J. *Irish Rock: History, Roots and Perspectives* O'Brien Press

Robinson, Tim *The Stones of Aran: Pilgrimage* Penguin.

Share, Bernard and Tucker, Alan (ed.) Somerville-Large, Peter. *Dublin*. Hamish Hamilton.

Somerville-Large, Peter. *The Grand Irish Tour*. Penguin.

Stephens, James, illus. Rackham, *Arthur. Irish Fairy Tales*.

Gill & Macmillan.

Woodham-Smith, Cecil. *The Great Hunger*. Hamish Hamilton.

Other Insight Guides

Nearly 200 **Insight Guides** and **Insight City Guides** cover the world, complemented by more than 130 **Insight Pocket Guides** and 133 **Insight Compact Guides**.

Insight Guide: Dublin covers in comprehensive detail the city's history, culture, people, places and attractions.

For those on a tight schedule, *Insight Pocket Guide: Ireland* sets out 17 timed itineraries, and *Insight Pocket Guide: Dublin* takes the same approach to the capital. Both contain recommendations from a local expert and have a full-size fold-out map showing the itineraries. *Insight Pocket Guide: Ireland's Southwest* covers the top tourist region of Cork, Killarney and Kerry.

Insight Compact Guide: Ireland, *Insight Compact Guide: Dublin*, *Insight Compact Guide: The West of Ireland* and *Insight Compact Guide: Belfast* are the ideal pocket reference works to carry with you as you explore. Text, pictures and maps are all carefully cross-referenced for ease of use. Great value.

Ireland and *Dublin* are two titles in the 130-strong **Insight FlexiMap** series. These easy-folding laminated maps are both practical and durable.

Ireland's Best-selling Books

Easons, the Dublin book retailer and wholesaler, compiled a list a few years ago of the top Irish classics of all time:
Gulliver's Travels by Jonathan Swift
The Vicar of Wakefield by Oliver Goldsmith
Castle Rackrent by Maria Edgeworth
The Complete Works of Oscar Wilde
The Complete Works of W. B. Yeats
Dracula by Bram Stoker
The Playboy of the Western World by J. M. Synge
The Complete Works of James Joyce
Three Plays by Sean O'Casey
Easons also compiled a list of Ireland's best-selling books of the 20th century.

This was dominated by Maeve Binchy, the former *Irish Times* journalist who has ploughed the same furrow as Edna O'Brien did a generation earlier, though in a more sentimental way:
The Glass Lake by Maeve Binchy
Little Irish Cookbook by John Murphy
Evening Class by Maeve Binchy
The Copper Beech by Maeve Binchy
Waiting for Godot by Samuel Beckett
Borstal Boy by Brendan Behan
The Ginger Man by J. P. Donleavy
Peig by Peig Sayers
Irish Proverbs illustrated by Karen Bailey
Angela's Ashes by Frank McCourt

ART & PHOTO CREDITS

Sam Abell/National Geographic 10/11, 108/109

Charles Bateman/Image Ireland 284

Bruce Bernstein 22

Bord Fáilte 69, 85, 90/91, 112, 113, 236R

Bob Brien/Image Ireland 278, 306L, 308

Chris Coe/Axiom 76/77

Christopher Cormack 168

Richard Cummins 6/7, 8/9, 15, 60, 142, 144, 149, 155L, 155R, 175, 179, 193, 201, 264, 267, 302, 317

Michael Diggin/Collections 186

Jim Fitzpatrick 98/99

Guglielmo Galvin 59

Gamma 17L

Robert Hallman/Collections 172/173

Blaine Harrington 152R

Brian Harris 248, 249

Peter Harvey/Collections 128/129

Michel Hetier 253

Christopher Hill 18/19, 52, 59, 127, 286/287, 294, 296/297, 319, 322, 324, 326R

Bob Hobby 130/131, 214, 219, 223, 269

Hubert Schaafsma Collection 26/27

Hulton Getty 38. 39, 42, 46L, 94, 95

Evelyn Humphries/Image Ireland 301

Irish Times 49

Thomas Kelly 1, 4/5, 14, 16, 17R, 23, 45, 55, 89, 93, 100, 101, 105, 106, 123, 134, 140, 141, 145, 152L, 162, 169, 177, 181, 184T, 184, 185, 187, 204, 208T, 210, 212, 213, 222, 235, 236L, 237, 238, 239, 240L, 242, 243, 245, 266T, 266, 268, 270, 271, 272, 274, 291, 328

Bill Kirk/Image Ireland 312/313, 314

Kobal Collection 80

Alain Le Garsmeur/Image Ireland 293L, 293R, 294T, 298, 304, 309

Barry Lewis 70, 74, 75R, 259

Mansell Collection 92

Tony McGrath 50, 54

Anderson McMeekin/Image Ireland 315

George Morrison 124

National Gallery of Ireland 142T

National Museum of Ireland 25, 40

Network Photographers 64/65

David Newell Smith 51

Jeremy Nicholl 53, 327

Northern Ireland Tourist Board 120, 285, 288, 289, 303L, 303R, 305, 321

Richard Nowitz 71, 146, 154, 165

Paul O'Driscoll 215

G. P. Reichelt 47, 244, 283

John Russell 216/217

Marc Schlossman/Collections 174

Michael St Maur Sheil/ Collections 107, 143R, 258, 262/263

The Slide File 17, 56, 102/103, 104

John Sturrock 48

Billy Strickland 110/111, 114/115

Heinz Stücke 218, 306R

Jacob Sutton 78/79, 84, 143L

Tony Stone Pictures 132/133, 164, 197, 198/199, 200, 241, 246/247, 275L, 276/277, 300, 307

Geray Sweeney 2/3, 12/13, 81, 82/83, 88, 116/117, 119, 121, 126, 143T, 144T, 145T, 147T, 147R, 148T, 148, 151T, 151, 153, 155T, 156. 157T, 157, 158T, 158, 159L, 159R, 160T, 160, 161T, 162T, 163, 165T, 167T, 167, 194T, 197T, 202T, 202, 203T, 203, 204T, 205, 206T, 206, 208, 209T, 211T, 213T, 214T, 220, 221T, 221, 224, 225T, 225, 226T, 226, 227T, 227, 232/233, 238T, 250T, 250, 251, 252T, 252, 253T, 255T, 255, 256T, 256, 257T, 257, 258T, 259R, 267T, 268T, 281L, 281R, 282, 299, back cover right

Geray Sweeney/Collections 73, 318

Michael Taylor/Image Ireland 320, 323, 325

Wayne Tolmie/Image Ireland 295

Topham Picturepoint 57, 58, 75L, 242T, 286T

Trinity College Dublin 24

Joseph F. Viesti 86/87, 150, 166, 178, 183L, 234

Marcus Wilson Smith 72, 122, 150T, 169T, 176, 177T, 178T, 180T, 180, 182, 183T, 183R, 185T, 187T, 190/191, 192, 195, 196T, 215T, 236T, 240R, 265, 271T, 273T, 273L, 273R, 274T, 275R, 279, 280T, 289T, 290, 292, 296T, 297T, 302T, 304T, 318T, 320T, 324T, 326T, 326L, front flap top & bottom, spine, back cover left, centre & bottom, back flap top & bottom

George Wright 66/67, 68, 118, 125, 207, 211, 254

Picture Spreads

Pages 62/63 Alain Le Garsmeur/ Image Ireland (Lemaneagh Castle), Thomas Kelly (knocker), The Slide File (all others).

Pages 96/97 Ronald Grant Archive (The Quiet Man), Pictorial Press (The Crying Game), Kobal Collection (all others).

Pages 188/189 clockwise from top left: Thomas Kelly, Jacob Sutton, Mary Evans Picture Library, Derek Speirs/Report, Derek Speirs/ Report, Jacob Sutton, Thomas Kelly.

Pages 228/229 Charles Bateman/Image Ireland (top right), Alain Le Garsmeur/Image Ireland (all others).

Pages 310/311 Christopher Hill (baby), Jeremy Nicholl/Katz (all others).

Map Production Berndtson & Berndtson Productions; Polyglott Kartographie

INSIGHT GUIDE
IRELAND

Editorial Director **Brian Bell**
Cartographic Editor **Zoë Goodwin**
Production **Mohammed Dar**
Design Consultants
Klaus Geisler, Graham Mitchener
Picture Research **Hilary Genin**

Index

a

abortion 57
Achill Island 257-258
Act of Union 22
Adare 222
agricultural subsidies 60
Ahern, Bertie 61
Ailwee Cave 226
All-Ireland Fleadh Ceoil 88
Allihies 208
Allingham, William 271
Altar 206
Amharc Mm, 273
Ancient Order of
    Hibernians 310
Andrew Jackson Centre 302
Angel 97
Anglo-Irish Agreement 57
Anglo-Irish rule 142
Anglo-Irish treaty 23, 46
Anglo-Irish War 23
Annalong 297
Annals of Innisfallen 210
Antrim 308
Antrim Coast Road 303-304
Aran Islands 226, 253
architecture 62
Ardara 272
Ardee 168
Ardglass 298
Ardmore 180
Ardmore Studios 96
Ards Peninsula 299
Arklow 175
Armagh city 293–294
art galleries 360
Arvagh 291
"Ascendancy" 47
Ashford 165
Athlone 244
    Castle 244
Athy 169, 182
Atlantic Drive 275
Aughnanure Castle 256
Auld Lammas Fair 305
Avondale 165
Avondale House, Co.
    Wicklow 63

b

"B" Specials 48
bagpipes 87

Bailieborough 292
Ballaghbeama Gap 214
Ballina 259, 265
Ballinamore 270
Ballinasloe 235
Ballinskelligs 212
Ballinspittle, Co. Cork 73
Ballybeg 186
Ballybrit 251
Ballycastle 305
Ballycotton 180
Ballydehob 205
Ballydonegan 208
Ballygalley 304
Ballyhack 177
Ballyholme Bay 301
Ballyhoura Way 187
Ballyjamesduff 292
Ballymacarbery 186
Ballymaloe Country House and
    Restaurant 126, 180
Ballymena 308
Ballymoney 308
Ballymote 265
Ballynahow 212
Ballyronan 309
Ballyshannon 271
Ballyvaughan 226, 228
Baltimore 204
Banagher 237
Banbridge 295
Bangor 301
Bantry 206
Bantry Bay 30
barm brack 127
Barrow, River 169, 184-185
battles
    Clontarf 27, 142
    Kinsale 27
    Boyne, the 22, 28, 167, 219,
        310
    Diamond, the 30
    Somme, the 40
    Vinegar Hill 175
Beara Peninsula 207
Beara Way 208
Beckett, Samuel 95
Belfast 315–327
    Albert Memorial Clock 324
    Belfast Castle 325
    Belfast Central Library 324
    Belfast Civic Arts Theatre 320
    Botanic Avenue 320
    Bradbury Place 319
    British troops arrive 50
    buildings 62
    Cave Hill Country Park 325
    Central Station 327
    City Hall 317

    Crown Liquor Saloon 126, 321
    Donegall Pass 320
    Donegall Place 317
    Golden Mile 318
    Grand Opera House &
        Cirque 321
    Great Victoria Street 321
    Group Theatre 317
    growth of 38
    history of 315
    hotels 349
    Lagan Lookout Centre 324
    Lagan, River 315
    Lanyon 317
    Linen Conservation Area 317
    Linen Hall Library 322
    Odyssey Pavilion 325
    Old Museum Arts Centre 318
    Ormeau Avenue 318
    Ormeau Road 325
    Parliament Buildings 326
    Peace Line 53, 327
    Pottinger's Entry 323
    Queen's University 319
    restaurants 127, 357
    Royal Belfast Academical
        Institution 322
    Royal Botanic Gardens 320
    Shaftesbury Square 321
    Sinclair Seamen's
        Presbyterian Church 324
    St Malachy's Church 318
    Stormont Castle 326
    Ulster Hall 317
    Ulster Museum 320
    Union Presbyterian
        Theological College 320
    Waterfront Hall 324
    World War II raids 49
    Zoological Gardens 326
Belleek 289
Belmullet 258
Belvedere House, Gardens 241
Benburb Heritage Centre 286
Bennettsbridge 184
Bessbrook 295
birdwatching 205, 270, 301,
    305
Birr 237
    Castle and Demesne 237
Black Head 226
Blacklion 291
Blackrock 161
Blackwater Bog 236
Blackwater Valley 179
Blarney Castle 27, 196
Blarney Stone 15
Blasket Islands 214
Blennerville 215

Blessington 164
Bloody Sunday, Derry 23, 54
Boa Island 288
bodhran 87, 256
Bonamargy Friary 305
Bonaparte, Napoleon 31
Book of Armagh 94, 144
Book of Ballymote 265
Book of Dimma 144
Book of Durrow 144
Book of Kells 26, 94, 144
Book of the Dun Cow 94
Borrisokane 238
Ború, Brian 22, 27
Boundary Commission 45–46,
   279
Boycott, Captain 37
Boyne, Battle of the 22, 28,
   167, 219, 310
Boyne, River 166
Bray 162
Breffni Castle 270
Bricklieve Mountains 265
Brontë Interpretive Centre 295
Bronze Age 26
Bruckless 272
Bruton, John 59
Bundoran 271
Bunratty Castle and Folk
   Park 88, 221
Burren, The 62, 226, 228–229
   Burren Centre 225
Burtonport 273
Bushmills 306
   Bushmills whiskey 121

C

Cahir 187
   Cahir Castle *187*
Cahercommaun 229
Caherdaniel 213
Cahersiveen 212
Caldragh Cemetery 288
Caledon 50
Cape Clear 205
Cappoquin 179
Caragh Lake 211
Carlingford 168
Carnlough 304
Carrick-a-rede Rope Bridge 305
Carrick-on-Shannon 270
Carrickfergus 302
Carrickmacross 293
Carrigaholt 224
Carrigglas Manor 242
Carrowbeg River 258
Carrowmore 265
Carson, Sir Edward 39, 169

Casey, Bishop Eamonn 74
Cashel 186
Castle Caldwell 288
Castle Coole 290
Castle Matrix 223
Castle Ward House 299
Castlebar 259
Castlecove 213
Castlepollard 242
Castletown House 169
Castletownbere 208
Castletownshend 204
Castlewellan 298
Catholic Church *see Roman*
   Catholic Church
Catholic Emancipation Bill 33
Catholic Relief Acts 29
Cavan 291
Cavendish, Lord Frederick 38
Céad Mile Fáilte 15
Ceide Fields 259
Celbridge 169
Celtic beliefs 71
Ceoltóirí Chualann 88
Charles Fort, Kinsale 201
Charles I 27
Charles II 28
Charleville Forest Castle 240
Chieftains, The 85
Children of Lir 242
Christian Brothers 74
Churchill, Lord Randolph 39
Churchill, Sir Winston 40, 45, 48
cinema, influence of 96
Clancy Brothers 88
Clare Island 258
Clarinbridge festival,
   Galway 126
Clear Island 205
Clew Bay 257
Clifden 256
Cliffs of Moher *218*, 219, 225
climate 330
clocháns **214**
Cloghmore 297
Clonakilty 202
Clones 292
Clonmacnoise 236
Clonmacnoise and West Offaly
   Railway 235
Clonmel 186
Clontarf 162
Cloughoughter Castle 291
Coalisland's Corn Mill Heritage
   Centre 285
Cobh 197
Coffey, Aeneas 119
Coleman, Michael 100
Coleraine 307

Coliemore Harbour 161
Collins, Michael 42, 43, 45,
   203
Collooney 265
Comber 298
Comhaltas Ceoltóirí Eireann 88
Commitments, The 80, 97
Connemara 254
Connery, Sean 96
Connolly, James 23, 40-41
Connor Pass 215
contraceptives, laws on 55
cooking 126-127
Cookstown 286
Cooldrumman 268
Coole Park 227
Cooley Peninsula 168
Coomanaspig Pass 212
Cootehill 291
Copeland Island 301
Cork
   Crawford Municipal
      Gallery 195
   Firkin Crane Centre 196
   Lee, River 193
   Opera House 195
   population 193
   Princes Street Market 194
   St Anne's Church 196
   St Finn Barre's
      Cathedral 193
   Tourist Information
      Office 193
   University College,
      Cork 194
Cork Dry Gin 121
Corkscrew Hill 226, 228
Cornafean 291
Corrymeela Community
   House 305
Craggaunowen Project 221
Craigavon 295
Crawfordsburn 302
Creevylea abbey 267
Croagh Patrick 71, 100, 257
Cromwell 22, 28, 162, 167,
   183, 228, 244
Crossmaglen 295
Crumlin 309
Crying Game, The 96–97
Cultra 302
Curracloe Strand 175
Curragh 169, 181
Cusack, Michael 110
Cushendall 304
Cushendun 305
Cyril Fry Model Railway
   Museum 163

d

Dáil Eireann 46, 146
Dalkey 161
Damer House 239
dance 87
Danny Boy 85
Darby O'Gill and the Little People 96
Dargan, William 147
Davitt, Michael 37
de Lorean, John 57
de Valera, Eamon 23, 41, 42, 45, 70
vision for Ireland 46, 50
Defenders, the 29, 30
Derreen Gardens 208
Derry city 280–283
1968 civil rights march 50
Bogside 281
Foyle Valley Railway Centre 283
growth of 281
Guildhall 282
Harbour Museum 283
Roaring Meg 281
siege of 281
St Columb's Cathedral 282
The Diamond 282
Tower Museum 282
Derrynane House 213
Dervock 308
Devenish Island 288
Devil's Glen 165
Devlin, Bernadette 50
Dingle 214
Dingle Peninsula 214
Disraeli, Benjamin 55
divorce 58
dolphins 225
Donaghadee 301
Donleavy, J. P. 20
Donnelly's Hollow 169
Doolin 226
Downhill 308
Downpatrick 298
Dowra 291
Dowth 166
Doyle, Roddy 97
Draperstown 285
Drimcong House Restaurant 127
Drogheda 167
Drombeg Stone Circle 203
Dromineer 238
Drowes, River 269
drug trade 61
Druid Theatre 251
Drumcliff 267

Drumshanbo 270
Drumsna 270
Dublin
Abbey Theatre 95, 154
American Embassy 160
Anna Livia sculpture 155
Arthouse 149
Ballsbridge 160
Bank of Ireland 143
Belvedere College 157
Bewley's Oriental Café 144
Brazen Head 88, 153
Busaras 154
Buswell's Hotel 146
Chester Beatty Library 161
Christ Church Cathedral 151
Church of the Carmelite Fathers 151
Church of the Most Holy Trinity 151
City Hall 150
criminal racketeering 61
Custom House 153
Dame Street 148
Dublin Castle 150-151
Dublin Civic Museum 145
Dublin Experience 144
Dublinia 152
Earlsfort Terrace 146
Early history 142
Eden Quay 160
Fishamble Street 149
Fitzwilliam Square 62, 147–8
Four Courts 159
Gaelic name 141
Gallagher's Boxty House 126
Garden of Remembrance 157
Gate Theatre 157
General Post Office 155
Georgian buildings 63
Grafton Street 144
Guinness's Brewery 153
Ha'penny Bridge 149
Half-penny Bridge 153
Henrietta Street 158
Henry Street 156
High Street 152
hotels 340–341
Irish Museum of Modern Art 160
Iveagh House 145
James Joyce Centre 158
Johnston's Court 144
Kildare Street 146
Kilmainham Gaol 160

Kilmainham Royal Hospital 159
King's Inns 158
Leinster House 146
Liberties 151
Liberty Hall 153
Liffey, River 141
Mansion House 146
Marsh's Library 151
Merrion Square 146
Moore Street 156
Municipal Gallery of Modern Art 157
National Concert Hall 146
National Gallery of Ireland 147
National Library 146
National Museum 146
National Wax Museum 157
Newman House 145
O'Connell Bridge 143, 153
O'Connell Street 143, 154
O'Donoghue's pub 88
Olympia Theatre 150
Peacock Theatre 154
Phoenix Park 160
Powerscourt Centre 144
restaurants 127, 350–351
Rotunda Hospital 156
Royal College of Surgeons 145
Royal Dublin Society 161
Royal Irish Academy 146
Shaw Birthplace 146
Shelbourne Hotel 146
St Anne's Church 146
St Audoen's Church 152
St Mary's Church 158–159
St Mary's Pro-Cathedral 156
St Michan's Church 158
St Patrick's Cathedral 151
St Stephen's Green 145
St Werburgh's Church 69
Spire of Dublin 155
Tailors' Hall 152
Temple Bar 63, 127, 148–149
Trinity College 143
University Church 145
Wide Streets Commission 63
World of Guinness Exhibition 153
Writers Museum 157
Zoological Gardens 160
Duiske Abbey 185
Dún Aengus 254
Dun Laoghaire 161

Dundalk 168
Dundrum 298
Dunfanaghy 274
Dungannon 285
Dungarvan 179
Dunguaire Castle 88, 227
Dunlap, John 283
Dunluce Castle 306
Dunmore East 178
Dunquin 215
Dunseverick Castle 305

e

Earhart, Amelia 283
Easky 265
Easter Rising 23, 40-41, 155, 160
Eat the Peach 97
Elizabeth I 27
emigration 18, 34, 60, 78, 197
Emmet, Robert 33
Emo Court 239
English, attitude towards 25
Ennis 222
Enniskillen 287
Ennistymon 225
Eriugena, John Scotus 71
Erne Shannon Waterway 269
Errigal 274
expatriates 17
Eyeries 208

f

fairy rings 101
Fanad Head 275
Fastnet Rock Lighthouse 204
feminism 55
Fenians 36
Fianna Fáil 40, 47
   meaning of 46
fiddle players 87
Field, John 151
Field, The 97
Fine Gael 46
Finney, Albert 97
Firbolg, the 25
fishing 241, 269, 366
Flight of the Earls 22
Flight of the Earls Heritage Centre 275
Florence Court 290
flying boats 224
folk cures 101
folk music 88
folklore 98
food 125–127
Fota Arboretum 197

Fota Wildlife Park 197
Foyle, River 280
Foynes 223
France, alliance with 30
Fraser, Lady Antonia 242
French Revolution, influence of 33
Friel, Brian 95
fuchsia magellanica 203

g

Gaelic Athletic Association 110, 112
Gaelic football 110, 112, *115*
Gaelic language 60, 93–94, 254
Gaelic League 22, 39
Gaels 26
Gaeltacht 93, 254
Gallarus Oratory 215
Galway Bay 226, 249, 251
Galway city 249–251
   Druid Theatre 251
   Lynch's Window 249
   population 250
   Race Week 251
   Spanish Arch 250
Galway hookers 227, 253
Galway International Oyster Festival 126
Galway, James 311
Gandon, James 143, 153
Gap of Dunloe 210
Gartan Lough 275
Giant's Causeway 305
Gladstone, William Ewart 25, 36, 39
Glandore 203
Glasnevin 162
Glassan 244
Glebe House Gallery 274
Glen of Aherlow 181, 187
Glenariff Glen 304
Glenarm 304
Glenbeigh 211
Glencar 214, 269
Glencar Lough 268
Glencolumbkille 273
Glencree 165
Glendalough 165
Glengarriff 207
Glenties 273
Glenveagh National Park 274
Glin Castle 224
Golden Age 26
golf 115
Good Friday Agreement 61
Gorey 175
Gosford Forest Park 295

Gougane Barra 206
Graiguenamanagh 185
Grange Stone Circle 222
Grattan, Henry 29, 143
Great Blasket 214
Great Famine 34
Great Rebellion, the 27, 30
Gregory, Lady 95, 154, 227
Greyabbey 299
greyhound racing 113
Grianán of Aileach 275
Griffith, Arthur 39–40, 42, 43, 45, 46
Guerin, Veronica 61
Guinness 119, 152–153
Guinness, Arthur 28, *152*
Guinness Storehouse 152–3

h

Hallowe'en 100, 127
Handel, George Frederick 149, 159
hare coursing 113
harp 85
Harris, Richard 97
Haughey, Charles 56–57
Hawk's Well Theatre, Sligo 267
Heaney, Seamus 95, *286*, 287
Hear My Song 97
Helen's Bay 302
Henry II 27
Henry VI 27
Henry VIII 27
Hidden Ireland 127
Hill of Slane 166
Hill of Tara 168
Holy Island 222
holy wells 71, *101*
Holywood 302
Home Rule 36, 38-40, 42
Hook Head Peninsula 177
Horan, Monsignor James 259
horses 105–109
   Galway races 251
Howth 162
   Abbey Tavern 88
   Howth Head 162
humour 15
hunger strikes 42, 55
Hunt Museum, Limerick 220
hurling 110, 112

I

Ilnacullin Gardens 206
Inch 214
industry 60

Inishcrone 265
Inisheer 226, 254
Inishmaan 254
Inishmore 254
Inistioge 185
Innisfallen Island 210
Innishmurray 268
IRA, the see Irish Republican
    Army
Ireland's Eye 162
Ireland's Historic Science
    Centre 237
Irish Citizens' Army 40
Irish Coffee 224
Irish Country House
    Association 127
Irish Film Board 97
Irish Free State 45
    creation of 43
Irish Home Rule Party 23
Irish Horse Museum 182
Irish Linen Centre 296
Irish National Heritage
    Park 176
Irish National Land League 22
Irish National League 38
Irish pubs 120
Irish Republic, beneifts of
    European Union 60
Irish Republican Army (IRA) 23,
    42, 48, 50, 53, 54, 279
    ceasefires 59, 61
    in movies 97
    origins of 36
    split in 53
    1956–62 campaign 50
Irish Republican
    Brotherhood 22, 35
Irish Volunteers 29
Iron Age 22
Island Magee 303
Iveragh Peninsula 208

j

Jackson, President Andrew 303
James I 27
James II 28, 281, 310
Jameson Heritage Centre 181
Janus figures 288
Japanese Gardens, Kildare 182
jaunting cars 209
Jerpoint Abbey 184
Jerpoint Glass 184
Johnstown Castle Gardens 176
Jordan, Neil 95–97
Joyce, James 93, *95*, 96, 155,
    158, 161

k

Kavanagh, Patrick 95
Kealkil 206
Kells 168
Kenmare 209
Kennedy, John F. 252
Kennelly, Brendan 95
Kerry County Museum 216
Kesh 288
Kierkegaard, Søren 17
Kilbeggan 240
Kilcar 272
Kildare 169, 181–182
Kilfenora 225
Kilfinane 187
Kilkee 224
Kilkeel 297
Kilkenny 181, 183
Kilkenny Rising 35
Killala 31, 259
Killarney 209
    National Park 210
Killary Harbour 257
Killeshandra 291
Killiney 161
Killorglin 211
Killybegs 272
Killymoon Castle 286
Killynether Wood 301
Kilmainham Gaol 160
Kilmakilloge Harbour 208
Kilmore Quay 177
Kilnaboy 229
Kilruddery House, Co.
    Wicklow 63
Kilrush 224
King James II 310
King Sitric 151
Kinsale 201
Kinsale Gourmet Festival 127
Kinvara 226
Kircubbin 299
Kirkistown Circuit 299
Knappogue Castle 88, 221
Knock, Co Mayo 71, *75*, 259
Knockmealdown
    Mountains 179
Knowth 166
Kylemore Abbey 257

l

Labour Party 47
Lahinch 225
Lake Isle of Innishfree 267
Lamb's Head 213
Lambeg drums 311
Land League 23, 37

Land reform 36-37
land, ownership of 28
Lane, Sir Hugh 157
Lanyon, Sir Charles 143, 303,
    317, 320, 324
Larkin, James 155
Larne 303
Le Fanu, Sheridan 146
Lecky, William 33
Leenane 257
Lemaneagh Castle 62, 229
Lemass, Sean 49
Letterkenny 274–275
Liffey, River 141
Limerick 219
    Hunt Museum 220
    King John's Castle 220
    People's Park 220
Lisburn 296
Lisdoonvarna 226
Lismore 179
Lissadell House 268
literature 93
Lloyd George, David 42, 45
Locke's Distillery 240
Longford, Earls of 242
Loop Head 225
Lough Allen 269
Lough Arrow 265
Lough Derg 222, 238, 272, 288
Lough Derravaragh 242
Lough Ennel 240–241
Lough Gill 267
Lough Gowna 292
Lough Gur 222
Lough Ine 204
Lough Navar Forest Park 289
Lough Neagh 295, 309
Lough Ree 244
Loughgall 295
Louisburg 257
Lower Lough Erne 287
Lusitania 197, 201
Lustybeg 288

m

Macaulay, Thomas
    Babington 25
MacCool, Fionn 98, 100, 297
Macgillicuddy's Reeks 210
MacMurrough, Dermot 22, 27
MacNeice, Louis 17
McAleese, Mary 23, 61
McBride, John 39
McCormack, John 156, 244
McGahern, John 269
McKinley, President
    William 308

McMurrough, Dermot 178
McQuaid, Bishop John 75
Maghera 285
Magilligan Strand 308
Mahaffy, Sir John 93
Malahide 162
Malin Head 276
Malone, Molly 144
Man of Aran 254
Man of No Importance, A 97
Manorhamilton 270
Marble Arch Caves 290
Marian shrines 98
Markievicz, Countess
    Constance 268
Marsh, Archbishop
    Narcissus 151
Martin, Violet 204
Marx, Karl 35
Maynooth 169
Mayo 257
megalithic tombs 206, 229
Mellifont Abbey 167
Michael Collins (film) 96
Midleton 180
Millmount 167
Milltown Malbay, Co. Clare 88
Mitchelstown 187
Mizen Peninsula 206
Monaghan 292
Monasterboice 167
Monasterevin 182
Moore, Thomas 151, 165, 169
Mount Eagle 215
Mount Gabriel 205
Mount Melleray 179
Mount Stewart 300
Mount Usher Gardens 165
Mountjoy, Viscount 154
Mountshannon 222
Mourne Mountains 297
Movilla Abbey 300
moving statues 98
Moyne Abbey 259
Muckno Lake 293
Muckross House 210
Muckross Park 209
Mullaghbawn Folk
    Museum 295
Mullaghmore 268
Mullingar 241
Multyfarnham 242
Murlough Bay 307
Murphy, Dervla 59
Murphy's whiskey 121
music, traditional 85, 226
Mussenden Temple 308

n

Naas 169
National Land League 37
National Stud 169, 182
nationalism 70
Navan 168
Neeson, Liam 96
Nelson, Lord Horatio 155
Nenagh 238
    Heritage Centre 239
Nendrum Abbey 298
Neolithic period 22
Newcastle 298
Newgrange 26, 166, 229
Newman, John Henry 145, 156
Newport 258
Newry 296
Newtownards 300
Nire Valley Drive 186
Nore, River 184
Normans 27
North Antrim Coast Path 307
North Down Heritage
    Centre 301
Northern Ireland
    abolition of Stormont 55
    Anglo-Irish agreement 57
    community divisions 53
    counties of 280
    growth of economy 50
    housing discrimination 50
    influence of Catholic
        church 53
    joins EEC 55
    roots of US presidents 284
    terrorist death toll 55
Northern Irish Civil Rights
    Movement 23

o

O'Brien, Edna 20, 222
O'Casey, Sean *95*, 154, 227
O'Conaire, Pádraic 252
O'Connell, Daniel 22, 33, 35,
    94, 146, 155, 169, 213
O'Connor, Frank 95
O'Flaherty, Liam 254
O'Neill, Captain Terence 50
O'Neill, Hugh 27
O'Riada, Sean 88
O'Shea, Kitty 155
Ogham alphabet 22
Old Head of Kinsale 202
Omagh 284
Orange Order 38, 310–311
    origin of 30
Oxford Island 309

p

Paisley, Rev, Ian 50
Pale, the 142
Parke's Castle 267
Parnell, Charles Stewart 23,
    36, 37–39, 63, 155
partition 43, 45
passage graves 229, 265
passport requirements 331
Patterson's Spade Mill 309
Pearse, Pádraic 23, 40, 69, 252
Peatlands Park 285
Peel, Sir Robert 33
Peep o' Day Boys, the 29, 30
Penal Laws 22
Pettigo 288
Pitt, William 30
Plantation of Ulster 22
*Playboy of the Western
    World* 95, 154, 254
Playboys, The 97
Plunkett, Oliver *167*
Pope John Paul II 71
population 78
Port 273
Portadown 27, 295
Portavogie 301
Portmagee 212
Portmarnock 162
*Portrait of the Artist as a Young
    Man* 93, 158
Portrush 307
Portstewart 307
potato cakes 127
potato famine 23
poteen 121, 255, 304
Poulaphouca, Lake 164
Poulnabrone Dolmen 228-229
Powerscourt 165
Progressive Democrats 61
Protestant church,
    disestablishment of 36
Provisional IRA 53
Puck Fair 211
pubs 119–122
    Crown Liquor Saloon
        (Belfast) 126, 321
    Doheny and Nesbitt's
        (Dublin) 122
    Durty Nelly's (Limerick) 221
    food 128
    Mulligan's (Dublin) 122
    Neary's (Dublin) 122
    number of 122
Puck Fair 211
public holidays 332
Purple Mountain 210

q

Queen Victoria 39
  plot to kidnap 35
Queenstown Story 197
Quiet Man, The 96
Quin 221

r

Radio Eireann 88
Raleigh, Sir Walter 180, 223
Randalstown 309
Rankin, Jeannie 127
Rathfriland 298
Rathkeale 223
Rathlin Island 305
Rathmullan 275
Rea, Stephen 97
Redmond, John 39, 41, 42
refugee problems 60
religion 69–75
  pagan Catholicism 71
  religious conflict 18
Republic of Ireland
  emigration 60
  founding of 23
  joins EEC 55
  withdrawal from British
    Commonwealth 49
Reynolds, Albert 57, 59
Ribbonmen, the 29
ring forts 229
Ring of Beara 207-208
Ring of Kerry 211–212
Riverdance 61, 80
road bowling 113
Roaringwater Bay 204
Robinson, Mary 23, 57, 60
Rock of Cashel 179, 181, 186
Roman Catholic Church
  abortion 73
  censorship 97
  congregation size 69, 72
  discrimination against 28
  divorce 73
  feminism 74
  influence of 47, 69
  loss of authority 75
  moving statues 98
  schools 70
  osky 270
  saveel 254
  oscoff (Belfast
    restaurant) 127
Roscommon 244
Roscrea 239
Rose of Tralee Festival 215
Ross Castle 210

Rossbeigh Woods 211
Rosscarbery 203
Rosserk Friary 259
Rosses Point 267
Rostrevor 297
Roundstone 256
round towers 26, 165, 184,
  222, 308
Royal Irish Academy 94
Royal Ulster Constabulary 50
Russborough 164
Ryan's Daughter 214

s

St Finbar's Oratory 206
St Macdara's Island 256
St Patrick 22, 26, 100, 266,
  298
Saltee Islands 177
Salthill 251
Sarsfield, Patrick 219
Scarriff 222
Scarva 310
Scattery Island 224
Schull 206
Scott, Sir Walter 34
Scrabo Tower 300
seafood 125
Shanagarry 180
Shannon Airport 219
Shannon Harbour 237
Shannonbridge 235
Shaw, George Bernard 17, 93,
  95, 146–147, 157, 227
Shercock 292
Sheridan, Richard Brinsley 94,
  292
Sherkin Island 205
shopping 209, 364
  in Dublin 144, 148
Silent Valley 298
Sinn Féin 23, 40, 42–43, 61,
  153
Sion Mills 284
Skellig Michael 212
Skellig Rocks 208
Skibbereen 204
Slane 166
Slea Head *201*, 214
Slieve Bloom Mountains 238
Slieve Donard 297
Slieve Gullion Forest Park 296
Slieve League 273
Slieve Miskish mountains 207
Sligo 265-266
Sneem 213
Society of United Irishmen 29
soda bread 127

*Some Experiences of an Irish
  RM* 204
Somerville and Ross 95, 204
Somerville, Edith 95, 204
Somme Heritage Centre 300
Spenser, Edmund 223
Sperrin Heritage Centre 285
Sperrin Mountains 285
Spiddal 254
sports 110, 365
Staigue Fort 213
statues, moving 71
Statutes of Kilkenny 22, 93
Stephens, James 35–36
Stormont Castle 48, 326
Stormont parliament, abolition
  of 55
storytellers 100
Strabane 283
Strangford 298
Strangford Lough 298
Strangford Lough Wildlife
  Centre 299
Streedagh Strand 268
Strokestown Park House and
  Famine Museum 243
Strongbow 27, 178
Struell Wells 298
Suck, River 235
Sugar Loaf Mountains 162
Swanlinbar 291
Swift, Dean Jonathan 29, 93,
  151, 169, 292
Synge, John Millington 95,
  154, 227, 254
  use of folklore 98

t

Tarbert 224
Temple of the Winds 300
terrorism 36
Terryglass 238
Thackeray, William
  Makepeace 126, 307
thatched cottages 62
Thatcher, Margaret 55
Thomastown 184
Thoor Ballylee 227
Timoleague 202
tin whistles 87
Tone, Wolfe 22, 29, 159, 206,
  275
Torc Waterfall 209
Tory Island 101, 274
tower houses 62, 221, 223,
  227
tourism 60
Tralee 215

Tralee and Dingle Light Railway 215
Tramore 179
Travellers 188-189
trawling industry 207
Treaty of Limerick 219
Trevor, William 95, 235
Trim 168
Trollope, Anthony 270
Tuam 33
Tuamgraney 222
Tullamore 240
Tullynally Castle 242
Twelve Pins 256
Tyrone Guthrie Centre 293
Tyrone villages 286

u

U2 (pop group) 60
Uillean pipes 87
Ulster Defence Association 54
Ulster Folk and Transport Museum 302
Ulster History Park 285
Ulster Volunteer Force 23, 39, 54
Ulster, province of 40

Ulster-American Folk Park 284
Ulysses 158, 161
union with Britain (1801) 31
United Irishmen 22, 30, 142, 153
Upper Lough Erne 287

v

Vale of Avoca 165
Valentia 212
Ventry 214
Vikings 22, 26, 142, 149, 178, 236, 268
Vinegar Hill, Battle of 175
Virginia 292

w

Warrenpoint 296
Waterfoot 304
Waterford 178
Waterford Crystal Factory 178
Waterville 213
Welles, Orson 157
Wellington, Duke of 146
Westport 258
Wexford 176

Wexford Opera Festival 176
Wexford Wildfowl Reserve 175
whiskey 119–121, 159
  brands of 121
White Bay 304
White Island 288
Whiteboys, the 29
Whitehead 303
Wicklow Mountains 164
Wilde, Oscar 39, 93, 146
William of Orange 28, 30, 281, 310
Wilson, President Woodrow 284
World War I 40
World War II 48

y

Yeats, Jack B. 147
Yeats, William Butler 39, 47, 78, 146, 154, 156, 157, 227, 266
  Abbey Theatre 95
  use of folklore 98
Yeats Memorial Building, Sligo 266
Youghal 180